ITALY

Publisher:	Aileen Lau
Editors:	Aileen Lau
	Emma Tan
	Bina Maniar
Editorial Assistance:	Cecilia Ng
	Shaw Soo Ling
DTP Design & Layout:	Sares Kanapathy
Illustrations:	Koh Hong Teng
Cover Artwork:	Susan Harmer
Maps:	Superskill Graphics

Published in the United States by
PRENTICE HALL GENERAL REFERENCE
15 Columbus Circle
New York, New York, 10023

ISBN 0-671-87903-0

Titles in the series:
Alaska - American Southwest - Australia - Bali - California - Canada - Caribbean - China - England - Florida - France - Germany - Greece - Hawaii - India - Indonesia - Italy - Ireland - Japan - Kenya - Malaysia - Mexico - Nepal - New England - New York - Pacific Northwest USA - Singapore - Spain - Thailand - Turkey - Vietnam

USA MAINLAND SPECIAL SALES
Bulk purchases (10+copies) of the Travel Bugs series are available at special discounts for corporate use. The publishers can produce custom publications for corporate clients to be used as premiums or for sales promotion. Copies can be produced with custom cover imprints. For more information write to Special Sales, Prentice Hall Travel, Paramount Communications Building, 15th floor, 15 Columbus Circle, New York, NY 10023.

Printed in Singapore

ITALY

Text by Andy Gravette

With contributions from:
Pierre Ketteridge
Aileen Lau
Emma Tan
Morten Strange
Laure Lau
Shaw Soo Ling

Editors
Aileen Lau
Emma Tan

Prentice Hall Travel

New York   London   Toronto   Sydney   Tokyo   Singapore

C O N T E N T S

INTRODUCTION

Ciao Italia! 1
Welcome to the land of history, culture, style and great taste

HISTORY, GOVERNMENT & ECONOMY

Deities, Dictators & Dominions – History & Government 7
CroMagnon - Romulus & Remus - Greeks - Etruscans - Early Republic - Gauls - Punic Wars - Pax Romana - Fall of the Roman Empire - The Popes - City States - Spanish & Austrian Domination - French Revolution - Kingdom of Italy - World War I - Mussolini & Fascism - World War II - The Italian Republic - Italy today
    Garibaldi – Italy's Hero 30

Cars, Salami and Wine – Economy ..
.... 33
Natural Resources - Agricultural Activity - Tourist Trade

PHYSICAL PROFILE

The Tiber Crossed – Geography 43
Mountain Ranges - Rivers and Lakes - Volcanoes - Coastlines
    The Spas of Italy 46

Of Birds and Bears – Flora & Fauna .
.... 51
Wildlife - National Parks - Birdlife - Conservation Bodies
    Birding in Italy 60
    Hunting in Italy 64

PEOPLE, LIFESTYLE & CULTURE

Shades of Latin – People 71
Phoenicians - Etruscans - Greeks - Byzantines - Arabs - Jews - Moors - Bebers - Ostrogoths - Goths - Visigoths - Gauls - Franks - Alemanni - Vandals - Alani - Strevi - Lombards - Romans - French - Austrians - Spanish Style & "Bella Figura" - Close-Knit Society
    The Mafia 76

A Nation Devout – Religion 83
Catholicism - Christian sects - Judaism - Muslims

A Day for every Saint – Festivals .. 89
Processions and pageants throughout the year
    Carnevale – The Story of Carnival
.... 90
    Dance, Costume and Folklore 93

Virgil to Verdi – Literary & Performing Arts 97
Literature - Music - Opera
    Dante, Poet and Philosopher 99
    The Spaghetti Western 102
    Italian Cinema 106

C O N T E N T S

Statues to Sarcophagi – Arts & Architecture 109
Greek, Etruscan and Roman Influences - Byzantine - Romanesque and Gothic - Renaissance - Mannerism and Baroque - Modern Art
The Florentine Artists 114

FOLLOW THAT BUG

CENTRAL ITALY
The Eternal City – Rome & Environs 131
Glories That Were - Opulence and Artistry of the Past - Museums - Fountains - Monuments - Churches - Piazzas - Pizzas - Palaces - Villas - Parks - Environs of Rome - Trastevere - Tivoli - Subian - Palestrina - Frascati - Albano - Castel Gandolfo - Velletri
The Vatican 148
The Roman Forum 163

Lake Country – Lazio 173
Inland Lakes and Scattered Hills - Etruscan Exuberance - Walled Cities - Abbeys and Citadels

Rural & Rugged – Molise 189
A Farming Community - Prehistoric Life - Iserna - Ancient Sites

Beeches, Bears & Ruins – Abruzzi ... .193
Gran Sasso - Maiella Massif - Climbing,

Skiing, Hunting Activities - L'Aquila - Adriatic Coast
The Abruzzo National Park 198

SOUTHERN ITALY
Rising above the Ashes – Naples 203
Mount Vesuvius - Magna Graecia - Castles - Museums - Galleries - Churches - Ruins - Kings and Capodimonte - Villas.
Pompeii 208
The Smoking Peak 213

Greco – Roman Resorts – Campania 217
Bay of Naples - Hercules' City - Land of the Sirens - Amalfi Coast - Salerno - Paestum - Cilento - Cuma - Caserta - Capua - Benevento - Santa Sofia.

Heel & Spur – Puglia 231
Flat "heel" of the Italian "boot" - Bari - The Gargano Promontory - Vieste - Manfredo - The Tavoliere - Foggia - Lucera - Barlo - Monopoli - Martina Franca - Alberobello - Castellana Grotte - The Salentine Peninsula - Brindisi - Lecce - Santa Cesarea Therme - Taranto.
The Trulli 236

Grecian Villages & Backwaters – Calabria & Basilicata 243
The "toe" of Italy - Calabria - Reggio - The Thyrrenian Coast - Praia a Mare - Cosenza - Scilla - The Sila Massif - The Ionian Coast

C O N T E N T S

- Catanzaro - Crotone - Gulf of Taranto - Basilicata - Potenza - Maratea - Metaponto - Matera

ISLANDS OF ITALY
A String of Pearls – Italian Isles .. 253
The Discovered and Undiscovered Gems of the Mediterranean - Capri - Ischia - Procida - The Tremiti Isles - Elba - Montecristo's Isle

Volcanic Beauty – Sicily 263
Italy's largest island - Breadbasket, Olive Oil and Wine Cellar - Palermo - Catania - Syracuse - Messina - Agrigento - Ragusa - Trapani - Enna
    Mount Etna............................. 272

Sards, Sardo, Sardinia – Sardinia .....
...281
Pre-historic and megalithic sites - Nuraghic Culture - Farming Community - Cagliari - Sassari - Alghero - Oristano - Olbia - Nuoro - Costa Smeralda
    Sardinian Panoply of Festivals ......
   290

NORTHERN ITALY
The Industrial North – Milan & Lombardy 295
Throbbing Metropolis of Business - Fertile Plains - Romantic Villas - Botanical Gardens - Pavia - Cremona - Mantua - Bergamo - The Italian Lakes

Alpine Panorama – Piedmont & Valle

D'Aosta 317
Scenic Routes - Europe's highest peaks - Turin

Little Austria – Trentino Alto Adige .
...329
Dichotomy of cultures - Trento - Bolzano

Karst and Castles – Trieste & Friuli Venetia Giulia 343
Dolomites and Alps - Dolines and Caverns - Slovenian Borders - Trieste - Muggia - Gorizia - Udine - The Carnia - Southern Flatlands
    The Carso 350
    The Quattro Castelli 353

Romance & Faded Elegance – Venice & Veneto 355
La Serenissima - Gateway to the East - Venice - Canals and Palaces - Piazza San Marco and Environs - Padua - Vicenza - Verona
    O Sole Mio! 373
    Venice in Peril? 374
    The Orient Express 375

Medieval Voyages – Genoa & Liguria
...383
Spirit of Columbus - Genoa - Riviera del Ponente - Riviera del Levante - Portofino - La Spezia
    Genoa's Greatest Son 389

Culinary Country – Bologna & Emilia

C O N T E N T S

Romagna 399
*Art Collections - Universities - Sausages
and Cuisine - Bologna - Ravenna - Rimini -
Ferrara - Modena - Parma - Piacenza*

Poetic Beauty – Florence & Tuscany
.... 417
*Literary and Artistic Magnificence - Archi-
tectural Masterpieces - Florence - Churches
and Palaces - Prata, Pistoia & Fiesole -
Arezzia - Siena - Pisa - Lucca*

**Landlocked Treasures – Perugia &
Umbria** 435
*Etruscan Heritage - Perugia - Citta di
Castello - Gubbio - Assisi - Foligno - Spello
- Spoleto - Norcia - Todi - Terni - Orvieto*

Raphael's Birthplace – Marche ... 447
*Frontier Lands - Ancona - Adriatic Coast -
Macerata - Urbino*

WHAT TO DO

Pasta to Marsala – Cuisine 445
Fooding, Wining & Dining

La Dolce Vita – Nightlife 463
Smart Bars, Clubs & Discoes

Unloading Lires – Shopping 471
Souvenirs, Foods and High Fashion

**Games People Play – Sports & Recrea-
tion** 477

From Soccer to Formula Races

EASY REFERENCE

Travel Tips 485
Supplement essential for travel planning
Directory 490
Useful listings
Photo Credits 498
Index 500

MAPS

Italy 128
Central Italy 132
Rome 136
Roman Forum 140
Vatican City 152
Southern Italy 200
Naples 204
Sicily 264
Sardinia 282
Northern Italy 292
Milan 296
Turin 318
Venice 356
Bologna 400
Florence 418

Canaletto. Caravaggio.

Botticelli. Bernini. Brunelleschi.

Donatello. Fra Angelico. Ghiberti.

Giorgione. Giotto. Mantegna. Michelangelo. Leonardo da Vinci. Raphael. Titian. Tintoretto. Veronese.

the vast history and culture, reflecting Etruscan, Greek, Roman, Doric,

Italian architecture is all about

Passeggiata, the traditional evening walk, along a Sicilian promenade.

Paradox

Although an industrious nation, most of Italy shuts down between noon and 4 pm for the siesta; no amount of haranguing will alter this.

Much of the terrain is mountainous, yet Italy is the world's largest producer (and indeed consumer) of wine; she possesses some of Europe's most beautiful beaches, which are at the same time among the more polluted. In the land of endless pasta, olive oil and ice cream, the young Italians are svelte, fit and healthy – only Italian couture seems to hang right on them – until they fill out more!

A volatile people, the Italians are famed for their gesticulations, self-expression, opinions and, when appropriate, haughty disdain; yet they are also the world's most solicitous hosts.

Catholic yet Socialist

A strongly Catholic country, Italy is predominantly socialist in its politics while to its north and east it acts as a gateway to Western and Central Europe, and as a gateway to Africa and to the Orient via its shipping lanes to the south. Still it maintains a highly regionalised character, with each province or area fiercely proud and protective of its individuality.

But, perhaps most noticeable of all

*C*iao! — the traditional Italian greeting, meaning welcome, cheers, or goodbye depending on circumstance is evocative of the richness, melliflu- ousness and melodiousness of the Italian language, and in turn, the nature of Italy itself.

Although Italy was only unified as a single nation-state in 1871, the con- stituent parts have acted as a magnet to travellers (be they conquerors, foreign dignitaries, artists, writers, poets or just plain humble tour- ists), for millennia.

Children of the Valle D'aosta region.

The roots of most European civilizations lie in this, the most paradoxical of countries. Para- doxical? Yes, because most aspects of Italy are contradictory, or at least multi- faceted. A country with one of the more problematic economies in Europe, boasts one of the highest stand- ards of living and leads the world in couture, cuisine, automotive design and a sense of style.

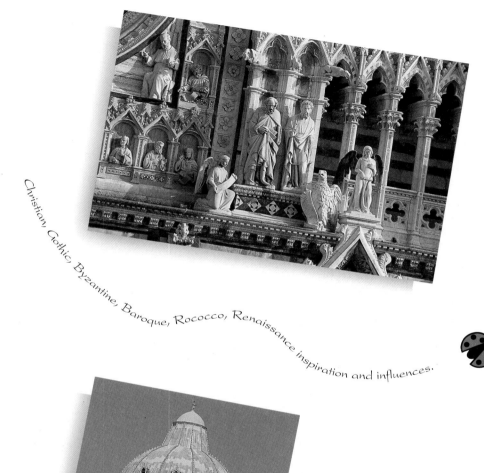

Christian, Gothic, Byzantine, Baroque, Rococco, Renaissance inspiration and influences.

a time for costumed balls, masquerades

Everyone loves the Carnevale in Venice,

The Trevi Fountain, well-banked with coins and wishes.

ports of Genova and Venice); the glorious landscapes of Lombardy and Tuscany; the beauty of Rome and the romance of the Bay of Naples; Calabria, with its harsh, bleak, but beautiful scenery and imposing aspects over the Tyrrhenian and Ionian Seas; and of course the islands: Sicily, Sardinia, and the smaller isles: Elba, Ischia, Capri and the Eolie islands. Whatever your interest, be it art, history, literature, architecture, or just touring and sampling the gastronomic and ecological delights of an area, feast on. Ciao Italia!

is the division between north and south: the north being one of the most industrialist areas in Europe, while the south remains one of the more depressed.

Perhaps this persistent dichotomy, explains Italy's continuous fascination to invaders through the ages, from the early barbarian hordes of Goths and Huns, through Charlemagne in the 8th century, Napoleon in 1796, the Hapsburgs, and not so long ago the Nazi occupation. However, a more likely draw was the dangling bauble of Italy's heritage of civilization and art.

Paleolithic, Neolithic, and Bronze Age peoples all settled on the Italian peninsula, followed by the Phoenicians, Greeks and Etruscans, many of whose ruins and relics remain standing today. But, it is the fabled glory of the Roman Empire, the solemn Gothic majesty of the Middle Ages, and the splendour of the Renaissance which captured the imagination.

Goethe, Byron, Lawrence, Joyce, even Hemingway were drawn to Italy to seek the elusive muse, while others such as Shakespeare drew inspiration from this history-steeped land, although they never travelled there.

Paleo di Siena, the colourful festival in Tuscany.

A Centre for the Arts

As a center for the arts, Italy has no peer – it has been said that of all the historic monuments and works of art in the western world, two–thirds are Italian, or else they are in Italy. When you consider Rome, Florence, Pisa, Bologna, Venice, Milan, Genova and Naples, and their respective architecture, museums, works of art and intrinsic natural beauty, this claim seems far from exaggerated. Italian paintings and sculptures have found their way to salons, palaces, museums and private collections the world over. It is also not untrue that Italian art provided much inspiration to European artists.

Italian food is a legend in its own right – pasta, pizza, capriccio, ribollita, risotto, vitello – the list could go on forever. The wines that complement these dishes are just as varied – Asti Spumante, Abruzzo, Barbera, Barollo, Bardolino, Chianti, Frascati, Lambrusco, Valpolicella – the names trip off the

Italian food is not only delicious but full of zest.

tongue! It has been said that if a different type of wine were drunk every night, it would take about 15 years to sample all the varieties in existence in Italy.

Today Italy offers the traveller the most varied experience of all European countries: the Alpine north, which, due to the historical (mainly Roman) trade routes has a multi-ethnic and cultural heritage (French, Swiss, Austrian, Slovenian); the Italian lakes; the western (Ligurian) and eastern (Adriatic) peninsulars rich in natural beauty and maritime importance (the historical sea-

and sheer fantasy, amidst the setting of the labyrinthian city of canals and palaces.

Italy has a vast cultural wardrobe of costumes ranging from medieval, religious, folk to fantasy!

I n the last few years, it was discovered that man inhabited an area around Isernia, in the region of Molise, in central Italy, about a million years ago. This is the earliest evidence ever found of man's in-habitation of Europe.

The Neanderthal man gave way to the Cro-Magnon around 18,000 BC and the Neolithic man arrived on the scene 11,000 years later.

Skills in metallurgy were acquired by 2,000 BC and, by the 8th century BC, the 'people' had formed separate tribes some of whom were the Samnites, Danunii, Messapii, Picentes, Sabines, Aequi, Volsci and the Latins who settled in various parts of the peninsular and the islands. On the two large islands, the Siculi had entrenched on Sicily, and the Sards on Sardinia.

Etruscan frescoes in the province of Viterbo depicts a distant but cultured past.

Legend of Romulus & Remus

According to Roman mythology, the city of Rome was founded by twin brothers Romulus and Remus.

Tradition has it that in the 8th century,

Statues of Romulus and Remus inside the Museo Capitolino.

the ancient Italian city of Alba Longa was ruled by King Numitor until his younger brother, Amulius dethroned him. Amulius killed Numitor's sons and forced Numitor's daughter, Rhea Silvia to become a Vestal Virgin so that she could never bear children who might threaten his rule. But she gave birth to twin sons: Romulus and Remus, fathered by the god Mars. Amulius killed Rhea Silvia and ordered the infants placed in a basket and thrown into the Tiber River to die. A she-wolf found them by the river bank and raised them. The scene of the she-wolf nursing Romulus, Remus became a popular subject for Roman artists. Faustulus, a shepherd, and his wife discovered them and brought them up as their own. However, when they became men and learned of their origin, they killed Amulius and reinstated Numitor to the throne.

Soon Romulus and Remus became leaders of a band of Latin youths and left to found a new city and home. But the twins had an argument about where the city should be built, and as a result, Remus was killed. Thus Rome came to be named after her first king, Romulus, and it was established on the Palantine Hill overlooking the Tiber. Romulus was a popular ruler and a good military leader, and under him, Rome thrived, but there were only male inhabitants in the city. Romulus and his followers decided to people the city by kidnapping and raping the women from the neighbouring Sabine tribe. Romulus reigned

The rape of the Sabine women, as depicted in a painting.

for 38 years, and during that time, Rome expanded and became the most powerful city in its region.

The Greeks & Etruscans

These two groups of outsiders played a vital part in thrusting Italy into the heart of the ancient world, and it was they who propelled the growth of civilization in Italy.

The Greeks and the Etruscans sailed across the sea in search of rich new land. By 750 BC, the Greek settlers had built cities in Sicily and on the west coast of Italy, and were the first to cultivate the previously wild vine and olive. They prospered wealthily from the fertility of

Relics depict dress and hairstyles of a lost era.

Mementoes of the Etruscan culture.

the land and traded with mainland Greece. But because the Greek colonists warred with their leaders and fought among themselves, they did not become a powerful political force in Italy. However, the Greeks were a dominant civilizing influence to the native Italians. They learned from Greek sculpture, architecture, ceramics, writing, and modern warfare, the last of which the natives would finally use against their Greek teachers.

Around 800 BC, the Etruscans settled and built cities on the west coast of Italy. It is still not clear where the Etruscans came from, but it is irrefutable that they brought a very advanced civilization to Italy. They specialized in metal crafts and hence thrived on trade.

Many elaborate paintings that depict men and women dancing, playing music, feasting while lying on reclining couches, hunting and battling revealed that the Etruscans enjoyed life immensely. Moreover, their lives were more devoted to religion than to politics.

To trade with the Greek colonists, they developed overland trade routes, one of which cut through Latium. By around 600 BC, Rome and other towns in Latium were controlled by the Etruscans. They built temples, roads and public buildings in Rome, and they introduced the idea of the citizen assembly. For 300 years under the Etruscans, Rome grew into a prosperous city. The people became so powerful that, by the 5th century, the Romans drove the

Decorations on an Etruscan vase.

Etruscans out. Upon the overthrow of the monarchy, Rome's leaders declared that no more kings would rule Rome, and the Roman Republic was established in 509 BC.

The Early Republic

In 493 BC, Rome formed an alliance with the Latin League, a federation of cities of Latium. Rome then used the league's resources to conquer her neighbours, who were consequently given Roman citizenship – Roman citizenship was made extremely desirable as it offered certain privileges and protection; in exchange, the conquered cities supplied the Roman army with soldiers. By 396 BC, Rome had become the largest city in Latium.

During the 3rd century BC, Rome had many triumphs over the Etruscans; she also defeated the Gauls who descended on Rome in 390 BC, and she disbanded the Latin League. In 290 BC, the Romans conquered the mountain people who lived in the south of Rome, then the Greek colony of Tarentum in southern Italy. By 275 BC, Rome ruled virtually all of the Italian peninsular.

Roman Expansion

During 200 - 100 BC, Roman expansion created a mighty empire. At the same time, in North Africa, the settlement of

Etruscan relics at the Museo di Villa Giulia, Rome.

Carthage, established by the Phoenicians, had grown to such a size that it challenged the power of Rome. In 348 BC, Rome made a pact with Carthage which was short-lived.

By concentrating on the Mediterranean Sea between Italy and Africa, the Romans were, by necessity, forced to deal with the Greek colonies in the south. Rome began to control larger parts of southern Italy and Sicily, so much so, that by 343 BC, the Romans had defeated the Greeks in their last stronghold – Campania.

To ensure easy access by its armies and to establish its foothold in the south, Rome built the Appian Way. It was begun by the Emperor Appius Claudius in 312 BC and completed by Augustus more than two centuries later when it was extended to run from Rome to Brundusium or Brindisi, the ancient Greek port.

Carthage then became a great sea power and trading center, and inevitably Rome and Carthage clashed in the struggle for mastery of the Mediterranean sea. Three struggles called the Punic Wars took place. The first of the three Punic Wars between Rome and Carthage began in 264 BC, lasting for 23 years. This galvanized Rome into improving its sea power and developing its navy. By the year 238 BC, both Sardinia and Corsica were annexed by Rome.

Sicily too, was captured by Rome in 212 BC, in the middle of the Second Punic War (218-200 BC). It was in this

Painting of Hannibal marching into Italy with elephants.

war that the Carthaginian leader, Hannibal, who had siezed the Rome-allied Spanish town of Saguntum, and then led his army, including a host of elephants, across the Pyrenees and down through the Alps to battle with the Romans in Apulia in 216 BC.

After several triumphs in the field of battle against the Emperor Fabius Maximus' forces, Hannibal's army became demoralized as Roman manpower and endurance finally wore him down, and he left the Italian mainland. In 201 BC, Hannibal was defeated by Scipio near Carthage. Rome began to concentrate on the development of its social structure and the Forum was established as the main civic center by the year 176 BC. Never existing long in peace, Rome

again went to war and finally conquered Greece (Macedonia) in 168 BC.

The Third Punic War escalated in 146 BC when Scipio destroyed Carthage after a two-year siege. This put Rome in control of the entire Mediterranean region and it dominated every country with a coastline on the Mediterranean by 133 BC, except Egypt.

Disintegration of the Republic

While Roman expansion triumphed overseas, discontent grew at home because the gap between rich and poor widened. The rich grew richer from looted property, tax revenues and slaves which

Portrayal of the assassination of Julius Caesar.

poured into Rome from conquered territories; and the poor became poorer as unemployment increased, due to the inflow of slaves who drove out the small farmers. Two Roman tribunes led by brothers, Tiberius Gracchus and Gaius Gracchus in 133 and 123 BC, tried to help the poor by promoting the distribution of state-land to the poor, but there were many who opposed them and they were eventually assassinated.

Friction at home, corruption among the leaders of the republic, betrayal by Rome's allies, and a war in Asia, all weakened the Roman Republic. In 82 BC, the Roman general Lucius Sulla became dictator, reformed the Senate, and brought some stability, but he retired after three years.

Around 60 BC, Rome's control expanded to eastern Turkey, Palestine and Syria under general Pompey, and from 58 to 51 BC, Julius Caesar's ascent began and he conquered Gaul, thus adding the massive region west of the Rhine to the Roman world. The Senate and Pompey feared his strength and ordered him to disband. In answer, he crossed the Rubicon (a stream that separated Italy from Gaul) and invaded Italy. Civil war broke, Caesar defeated Pompey, and in 45 BC, he became sole ruler of the Roman world. He founded his own forum as dictator, and it was firmly established that the emperor was the only true leader of the republic. In 44 BC, Caesar was assassinated by a group of aristocrats who hoped to revive the Roman Republic. A struggle for power ensued for more than 16 years. By 31 BC, Caesar's adopted son and heir, Octavian, defeated the forces of Anthony and Cleopatra in the Battle of Actium, and became the unchallenged leader of the Roman world.

The Imperial Age of Rome really began in the year 27 BC. Octavian became the first Roman emperor, and changed his name to Augustus, which means "exalted". Despite his power, he preferred the title "princeps" which means "first citizen". Twenty years of civil war had devastated the republic, and only a strong central authority seemed capable of controlling the government and empire.

Pax Romana

The reign of Augustus marked the beginning of 200 years of "Pax Romana" or "Roman Peace". Augustus set up an orderly government and the rule of law, with the emperor holding supreme power. He commanded the army, governed the provinces, and placed loyal supporters in the Senate. The civil service was orderly and staffed by qualified administrators to help him control the empire and he patronized the arts, architecture and literature which flourished well. Many great writers were linked to the "Augustine Age" – Virgil, Ovid, Livy and Horace, who all wrote of Augustus' achievements. Trade too, reached a high point during this period.

In 14 AD, Augustus died, but had groomed his stepson Tiberius to succeed him, thereby ensuring a smooth transfer of power and a succession of emperors. Augustus' family, the Julio-Claudians ruled until 68 AD, followed by the Flavians who stayed in power until 96 AD. The Antonines who were celebrated for their wisdom, took the Roman Empire to greater heights from 96-180 AD.

Limited expansion took place after Augustus. Emperor Claudius invaded Britain in 43 AD, and in 106 AD Trajan took Dacia (part of modern Hungary and Romania). With military and political stability, farms and estates improved; roads made efficient communications possible, and new towns and cities were founded, even in remote ar-

Augustus, whose reign marked a high point in Roman history.

The Triano columns with ancient scenes of Roman history carved in encircling bands.

eas. Provincial governors served long terms and became familiar with territories they supervised, and the civil service became very proficient at running the daily business of the empire.

The emperors grew supremely powerful, and were regarded and worshipped as gods after their deaths. This provided a common base of loyalty among the people of the vast empire who had very diverse religions, traditions and origins.

Around this time, a new religion sprang up in the eastern regions of the empire based on the teachings of Jesus Christ. Although Jesus was crucified about 30 AD, his disciples spread Christianity throughout the empire. Persecution of Christians began first from local malevolence, then orders from Rome.

Increasing disorder

When Emperor Commodus died in 192 AD, disorder broke out. The central authority could no longer hold the empire together because of its immensity. Many emperors tried to seize the throne by force; generals fought among themselves for power, and from 235 to 284 AD, 60 army commanders were named emperors by their troops. While the defenses of the empire weakened, the Goths, a Germanic tribe invaded Roman territory many times, and the Persians raided Syria and Mesopotamia.

Diocletian, a general who was proclaimed emperor in 284 AD by his troops, decided to restore order by dividing the empire into east and west, and then reorganising the empire into small units, with each unit having its own government and army. He named Maximian as co-emperor to reign over the western part, and appointed two deputies to succeed them. Heavier taxes were consequently needed to finance the larger government and army.

Through the 2nd century, Christians were brutally persecuted and many blamed them for the evils of the time by having offended the ancestral Roman gods. By 303 AD, Diocletian banned Christian worship.

Diocletian's system of shared rule and succession immediately failed as several men attempted to take the throne. In 306 AD, Constantine I was declared emperor over the western provinces. He conquered his major rival and received a vision that promised him victory, only if he fought under the sign of the cross. By 313 AD, Christians were given freedom to worship.

Constantine later defeated his co-emperor Licinius (of the eastern provinces),and in 330 AD moved his capital to Byzantium and renamed the city Constantinople. Constantine died in 337 AD, and his sons and nephews struggled against each other for the throne. One of his nephews, Julian became emperor in 361 AD. He tried to reestablish the ancestral Roman religion and forbid Christianity, but by then Christianity had become the official religion of the empire.

Fall of the Roman Empire

The West Roman Empire grew weaker and weaker as Vandals, Visigoths and other Germanic tribes invaded Gaul, Spain and northern Africa. In 410 AD, the Visigoths looted Rome.
The fall of the Roman Empire is usually dated 476 AD, the year that the last ruler of the West Roman Empire, Romulus Augustulus, was forced from the throne by Germanic chieftain, Odoacer, and the West Empire was carved up into several kingdoms. The East Roman Empire existed as the Byzantine Empire for some time. However, by 1453, the Turks took Constantinople and the disintegration of the Roman Empire became evident.

Rise of the Popes

Odoacer, the Germanic leader who overthrew the last Roman emperor, ruled for 17 years until he was murdered by Theodoric, king of another Germanic tribe. Theodoric governed Italy peacefully with an Ostrogoth army and an Italian administration. However, the kingdom grew weak after his death in 526 AD, and by 553 AD, the Byzantine emperor Justinian who ruled the East Roman Empire conquered the Ostrogoths and so it was that the old empire reunited. In 572 AD the Lombards, another Germanic tribe, invaded and terminated Byzantine rule.

A new political and religious power

Lorenzo di Medici, also known as Il Magnifico.

Galileo Galilee.

and his son Louis I succeeded him.

Louis then divided the empire among his sons who fought among themselves for more land. These battles continued until Otto the Great was crowned emperor in 962 AD, marking the start of what was later called the Holy Roman Empire.

Revival of the Arts

Around 1000 AD, Italian cities grew independently in wealth and political importance and many, like Pisa, Milan, Venice, Genoa and Florence became city-states. Each having their own trade, banking and foreign policy. The city-states supported the arts: Renaissance

came into being in the 4th and 5th centuries. The popes began to expand their authority and opposed foreign invasion and foreign rule. For 200 years they resisted the attempts by the Lombards to capture Rome, as they had of most of Italy.

Enlisting the help of two Frankish kings, Charlemagne and Pepin, the popes halted the Lombards. By 774 AD, Charlemagne had completely overwhelmed the Lombards and took Lombardy. Recognising Charlemagne's power, and wanting to seal an alliance with him, Pope Leo III crowned him emperor of the Romans in 800 AD. With newly acquired land, the popes set up political rule in the Papal States in central Italy. Charlemagne died in 814 AD

Christopher Columbus.

artists were patronised, and thrived in all fields. There was a revival in interest of classical Greek and Roman art, literature, and thought.

Inventions such as printing evolved and expanded and research was conducted in science and maths, and the first great European voyages commenced. Three of the world's greatest artists, Leonardo da Vinci, Michelangelo, and Raphael were working in the city-states of Italy at the same time! Italian Renaissance styles in art, architecture, literature, philosophy, music, political science were pillars of European cultural and scientific developments.

City-States

The city-states became some of the most important and attractive prizes in Europe. Each were often weakened by internal strife between citizens and became vulnerable to foreign attacks. The most well known of these was the fight between the Guelphs and Ghibellines – the Guelphs sided the sovereign papal power while the Ghibellines supported the emperor.

In 1494, when some city-states requested foreign assistance to settle some violent internal disagreements, King Charles VIII of France invaded and showed the city-states that they were quite vulnerable in their fractiousness. For many years thereafter, France and the Holy Roman Empire fought incessantly over Italy.

Spanish and Austrian Domination

The Spanish king of the Habsburg family, Charles I, was crowned Emperor Charles V of the Holy Roman Empire in 1519; he warred with Francis I of France, and approximately 38 years later, almost all of Italy was under Spain. Spanish Habsburg power began to decline in the late 1500's and Italy came under Austrian Habsburg rule by the early 1700's. It was a time when the Austrian king controlled Italy through local Italian rulers.

Napoleon and the French Revolution

Around 1789, these rulers had started to side with European kings who opposed France; when the French king was overthrown and France became a republic, secret clubs sprang up throughout Italy supporting an Italian republic.

French Republican armies began to advance across Europe in 1796; Napoleon invaded northern Italy and ousted the Austrian rulers. Italian republics with constitutions and legal reforms were set up. In 1804, Napoleon became emperor and part of northern Italy became the Kingdom of Italy while the remainder became part of France. Only Sicily and Sardinia remained free. Under Napoleon, many Italians for the first time, since the days of ancient Rome, began to see the feasibility of a united and free Italy - laws and money were the same in all parts of the country, people from different parts of the country served in one army, and representative assemblies had been set up. French rule lasted for less than 20 years until Napoleon was defeated in 1814 by the major powers of Europe.

A New Order in Europe

Representatives met at the Congress of Vienna and it was decided that Italy's former rulers would be reinstalled, and the kingdom of the Two Sicilies were formed. This consisted of Naples and Sicily under the rule of the Bourbon royal family, and the region of Pied-

mont in the north-west, including Sardinia, under the rule of the royal House of Savoy. Venetia and Lombardy came under Austrian rule, while most of the Papal States was returned to the Pope. Several remaining northern states were placed under dukes loyal to Austria.

During this time, Piedmont became the focal point of reforms. In the 1820's and early 1830's, Giuseppe Mazzini, an Italian patriot who was bent on creating an independent and unified Italian republic, instigated a few unsuccessful revolts against local rulers.

Italy in Revolt and Unity

During 1848, there were revolutions in France, Austria, in many German states

Commemorative stamp of San Marino.

Guards of San Marino.

and in all major Italian cities. By the following year, Austria had regained control over most of Italy. The kingdom of Sardinia was defeated and King Charles Albert was succeeded by his son, Victor Emmanuel II. The King of Naples rejected the constitution he was forced to endorse the year before, jailed the revolutionaries and ruled harshly. The Pope and the Grand Duke restored their control over Rome and Tuscany respectively, and Austria suppressed the revolutionary government of Venice.

Many Italians realized that in order to have any improvements they had to expel the Austrian rulers. The King of Sardinia had kept the constitutions he granted the people in 1848, including the tri-coloured flag, the symbol of Ital-ian patriotism, and the prime minister, Count Cavour, tried to set up the kingdom as a progressive, independent state, and even tried, as a spokesman for Italy against Austria, to have the kingdom accepted into European councils. Consequently, national unity under the King of Sardinia became the goal for most Italian patriots. When Count Cavour arranged a defence agreement with Napoleon III, Austria feared that it would lose Italy and in 1859, declared war on Sardinia. Austria lost and was pushed almost as far east as Venice. The dukes who had supported Austria were ousted by local revolts.

In 1860, the entire northern part of Italy, with the exception of Venice, down to the Papal States in the south became part of the Kingdom of Sardinia.

In the same year, Giuseppe Garibaldi with a thousand volunteers defeated the Bourbon rulers and their far larger professional army, and brought freedom to Sicily. He proceeded on and captured southern Italy and Naples. (see 'Garibaldi - Italy's hero' on page 30).

The Kingdom of Italy

In 1861, with a unanimous vote, Victor Emmanuel II, King of Sardinia, formed the Kingdom of Italy and became king over the whole peninsular, with the exception of Venetia, the city of Rome and the tiny San Marino. Six years later, he supported Prussia's war against Austria, where the agreement was that if Prussia defeated Austria, Italy would have Venice. Austria's defeat only took one month, and Venice became part of Italy. In 1870, war broke out between France and Prussia. France withdrew its troops from Rome, and the Pope was left defenceless to the advancement of the Italian army. The Pope's territory was reduced to the Vatican, the Lateran palaces and the papal villa at Castel Gandolfo. Rome became the capital of Italy in 1871, and finally Italy included the complete peninsular.

The Kingdom of Italy was left with the huge debt caused by the wars. This problem was exacerbated by the fact that Italy had few natural resources. A north-south divide emerged with the south being much poorer. Regional disputes occurred, plus it was behind many other industrialized nations of the time. In fact, Italy was far from being unified. The Parliament did not represent all the people as only the rich were allowed to vote. There were many who detested being ruled by the Piedmontese leaders of the Kingdom of Sardinia, and the Pope refused to recognize the legality of the new country and forbade Roman Catholics from voting in the national elections. Moreover, Socialists and labour movements began to emerge in all parts of the country. Even though things gradually improved by 1915 both socially and economically, and working conditions improved, production increased, and more people became educated, the government was still unable

Victor Emanuele II.

to win confidence and support from its people. There was the additional problems when it came to the country's foreign policy. The Italian government wanted to increase its popularity by setting up a colony in North Africa, it also wanted to expand Italy's role in world affairs and by 1882, Italy joined the Triple Alliance along with Germany and Austria-Hungary.

From 1887 to 1896, Italy ventured out and made forays into North Africa, that is, Ethiopia and Libya. Italy won over Libya and the Dodecanese Islands from the Turks in 1912.

World War I

World War I lasted from 1914 to 1918. Germany and Austria-Hungary marched against the Allies – France, Britain and Russia (as it was before it became the Soviet Union in 1922). Even though Italy was in the Triple Alliance which included Germany and Austria-Hungary, she stayed out of the war for almost a year; this was because Italy was friendly with France while it was the Austrian-held territories, Trieste and Trentino, that Italy wanted most. The Italians had a divided opinion about the war. Some sided with the Allies, others supported neutrality. The Allies made a secret promise to Italy that if they won the war, Italy would have Trieste and Trentino, portions of Istria, Dalmatia and Albania, plus territory in Africa, as well as financial aid. The war

King Umberto in 1867.

sacrificed more lives and incurred more expenses than expected and very little was gained. For two years against Austria along the north-east border of Italy, the Italian army only progressed 15 kilometres, and in 1917, they had to retreat. But before the end of the war Italy won some important victories.

When the war ended, Italy was given almost 23,000 square kilometres of vital Austria-Hungary territory, including Trieste and Trentino, but this was far less than what the Allies had promised. Italians, especially veterans, were therefore left more dissatisfied and bitter with their governments than before the war. Also post-war unemployment in Italy skyrocketed.

The 1919 elections, first in which all

The world wars took a toll on Italy.

adult males were allowed to vote, saw landslide victories for two new mass parties: the Popular Party, which had links with the Roman Catholic Church, and the Socialist Party. Still, too many different parties in Parliament impeded progress in the formation of an effective national leadership. The people once again threatened to revolt; there were workers strikes and land demands by farmers throughout Italy.

Mussolini and Fascism

The new movement called Fascism sprang up, led by a former Socialist, Benito Mussolini. This movement was favoured by many. The movement stood for strict government, ordered control of labour and industry, and promised peace and discipline.

In October 1922, the Fascists marched on Rome and King Victor Emmanuel III made Mussolini premier of Italy. Three years later, Mussolini was ruling Italy as dictator and was called 'Il Duce' (The Leader). The Fascists used secret police and scare tactics to oppress resistance; they controlled schools and the media and used propaganda skilfully; employers, workers, and youths were organized into groups that strongly supported Mussolini. The Italian Fascist movement inspired similar developments in Europe and in Latin America. Many other countries were impressed by Mussolini's achievements in apparently fulfilling his promise of order and military might. Most of all with the Lateran Treaty of 1929, Mussolini brought together the Church and the government for the first time since 1870, when Italy took over Rome.

For ten years, from 1935, Italy was almost constantly at war. In 1936, Mussolini took Ethiopia and he helped Francisco Franco win the Spanish Civil War, and later that same year, he signed an agreement with Hitler, the German dictator, and made Italian foreign policy identical with that of Germany. This paper was called the 'Rome-Berlin Axis' which suggested that all Europe would rotate around a line drawn between the two capitals. In 1939, Mussolini captured Albania.

World War II

On September 1, 1939, Hitler's army invaded Poland, France and Britain declared war on Germany. On June 10, 1940, less than two weeks before Germany captured France, Italy joined the war. Italy was defeated in Ethiopia, Eritrea, Greece and North Africa; in reality Italy was not ready to go to war, militarily nor economically. On July 10, 1943, the Allies invaded Sicily, and two months later they landed on the mainland. Italy surrendered that same day. During this time, Mussolini was put into prison under the orders of King Emmanuel III, but he was rescued by German paratroopers and fled to northern Italy. On October 13, Italy went to war against Germany and was defeated. Germany replaced Mussolini as head of a puppet government.

The Allies advanced and there was civil war in Italy - the 'Resistance', an anti-Fascist, anti-Nazi movement fought against the remaining Fascist forces. Some of the members of the Resistance were members of the Communist Party.

Mussolini with Hitler.

By 1945, Mussolini was caught by the Resistance trying to escape to Switzerland and was shot.

A peace treaty was signed in 1947 and Italy lost Eritrea, the Dodecanese Islands, and Libya. Italian Somaliland was put under Italian administration and also United Nations territorial trust from 1949 for ten years.

The Italian Republic

In May of 1946, King Victor Emmanuel III gave up the throne to his son Humbert II On June 2, Italy held its first free election in twenty years. The people voted for a republic, and they elected a Constituent Assembly to form a new democratic constitution. The constitution was adopted by the Assembly in 1947.

The Christian Democrats, the Socialists and the Communists were the most powerful political parties in the Italian republic. However, the Christian Democrats, usually in a coalition with smaller parties, has had a majority in every cabinet since the second World War, and they held the top positions.

The most powerful man in the government from 1948 to 1953 was the head of the Christian Democrats, Premier Alcide De Gasperi. He drew up plans for industrial and agricultural growth; under him, Italy formed closer ties with the United States and other Western European countries. He also expelled the Communist Party from the government. De Gasperi died in 1954 and the Christian Democratic party weakened. This allowed other parties more say in policies. But still the Communist Party, despite its large size, was not allowed any of the important seats in the government.

Political, Economic and Social problems

In the 1940's and 1950's, Italy was receiving and depending on aid from the United States. In 1950, Italy became a founding member of NATO and the European Payments Union, now known as the European Monetary Agreement. Italy became a member of the United Nations in 1955 and in 1958 helped found the European Economic Community with other European nations.

The Italian economy grew and by the 1960's, industrial production had risen to twice its prewar level and Italy's economic growth was the highest in Europe. Industry took over agriculture's position as the country's most important economic activity.

However, Italy's rapid growth and

Aldo Moro, who met with an unhappy ending.

changes brought its own problems. The gap between the richer north and poorer south widened despite government aid to the south. Social unrest spread. Questions about the workers' share in the nation's increasing prosperity became more important. There were rising shortages in housing, and bigger demands for social reforms. Strikes and protests by labour union members became more common, which brought increases in wages and benefits for workers.

In 1962, the Socialists were given a role in the government, their coalition with the Christian Democrats created a fairer tax system; higher education became more available, and regional governments were given more authority thus becoming more efficient. Inflation

became a major economic problem.

A worldwide increase in the cost of petroleum was largely to blame for the spiralling inflation in Italy as she imported most of her petroleum. Moreover, the increased wages and the government's inability to raise taxes added to the inflation. The government at this time had also increased its financial burden by taking on many collapsing and unprofitable businesses.

The Government

The government started to lose support of the people and was regarded by the majority as being incompetent.

In the 1970's, the Communist Party received increased support from the people and their influence in Italian politics expanded. The Communists in Italy were largely dependent on Eastern European and Soviet Communism. By 1977, the Communists agreed to support the national government in return for having the right to vote in major issues. But they were still excluded from the Cabinet. In the 1980's, the Communists' voice weakened significantly.

From the late 1960's, the politcal role of the Roman Catholic church abated. By 1970, divorce was legalised and in 1974 the Italian Parliament went against intense opposition by the church and voted to allow abortions. In 1985, an agreement was passed that the 1929 provision which made Roman Catholicism the state religion of Italy was no

Bettino Craxi who, with the Socialist Party, led the country from 1983 – 1987.

The Christian Democrats in Congress.

longer valid. Although opposed by the Christian Democrats and the United States, the government, working with the Communist Party, has been able to use harsher policies to control inflation and build a more efficient economy.

This move has also been highly unpopular with the Red Brigades – a small extreme left group of terrorists who oppose all the political parties. They shot some government officials and leading business executives, carried out some bombings of public places, and in 1978 they kidnapped and murdered Aldo Moro, a former premier who was expected to become Italy's next President. He was also the man who tried to bring the Christian Democrats and the Communists together. Follow-

ing this, the government led a crack-down on terrorists. As a result, hundreds were arrested and convicted. By the late 1980's, terrorism had diminished to insignificance.

However, organised crime has for a long time been a huge problem in Italy. Organised crime ranged from corrupting and bribing officials to obtain lucrative construction contracts to drug trafficking. General Dalla Chiesa who was fighting against the Mafia, was killed by them in 1982. The government began mass prosecution of people accused as members of the Mafia and many of them were convicted.

Today, Italy continues to face social problems due to the north-south divide of wealth, and administrative problems

Garibaldi – Italy's Hero

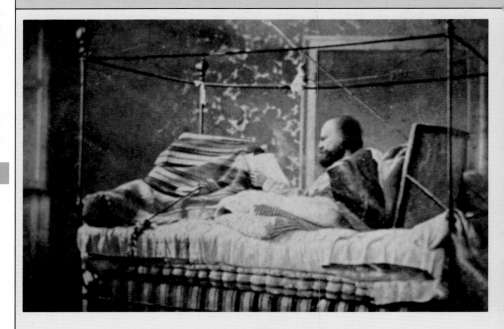

Giuseppe Garibaldi, "the sleeping lion whose breathing makes the oceans swell".

Sardinia's most famous champion, Giuseppe Garibaldi (1807-1882) was a military hero who fought to unite Italy. He was born in Nice, France and he began life as a sailor, until his patriotic views and friendliness with Giuseppe Mazzini, an Italian patriot who was bent on the liberation of Italy, placed him in the role of conspirator. In 1834 he fled to South America after taking part in an unsuccessful rebellion against the King of Sardinia, where as a soldier and privateer, he fought for rising republics gaining expert experience in clandestine warfare. He became famous for fighting for the Brazilian state of Rio Grande do Sul against the Brazilian government, and he also fought for Uruguay which was struggling for independence against Argentina.

Garibaldi returned to northern Italy in 1848 to help the Lombards fight their Austrian rulers. He led an Italian legion that failed to defend the newly formed Roman Republic against French and Austrian troops sent to reinstate the Pope.

because of an unstable, and frequently changing government generally not dealing with problems in Italy.

In 1981, for the first time since World War II, Italy had a non-Christian Democrat as premier, he was Giovanni Spadolini, the leader of the Republican Party. From 1983 to 1987, Bettino Craxi of the Socialist Party took Spadolini's place. His government held office for the longest period since the Italian republic was established. Since he retired, Christian Democrats have held the office of premier in Italy.

He fled again, this time to Staten Island, New York, and worked as a candlemaker for 5 years.

Upon returning to Italy, he based himself on the island of Caprera, just off the north coast of Sardinia. The famous house 'Casa Bianca', in which he resided for 33 years can be seen on the island. As he had recently arrived from America, it was built in South American style.

In 1859, Garibaldi took part in the Sardinian war against Austria. Then in 1860, he and his 'thousand' red-shirted volunteer troops conquered the Kingdom of the Two Sicilies for the Kingdom of Italy, which was just coming into being. They sailed from Genoa and landed in Sicily, swiftly defeating the Bourbon forces. His army had grown to 20,000 and he was determined to overthrow the Kingdom of Naples, and establish the union of Italy under Victor Emmanuel II. He landed with his forces in Calabria and entered Naples in February 1861, taking the city without firing a shot. This was the first time an army entered a city by train.

He resigned his command to King Victor Emmanuel II. But in 1862 and again in 1867, against the wishes of the king, he tried and failed to capture Rome from the Pope. Rome only became part of the Kingdom of Italy in 1870. In 1874, Garibaldi was elected to the Italian parliament.

He died in 1882 and was buried on his favorite island of Caprera. His tomb with its naval guardian, has the inscription -"the sleeping lion whose breathing makes the ocean swell". Nearby, is the pine tree which he planted in 1867 for his daughter, Clelia. Clelia lived on the island until her death in 1957. The museum on the island displays artifacts and photographs from the patriot's lifetime and his bed is housed in a large glass case.

Political tenterhooks

Italy has had more than 50 governments since the second World War but most of the leading figures in politics have ridden the waves and keep appearing in a succession of governments. On an average, Italy's cabinets have lasted no more than ten months. Italy has eight main national political parties. These include the Christian Democrat, the Social Democrat, the Republican, the Communist, the Socialist, the Liberal, the Monarchist and the Neo-Fascist.

Recently, several breakaway parties were formed, or revamped, such as that of the porn star, 'Cicciolina' and her 'Party of Love', then the entry of Alessandra Mussolini, the Duce's granddaughter, into politics, the rise of Neo-Fascism and the entry of Moana Pozzi into the political arena. Only in 1948, when the Christian Democrats won a landslide election, have any of the eight parties had a majority of votes since World War II. Christian Democrats, strongly supported by the Catholic Church, now hold more than 30 percent of the electoral votes. The Communist Party is the largest in Europe. Its stronghold is central Italy as the Democrats score in Rome, Lazio and Abruzzi. The Socialist Party holds third place with 10 percent of the votes. Up to 90 percent of the electorate normally turn out to vote.

Although the Communists have never had a majority to form a government, neither have the Democrats, thus always resulting in political tenterhooks. The Socialist Party maintains the political balance. There are few debates in government and the Prime Minister can make no decisions without approval of the parties.

Economy

The Italian economy has had a checkered career in the last forty years, and still shows a strange mixture of aggressive innovation and stubborn traditionalism. While having one of the poorest European economies, it still enjoys one of the highest living standards in the Western world (on paper at least). These facts, while appearing contradictory, hide an important and ongoing schism - the ever-present north-south divide; resulting in a highly-successful industrial north, and a rather desperately poor agricultural south.

Citrus fruits are important export crops for Italy.

33

Natural resources

Italy's natural resources have traditionally been scanty for both agricultural and industrial purposes. With a large proportion of the land given over to mountainous terrain, and much of the remainder marshy, it is only the consistent effort of centuries that has established and maintained soil fertility. Land reclamation schemes, such as in the **Po Valley**, the

Motor industry in Modena.

Maremma plain in **Tuscany** and the **Pontine** marshes, carried out in the 19th and 20th centuries testify to the hard effort of generations.

Agricultural activity

That said, agriculture remains the main economic activity for much of the country, especially in the south. Citrus fruits (especially lemons), olives, potatoes and tomatoes are important crops, but it is wheat that is the main agricultural product (think of all that pasta!) – **Sicily**, in fact, is known as Italy's breadbasket!

Hemp is important (Italy is Europe's second largest producer after the old Soviet countries), and so is the produc-

tion of silk, although the stiff competition from Japan has, for decades, been eroding this market. And let us not forget the mighty vine - Italy is the world's largest producer (and consumer) of wine! Fisheries, while unimportant in comparison to the North Atlantic countries, are the main form of support for many in the coastal areas, the main haul being sardines, anchovies and tuna. There is little cattle overall, the main herds being in the north for dairy produce, while sheep are reared in the south and in the islands.

The reliance on the country's agriculture is imposed because industrial resources have long been limited, with the absence of coal and iron in any quantity, hampering the early days of industrialization. Some anthracite used

Italy is a producer and also a great consumer of olive oil.

Prosciutto ham awaiting its moment of savour.

Fish market in Syracuse, Sicily.

to be mined in **Piedmont**, but apart from that, all fuel has to be imported. Italy does, however, have limited deposits of natural gas in Lombardy, the lower Po Valley, and in the south.

Alternative power

With little power-producing fuel, Italy has been forced to look elsewhere for power sources. The big success story is HEP – hydroelectric power: putting their mountainous country to good use, the Italians have created their own "white coal". However, Italy does produce significant quantities of asbestos, aluminium, bauxite, cadmium, iron-ore, pig-iron, mercury, zinc, gypsum, mar-

ble, potash, salt, sulphur and talc, all of which are exported in significant quantities internationally.

Apart from the traditional raw-materials, Italy during the last century, has created a mini-revolution in the manufacturing industry. The manufacturing industries are, to a large extent, confined to the northern plains, with Turin and Milan being the major centres. Its major industries are iron and steel, motor vehicles, chemicals, the production of machinery, the refining of oil and gas, textile yarn and fabrics, producing clothing, especially footwear and accessories, and all the all-important food processing.

Today, manufacturing, mining and trade are Italy's most important economic activities. In **Turin**, the famous Fiat car giant has expanded (they also own Alfa-Romeo, Lancia and Ferrari); the industry in Naples is dominated by the Alfa-Romeo car business; in **Taranto** the steel industry dominates, and in **Ivrea**, electronics is king, along with the large Olivetti typewriting and computer company; in **Varese** the accent is on a prosperous engineering industry as are the towns of **Bergamo**, **Lecco** and **Brescia**, and **Syracuse** is predominantly a centre for the production of petro-chemicals.

There is a big textile industry, based mainly on cotton and silk, while **Milan** is, of course, the fashion-house of Europe. Numerous manufactured goods are exported, from clothes and accessories, to furniture, household appliances and photographic film. The trademarks, linked with the production of these goods are household names world-wide. Textiles, cars, leather goods, plastics and chemicals are among the most exported manufactured Italian produce.

The country's excellent system of transport, both by road and by means of its well-run railway, ensures quick and efficient delivery of its manufactured goods throughout the country and to those countries which import from Italy. Swift delivery of Italy's goods through Europe is also enhanced by the country's location – central and south to the countries of the **European Common Market**, and by its excellent maritime connections through such major commercial seaports as **Genoa**, **Venice** and **Trieste**.

Overall, inflation and unemployment in Italy is chronically high and many Italians work outside their own country, sending money back to their families in Italy. The agricultural prosperity is a major achievement in Italy and remains the backbone of the country, supporting a large number of the population.

Picking grapes for wine-making.

Garden plots to vast rice fields

The land-reform program after World War II did most to develop the country into a major producer and, in the south, **Bari**, **Naples** and **Taranto** became major industrial centres, while **Turin**

Genoa, one of Italy's older ports.

nantly cereals, wheat, maize, rice and potatoes, plus livestock of cattle and pigs. Cooked meats, like salami, Parma ham and the famous Italian cheeses represent a significant proportion of the animal products which are exported as well as consumed locally. The hides of cattle and pigs also go towards the export drive, being converted into leather goods which are highly prized abroad. Wheat production is of prime importance as this is the raw material for the flour from which Italy's pasta is made.

Italy is a major world supplier of sugar beet, grown both in the north and the south. In the warm south, citrus fruits, olives, tomatoes and tobacco are raised; also goats, donkeys and mules. Wine is produced throughout the country but primarily in the south. Italy

and **Milan**, in the north, attracted many thousands of workers from the fields of the poorer south.

More than 15 percent of Italians now work on the land, mostly on small peasant or family farming plots, or vineyards, although great swathes of cultivated land linked to co-operative farming schemes cut across areas such as the **Marches**. Some large centres are renown for the manufacture of certain products from agricultural produce - **Como**, for silk, and **Biella** for wool, for example. Certain areas are famous for their production of perfumes which rely on extensive fields of flowers. However, the raising of food and wine crops are predominant.

Produce in the north are predomi-

Fashion is one of Italy's bright and high-stepping industries.

Italy is one of the largest wine exporters in Europe.

supplies the world with more wine than any other country. Italy is also a world producer of vegetables like aubergines, cabbage, carrots, cauliflowers, onions, pumpkins and tomatoes, and of fruits like apples, apricots, citrus fruits, melons, peaches, pears, plums, watermelons and nuts. Italy has long been a major supplier of fish, seafoods and fish products to the world market, and several vast desalination plants along its coast and on its islands, produce significant amounts of salt, both for domestic consumption and export.

Tourist lira

Today, tourism is a thriving industry, being the third most important destination in Europe and fourth in the world. Almost four percent of the Italian population work in the tourist industry. The country offers ski and mountaineering resorts in the north, some of the most beautiful of all of Europe's beaches, basking under a pleasant Mediterranean climate all around its enormously long coastline, historic centers unsurpassed on a world scale, a network of heritage, the love of art, music, theater, opera, literature and architecture which runs throughout the land – a 'land of light and culture', and the attraction of a lively and gregarious people who have a dedication to producing some of the best wines and dishes to be found anywhere in the world.

Italy's revenues over the past decades also come from being heavily-touristed.

Geography

Italy is divided into twenty regions, most of them on the mainland (**Valle d'Aosta, Piedmont,
Liguria, Lombardy, Trentino-
Alto Adige, Friuli-Venezia
Giulia,** Veneto, Emilia-
Romagna, Tuscany, Marches, Umbria,
**Latium, Abruzzi, Molise, Campania,
Apulia, Basilicata, Calabria**) plus the
islands of **Sardinia** and **Sicily**. Boot-
shaped and extending far out into the
Mediterranean, Italy stretches from the
Alpine zones al-
most to the shores
of Africa, hence the
climate of the
country varies considerably.

43

The north is generally continental,
with cold winters and hot summers. In
the south, the climate offers hot and dry
summers and warm, damp winters. Even
in the southerly islands of Sardinia and
Sicily, snow can fall during the winter-
time. **Messina**, in Sicily
can be the hottest
place in Italy, with
temperatures rising
during August to
around 30 degrees
centigrade. The 800
kilometre (500 mile-
long) Italian penin-
sular is surrounded
on three sides by four
seas: the **Ligurian**, the
Tyrrhenian, the **Ionian**
and the **Adriatic**.

Dawn mists in Alpine Italy.

The Dolomites in the San Martino area.

Water is, and always has been, a paramount element in the Italian way of life. Without water it is impossible to grow grapes, from which the Italian's largest export is made! With almost twenty major rivers, and numerous lakes, Italy is blessed with an abundance of water in most areas. The Romans even adopted the **River Styx** of Greek mythology to signify the barrier between life and death. The main river systems of Italy are the **Tiber**, the river which runs through Rome, rising in the high **Apennines** and winding its way south across the country before disgorging into the **Tyrrhenian Sea** near Rome; the **Adige**, which runs down from its source on the Italian-Swiss-Austrian border; the **Brenta**, running south-east from **Trento** to its mouth below **Venice**;

Rippling sand-dunes in the nature park, Maremma.

The Spas of Italy

The link between water, spas and perceived health is one that goes back to the dawn of mankind, pervading legends, myths and religions, and the works of poets, philosophers and scientists. **Vitruvius**, a 1st century BC Roman writer and architect, noticed that temples sited close to mineral springs received more ex-votos than others for recoveries from illness, and ascribed this to the "spirit" of the springs. **Herodotus** first established the concept of hydrotherapy, detailing not only the properties of the various waters, but also the length of the cures proposed. **Galan** and **Aristotle** also lent weight to the use of hydrotherapy by attributing all sorts of properties to the mineral spring waters and mud applications, and extolled the qualities of hot vapours.

The first spas were those of the ancient Greeks in **Thessaly**, **Asia Minor** and near the **Aegean Sea**. As favourite resorts, these spas were distinctive in the beauty of their execution and the precious works of art on display, a habit carried on by the Romans and other lovers of water and baths. The later Romans adopted the culture of the spa with great fervour, a kind of "thermal mania", prompting **Pliny** to write "For more than 600 years the only doctors the Romans ever saw were their baths".

It is no wonder then, that the modern Italian would never even consider a pilgrimage to the famous thermal baths of Greece and Turkey or the saunas of Finland, when he or she has all the hydrotherapeutical choices imaginable at home - steamrooms and saunas, high velocity sprays and whirlpools, mudbaths and mudpacks, honeyrubs, paraffin and sulphur packs, vapor inhalations or just plain regimes of mineral water diets. Aside from the possible rejuvenative effects of these treatments, the accompanying sporting activities available (swimming, walking, hiking, tennis, horse-riding etc) must have a marked therapeutic value themselves!

For those with a yen to "take the waters", below is a quick round-up of some of the more popular resorts: The **Abano Terme** in **Veneto** (just outside **Padua**) is the Mecca of mud and massage, and boasts 130 mineral springs. One of the most important spas in Europe, it has been a favourite since Roman times. **Grado**, in

Thermal springs of sulphur and mud in Saturnia, Tuscany.

Friuli-Venezia Giulia, is a renowned island off the Adriatic coast (connected to the mainland via a three-mile causeway), famed for its sand treatments and seawater immersions. **Levico** and **Vetriola** in **Trentino**, and **Merano** in **Alto Adige**, date from the turn of the century, and specialize in mudbaths, rubdowns and "radioactive" water therapy. The waters are high in arsenic and iron, said to be good for the blood and circulation. **Saint-Vincent** in the **Valle d'Aosta** is recommended for digestive complaints (probably induced by the richness of the food at the town's restaurants), while the baroque spa of **Salsomaggiore** in **Emilia-Romagna** is fabled for its mud remedies and warm saltwater immersions. **Tuscany** has more than its fair share of **Terme**, the better known ones are **Cianciano**, **Montecatini**, **Saturnia** (sulphur and mud cures), **Montepulciano** and **Petriolo**. The Italian islands are also well served, with **Terme** on **Elba** and **Ischia**, as well as **Sicily** (**Castroreale**), the **Eolie Islands** and **Sardinia** (**Sardara**, **San Saturnino** and **Aurora**).

Sardinian waters are crystal clear, peacock blue or emerald green.

and the **Po**, Italy's longest water course, stretching from the French border all the way east to its delta at **Porto Tolle** on the **Adriatic** coast.

The waters around Italy abound in fish and are ideal for sailing and cruising. Some beaches offer waves suitable for surfing or windsurfing, others are rocky and buffeted by the sea. Some of the highest sea cliffs in Europe are in Italy where a combination of sea and wind has battered and smoothed the rocks into fantastic and weird shapes. The Adriatic sea to the east can sometimes be disappointingly grey-blue, whereas the waters off the Sardinian coast can be crystal clear, peacock blue and a mesmerizing emerald green. The land too has held almost magical prop-

erties with the ancient Italian inhabitants and those of the classical period with its abundance.

In the north, the spectacular Alpine scenery is fissured with glaciers among jagged peaks and pasture-filled valleys interspersed with deep lakes. Most fertile of areas is that expanse of the Lombardy plains extending from the **Gulf of Venice** on the **Adriatic Sea**, to the foothills of the French and Swiss Alps. Apart from natural lakes, there are many artificial reservoirs in the mountains and hydroelectric schemes have been installed in many regions.

With the broad exception of the **Po Valley** in the north, Italy is almost exclusively mountainous: the massif of the Alps dominate the northern part of

Elba Island whose features are typical of any Mediterranean island.

the country, while the **Apennine** chain forms the backbone of the peninsula, extending its entire length.

The Apennine is granite, gneiss, sedimentary limestones and sandstones, dolomite, marble and lava. Earthquakes have been known to be a regular haz-

ard. To the west of the mountain spine, volcanic activity is prevalent in some regions. There are two famous volcanoes in Italy, **Mount Etna**, on **Sicily**, Europe's largest active volcano, and **Vesuvius**, on the southern mainland near **Naples**. In the northern Alpine

coastal plains, the low hilly country and terraces up mountainsides are all cultivated wherever possible; the mountainous regions are devoted to lumber and forested areas, and the bare rocky peaks, wherever possible, are adapted, during appropriate conditions, as ski slopes.

This topology determines the prevailing weather patterns, and helps to ensure the (generally) mild conditions. The natural barrier of the Alpine massif shield the Italian lakes from the worst excesses of the northern winter, while both the Maritime Alps and the emerging Apennine range protects the Ligurian coast, intensifying the effect of its Mediterranean aspect (watch out for the acres of glass houses that bedeck the hillsides in Liguria – market gardening, particularly fruits and flowers, are its main export). In the north, the exposed Po Valley is subject to the rigours of the typically harsh continental winters, with the proximity of the (Adriatic) coast having little mellowing effect. Further south, the Mediterranean influence is more clearly evident (at least along the coastal plains – it may be surprising to learn that there are ski resorts in the Apennines as far south as Florence and Rome; and wait for it....Calabria in Sicily!). Another climatic factor is the occurrence of several localised, periodic wind patterns, the best known of which are the **Scirocco**, a damp, dirty wind which blows across the Mediterranean from North Africa; the cold, dry **Tramontana** from the north; and the **Bora** from the north-east Adriatic.

region are some of Europe's highest peaks, the **Matterhorn** and **Mont Blanc**. Forests adorn the sides of the hills, pines and firs of course, but perhaps also chestnut groves on the lower slopes, turning to beech and mountain larches as one climbs to the higher ground. Wildlife and game abound (see "Of Birds and Bears" on page 51), and national parks have been established throughout. The

OF BIRDS AND BEARS

From the wolf that suckled Romulus and Remus, the founders of ancient Rome, to the ever-present singing finch, from the Sardinian wild boar to the Marsican bear, from the Mediterranean octopus to the golden eagle - the wildlife of Italy is about as varied as can be found anywhere in Europe.

Ibex, chamoix, marmots, fox and hare inhabit the high **Alps** and **Dolomites**; the almost-extinct European brown bear and the wolf can be heard (and occasionally seen) in the central **Apennines**, while the fabled wild horses of **Sardinia** still canter the high plateaus.

Frogs, toads, newts and even salamanders thrive, snakes and lizards abound, while the European pond turtle, or terrapin, is not an uncommon sight on the inland lakes. Marine life is varied all around the Mediterranean, yet angling is a challenging skill, due to decades of over-fishing and the appalling pollution of many coastal areas.

Italy is an ornithologist's dream, with all

Flora and Fauna

51

Autumn gold in northern Italy.

Chestnuts popping from their husky shells.

manner of bird life to be seen. Songbirds have long been associated with Italy, although stocks have been depleted in many areas both by uncontrolled netting by the locals, as well as the ravages of the increasing bird of prey population.

Italian National Parks

Five national parks have been established in Italy, valuable "safe havens" for the flora and fauna of the regions. Strictly protected, they go a long way to safeguard the future of some of Italy's most threatened species, such as the golden eagle, brown bear, wolf, and water buffalo.

Gran Paradiso

The **Gran Paradiso National Park** is the oldest and best known in Italy. Covering some 173,000 acres in the **Graie Alps** between **Aosta** and **Turin**, it is divided by five major valleys giving a varied panorama of mountain peaks, waterfalls and icy torrents, glaciers, snowfields, water meadows, and forested valleys. The history of the park is inextricably linked with that of the ibex, or **Bouc-Castagn**.

Almost extinct in the early 19th century, a timely royal edict banning the hunting of this relative of the goat helped increase its numbers, and the founding of the park by **King Victor**

Camomile, a herbal favourite for tea.

Emmanuel III in 1922 ensured its survival in this region. Today there are over 3,000 ibex, as well as 6,000 chamois, protected in the park. Foxes are common, impressive in their white winter coats as they emerge from the high forests of larch, spruce, silver fir and scotch pine, and will, along with stoats often prey on baby marmots, those comical rodents apt to break into agitated barks and piercing whistles at the first sign of danger. The white hare too has its home here, while in the lower forests of alder, silver birch, ash and aspen, the squirrel leaps from branch to branch.

Most impressive of the birdlife is the golden eagle, of which there are five or six breeding pairs. Other common birds are the Alpine Chough, the Rock Partridge and the ptarmigan.

The alpine flowers provide an ever-changing kaleidoscope of colour through the seasons. In spring, melting snowfields give way to grassy meadows forming a verdant backdrop to the alpine anemones, buttercups and black vanilla orchids. Arnica, gentians, catchfly and bellflowers make their appearances, attracting a variety of insects such as butterflies and bees.

Not everything is perfect in this seeming Eden. Poaching is endemic, and difficult to control in this high mountainous region so close to the borders. Park keepers are vigilant, and publicity is being employed to attract more visitors, and much-needed revenue, to this beautiful alpine area.

Sunflower fields colour the landscape throughout Italy.

Cactus blossoms in Puglia and in the less wintry south.

Stelvio

Covering a massive 338,000 acres, the **Stelvio National Park** occupies the central Alps, spanning parts of **Lombardy** and **Trentino-Alto Adige**.

Rich in flora and fauna due to its very size, the park suffers from the incursions of the industrial age in the form of mines, quarries, HEP stations and the environmental bane of the numerous ski resorts. Despite this, there are extensive tracts of unspoilt land, housing all manner of alpine animals, birds, insects and plants, and on the human side, many traditional rustic and agricultural skills have been preserved, such as traditional cheesemaking

and manual scything. Much of the park is filled by high peaks, perfect for the ibex and chamoix, which, as in **Gran Paradiso**, predominate.

The 100-odd ever-receding glaciers that are found in the park have carved out the typical glacial features – "U"-shaped valleys, scree, lateral and terminal moraines, all of which provide extremely fertile ground for the abundance of alpine flora. Meadows and rich pastures sport daisies, yellow buttercups, pasque-flowers, globe-flowers, gentians and violets, striped daphne, clematis and the poisonous aconite. Further up, driadi, blue gentianellas, catchfly, androsace and alpine anemones can be found, while the highest slopes are reserved only for mosses and lichens.

Conifers weathering the winter in northern Italy.

A lone eagle soars, scanning the snowline, causing the marmots to explode into raucous whistling, startling an early stoat, which tumbles away across the rocks.

Abruzzi

The **Abruzzo National Park** in the central **Apennines**, is the most central of all Italy's national parks. Lying at altitudes of between 2,100 and 7,000 ft, it is predominantly a limestone area, showing all the karst phenomena typical of such areas: plateaus, sinkholes and dolines, and innumerable grottoes.

Unusual for a limestone area, as much as 66% of the park is covered by woodland. Willows, poplars, limes and hazelnut grow along riversides, while further up beech, maple, yew and holly blanket the hills, interspersed with clumps of violets and primroses. Above the mighty beech forests, the pines take over, clinging tenaciously to the steep dolomitic rock.

It is the rare wildlife that epitomizes this park. The European brown bear is only found in two parts of Italy – in a small area of Trentino, where there are believed to be about ten specimens, and here, where there are about 100 Marsican bears, a localized sub-species. There are about 30 wolves in the park, shy, retiring and difficult to spot (although they are often heard at night, howling!). Chamoix are common, as are deer – Roe, German and Slav deer

Poppies redden the meadows in the summer.

Birding in Italy

In terms of birds, Italy is part of the western **Palaearctic** zoogeographical region which includes the rest of Europe, North Africa and the Middle East.

Within this region the birds are largely shared; you cannot travel to Italy and see any bird species that does not also occur other places in the Mediterranean vicinity. The closest thing Italy has to an endemic species is the **Italian Sparrow** *Passer italiae* which some scientists regard as actually a subspecies of the widespread **House Sparrow** *P. domesticus*.

However, Italy is a country of varied landscapes with impressive Alpine terrain in the north and dry hills and coastal wetlands further south. Each location has its own composition of birdlife and most are beautiful to visit and easy to cover for the nature enthusiast, with easy access and convenient accommodation nearby.

Mountains and forests

Probably the most impressive alpine location is the north-western corner bordering France, around the **Gran Paradiso National Park**. This 567 square kilometres protected area comes complete with a 4,078 meter snow-covered peak and forested slopes with some picturesque hiking trails to take you through this grandiose setting. **Gran Paradiso** is accessible from the city of **Turin** via the town of **Noasca** up through the foothills to the **Col du Nivolet**. There are plenty of chalet-type and hotel accommodation and restaurants available.

Gran Paradiso is home to some rarely seen mammals and also many birds occurring mainly or exclusively in this montane habitat. In the high Alpine zone above or near the treeline you should look out for **Alpine Chough, Ptarmigan, Rock Partridge, Snow Finch** and the magnificent **Golden Eagle** soaring above. They are Alpine specialists that you will find in few other places in Italy.

In the pine forests further down there are **Hazel Hen** and several species of owls and woodpeckers - and do not forget to watch the delightful little birds like **Wall Creeper, Crested Tit** and **Citril Finch**.

Owl perched on a barn window.

At the lower elevations on the eastern side of Turin near the main road towards Milan, there is also a natural breathing space in this otherwise heavily populated and industrialized part of Italy. It is the **Greggio Nature Reserve** along the western bank of the **Sesia River**; just follow the signposts from the motorway leading you north. It is an area of open woodlands and marshes along the river banks. **Greggio** is home to interesting south European birds like **Hoopoe** and **Melodious Warbler** and there is an important breeding colony for **Little Egret** and **Black-Crowned Night Heron**, which come alive with activity in the spring and early summer months. Also watch for **Penduline Tit** and **Savi's Warbler** near the marshes.

Further south in Italy there is a fine natural area in the **Appenine Mountains** east of Rome, the **Abruzzo National Park**. The town of **Pescasseroli** on highway 83 has hotel accommodation and is an ideal jump-off point for visits into this reserve which is well suited for nature walks and birdwatching.

Parts of the **Abruzzi** extends above the treeline to over 2,000 meters and has Alpine bird species like **Chough**, **Blue Rock Thrush**, **Black Redstart** and **Alpine Accentor**. Look out for the rare and endangered **Lesser Kestrel**. In gorges and denser forests at slightly lower elevations, interesting birds include **Rock Pipit**, **Middle-spotted Woodpecker** and several **shrikes**, but there is generally a good density of more common European woodland birds.

Apart from resident birds, migratory species can be seen many places in Italy. The country is visited every year by migrants from the northern **Palaearctic** region passing through in spring and autumn. The island of **Capri**, less than an hour's sailing off the mainland from **Sorrento** has been known for many years to attract scores of migratory birds, especially during the spring period March-May. There is a bird observatory on the island where ringing and population studies take place. But generally birds can be seen everywhere on **Capri** during that part of the year, from **warblers** and **flycatchers** in the bushes to raptors like **Honey-Buzzard**, **Black Kite** and **Egyptian Vulture** flying overhead.

Lakes and lagoons

Migrants are also prolific all through the winter season in Italy's wetlands. **Venice** is of course known for its urban waterways but the coastal area along the **Adriatic Sea** is also an important feeding and roosting ground for thousands of water birds. It is one of Europes best wetlands with enormous flocks especially of ducks like **Wigeon**, **Pintail** and **Tufted Duck**. Shorebirds feed on the low-lying shores and there are many species occurring here which are difficult to see in other parts of Europe, like **Marsh Sandpiper**, **Temminck's Stint** and **Broad-billed Sandpiper**. Boat trips can be arranged from Venice itself and there are also roads leading around the lagoon areas.

Some amount of hunting takes place around the wetlands; many ducks and shorebirds are shot every year. Previously these parts of south-

Great Crested Grebe.

The wetlands make great roosting grounds for many birds.

Ducks, shorebirds and herons

ern Europe had a dubious reputation in wildlife protection. Small **songbirds** were caught for food and some birds like **raptors** protected in other parts of Europe were shot out for sport. With the integration going on in Europe lately, these habits are changing and the notion is catching on that nature can be enjoyed just by observing it - you don't necessarily have to eat it! Further to the south of Venice lies the **Valli di Comacchio** which is a large lagoon with brackish water, exceptionally good for birds. There are many migrants during the winter, but this place is also good during the summer when many Mediterranean wetland birds breed in the marshes. Look out for **Avocet**, **Pratincole**, **Black-Winged Stilt** and some **gulls** and **terns** difficult

....Birding in Italy

Black crowned Night Heron.

bler which you don't find in northern Europe.

More information

There is no shortage of bird books featuring birds of Europe and the rest of the western **Palaearctic** region. One of the newest and most comprehensive ones in English is "Birds of Britain and Europe" by C. Perrins, Collins 1987.

For travel information on where to go for bird-watching, John Gooders has published several volumes (**Andre Deutsch**) in the "Where to Watch Birds" series that also cover Italy. There is an ornithological society in Italy that can be contacted for the latest news at **Associazione Ornitologica Italiana**, Via Belfiore 11, Milan. Check with the tourist offices too.

to find in northern parts of Europe.

Further south in Italy there are some similar coastal salt water lagoons at **Orbetello** not too far north of Rome. In the recent years, tourism in Italy has grown tremendously as it has over most of the Mediterranean regions and this area is no exception. Part of the **Orbetello** is a nature reserve as is the deeper lagoon of **Burango** just to the south. There are many ducks, shorebirds and herons here. Some birds of prey special to the marsh habitat are also seen here like **Hen Harrier**, **Marsh Harrier** and in drier parts also **Montagu's Harrier**.

At the bottom of the "boot", the **Gargano peninsula** to the east is a scenic region with salt pans along the coast, rivers and lakes and some hills that rise up to over 1,000 meters. It is a relatively wild and picturesque region which is not as touristy as some parts of the west coast. But it is great for outdoor hikes and birdwatching. Good birds to look out for include **Black-eared Wheatear** and **Lesser Grey Shrike** in the hills and **Great Bittern**, **Little Bittern** and **Black Tern** among others near the marshes.

Further south, some 15 km south-west of Matera there is a large lake at **San Giuliano** which is worth checking out. There are many **Great Crested** and **Little Grebes** on the large water surface as well as **Gargany** and other ducks. The surrounding woods have **Indian Roller**, **Woodchat Shrike** and **Fan-tailed War-**

Little Egret.

The pensive wolf in its golden coat of fur in the Abruzzo National Park.

are all to be found. Foxes, badgers, otters, martens, wildcats, polecats and snow voles are all represented, as are birds of prey – golden eagles, eagle owls, tawny owls, goshawks, sparrowhawks. The park's most prized and rare birds must be the white-backed woodpecker and the rock nuthatch, while tits, chaffinches, missal thrush and ringed dove are all common. On the higher peaks can be seen the crimson-winged wallcreeper, the redstart, the waterpipit, the Alpine Accentor, the whitetail and the familiar Rock Partridge.

Circeo

Named after the sorceress of myth and legend, **Circe**, this national park occupies a headland on the **Tyrrhenian** coast in central **Lazio**, just below Rome. Created in 1934 under the Mussolini regime, it covers some 20,000-odd acres, and incorporates mountainous hills, scrubland, tracts of forest, bogs and marshland, dunes, coast and lakeside.

Cuckoos, Comorants, Chaffinches...

A magnet to birdwatchers, migratory birds such as the thrush, woodcock and chaffinch can be observed in autumn wheeling past on their southern journey; while spring sees the quail, turtle dove, cuckoo and golden oriole.

Hunting in Italy

As with all Europeans, Italians love the hunt, be it the solitary pleasure of stalking a deer, the companiable exercise of duck hunting with a favourite bird dog, or the thrill of an organised wild boar hunt. Every Sunday you will see the Italians out with their shotguns, striding off across the fields for a morning's sport. Also popular but less socially accepted, is the widespread practice of indiscriminate netting of songbirds, which in many areas has decimated the native bird populations.

Italy's love affair with hunting dates back to the time of the Romans, when the hunt was seen as every citizen's right, and special parks were established to facilitate this. Today stringent controls have been imposed at both regional and national levels, and the bureaucracy encountered in obtaining the necessary permits can be daunting; although for the patient and persistent, the rewards can be great. The Italian hunting season stretches from September to February (but it is advisable to check for regional variations and specific exceptions).

Lombardy is a favourite among duck, pheasant and grey partridge hunters, thanks to its low, marshy aspect, while **Lazio** is also popular. So too is **Puglia**, an extensive wilderness attracting hunters in their droves for the various game birds, hare, deer and wild boar. The best region for wild boar, also the most exciting quarry to be found in Italy, has to be the **Maremma**, in **Tuscany**, with its vast secluded tracts and extensive pine forests offering excellent cover. **Sardinia** is popular too, due to the ideal remote conditions, secluded highlands, ideal for the small, wiry wild boar peculiar to the island. This is a paradise for the nature lover, with its incomparable flora and fauna. Hunting is not permitted in Alpine regions except to residents.

For details on hunting in general, specific regions and types of game to be found, seasonal restrictions, firearms, permits etc, contact the **Federazione Italiana della Caccia**, or **Federcaccia (Italian Hunting Federation)** in Rome, or the **Ente Produttori Selvaggina** in any city.

Cormorants abound, as do all manner of wading birds: mallard, teal, widgeon, Pintails, egret and Black-Winged Stilt. The inland lakes are home to ruddy shelduck, spoonbill and grebe, while the osprey circles overhead. In the forests the green woodpecker can be heard, while fauna include badger, marten and wildcat. Roe and fallow deer may be glimpsed, as can the mongoose. Poor management and unwise development took their toll on the park for decades, since the mid-seventies wide-ranging conservation projects have been adopted, and Circeo a healthy future.

Calabria

The wolf is the symbol of the **Calabria**

White mountain goats are to be found in the mountainous areas.

National Park, the southernmost of the Italian parks, and is by far the most important animal in it. Spread over three areas, **Reggio Calabria**, **Cosenza** and **Catanzaro**, the **Calabria** park is Italy's most recent, established in 1968.

The park is heavily wooded, comprising larch, beech, silver fir, Italian alder, field maple, chestnut, Hungarian oak and cerris or turkey oak. River areas are lined with willow, ash and elm, while in the highlands fir and pine bedeck the slopes. Grassy glades are populated with pansies and asphodels.

A mature deer in Abruzzo National Park, where a wide range of wildlife and woodland abounds.

A family of horses in Maremma, Tuscany.

Also great spotted woodpecker's, black woodpeckers, nuthatches, tits and jays. There is a surprisingly large population of birds of prey, with kite, goshawk, sparrowhawk, eagle owl, tawny owl and buzzard making their homes in the **Sila** forests. Another inhabitant of the Sila forests is the wolf, about 200 or so, who are rarely seen, but whose bays reverberate through the night, an eerie and often frightening sound. Fallow and Roe deer, the natural prey of this magnificent canine, are increasingly rare, but their numbers are maintained to some extent by breeding programmes and a policy of restocking herds. Badger, marten and wildcat can also be found, as can the forest dormouse.

Conservation bodies

The presence of the national parks has done much towards preserving and nurturing the wildlife of Italy, especially with organizations such as the **Park Administrations**, the **Italian WWF** (part of the **Worldwide Fund for Nature**), **Italia Nostra**, the **Club Alpino Italiano**, and other regional, national and international conservation bodies giving their support and encouraging investment. It is up to the Italian people themselves and foreigners, to ensure that interest in and use of these wonderful natural facilities is maintained, and that the encroach of man's agricultural, industrial and residential developments is halted.

Light and shade - a reflection of the people of Italy, in the sun and the shade, with light skins, blue eyes and blonde hair, with swarthy skins, brown eyes and raven hair. Man has inhabited the Italian peninsula for a thousand millenniums. Since then, many different races have swept across the land.

People

71

From the east came the **Phoenicians**, the **Etruscans**, the **Greeks**, the **Byzantines**, the **Arabs** and the **Jews**; from the south came influ-

Italian farmer from the Tyrolean North.

ences of Egypt, Libya and North Africa with the **Moors** and **Berbers**; from the north came the **Ostrogoths**, **Goths**, the **Visigoths**, the **Gauls**, the **Franks**, **Alemanni**, **Vandals**, **Alani**, **Suevi**, the **Lombards**, **Normans**, **French**, **Austrians** and the **Spanish**.

Typically, the Italians are a Latin race, uninhibited and easily excitable; a warm-hearted and enthusiastic people, devoted to the family social circle and especially to

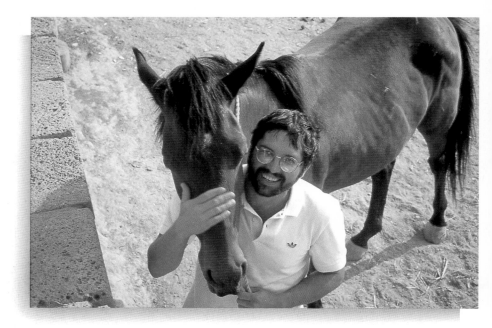

An Italian trainer with his horse.

the older members of the community and to children. On the whole, the Italians are an industrious race and, in compensation for hard work, enjoy celebrating and partying at every opportunity. The influence of the church is paramount and social guidelines are strict, although some female visitors may dispute this should they become the attention of the archetypal Italian 'Romeo'.

The Italians are generally very helpful to tourists and will make an effort to indicate directions or even go out of their way to make the visitor feel at home. A gregarious people, the countryfolk are most hospitable and generous and often offer to share their vivacity and celebrations with visitors, giving a privileged insight into the way the Italians think, work and play.

A unified individuality

It is not only ignorant, but impossible, to lump Italians together as one people, as was done in 1790. Each Italian person, each regional character, each townsman or villager, is fiercely individualistic. The collective noun of 'Italians' is abhorrent to many, particularly those from outlying regions and islands. The past, and especially family history is most important and lives on in the minds and hearts of all Italians. This is not only reflected in the fact that the Italian people are surrounded with the trappings and glories of the past, but

It is common to see attractive ladies whizzing through city traffic on scooters.

A young lad working on the family farm in Stelvio.

that the way and direction of life is governed or influenced in some way by past deeds.

History both binds and divides the Italian people. Feudal conflicts of centuries ago between families of villages, or groups, defined demarcations which are rigorously adhered to till this day. Each tiny community has its own church, with its bell-tower, and it is to this that each member of the community rallies, and with which he identifies, especially when preserving his village's individuality over that of another. This is known as the 'bell tower syndrome' or 'campanilismo'. This applies to city and townsfolk as well as country people. The **Romans** are fiercely Roman and stand by their imperialistic ancestry;

the **Pisan** and **Genoese**, even today, relate to their days of maritime superiority; and the **Venetians** and **Florentines** parade their great Renaissance past. Arguments, often heated and lengthy, are as important an ingredient of the Italian way of life as olive oil in Italian cooking. On street corners, on park benches, in bars and in traffic jams, as much as in the council chambers, the municipal halls and centres of government, the sound of argument is all-pervading. It is, again, the sound of individuality, of voicing a right to be different, and therefore to disagree.

The most universally prominent characteristic of all Italian people is the staunch and overriding love of one's family unit, one's direct family and re-

In Sud Tirol, the northern Italians are of Austrian and Germanic stock.

The Mafia

In the earliest days of the 'Mafia', the **'Cosa Nostra'**, or the 'Brotherhood', country folk, threatened of their livelihood by invading races, such as the Spanish occupation of Sardinia, formed small pockets of resistance to protect their communities. This society, known only to the confidants of each village, developed its own law and social codes. The guidelines for these 'secret' societies became known as the 'Law of the Machia', or the law of the brush-wood (machia) – a type of scrub which covers the mountainsides in southern Italy and its main islands of Sicily and Sardinia.

This family system of social mores, ethics and inter-village trade spread throughout the wilder, isolated regions of Sicily and Sardinia and became a strong network of self-support-ing, self protecting and self-governing groups. These pockets of resistance became powerful, particularly within their own mountain confines and a self-disciplining set of rules was drawn up which became universally accepted within the rural communities.

The judicial system adopted by the groups of Mafia-communities became associated with harsh justice which was called the *vendetta*. This eventually became synonymous with inter-family squabbling and with social and territorial feuding within the Mafia.

Today, the Mafia is reputed to be a powerful force within the Italian economic and financial system and just one aspect of its operations, the notorious drug-trafficking business, is said to require the laundering of a percentage of Italy's total national revenue. '*Omerta*', or the code of silence is practiced throughout the Mafia broth-erhood; if broken, it was punishable by death. This was once the ultimate 'wall of silence' which surrounded Mafia dealings, and pro-tected the Mafioso (Mafia practitioners) from the law.

This wall now seems to be crumbling, even on the verges of the Mafia's stronghold, Sicily, and the criminal retreats around the **Bay of Naples**, where the Mafia's counterpart, the 'Camorra' are thought to be.

Despite all the recent horrific murders of eminent personalities, and especially those con-tracted to break the Mafia's hold and its control of organized crime, the law seems to have gained some ground in the war against crime on Italy's streets and in its corridors of power.

Recent arrests of some of the most powerful and influential people, not only within the Mafia, have shown that the Mafia system knows no boundaries and has now developed from its humble 'brushwood law' origins, to reach its tendrils into the highest offices in the land.

Despite concerted efforts by the law en-forcement agencies and their successes against organized crime, the undercurrent of Mafia-associated activities goes on. It spreads from the youngsters in the streets who begin their addic-tion to drugs before their teens and support their habit by bag and watch-snatching, to the 'middle-class criminal' of whom there are esti-mated more than 1 million, earning a substan-tial annual salary from mixed crime, to the 'dons' or 'godfather-type' individuals who still are convinced they stand above the law.

lations. The protective and, to some outsider's eyes, over-zealous care and concern for the young and old of a family is typically Italian.

Style and 'Bella Figura'

Appearance in public is of paramount importance to all Italians, irrespective of age or sex. The 'bella figura' tag means to be immaculately and often expensively turned out in **Armani**, **Byblos**, **Fendi**, **Gigli**, **Gucci**, **Valentino** and the like.

The Italians adore being fashion-able and their evening ritual of the *passeggiata*, or parade/stroll, down the

main streets, avenues, squares and boulevards, serves as the ideal opportunity to see and be seen in one's 'Sunday best'. This is where the Italians take time and care to appear outstanding in dress and taste, 'do' the *passeggiata* with nonchalance and yet with style.

These evening walks are an essential way of Italian life and enables people to mix casually, and in a relaxed atmosphere after a day's work, in the cool of the evening. The *passeggiata* is an important part of the Italian lifestyle and involves the old and young, but is predominantly and traditionally performed at a forum where couples could meet each other under the strict eyes of their anxious parents.

The style and pride with which the Italians take their evening strolls is also reflected in their passion for eating out and being seen to be eating out. This maybe through entertaining at the finest restaurants, or taking coffee at the outside tables and chairs of the 'in' cafe, or by parading the entire family with lavish meals at top eateries hence demonstrating the head of the household's status and wealth.

However, the family circle appearance and the attention focussed on children and women in public, belies the fact that the Italian men are vigorously chauvinistic and the old adage about the Italian 'bottom-pincher' is as true today as it was fifty years ago when it became 'de rigeur' to include one in any

Keeping abreast of the daily news.

movie which included Italians or scenes of Italy!

A close-knit society

The family and the church, apart from a fiercely protective political attitude, hold the Italians together, although they are almost universally pro-unification of Europe. Children and the elderly are benignly regarded and belong in the 'bosom' of the family group. They are the family's prized 'possessions' and are

A dark Sicilian beauty.

carefully and affectionately pandered to. However, fewer and fewer couples are having more than two children, confounding the traditional image of the vast Italian families with hordes of youngsters.

Italians have a great sense of occasion and not only the major events of the calendar and family occasions like births, marriages and deaths bring the family unit together, but any excuse for a family reunion is a cause for celebration and inevitable feasting. People are tending to leave the cities for the peace of the countryside, and nowadays youngsters are not leaving home to search for work in the big cities as they used to in the 1950's and 60's. Many young sons in Italy are university students and Italy has the highest pro-

portion of university students of any Common Market country. Village life has changed little over the centuries except that family life and values are not as strict and regimental as it was twenty or thirty years ago. The layout of a village has likewise remained basically the same.

Every village always has a piazza, and facing it is usually the church, the Municipo, or Town Hall, the *carabinieri*, or police station, a bank, a few shops and several bars or cafes. The only houses around the piazza are usually the grand town houses of local landed gentry. Women tend to stay indoors or bustle around the markets and food shops, whilst the men congregate in bars and on benches in the village or town square.

Traditional dress is usually worn at town festivals in Alto Adige.

Mother and daughter dipping under the generous Italian sunshine.

Religion

83

I t is true that in Italy you cannot go very far before seeing a church or chapel (every village or even hamlet has at least one) and road-side shrines (usually erected in the memory of road accident victims) are commonplace.

An inherently devout people, Italians take their religion extremely seriously. The great majority of the population are Roman Catholic, a fact hard to ignore in the face of so much religious art and architecture on any visitor's itinerary.

The Holy Mother and her adoring one, an oft-repeated subject of frescoes and sculptures.

Catholicism

Having said that, there are other religions and denominations represented. In parts of Calabria and Sicily there are Catholic populations following the Greek or Byzantine rite, while remaining in communion with the See of Rome. There are some pockets of Protestants in the north Waldenses (who follow Calvinist doc-

Religious art, most reverently portrayed inside the church of
San Clemente in Rome.

Il Papa preaching to his flock who gather faithfully outside his Vatican balcony.

trine) in western Piedmont, and a Lutheran group in Lombardy. Baptist, Anabaptists and Methodist churches can be found, while there are large Jewish communities in Rome and in the cities of the industrial north. Muslim temples too can be found, in the larger cities and in the south.

Worship and services

Rome is the capital of the country, and at the centre of Rome is the Vatican, home of the Pope, leader of the Roman Catholic faith worldwide. The Vatican City State is recognized in the Constitution of the Italian Republic as an independent and sovereign state, with provision for relations with the Italian State by means of an Italian embassy at the Holy See.

Although the Roman Catholic Church is defined in the Constitution as the "sole religion of the State", various "Edicts of Toleration" dating from the 18th and 19th centuries ensure the freedom of the various religious minorities in the country. A study of religion per se in Italy is to delve into her long and ancient history, government and even politics. In this book the subject is covered throughout the history and regional chapters. Information on places of worship and service times can usually be obtained from the churches, synagogues, mosques or temples themselves, from the reception desk of your hotel, or from the local tourist offices.

Festivals

Being a staunchly Roman Catholic country, Italy celebrates many saint's days and most cities, towns and villages have a patron saint after which their main church is named and whose saint's day is celebrated in the local vicinity. It would be impossible to list the multitude of festivals and sacred holidays celebrated in Italy, both locally and nationally, but the following gives an idea of their great diversity.

Arezzo holds the **Saracen's Joust** on the first Sunday in September. Dating from the 12th century, this involves knights dressing up in authentic costume and competing for the team.

The teams represent the four quarters of the town and knights from each team ride against an effigy of a Saracen which is armed with a pivoted flail which can unseat a careless knight. In Ascoli Piceno, the town's most spectacular

A procession in Naples to honour their patron saint.

89

Carnevale – The story of carnival.

With pagan derivations steeped in the mists of time, carnival, as we know it now, is a Christian invention and the word comes from the Latin 'carnevale' - 'carne' meaning meat, and 'vale' meaning farewell, hence farewell to meat. The celebration, held before Easter, recognises the final days of the permitting of meat-eating before Ash Wednesday and the start of the 40 days of fasting during Lent.

Italy's most flamboyant example of this festival is held in Tuscany's **Viareggio**. The port adopted the traditions of ancient Rome, especially the 'Corso', a procession which included grand costume parades and decorated floats.

Carnival began in Viareggio in 1874, when the committee was founded. The parades began as satirical representations mocking authority and institutions. Some floats praised the marvels of the age, like science. The broad shoreline boulevard became the most popular location for the more spectacular parades and the 'Corso' moved there from the old part of the city. The region's famed skill in marble carving was turned to the fabrication of giant *papier mache* sculptures created by artisans known as '**Maghi**' or magicians. Caricatures are favourite with the Maghi and some effigies can be as tall as a three-storey house.

pageant is the **Quintana Tournament** held in early August. Jousting is also part of the celebrations of this event which dates from the 15th century.

Assisi's contest is more musical and is known as the **Calendimaggio**. It is held in Easter Week (March-April).

In Bari, townsfolk dress in historical costumes and parade in the **Feast of St. Nicolas** celebrations on May 8 and 9.

The regatta in Venice, an event of noise and colour.

Decorations in Lazio to commemorate the ascension of Christ.

Easter remembrances in Naples.

Dance, Costume and Folklore

The famous Tarantella dance is part of the carnival celebrations of Viareggio. Local neighbourhoods begin competing with their floats three weeks before *Martedi Grasso* (Mardi Gras) and masquarades spill into the streets with their own versions of Harlequin – Burlamacco, Arleccionio and Pulcinella. The song of the town's carnival is heard everywhere, "*Carnevale e il vecchio, che la vita ci Rida!*" (Carnival is the old fool who gives us life).

Each region and their various areas seem to have their own version of local folk songs and individual dances, which often go hand-in-hand with processions and pilgrimages. Folk dancing displays can be attended in most towns and villages and the Italian Tourist Board has done much to promote the interest in, and the preservation of, local folk dancing and the traditional costumes which relate to each village or region. Folkloric groups can be found throughout the country, especially on the islands of Sicily and Sardinia.

Bergamo's main event is the great international cycling race, the **Baracci Trophy**, held in mid-October. From October to November the town holds the **Opera Festival**. Cagliari, the capital of Sardinia, has held the **Festival of St. Elisio** from May 1-4 since 1657. In thankfulness for deliverance from the plague, thousands of traditionally dressed pilgrims follow the saint's effigy to the town of Nora. In Cocullo, the **Procession of the Snakes** in May, has reverted from its pagan origins, and today, villagers follow Saint Domenico's statue carrying live snakes.

Florence celebrates the 12th cen-

Masquerade in Venice, fancy dress on a gala scale.

A touch of Hollywood in Venice at its annual film and arts festival.

tury **Scoppio del Carro** festival on Easter Sunday. Commemorating the Crusader's return, a wagon, decorated and filled with fireworks is placed outside the cathedral. The firework display is detonated by the priest from the altar. Costumed participants twirls flags and standards. This city also holds the **Game of Calcio** in June. This celebrates, with a costumed game of football, the fact that, in 1530, the inhabitants defiantly played football while being besieged by Charles V. Gubbio holds a crossbow contest in medieval costume in the city square during May and, on May 15, three wooden shrines are carried, in honour of the saint, to the top of Mt. Ingino during the festival of **Ceri Race**. The **Ivrea Carnival** is held in February which celebrates the town's liberation, with a furious battle of oranges as the grand finale. La Spezia's **Rowing Race** is held on the first Sunday of August. Merano's **Farmer's Horse Race** is a vigorous event held on Easter Monday. In Naples the **Piedigrotta** is the famous Neapolitan singing contest held in the first two weeks of September, with fireworks and colourful processions.

Nuoro, on Sardinia, celebrates the **Festival of the Redeemer** in August, with parades and costume displays.

Palermo, on Sicily, celebrates the end of the plague after **Saint Rosalie**'s remains were discovered in 1225. This folkloric and religious festival is held in the capital from July 11-15. In Piana degli Albanesi a grand parade celebrates

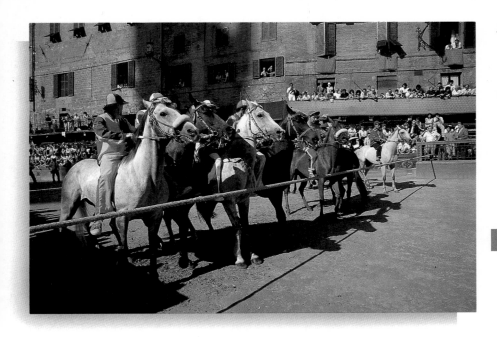

Horses, riders and colourful costumes make the Paleo di Siena an event worth catching.

the **Epiphany** on January 6 with an unusual Byzantine ritual.

Pisa is famous for its **Regatta**, in mid-June, where highly decorated boats are rowed against each other by teams representing the four corners of the city.

Rome celebrates with military parades and bands, its **Republic Day**, on June 2. In Sansepolchro, in September, a medieval crossbow competition is held. Sassari, on Sardinia, is the scene for the **Sardinian Cavalcade**, where more than 3,000 parade with music and folkloric displays on Ascension Thursday. Since 1580, the end of the plague in Sassari, huge candlesticks are paraded through the city on August 14.

Siena's **Bareback Horse Race** dates from the 15th century and involves sev-enteen riders racing around the town before feasting, parades and colourful flag-waving competitions. The race is held on July and August 16.

Spoleto celebrates its festival in June and July with art exhibitions, music, theatre, ballet and cinema. Venice holds its famous gondola and state barge **Regatta** and **Water Pageant** on the first Sunday in September, with a series of processions and races. The **Venice Biennale** is an international art and film festival held August - September.

In Verona, between July and August, is the city's celebrated **Opera Season**. Viageggio's **Carnival** is held in February and consists of spectacular displays and processions, fireworks, and cultural events.

I talian art, architecture, literature and music are all intertwined, even with its history; never more so than during the Renaissance period, when the ideal was to turn one's hand to all branches of the creative (and scientific) arts, with the result that in any account of Renaissance art, the same names will recur again and again, whether the subject be painting, sculpture, architecture, poetry, prose or philosophy.

Literary & Performing Arts

97

Virgil, the acknowledged master of Roman poetry.

Literature

One must remember that between the fall of the Roman Empire and the Unification of 1860, Italy was a patchwork of independent city and regional states, so that the literature of this people is, by definition, patchy and regional, with different cultures, and indeed dialects and even languages pertaining (it was **Dante** who promoted, and helped establish, Tuscan as the universal language).

Not much is known

Some of the finest violins come
from Cremona.

alded the Renaissance, which manifested itself in literature with a new, revived interest in education, history, literary critique and above all, philosophy. By the latter half of the century and the High Renaissance, the field was dominated by those who had come to prominence in other fields (be they artistic, religious or political), notably **Lorenzo de Medici** and **Girolamo Savonarola**, as well as the more universally recognized **Michelangelo** and **Leonardo da Vinci**. Another giant of Italian literature of this time was **Niccolo Machiavelli**, the noted (or notorious, according to opinion) militarist ("The Art of War").

The 16th century saw a shift towards the refinement of the art of the playwright, expanding it from its roots in the mystery plays of the Middle Ages. The development of literature in the 17th century was hampered, if not totally stifled, by the ascendancy of the Inquisition, but the fields of science, theology and mathematics fared somewhat better, despite, rather than because of, the wave of fundamentalism sweeping Europe then.

Italian romanticism developed in the late 18th century, typified by the works of **Foscolo, Pellico, Manzoni** and **Leopardi**, which often reflected the political turmoil and unrest of the time (Austro-Hungarian rule in the north, interspersed with the Napoleonic wars). Romanticism died with the unification of Italy. Following a period noted mainly for the patriotic nature of the works (by

of early Etruscan literature, but that of the Greeks and the Romans is well documented, with **Virgil** the acknowledged master of Roman poetry.

The Middle Ages was the time of love poems and the traditions of "courtly love", centered around Sicily and the south, as well as in Tuscany. **Cecco Angiolieri** was an early exponent, while the genre was best demonstrated in the 14th century by **Petrarch** (Francesco Petrarca) and, more famously, by **Dante Alighieri**, both of whose earlier works often revolved around the disappointment of unrequited or forbidden love. Dante is best known for his "Divine Comedy", charting a personal voyage through hell, purgatory and heaven.

The dawn of the 15th century her-

Dante, poet and philosopher

Italy's best-known poet and philosopher, Dante Alighieri was born in Florence in 1265. He married Gemma Donati around 1283, but was Beatrice Portinari who was to be the love of his life. His first work, "La Vita Nuova", is a personal journey tracking Dante's love for Beatrice from their first meeting in 1274 to her death in 1290.

In essence, it charts the transition from courtly love (or love of woman) to Christian love (love of God). Better known is his prose work, "Il Convivio" (The Banquet) in which he describes how philosophy came to replace Beatrice as his "mistress". Beatrice is a character, and a theme, to which he returned throughout his life.

Dante's masterpiece, however, is the "Commedia" (known today as the Divine Comedy), a work of three canticles of which the "Inferno" is the best known. It is an allegorical treatise on "the state of souls after death", it postulates that Dante, through some act of Divine Grace, is allowed to travel on a journey to God through the three realms of the afterlife: hell, purgatory, and paradise, before finally achieving divine beatitude. As well as the spiritual symbolism, the work incorporates allegories of the political, social and military aspects of his time (and also manages to fit Beatrice in as one of his spirit guides).

Born to a family of modest means, Dante became interested in politics at an early age, and served in various capacities on the Florentine City councils for several years, as part of the dominant "White" civic faction. He undoubtedly made several enemies in that time, as when the "Blacks" came to power while he was on a mission to visit Pope Boniface III, he was exiled "In Absentia". He was never to return to Florence. He travelled widely, residing at times in Verona and eventually in Ravenna.

It was during this exile that he wrote his masterpiece, and he died in Ravenna in 1321. His ashes lie in a monument built on the site of the cell where he was buried in the Church of San Francesco in Ravenna.

Minstrels entertain in a Ligurian restaurant.

Giuseppe Verdi, opera composer extraordinaire.

Prati, **Mameli** and **Carducci**), came Realism. Adopting an almost documentary style, this school focussed not on philosophies and personal convictions, but rather on social conditions and their effects on the protagonists. It is hardly surprising that the backdrop to these novels were usually the extreme south, Sicily and Sardinia – traditionally the poorest areas.

The advent of Fascism in the first part of this century also heralded the Futurist movement, the best exponents of which were **Svevo** and **Pirandello**. The Mussolini years were a dangerous time for "reactionary" and "subversive" authors, indeed for anyone voicing dissatisfaction with the state, and many were either imprisoned, exiled or killed.

The main poets of this time were **Salvatore Quasimodo, Eugenio Montale** (both awarded the Nobel prize for literature) and **Giuseppe Ungaretti**; while the most successful prose writer (for his novel "The Leopard") was **Giuseppe Tomasi di Lampedusa**.

Since the War, Italian literature has maintained its high standard, with authors such as **Italo Calvino** and **Alberto Moravia** depicting the lives of the working classes in modern Italy, while **Primo Levi** wrote harrowing descriptions of life as a Jew in the concentration camps during the holocaust.

One of the best-loved contemporary Italian novelists (and the best-known outside his own country) is **Umberto Eco**, whose first book, "The

Luciano Pavarotti, whose unmistakable voice is familiar the world over.

Music

Name of the Rose" immediately hit the international best-seller lists, and was subsequently made into a film.

Italian music can trace its roots back to the Etruscans and Greeks, both of whom influenced the early Roman Empire, although this was as an accompaniment, or perhaps integral to, the earlier dramas and recited poetry. Performance music gained a wider appeal in the 1st century AD when Augustus and Nero encouraged and sponsored public concerts and contests (remember that Nero is said to have fiddled away while Rome burned!).

The music of the Middle Ages was almost exclusively religious, that is, Christian in nature, being in the main constrained to the antiphonal (or responsive) chants of the congregation during Mass. Difficult to control (for these chants were for religious purposes, and not intended for personal enjoyment), this was later refined into the **Gregorian** chant, named after Pope Gregory I (560 - 604), and performed by a dedicated all-male chorus, the Schola Cantorum.

Polyphonic music emerged slowly in Italy, where the strong and restrictive papal rule held sway, although it was well established in France. It only appeared to any real extent in the form of secular, or non-religious, music in the

The Spaghetti Western

Who can forget the haunting strains of Ennio Morrecone's theme tune to "The Good, The Bad, and The Ugly", Sergio Leone's most memorable film?

The "Spaghetti Western" was a phenomenon of the 1960's and early 1970's, when, casting about for new material, Italian producers saw the huge success of a networked German TV western, "Winnetou". Deciding that there was a considerable market for homegrown "cowboy" films, directors were set to work. Filming primarily in remote parts of southern Spain (these were normally Italian-German-Spanish financed films) or Sardinia, budgets were low, dialogue infrequent and plot subtleties kept to a minimum.

Little could the film companies have known just how successful their celluloid offerings would be, gaining almost immediate cult status on both sides of the Atlantic!

It would be fair to say, however, that only one director, Sergio Leone, gained lasting recognition, with his 1964 hit "A Fistful Of Dollars". This was the film that brought Clint Eastwood, a hitherto relatively unknown TV actor ("Rawhide") to fame, as the taciturn, cheroot-chewing "Man with no name". This was followed in 1965 by a sequel, "For A Few Dollars More", which introduced another future western stalwart, Lee Van Cleef, as well as an established European (later Hollywood) legend, Klaus Kinski (albeit in a minor role). "The Good, The Bad, And The Ugly" (Eastwood, Cleef and Eli Wallach) in 1966 completed the trilogy, and was probably the best-plotted of the three.

The scores for all three were composed by Ennio Morricone, whose style became indelibly distinctive of the genre.

Leone appeared to lose his "magic touch" on his association with Hollywood, following up with his sprawling 1969 epic "Once Upon A Time in the West", starring Henry Fonda, Charles Bronson, Jason Robards and Claudia Cardinale. A revertion to an earlier style with the 1971 "A Fistful Of Dynamite" (James Coburn, Rod Steiger), while amusing and exciting enough in places, lacked the earlier grit and was a box-office flop.

Leone went on to other, diverse projects, including the 1984 gangster epic "Once Upon A Time In America" (hardly an inspired title, considering its provenance, but it did star Robert de Niro!), but never seemed to regain the flair of his earlier features.

The Spaghetti Western, having served its purpose of rekindling public (and Hollywood) interest in the classic western tale, died peacefully in the early 1970's.

11th and 12th centuries, in the courts of the city-states, where troubadours and minstrels entertained the nobility.

Secular music came into its own in the early stirrings of the Renaissance of the 14th century, in the form of the **Ars Nova**, a polyphonic style initially owing much to the progress made in France, but gradually evolving its own styles and character in the **Madrigale**, the **Ballata** and the **Caccia**. It was not until the 15th century that polyphonic styles were finally adopted by the Church.

Opera

The concept of opera was a direct child of the Italian Renaissance – seeking to recreate the feel of the Ancient Greek theatre, the Camerata, a group within the court of Giovanni de' Bardi in Florence, whose leading protagonist was Galileo Galilei's father, developed a new form, whereby the storyline was sung or chanted, although complex polyphony was avoided for clarity of narrative. A

La Fenice, Venice, during interval time.

La Scala, Milan, mecca of opera houses the world over.

Italian Cinema

Italy has long been known for its passion for the cinema, both in terms of movie house attendances and in the production, direction and behind-the-scenes influence on the industry.

From the earliest days of film making, the Italians were highly respected for their well-crafted silent films and historical dramas (usually recreating the heady days of the Roman Empire) that drew on the strong operatic traditions of the country.

The Fascist regime of the 1920's, 1930's, and early 1940's was slow to realise the propaganda value of the cinema, but in the mid-1930's Mussolini did instigate the famous Cinecitta film studio complex on the outskirts of Rome, rekindling interest (and investment) in the home-grown film industry.

At the tail-end of Mussolini's rule, Visconti's "Obsession" in 1943 paved the way for the neo-realist school of the post-war years. Based on true-to-life, gritty stories, shot on location rather than in studios, often using amateur or even non-actors, and lacking the gloss and glamour of the Hollywood offerings, these films were best exemplified by the works of **Visconti** ("Obsession", "Death In Venice"), **De Sica** ("Shoeshine", "The Bicycle Thieves", "Miracle In Milan") and **Rossellini** ("Rome, Open City", "The Earth Trembles").

After the demise of neo-realism in the early 1950's, directors such as **Federico Fellini** and **Bernardo Bertolucci** came to the fore, and apart from the brief hiatus of the "Spaghetti Westerns" of the 1960's and early 1970's, they have more or less dominated Italian film-making to the present day (from Fellini's "La Strada" in 1954 to Bertolucci's "The Last Emperor" in 1988).

religious form of opera, the *oratario* soon followed, using as its subject matter biblical stories rather than legends and mythology, and without the opulent sets and extravagant costumes.

The first great figure in Italian opera was **Monteverdi**, whose masterpiece was "Orfeo" in 1607. The popularity of opera spread, with Rome soon becoming the stylistic capital. In the 17th century this mantle passed to Venice, due in no small part to Monteverdi's appointment as choirmaster to Saint Mark's in 1613, and the world's first public opera house was opened in 1627, followed by others throughout Italy. The following century was an age of great diversity and experimentation, with the development and adoption of the now-universal Italian musical terms; now the best-known opera houses are opened, such as **La Fenice** (Venice), **La Scala** (Milan), and **San Carlo** (Naples). Opera *seria* already well established, it was in the 18th century that opera *buffo*, or comic opera, was developed, as a stopgap during scene changes in the main work. The most notable expo-

Frederico Fellini, who like many other Italians, brought great
imagination and sensitivity to the cinema.

nent was **Mozart** (particularly his work in Milan with **Lorenzo da Ponte** –"le nozze di Figaro", "Don Giovanni" and "Cosi fan tutti") while **Vivaldi** remains the major influence in opera seria. Naples had by now inherited the mantle of the heart of opera, although there were schools flourishing in Venice and Milan. The 19th century heralded the golden age of Italian opera, with composers such as **Paganini**, **Rossini** ("Il barbiere di Siviglia", "William Tell"), **Bellini**, **Verdi** ("Rigoletto", "La Traviata") and **Puccini** ("La Boheme", "Madame Butterfly", "Tosca") dominating the scene. **Toscanini** was the major force in the early 20th century, and as the artistic director of La Scala, was pivotal in introducing new operas to the Italian public. The Italian preoccupation with opera continued until between the two World Wars, with the result that Italian music became rather stultified and insular, unaffected by trends and movements outside of the national framework. A younger generation of composers, headed by **Pizzetti** and **Respighi** opened up the influences from the rest of Europe, while the Fascist regime encouraged new music and the revival of some of the old masters. Denationalization of the Italian music industry after the war saw a further opening up of the medium, leading to the experimentation familiar today (such as the fusion of classical and modern electronic styles found in the work of **Rondo da Ponte**).

Italian art and architecture is inextricably linked, particularly around the time of the (Florentine) Renaissance, but the divided nature of the individual city-states gave rise to a great number of regional variations and schools of thought.

In the field of art, Italy has given the world more than any other nation, much of it still resides in Italy. Students of art have always tried to spend some time in Italy to complete their studies, be they painters, sculptors or architects. Patrons throughout the western world have commissioned Italian art, often luring the artists away to carry out their work in foreign courts, Leonardo da Vinci is a case in point.

Some of Raphael's paintings are national treasures.

Greeks, Etruscans and Romans

Much of what is known today about **Greek** art and architecture stems from the remains that have been found in Magna Graecia (Greater Greece), their colony in southern Italy. It was at this

The Arch of Titus, in the Roman Forum.

time that the best examples of the **Greek Doric** order were built – temples typified by their elegantly fluted columns, slightly distended in the main shaft - good examples have been excavated at Paestum near Naples and in Sicily (Agrigento, Segesta, and Syracuse being the best preserved).

Surviving Greek art is mainly elaborately painted vases, plaster wall frescoes and statuary and sculpture. The best known archaeological sites where such pieces have been found are Herculaneum and Pompeii, and more recently, Paestum.

The **Etruscans** were a race living to the north of Magna Graecia, and they established a network of cities in the centre. Not as advanced as the Greeks, they obviously revered the artwork of their southern neighbours, as many items of Greek statuary and vases have been found in their tombs. Not much is known about their architecture, as little survives, due to the nature of the materials used - wood, clay, wattle. Only the massive stone foundations and terracotta archwork that remain give clues to their mastery of the stonemason's art.

The **Romans** were more art collectors than artists, preferring to import Greek objects, as well as using them for inspiration for their own works. Some **Roman styles** were developed, such as portrait busts, an idea borrowed from the Etruscans (little else of theirs could have pleased the Romans, as they appear to have gone to considerable lengths to obliterate any signs of the Etruscans' existence!).

The Romans also seem to have extensively developed the use of painting in frescoes, creating stunning "**trompe l'oeil**" set pieces in buildings, and became masters at mosaic inlays (in floors, walls etc).

The Romans' main claim to artistic fame was in architecture. The Romans are well known for their civil engineering feats, including irrigation and drainage, plumbing, aqueducts, viaducts, roads and bridges.

A Byzantine mosaic of St. Peter.

In the execution of the artistic side of their architecture, they merely adapted Greek ideas and principles to their own ends, rather than the wholesale copying and reproduction so often found in their art. Of the classic Greek orders, they used the more ornate **Corinthian** and **Ionic** orders, mainly as decoration of their own imposing styles (the Romans developed the **Colossal** order, a solid, chunky style, in keeping with the large scale of their buildings), and the column lost its functional aspect, being relegated to a purely decorative structure.

Instead, the Romans developed the use of the rounded arch and the dome. This is best seen in the construction of the *basilica*, the basic Roman building,

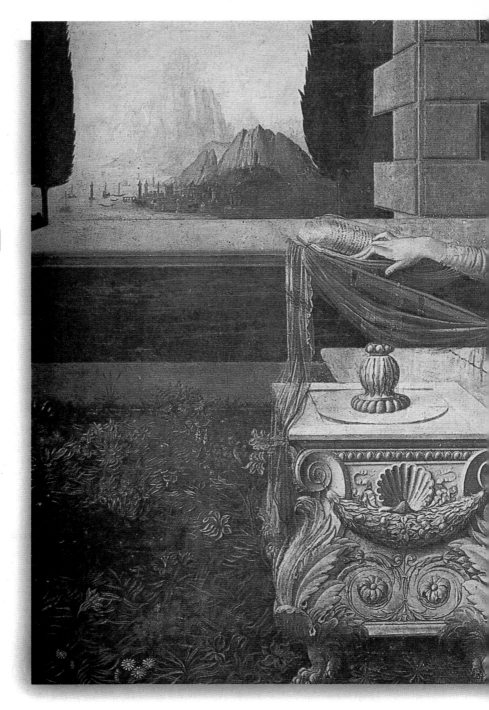

Leonardo da Vinci's celebrated "Annunciazione".

The Florentine Artists

Known as the "Athens of Italy", a seat of learning and home to the oldest societies and academies, and second only to Rome for wealth of monuments and art treasures, Florence is the place that nurtured Italy's and the world's finest artists and sculptors.

Florence's **Golden Era** was during the **Renaissance**, and the artist credited with founding Renaissance art was **Brunelleschi**, although Donatello (c. 1386-1466) was to be the most influential of the early Renaissance sculptors. A student of **Lorenzo Ghiberti**, his early works, still showing strong Gothic influences, were in wood, or more usually, marble (including his best-known early work, "Saint George killing the Dragon", in the Or San Michelle, the church of the Florentine Guilds). Taking the relief panels of Ghiberti as a departure point, **Donatello** devised the stunning *stiacciato* style of relief. In the 1420's he became a major sculptor in bronze, starting with a larger-than-life statue of Saint Louis of Toulouse, the first work showing the new architectural style pioneered by Brunelleschi, but without any of the residual Gothic forms. Another important work was his bronze David of 1430-32, the first free-standing, large-scale nude statue of the Renaissance. Other major pieces are the Annunciation in the Church of Santa Croce, Venice; the Tabernacle in Saint Peter's, Rome; and various pieces for the baptismal font in the Church of San Giovanni, Siena.

Fra Angelico (1400-1455) was born Guido di Pietro in Vecchio, Tuscany, and is acknowledged as one of the finest of the 15th century religious painters. His work is characterised by the simplicity of form and structure, and the use of vivid colours. His work was for many centuries considered "naive" and simplistic, only gaining wide appreciation in the 19th century.

Familiar subjects recurred in his work throughout his life: the Annunciation, the Crucifixion, the Virgin and Child. One of his best works was the altarpiece of the Annunciation in

Fra Angelico was one of the finest religious painters, whose works included the Last Supper inside the Museum of San Marco.

the Church of Santa Domenico at Cortona. He painted on altarpieces, mainly triptychs and polyptychs, although he was later to work on single panels, a new concept (a good example is "the Coronation of the Virgin").

Botticelli (a nickname meaning "little barrel") was born in 1444/5, and is best known for his "Birth of Venus" (now in the Uffizi Gallery). He had a distinctive, linear style in his figures, and soon came under the patronage of the Medici family ("The Adoration of the Magi" in the Uffizi depicts characters comprising the Medicis and a self-portrait). Other paintings from this period include "Allegory of Spring" ("Primavera") and "Pallas and a Centaur" (both also in the Uffizi). Aside from painting, he carved a great number of woodcuts to illustrate editions of Dante's "Divine Comedy".

Leonardo da Vinci (1452 - 1519) is the man most often identified as the embodiment of the Italian Renaissance. He applied himself to all the arts and most of the sciences, a fact that has often been used to explain the astonishing number of works that were never completed. He spent much of his life in Florence and in Milan, but spent a while in Rome, and ended his days at the French court of Francois I.

His most famous paintings are, of course, "The Last Supper" and the "Mona Lisa", although he was also an accomplished sculptor (no examples survive) and a master anatomist (his sketches indicate that he was at least a century ahead of his time in this field, and bordered on discovering the secrets of the human circulatory system).

Many other of his sketches are of a scientific or military nature, describing ideas for heavier-than-air flight, military transports, and civil engineering projects.

Florence's most famous son was, of course, **Michelangelo** (Michelagniolo Buonarroti), born in 1475. His early works were paintings, although his predilection was towards sculpture. Spending a year in Bologna, he was enticed to Rome in 1496, returning to Florence after an illness, and at the bequest of his family. He worked for a while on figures for a shrine in a cathedral in Venice, but cut this work short to come home to execute his most famous sculp-

Michelangelo's David.

ture, the statue of David (known as the "Giant") in 1504.

He was summoned to Rome to work on his most enduring work, the painting of the ceiling of the Sistine Chapel in 1508. The only major project of his life that he was able to see to completion as originally conceived. It depicts the stories of the book of Genesis, from Creation to The Flood, a task which, almost single-handed, took a mere four and a half years. He returned to Rome some years later to paint his most famous fresco - "The Last Judgement" in the Sistine Chapel, although this has weathered less well over the centuries than his work on the chapel's ceiling.

He spent his later years here in Rome, turning his hand to architecture, and was appointed Chief Architect of Saint Peter's Cathedral. Despite continued ill-health, he lived to a ripe old age considering the times, dying in 1564 just short of his 90th birthday.

Botticelli is best known for his "Birth of Venus", now in the
Uffizi Gallery, Florence.

Architectural intricacies are accented by evening illuminations at the Doges Palace, Venice.

which is in essence an inverted Greek temple, with ornate Corinthian columns and pillars on the inside, the infrastructure being a solid structure constructed around the forms of the structural arch and the vaulted ceiling.

Buildings were basically functional in nature, constructed from bricks and concrete – it was not until the reign of Augustus that more decorative and opulent materials such as marble began to be employed. Other firsts were the building of open amphitheatres (such as the Colosseum in Rome) and public baths

(Thermae), with elaborate plumbing feeding hot and cold spas, a tradition that continues to the current day (see "Spas of Italy" on page 46).

Examples of all the above are widely in evidence, and the archaeological finds at Herculaneum and Pompeii disclose many such sophisticated structures, as well as a highly-developed social and civic infrastructure.

Byzantine, Romanesque and Gothic

The early Christians were forced to practise their religion underground, in catacombs hollowed out of rock, for fear of discovery by the Roman establishment. **Christian art** at this time was limited to wall frescoes, showing little stylistic innovation, while the art of sculpture was more or less forgotten, save for the embellishment of *sarcophagi* and tombs. As the Christian faith was recognised, and its adherents were allowed to worship freely, places of worship tended to be designed on secular lines, most often based on the form of the *basilica*. Statuary was still eschewed, but mosaic work became the most predominant art form. Many examples of this style of church and decorative art remain, although most have been added to and altered down the centuries, with the best-preserved being Santa Sabina in Rome. It was during this period that transepts were introduced, emphasising the shape of the cross, also the first separate, oc-

The Vatican Museum collection of art and sculptures are some of the finest.

tagonal baptistries.

The next architectural developments occurred when Ravenna became the imperial capital under the rule of the **Byzantine** empire, the main features resulting from this eastern influence being the further development of the dome, and later, the independent campanile, or belltower. The best examples of **Byzantine architecture** are to be found in Venice and its environs, with the Basilica di San Marco being the prime example.

The **Romanesque** era in Italy began at the end of the 9th century, and heralded the emergence from the Dark Ages. It was typified by the proliferation of baptistries and campaniles, and the extensive use of white marble on exteri-

Caravaggio's "Testa di Medusa".

"Pieta" by Michelangelo in the Academy Gallery, Florence.

Brunelleschi, the Renaissance architect designed this 15th century hospital, one of the first such.

ors – the buildings in Pisa, and in particular the Leaning Tower, are good examples.

The Romanesque period is rather hard to quantify, with numerous regional variations – Byzantine influences in southern Italy, while in Sicily the Romanesque style was tempered by Norman and Saracen touches. It was at this time (around the turn of the 12th century) that sculpture first came back into favour, initially by **Wiligelmo da Modena**, whose bas-reliefs on the Cathedral of Modena displayed a fluidity of movement and clarity of expression unknown in the earlier Byzantine works.

Other sculptors came to prominence in the **Gothic** period, notably **Nicola** and **Pisano**, whose works clearly reflected classical influences. Painting also enjoyed a revival, with the main pre-**Renaissance** artists being **Cimabue** and **Cavallini**, and later, Cimabue's pupil **Giotto**, who was the first to break entirely with the Byzantine traditions, and managed to bring a sense of depth to his paintings. **Gothic architecture** did not really catch on in Italy, due in part to a climate which did not lend itself to the style already evident and more suited in Northern Europe. There were, however, a number of Gothic-inspired cathedrals built in the 13th and 14th centuries, in particular those at Siena, Florence, Orvietto and Milan. Non-religious or secular architecture also flourished, with the Doges' Palace in Venice possibly the best example of the style.

Religious scenes captured in Raphael's frescos in the Vatican Museum.

The Renaissance

The **Renaissance**, sometimes known as the **Florentine Renaissance** after its birthplace, was a time of artistic giants, and universalists who applied themselves to all branches and aspects of the arts and sciences.

While **Giotto** was the first to break the Byzantine preconceptions of his age, it was left to others to instigate a "renaissance", or rebirth of interest in the classical civilisations. The first of these artists in the 15th century were the sculptor **Ghiberti**, and more importantly, his student **Donatello**, who pioneered the *stiacciato* style of bas-relief, and who made extensive studies of the ancient Roman styles to produce his stunning free-standing statues.

In the field of painting, great strides were being made in new techniques and styles: **Masaccio** toyed with volume and space, **Uccello** developed the perspective line, while **Fra Angelico** brought a new vivacity to the expression of colour, a theme expanded by **Botticelli** in his masterpieces.

The Renaissance probably had a more profound effect on architecture than the other branches of the arts, with so many existing buildings and ruins to be studied and to give inspiration. **Alberti** and **Brunelleschi** were the first two Renaissance architects; Brunelleschi building the Spedale degli Innocenti, the first true Renaissance structure, as

The Duomo in Florence, an architectural showpiece of artistry and the
elegant use of marble and alabaster.

Michelangelo's masterpieces on the walls of the Sistine Chapel.

well as the dome of the Florentine cathedral, while Alberti is credited with first using harmonic proportions, a measurement system based on ancient music theory. Other reknown architects of the time, all influenced to a smaller or greater extent by Alberti and Brunelleschi, include **Michelozzo di Bartolomeo**, **Antonio Averlino Filarete**, **Donato Bramante**, and of course, **Leonardo da Vinci**.

The 16th century (known as the "cinquecento") was the time of the **High Renaissance**, when the activities of the painters, sculptors, architects, poets and writers reached their peak. Talents, and indeed genius, were nurtured by the great ruling families of the time: the **Medicis** in Florence, the **Sforzas** in Mi-

lan, and the **popes** of Rome. The giants of this later age included Leonardo da Vinci, **Michelangelo**, and **Raphael**; while in Venice a new school was appearing that would produce such masters as **Giorgione**, **Titian**, **Tintoretto** and **Veronese**.

One effect of the High Renaissance on architecture was to spread it from Florence and Rome throughout the rest of Italy and Europe. The biggest single new development was the resurgence of the classical villa, and the Medici family had several commissioned, designed by **Giuliano da Sangallo** and **Michelozzo**, although it is **Andrea Palladio**'s work that can be found throughout Venetian region, inextricably linked with architecture of High and **Late Renaissance**.

Bernini's colonnade in St. Peters in the Vatican.

Mannerism and Baroque

As the art and architecture of the Renaissance became more sophisticated, their exponents experimented with laid-down rules, distorting and fragmenting line and space, and reverting to harsher colours. First expounded by **Michelangelo**, **Raphael** and **Tintoretto**, **Mannerism** enjoyed a brief popularity, before being eclipsed by the **baroque** period.

The baroque period began in late 16th century, as a reaction against Mannerism, but also at the instigation of the Catholic Church and in the face of the increasing economic and political sway of papal rule. A new style was needed, conveying splendour, stature and power,

and the artists and architects of the time were only too pleased to comply. The ornate, curved forms that resulted gave a breathtaking impression of fluid movement and swirling light patterns. Baroque was essentially a Roman phenomenon, with good examples in the facade and nave of Saint Peter's Basilica by **Maderno**, as well as various works in the Vatican by **Bernini**, **Cortona** and **Borromini**. Baroque styles did spread away from Rome to the rest of the country, with particularly interesting examples to be found in Venice (Longhena's Church of Santa Maria della Salute on the Grand Canal), Genoa (the University), Turin and Naples (the Palazzo Reale at Caserta).

The tail-end of the baroque period

The swirling grace of entrance ramps to the Vatican Museum.

was the **rococo**, a highly-stylised form, which was followed by the 18th century neo-classical movement, a school largely centred on Venice, and whose main exponents were **Tommaso Temansa**, **Antonio Selva** (La Fenice Opera House), and **Giuseppe Jappelli** (Caffe Pedrocchi in Padua). A reaction against the stylistic excesses of the baroque and rococo styles, **neo-classicism** was inspired by the archeological findings at Paestum and in Sicily. The Industrial Revolution of the 19th century gave architects new materials and new ideas. **Art nouveau** followed as an architectural style at the turn of the century, followed by **Futurism**. The arts of the later 20th century have echoed that of the rest of Europe and the western world, with **realism**, **abstract**, **minimalism** and **conceptualism** all having their own movements and adherents.

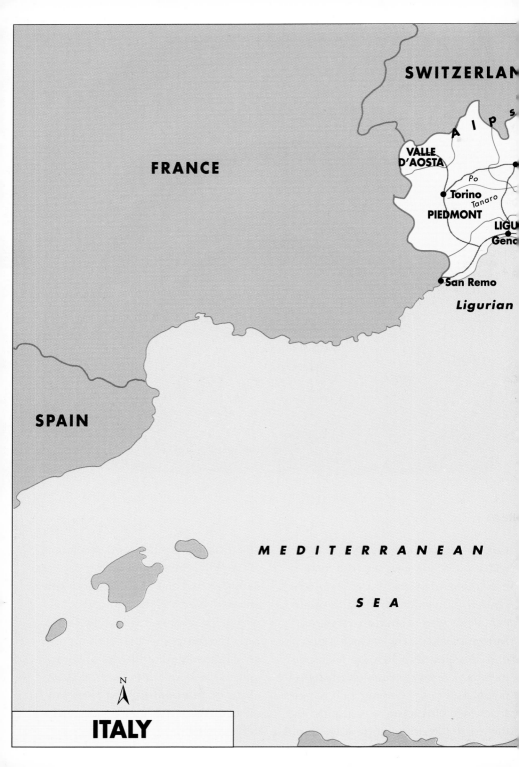

SWITZERLAN

A l p s

FRANCE

VALLE
D'AOSTA

Po

Torino
Tanaro

PIEDMONT

LIGU

Geno

San Remo

Ligurian

SPAIN

MEDITERRANEAN

SEA

N

ITALY

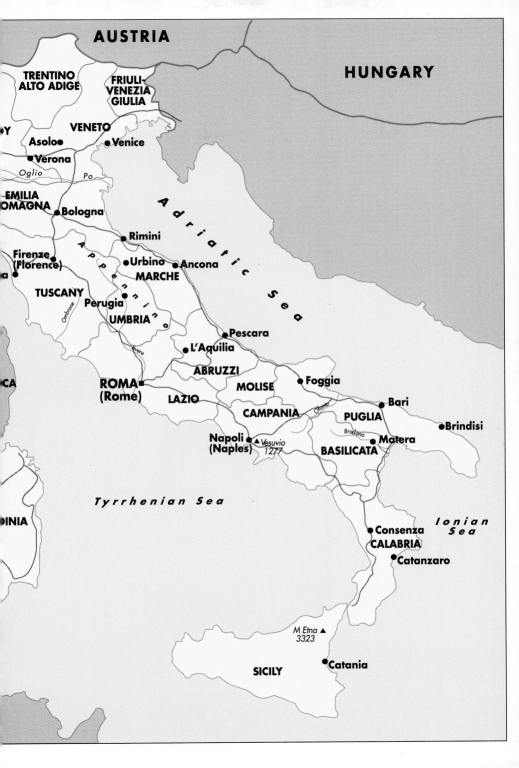

Lord Byron had obviously not heard of the city's classic epitaph – 'Rome, the Eternal City'. Unlike any other capital city in the world, Rome is a bizzare collection of architectural remnants left by a succession of occupants over its 2,600 years of history. Rome is rather like a crumbling wedding cake, originally built on seven hills, with each tier representing an era and each tier, before crumbling completely, being adopted into the subsequent era, for instance, ancient Roman tiles and pillars being built into early Christian churches and baroque ornamentation being adapted into later villas.

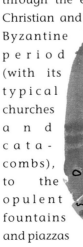

Trevi Fountain, of baroque opulence, which took Niccolo Salvi nearly forty years to complete.

This is clearly visible from the majestic ruins of imperial Rome, through the early Christian and Byzantine period (with its typical churches and catacombs), to the opulent fountains and piazzas designed by the

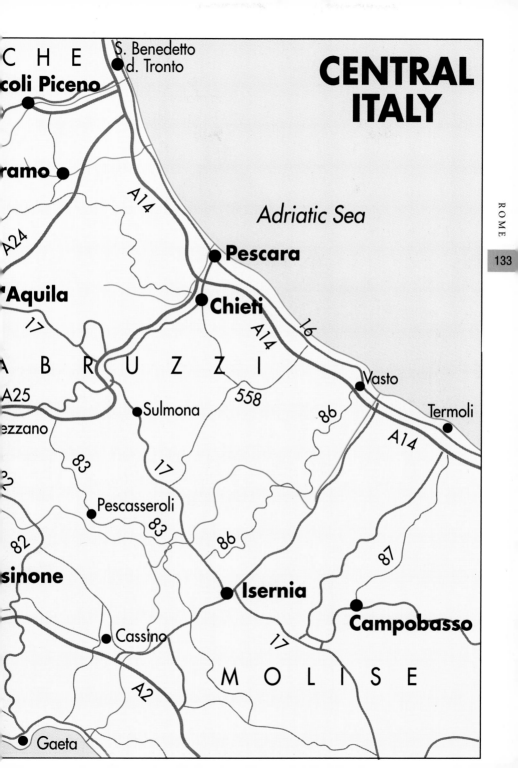

CENTRAL ITALY

C H E

oli Piceno

S. Benedetto
d. Tronto

ramo

A14

A24

Adriatic Sea

Pescara

'Aquila

Chieti

A14

16

17

A B R U Z Z I

A25

558

Sulmona

Vasto

Termoli

86

A14

ezzano

83

17

Pescasseroli

83

86

87

82

sinone

Isernia

Campobasso

Cassino

17

A2

M O L I S E

Gaeta

St. Peter's dome seen from the Tiber at dusk.

Evening crowds on the Spanish Steps in summertime.

popes between the 16th and 18th centuries, and through the rich style introduced by famous Renaissance artists supported by the Vatican, up to the more recent Rome of the mid-19th century, with its ornate theatres and monuments.

There are a thousand sites in Rome that should be seen: a hundred churches, museums and galleries, and theatres and monuments by the score. Just to list the numerous treasures of this spectacular and vibrant city, would take a volume of its own. In this chapter, it is best to cover the more famous and easily visited sites in a short series of tours.

As with many capital cities of the world, a mighty river, the **Tiber**, cuts through the metropolis north to south

making it easier to divide Rome into quarters: starting with the largest concentration of ancient Roman remains and magnificent churches in the southeast, continuing to the north-east sector with its palaces and museums, crossing the river to the north-west quarter dominated by the **Vatican**, and finally finishing in the south-west district which consists mainly of the **Trastevere** neighbourhood.

Nestling cosily into the bend formed by the River Tiber, which indents into the centre of Rome, is the **Centro Storico** district.

To the east of this lies the main shopping area, and typical narrow streets and alleyways scattered around the **Spanish Steps** lending their

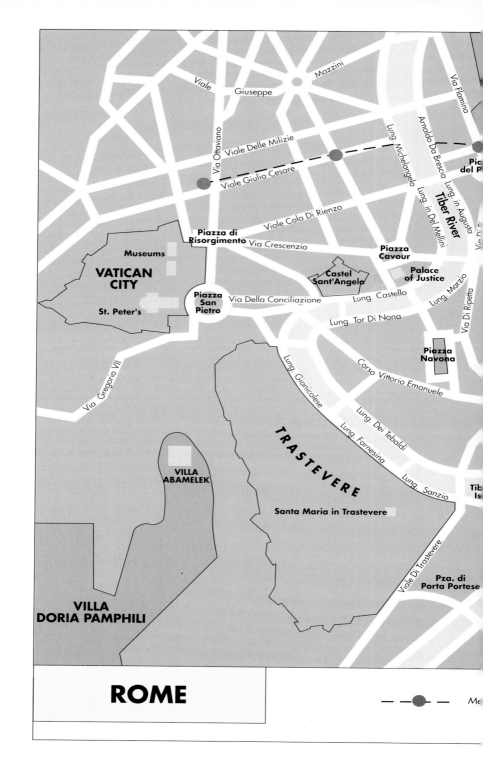

ROME

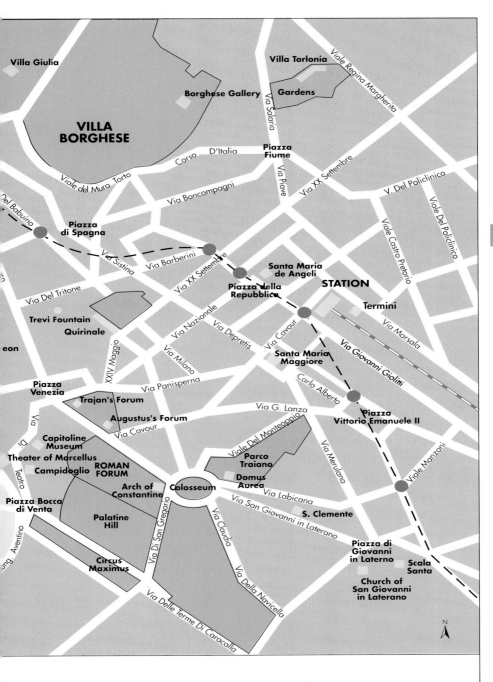

Villa Giulia

Villa Torlonia

Borghese Gallery   Gardens

Viale Regina Margherita

Via Salaria

**VILLA
BORGHESE**

Corso   D'Italia

**Piazza
Fiume**

Viale del Muro Torto

Via Piave

Via XX Settembre

V. Del Policlinico

Via Boncompagni

Viale Del Policlinico

Del Babuino

**Piazza
di Spagna**

Viale Castro Pretorio

Via Sistina

Via Barberini

Via XX Settembre

**Santa Maria
de Angeli**

STATION

Via Del Tritone

**Piazza della
Repubblica**

Termini

Via Marsala

Trevi Fountain

Via Nazionale

Via Depretis

Via Cavour

Quirinale

**Santa Maria
Maggiore**

Via Giovanni Giolitti

eon

XXIV Maggio

Via Milano

Carlo Alberto

**Piazza
Venezia**

Via Panisperna

Via G. Lanza

**Piazza
Vittorio Emanuele II**

Trajan's Forum

Augustus's Forum

Via Cavour

Viale Del Monteoppio

Via Merulana

Viale Manzoni

Via

Di

**Capitoline
Museum**

**Parco
Traiano**

Theater of Marcellus

**ROMAN
FORUM**

Campidoglio

**Domus
Aurea**

Teatro

**Arch of
Constantine**

Colosseum

Via Labicana

S. Clemente

**Piazza Bocca
di Venta**

Via San Giovanni in Laterano

**Palatine
Hill**

Via Di San Gregorio

Via Claudia

**Piazza di
Giovanni
in Laterno**

**Scala
Santa**

Aventino

**Circus
Maximus**

Via Della Navicella

**Church of
San Giovanni
in Laterano**

Via Delle Terme Di Caracalla

N

us

The Colosseum, an amphitheatre built in AD 80 by Emperor Vespasian.

labyrithine atmosphere to the overall picture making up the colourful tapestry which is Rome. South of this is the most famous of Rome's monuments, the **Colosseum**, international symbol of this 'mother of cities'.

The Colosseum is the centrepiece of this district which includes the **Roman Forum** and other ancient monuments on **Capitoline** and **Palatine Hills**.

North of the city stands the grand edifice of the **Villa Borghese**. West of the city, across the river from the Centro Storico area, is the **Vatican**, and south of this, stretching along the west bank of the Tiber, is the **Trastevere** district, renown for its nightlife and restaurants. To the west of Trastevere lies the grounds of the **Villa Doria Pamphili**.

Glories that were Rome

Starting at the symbol of **Romulus** and **Remus**' ancient city, the Colosseum, the visitor can expect to take several tours from various landmarks in the city, leaving little time to hesitate at each site, museum, gallery etc.

Rome's major monuments alone could take a full week to see.

The Colosseum, once an amphitheatre, and site of bloodthirsty games and competitive races, is the Roman world's largest surviving structure, built to accommodate 55,000 spectators in an arena with a girth of almost one-third of a mile and with 76 entrances. The Emperor Vespasian began construction of the Colosseum in 72 AD and it was completed by his son, Titus, about eight years later. Through the Middle Ages, a succession of popes stripped the bronze decorations and marble facings from its walls and used them in other buildings. The removal of the central floor revealed the maze of tunnels underneath the arena.

To the east of the Colosseum is the **Ludus Magnus**, once a three storey barracks built to house the gladiators. Nearby, in the **Parco Traiano**, is the **Domus Aurea**, or **Golden House of the Emperor Nero**. The remnants of 2,000-year-old mosaics and frescoes are all that remained of the house which was once floored with mother-of-pearl and contained solid gold furniture. The site of the Colosseum was, at the time of building the house, an ornamental lake. The word 'grotto' comes from the 'grotesque' of the decorations found in these ruins.

South of the Golden House, across Via Labicana, is the church of **San Clemente**, originally dating from 375 AD. This church is a sandwich of art and culture down through the centuries. Beginning with 1st century **Roman Mithraeum** down to the lowest strata, above an ancient underground water system, the church possesses a 7th century choir screen, frescoes dating from 900 AD, a mosaic from the 12th century, and Masolino's 'Life of St. Catherine', painted in the 1420's.

West from the Colosseum is the grand **Arch of Constantine**. Erected in 315 AD, it is the largest and best pre-

Italian carabinieri on parade.

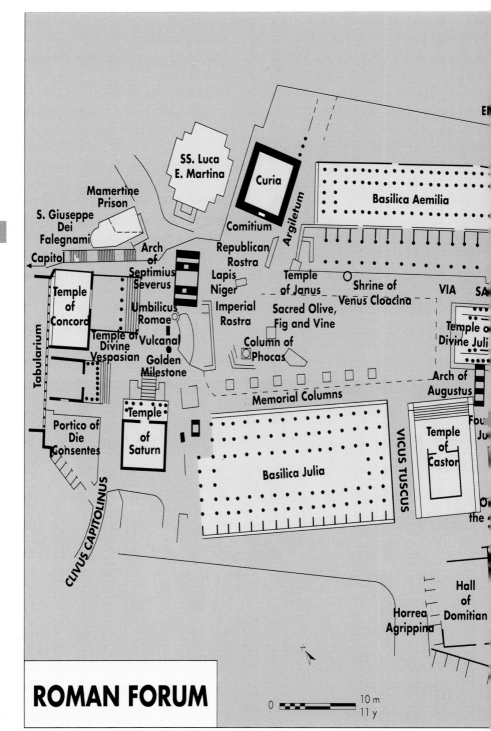

SS. Luca
E. Martina

Curia

Argiletum

Basilica Aemilia

Mamertine
Prison

S. Giuseppe
Dei
Falegnami

Comitium

Capitol

Arch
of
Septimius
Severus

Republican
Rostra

Lapis
Niger

Temple
of Janus

Shrine of
Venus Cloacina

VIA SA

Temple
of
Concord

Umbilicus
Romae

Imperial
Rostra

Sacred Olive,
Fig and Vine

Temple o
Divine Juli

Tabularium

Temple of
Divine
Vespasian

Vulcanal

Column of
Phocas

Golden
Milestone

Temple
of
Saturn

Memorial Columns

Arch of
Augustus

Portico of
Die
Consentes

VICUS TUSCUS

Temple
of
Castor

Fou
Ju

Basilica Julia

CLIVUS CAPITOLINUS

O
the

Hall
of
Domitian

Horrea
Agrippina

ROMAN FORUM

0   10 m
     11 y

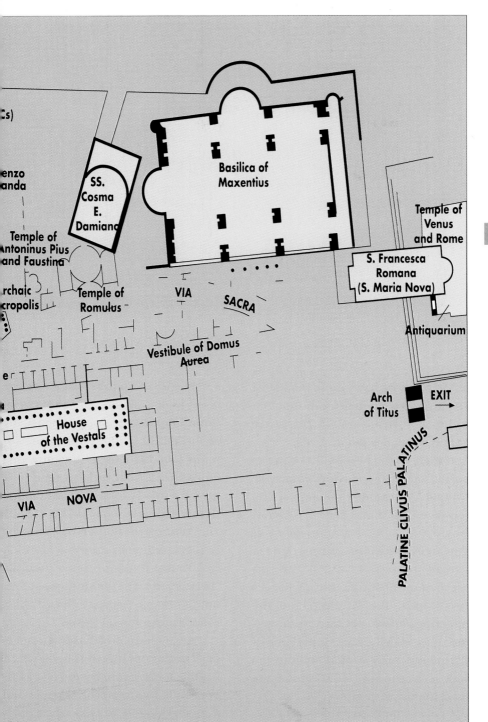

(s)

enzo
anda

Temple of
Antoninus Pius
and Faustina

Archaic
Acropolis

SS.
Cosma
E.
Damiano

Basilica of
Maxentius

Temple of
Venus
and Rome

S. Francesca
Romana
(S. Maria Nova)

Antiquarium

Temple of
Romulus

VIA

SACRA

Vestibule of Domus
Aurea

House
of the Vestals

Arch
of Titus

EXIT

VIA   NOVA

PALATINE CLIVUS PALATINUS

Magnificent statuary at the Capitoline Museum.

served triumphal arch of ancient Rome. To the south of the arch are the ruins on **Palantine Hill**, said to be where Romulus founded Rome.

There are some exquisite gardens on the site of the **Flavian Palace**, or **Domus Augustana**, and the best preserved ancient ruin is known as **Livia's House**. Further south are the remains of the **Circus Maximus** which was built to seat an audience of 250,000. This vast arena stands between two of Rome's seven hills, the Palatine and the **Aventine** and was last used for chariot-racing in 549 AD. Back to the Arch of Constantine and a short walk to the west, is the entrance to the ruins of the huge **Roman Forum**.

To the north-west of the Roman Forum is the **Capitoline Hill**, location of two important sites. On the piazza of **Campidoglio**, up steps designed by Michelangelo, is the **Capitoline Museum**, founded in the 17th century and based on a drawing by Michelangelo. It contains some excellent ancient sculptures including the famous 'Dying Gaul'. The **Palace of the Conservatory** nearby displays pictures by Caravaggio, Titian and Reubens and has some exquisite Greek bronzes. The **Senatorium**, or town hall is also on the same piazza which overlooks the Roman Forum.

Across the road of the same name is the **Theater of Marcellus** upon which site the Renaissance **Orsini Palace** has been built. Two rows of arches still stand from the original structure which dates

The construction of the Capitoline Museum was based on a drawing by Michelangelo.

from 11 BC. Other temple ruins to be seen in this area include the well-preserved **Temple of Fortuna Virile**, on **Piazza Bocca della Verita**, a few blocks from the Marcellus Temple. From here one can wander down to the banks of the Tiber and view the city's lone island, the **Isola Tiberina**.

The **Temple of Vesta** can be visited a little further south along the river bank, near the Romanesque **church of Santa Maria** in **Cosmedin**. Set in the wall of the church is the mask called the **Mouth of Truth** which is said to be capable of biting off the hand of any liar who dares place his fingers in its gaping maw. Continuing back down the street named after the Theater, past the Capitoline Hill and steps to the grandi-

ose **Victor Emmanuel Monument** to the right, one continues along the south side of the **Piazza Venezia** with the **Church of Santa Maria** in front. To the right is **Trajan's Column**, an exquisite tribute to the master craftsmen of Roman times, and, of course to the victories of the Emperor. It is possible from here to enter the sites of several ancient remains. The vast, roofless basilica **Ulpia** stands in its own beautiful forum and grounds. This should be visited before one enters the tunnel which leads to the great semi-circle which was the **Trajan Market**. Although the shops and remains of the large library building laid out in the 2nd century are of interest, find the entrance to the buildings below street level for a more intimate view of

Mosaics depicting 2nd century AD theatre masks from Dall' Aventino, Capitoline Museum.

what life must have been like in a Roman market.

The 12th century **Tower of Milizie** stands nearby and there is an excellent view from the top of this medieval base for the **Knights of Rhodes**. Walk back to the Piazza Venezia, turn left down the **Via Dei Fori Imperiali** which leads back to the entrance of the Roman Forum. On the left hand side, up a short turning, are the remains of the first Roman Forum, that of Julius Caesar's. On this site stood the **Temple of Venus** and the **Roman Stock Exchange**. Further along, on the **Via Tor de Conte**, is the **Forum of Augustus** which once contained an immense statue of the Emperor and a temple to **Mars the Avenger**.

One should now re-trace one's steps onto the Via Dei Fori Imperiali in order to view the ruins of two large forums which bound the north-east flank of the great Roman Forum. These are the **Forum of Nerva**, built between 96-98 AD. Twin Corinthian columns mark the site of the **Temple of Minerva**. The site off the forum next door to the Nerva, the **Forum of Vespasian**, is now virtually obliterated. Continuing south-east, along the main road, the visitor then find his way back to the starting point of the first tour, the Colosseum.

Grizzly catacombs and gory relics

In order to visit the monuments and

More modern treasures of Italy.

historic sites which lie to the south of Rome, it is essential to use transport as they lie too far from the city centre and are too dispersed for a comfortable walking excursion. Only the places of most interest in this part of the city are covered here.

Directly south of the Colosseum, across the **Celio** district of Rome, is the **Terme**, or **Baths of Caracalla**. Dating from 212 AD, this large structure was not just a public bath but offered a variety of entertainments for the populace of ancient Rome. Sections of the original mosaic can be seen, and today the imposing remains serve as a backdrop for opera performances.

To the west is another of Rome's seven hills, the **Aventine**. On its north flank is the 5th century **Basilica of Santa Sabina**. Inside the Basilica its great 1,500 years old carved doors can be seen. Also on the Aventine hill is the house of the **Knights of Malta**. Take a peep through the keyhole in the main gate for a splendid view of the dome of **Saint Peter's**. South, through the **Testaccio** neighbourhood and around the **Monte Testaccio**, stands a 35-metre high mound made of Roman amphorae shards discarded over 600 years. Continue on to the **Mattatoio**, a giant ruin, once a slaughterhouse, now designated as a new mixed market of shops and stalls. The **Protestant cemetery** nearby is where Keats and Shelley, Edward Trelawney and Gransci are buried. The cemetery is overshadowed by the bulk of

Summer tourist traffic on the Via Veneto walkways.

the **Caius Cestius Pyramid**.

Follow the ancient **Aurelian Wall**, built by Emperor Aurelia in 275 AD to enclose Rome's seven hills, to the east, and it will bring you back to the Baths of Caracalla. Follow the line of the wall further south and east and you will find a road that leads through the wall to the south. This is the 'Queen of Roads', the **Via Appia**, a Roman supply route to the Aegean port of Brindisi. This road takes the visitor to the five catacomb complexes on each side of the road. These early Christian burial tunnels create a phenomenal maze and were constructed between the 1st and 4th centuries.

Returning towards the Colosseum, through the Aurelian Wall and past the **Celian Hill**, the **church of San Gregorio Magno**, should be visited for it was here that St. Gregory instructed St. Augustine to convert England to Christianity from his marble throne, which is housed in a side room.

Nearby is the **church of San Giovani e Paolo** which contains relics and a sanctuary of two of Constantine's emissaries, beheaded here in 361 AD. To the east of this, originally a Roman church, stands the **Church of San Giovanni in Laterano**. This was founded by Constantine the Great. It shows clearly a mixture of architectural styles; it has a 4th century baptistry, a medieval cloister and a baroque interior. Although very old, it has an 18th century facade, its doors are from the Forum's Senate House and there is an interesting fresco by Giotto inside, apart from many other ancient relics and artifacts. The church's prize relics are the goriest yet, that is, the preserved heads of Saint Peter and Saint Paul.

Even further east, in an enclave almost surrounded by the Aurelian Wall and near the **Porta Giovanni** gate, is the **church of San Croce** in **Gerusalemme**. This church was built by the Emperor Constantine and houses relics of the cross. A short walk north is the most impressive of all the Roman gateways in the Aurelian Wall, the **Porta Maggiore**, constructed in the 1st century. This tour has taken in most of the more celebrated monuments, churches and ruins in the south of Rome and to the east of the Tiber River.

Museums, fountains and more monuments

Starting from Rome's central railway station, located at the eastern edge of central Rome, it is a short walk to the Information Office in the **Piazza della Repubblica**. The **church of Santa Maria degli Angeli** stands here. Designed by Michelangelo, this church stands over the site of the largest Roman public baths in the city, the **Baths of Diocletian**. This is also the site of the **Museo Nazionale**, the National Museum, with its immense collection of art, artifacts, mosaics and frescoes. Just around the corner from the square is Rome's famous **Opera House**.

It is not far to walk from here to the **church of Santa Maria Maggiore**. This magnificent edifice, one of Rome's largest religious basilicas, stands on **Esquiline Hill** and its interior displays some excellent Byzantine mosaics. Retracing one's steps across the **Viminale** district up to **Quirinale Hill**, we reach the first of Rome's many palaces to be visited. This is the **Palace of Quirinale**, a 16th century mansion, now home to the Italian President. To the north of this is another palace, the **Palace of Barberini**, now the **Galeria di Arte Antica**, or Art Gallery, which contains paintings by many of Italy's famous artists including Titian, Tintoretto and Raphael. In the **Piazza Barberini** is Bernini's **Fontane del Triton**, the famous Triton Fountain.

It is a fair walk north-east from here in order to visit the famous **Spanish Steps**, the unwitting amphitheatre of the capital, as the 138 steps up to 1504 **church of Trinita dei Monti** are used

The Vatican

With a total area of just over 100 acres, the Vatican is the most powerful independent state of its kind in the world. The state is also the smallest in the world, having become a sovereign state in 1929. The headquarters of the Roman Catholic world of some 800 million people, comprises **Saint Peter's Square**, the **Vatican Palace**, the **Papal Gardens** and **Saint Peter's Basilica**. The Vatican State also owns 12 more buildings in and outside Rome. The Vatican's population stands at about 1,000 and they have their own flag of yellow and white, its own coinage, stamps, newspaper, radio and railway station, and police force.

The popes are protected by the **Swiss Guard**, recruited from the Roman Catholic cantons of Switzerland, in their colourful yellow, blue and red-striped doublet and hose uniforms, designed by Michelangelo. The State's national anthem was composed for Pius IX by Gounod.

Ever since the 5th century, the popes have lived here apart from a brief respite during the 14th century. They and the Vatican inhabitants enjoy a duty-free status while around 4,000

The Vatican dome rising from behind the images of 140 saints.

The altar by Bernini and the cupola by Michelangelo.

brought to Rome from Heliopolis, by Caligula and which had once overlooked the martyrdom of St. Peter. Adorning the roofs of the 284 **Doric-pillared Bellini colonnade**, are 140 images of saints, looking down towards the twin 17th century fountains in the Square.

Apart from the **Vatican Gardens** there are several museums and galleries within the Vatican area: the **Egyptian Museum** is one of the first approached from the entrance; the **Carriage Museum**; the **Ciaramonti Museum**; the

The oval-shaped complex of the Vatican.

people are employed to work in the City. Every Sunday, at noon, the Pope recites the 'Angelus' from the window of his study on the top floor of the Vatican, overlooking St. Peter's Square.

The '**Square**' is, in fact, an oval, embracing an area which, some say, could accommodate 300,000 people. The centre is dominated by an **Egyptian obelisk**, more than 3,000 years old,

Michelangelo's masterpiece of St. Peter.

The statue of Athena at the
Vatican Museum.

The Swiss
Guards
protect the
Vatican
City.

The Vatican library houses immense
volumes of religious literature.

Ethnological Museum; the Etruscan Museum; the Gregoriano Museum; the Pio Clementino Museum; the Pio Cristiano Museum; the Museum of Christian Art, and the Gallery of Modern Religious Art; the Borgia Apartment is preserved as a museum as is the Bracio Nuovo and the Casino of Pius IV.

The Loggie of Raphael should not be missed, nor should the Pinacoteca, probably the finest picture gallery in Rome, and the Stanze di Raffaello for its stunning frescoes. There is also the immense Vatican Library and the Map Room. Chapels open to the public include the famous Sistine Chapel and the Chapel of Nicholas V.

Michelangelo's frescoes in the
Sistine chapel.

The Vatican Museum amidst
its garden setting.

Monument to Victor Emmanuel II.

N

Viale Vaticano

Viale del Bosco

Viale del Giardino Quadrato

Via

Ca
Pic

Acco

Viale Vaticano

Madonna
della
Guardia

Mon. a
S. Pietro

Piazza della Zecca

Viale Vaticano

IV

Leone

Grotta
di Lourdes

di

Viale dell' Osservatorio

Salita de

Via d

Viale dell' Osservatorio

S. Maria

Governatorato

Piazzale del Governatorato

Collegio
Etiopico

Viale Vaticano

Tennis

Mura

Radio

Viale Marconi

Viale del Seminario Etiopico

S. Stefano

Largo S. S

Masaico

Via del Mosaico

Piazzale
della
Stazione

Stazione

Viale Vaticano

VATICAN CITY

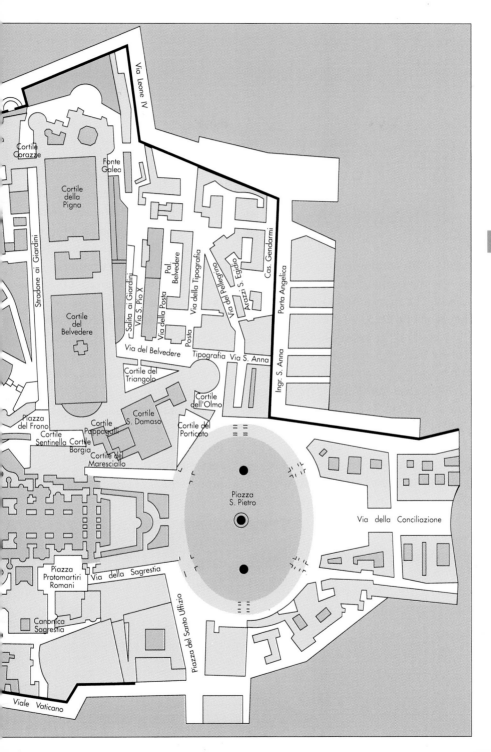

Via Leone IV

Cortile Corazze

Fonte Galea

Cortile della Pigna

Stradone ai Giardini

Salita ai Giardini

Via S. Pio X

Via della Posta

Pal. Belvedere

Via della Tipografia

Via del Pellegrino

Arazzi S. Egidio

Via S. Egidio

Cas. Gendarmi

Porta Angelica

Cortile del Belvedere

Via del Belvedere

Posta

Tipografia

Via S. Anna

Ingr. S. Anna

Cortile del Triangolo

Cortile dell'Olmo

Piazza del Frono

Cortile Sentinella

Cortile Pappagalli

Cortile Borgia

Cortile S. Damaso

Cortile del Porticato

Cortile del Maresciallo

Piazza S. Pietro

Via della Conciliazione

Piazza Protomartiri Romani

Via della Sagrestia

Canonica Sagrestia

Piazza del Santo Uffizio

Viale Vaticano

Porta San Paolo and the Pyramid of Caius Cestius.

traditionally as rows of seats from which to view the comings and goings of the capital. The Spanish Steps were built by the French in 1725.

Nearby is the **Keats-Shelly Memorial**, the house where Keats died in 1821. This house is now a museum and shrine to the English Romantic poets. Return now to the Triton fountain and walk west, along the Via del Triton and turn to the left just before the end of the street. This gives you a chance to toss a coin into the **Trevi Fountain** in order to ensure your return to Rome. The Trevi is one of the world's most opulent fountains and an enduring symbol of Rome's exotica. It was again made famous in the 1960 Fellini film 'La Dolce Vita' – 'The

Sweet Life', starring Anita Ekberg and Marcello Mastroianni cavorting in its waters. This is a marvelous celebration of baroque sculpture which took Niccolo Salvi from 1723 to 1762 to complete. In the **Accademia di San Luca**, to the right of the fountain, is the famous 'Venus' by Guercino, and also works by Titian and Raphael, among others. Across the Via del Corso, to the west, is Bernini's **Palace of Montecitorio**, home of the Italian Parliament since 1871. A short distance south of this palace is one of Rome's most famous monuments, the **Pantheon**. Countless acts of vandalism through the ages, and ill-advised 'improvements', notably by Bernini have

The old Appian Way leading to the Roman tombs.

The Naiad Fountain by Piazza della Repubblica.

The Presidential Guard marches by the Quirinale Palace.

still not managed to depreciate the grandeur of this spectacular structure.

The Pantheon is the best preserved classical building of all. Pictures and tombs inside the Pantheon are dwarfed by the building's vast dome, until recently the largest in the world, a record it held for almost 2,000 years since its construction in 27 BC by Agrippa. Behind this magnificent edifice is Bernini's most celebrated fountain, the **Elephone Fountain**. Nearby, and built on the site of the Roman **Temple of Minerva**, is the only Gothic church in Rome, built in 1280, the **church of Santa Maria Sopra Minerva**, contains an important work by Michelangelo, 'Christ with the Cross'. Yet more fountains! In the **Piazza Navona**, just west of the Pantheon, there

are three fountains, one of which, symbolising the great rivers of the world, is by Bellini's opposite number, Borromini. On the piazza is the **church of Sant' Agnese**, also an early 17th century work by Borromini. A little to the south of the piazza is the **Museum of Rome** which

Baroque fantasy rising from the waters of the Trevi Fountain.

depicts the life and times of Rome through the ages.

Cross the **Piazza San Pantaleo** to the **Corso Vittorio Emanuele**. Just across from the piazza is the **Barraco Museum** of ancient sculpture. Continuing east along the Corso will take you past the **Palace of Massimo**, on the left, built on the curve traced from the Roman theatre once on this location. It was constructed by the Renaissance architect Baldassare Peruzzi. Opposite the Palace is the **Church of Sant'Andrea della Valle**, Puccini placed the first act of

The Pantheon illuminated.

Tosca here, under Rome's second tallest dome, designed and built by Lanfranco in 1621-25. Should you want to, the Victor Emanuele route will lead eventually into the **Via Nazionale**, which runs up to the **Piazza della Repubblica** and the beginning of this tour.

Piazzas, palaces and pizzas

Starting from the Piazza San Pantaleo and crossing to the south side of the Corso Vittorio Emanuele, the vast building dominating the street is the **Cancelleria**, or **Papal Palace**. Head south to the bustling **Campo dei Fiori** and to the east of the square, is the site of **Pompey's Theatre** over which a jum-

ble of buildings have been since built. The theatre was ancient Rome's largest, and Julius Caesar was assassinated in the curia here in 44 BC. One block away, across the Piazza Farnese is the French Embassy, now in the **Renaissance Palace of Farnese**, originating in 1514 but added to by Michelangelo.

A short walk from the piazza is the **Palace of Spada** dating from 1540. It houses the **Galleria Spada**, a precious collection of paintings from the 16th and 17th century. From the Campo dei Fiori, head due east to the Via Arenula and continue east across the road into Via Falegnami, then the Via Delphino, and into the **Piazza Venezia** – Rome's physical centre. Just to the west of the square is the baroque, 1568-84, **Church** of Gesu. The treasures in this ornate edifice include the largest piece of lapis lazuli just over the Spanish-style altar under which the Jesuit's founder, St. Ignatius, is buried. In the Piazza Venezia is the **Palace of Venezia**.

This short walk can be added to the previous tour but does, altogether, make for a very long and exhausting day. It is therefore better to split Rome into smaller areas to visit individually, especially if some time is spent at each point.

Once in Rome, however, there are few visitors that will resist the temptation to sample at least a few of the thousand different varieties of pizzas advertised in the hundreds of streetside cafes and restaurants. The problem remains to balance the pizza intake with the amount of walking necessary!

Sidewalk culture at the Piazza Navona.

Grand villas, parks and more museums

The northern part of the Rome on the east bank of the Tiber, is dominated by the parks and gardens of opulent villas.

Furthest east of these, and immediately north of the main railway station, is the moderately-sized **Villa Tarlonia**, not far from the **Piazza Fiume**. From this square, the **Corso D'Italia** follows the old Roman city wall to the entrance of the extensive grounds belonging to the **Villa Borghese**. There are three museums in this parkland: The **Galeria Borghese** is a spectacular art gallery housed in the villa itself, and a museum containing many statues. The gallery displays works of art by Caravaggio, Correggio, Raphael and Titian. The **Galeria Nazionale d'Arte Moderne**, on the other side of the park, contains paintings by Cezanne, De Chirico, Modigliani, and Mondrian, amongst others.

The **Museo Nazionale di Villa Giulia**, is housed in the villa of the same name towards the west side of the park. This museum is dedicated to the Etruscan collection – the largest of its kind in the world. Other places to visit in this part of the city's outskirts, is the **Villa Ada** and the **National Zoo**.

Towards the river is the **Piazza del Popolo** containing the **church of Santa Maria del Popolo**, dating from the 1470's. The **Chigi Chapel** here was designed by Raphael and the church's

Villa Borghese gardens.

treasures include paintings and frescoes by Caravaggio and Pinturicchio. The 3,200-year-old Egyptian obelisk here is that of Rameses II, brought to Rome by Augustus from Heliopolis and erected in the piazza in the 1580's. Travel south down Via Ripetta, to where it joins the riverside road and find the **Mausoleum of Augustus** set in gardens to the left.

Crossing the Tiber

There are many bridges which cross the Tiber, and, in central Rome there are around twelve. The northernmost of these can be taken from the Augustus Mausoleum and the **Aris Pacis**, or **Altar of Augustan Peace**. This bridge is known as the **Ponte Cavour**.

The road across leads into the **Piazza Cavour** and the **Palace of Justice**. Joining the riverside road, and moving southeast, the great bulk of the **Castle of Sant'Angelo** comes into view.

To the riverside of the road, as the Ponte Cavour leads to Augustus' Mausoleum, so the bridge leading across the Tiber to the Castle, links Rome with the site of **Hadrian's Mausoleum**, now the Castel Sant'Angelo.

Named after the Emperor Helius, who built the bridge, ten statues of angels bearing symbols of Christ's Passion decorate the arches and were placed there by Pope Clement IX in 1669. The fortress' cylindrical shape maintains that of the original Etruscan tomb and the tower contains the urns of the Emperors Hadrian and Septimus Severus. The castle has a grim and checkered history which goes back to the mausoleum date of the 2nd century.

Once a residence connected with royalty and the papacy, and wreathed in stories of the Borias, the castle is linked to the Vatican by an underground passage. This imposing fortress now houses an art gallery, an armament display and a mausoleum. The covered escape route, well used by past popes, can be seen on the walk to the Vatican itself.

The Via della Conciliazione leads from the Castel Sant'Angelo and the River Tiber, to the **Piazza San Pietro**, or **Saint Peter's Square**. Probably the most famous square anywhere in the world, this piazza is embraced by a baroque facade by Bernini.

The Trastevere

The last 'quarter' of Rome to be dealt with in this chapter is that lying to the south-west. The **Trastevere** is popular with Romans and visitors alike for its restaurants, bars, cafes and clubs.

Apart from its celebrated eating, drinking and nightlife entertainment establishments the Trastevere has a small theatre known as the **Pasquino**.

There are two famous old churches to be seen in this sector of Rome. There is the 12th century **Church of Santa Maria** in Trastevere, set in the piazza named for the church and its octagonal fountain featured in Fellini's film 'Roma'. And nearby is the parkland-surrounded **Church of San Pietro** in Montorio.

Rome's environs – Ostia Antica

Located near the coast, on the banks of the Tiber, and in a strategic position when the sea flowed up to its docks, Rome's major port was founded 400 years after Rome itself was established. From its 4th century beginnings, **Ostium** grew into a large city and is now a cocoon of everyday Roman life with the

Ponte Sant Angelo across the Tiber River.

entrance originally through the **Porta Romana** gate. This is passed on the via Ostiense, opposite the **Necropolis**. One must visit the **Baths of the Imperial Palace, Cisiarii, Neptune, Mithras** and **Marciana**, and also the **Maritime Baths**; the **Hot Springs**, or **Therme of Sette Sapienti** and that of **Faro**. The houses include those of **Diana, Apuleius, Bacchus / Serapis**, that of **Cupid** and **Psyche**, the house of **Dipinti, Giardino**

Hadrian's tomb, on the way to the Tivoli gardens, east of Rome.

and that of the **Muse** amongst others. Warehouses, barracks, taverns, bordellos, figure among the remains of the theatre, forum, **Mithraeum** and **Thermopolium** structures. The entire complex can take several hours to view properly and then there is the **site museum**, which is a must on this tour.

Tivoli

World famous for its magnificent gardens and waterfalls, **Tivoli** was a favourite location for the wealthy of ancient Rome to establish their holiday villas. One particular villa, or estate, attracts visitors to take this short journey east of Rome, and this is the **Villa Adriana**, or **Hadrian's Villa**, built between 118 - 134 AD.

This is a great complex of intricate design reflecting Hadrian's love of architecture. The huge imperial palace is surrounded by a Greek theatre, a library, the **Lyceum**, the **Maritime Theatre**, the guest houses of the **Hospitalia**

The Roman Forum

The Forum was the commercial centre of the Roman Empire's magnificent city. The most notable sites are the **Temple of Antoninus Pius** and **Faustina**. It was built in 141 AD, and later converted into a church. The grand **Basilica Aemillia** is to the right and further on, the **Curia**, or **Senate House** dating from the 3rd century. The ruins of the **Temple of Janus** are in front of the Curia, and nearby is the spectacular **Arch of Septimus Severus** built in 203 AD to commemorate the Emperor's victory over the Parthians. In front of the arch is the **Lapis Niger**, or Black Stone, the oldest and most sacred point in the entire forum.

The **Temples of Concord, Saturn** and that to the **Divine Vespasian** are located at the north-west end of the site, below the **Capital** itself. Towards the centre of the site are a row of memorial columns fronted by the **Column of Phocas**. The vast **Basilica Julia** is sited south of the columns and is next to the **Temple of Castor** and **Pollox** with its three remaining columns, dating from 5 BC. Walking up to the Via Sacra from this temple the **Arch of Augustus** lies to the right.

The next temple one comes across is that of the **Divine Julius**. Through the Arch of Augustus is the **Temple of Vesta** and the **House of the Vestals** with its courtyard and ceremonial pools. Back to the end of the Via Sacra and towards the entrance are the **Archaic Necropolis** and the remains of the **Temple of Romulus** in front of the **Church of Saints Cosma** and **Damiano**. Via Sacra curves around to the east and, on the left hand side is the great **Basilica of Maxentius**. One triple-valued aisle is all that remains of this huge building constructed in the 4th century.

Passing the location of the **Temple of Venus** and **Rome**, which is backed onto the **Church of San Francesca Romana**, and stands to the left, the final monument presents a grand exit to the Forum site. The **Arch of Titus** was erected in 81 AD and now, forms a gateway for those leaving the Forum. This grand arch was built after the Emperor's death to commemorate his capture of Jerusalem.

The Roman Forum was the centre of activities during the Roman Empire.

ROME

164

Canopus fish pond at Hadrian's Villa.

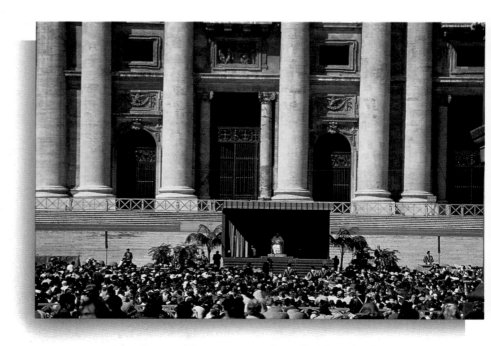

The Pope addressing crowds at St. Peter's Square.

Near a marketplace in the Trastevere district.

and **Temples to Apollo and Venus.** Hadrian had the entire area landscaped into valleys like that of the reconstructed Vale of Tempe in Greece and the Valley of Canopus, a canal in Egypt. Water is the theme of Hadrian's Villa, as it is of the **Villa d'Este** in Tivoli itself. A cardinal governor of Tivoli built this extraordinary complex of fountains and water gardens, lakes and waterfalls in which he located his Renaissance villa.

Subiaco

This monastic town lies due east of Tivoli, and one passes the site of the **Sabine Farm** which Maecenas donated to Horace in 33 BC. Many other hillside towns, villages and outposts lie dotted around this **Valley of Aniene**, like the **castle of Licenza**, with its **Antiquarium Museum; Anticoli Corrado**, with its 11th century frescoes in the **Church of San Pietro**; and **Saracinesco**, founded in the 9th century by the Saracens. Finally, **Subiaco** was where Saint Benedict retired to in the late 5th century. In the 1460's, the first printing press was brought to this town from Germany. Once, the town had 12 monasteries, now reduced to two, the **Convento di Santa Scholastica**, with its cloisters dating from 1052, the 13th century, and from 1580; and the **Convento di San Benedetto**, with its 13th century Lower Church and 14th century Upper Church. **Saint Benedict's Holy Grotto** is nearby

Villa D'Este in Tivoli.

with frescoes dating from the year 700 and others painted in 1210. Just on the town's outskirts is the **Church of San Francesco** with more interesting and rare paintings.

Palestrina

South of Tivoli is one of the Latin World's oldest towns. Predating imperial Rome, Praeneste, now **Palestrina**, was traditionally founded by the son of Ulysses and Circe, Telegono. This area is the massive site of the **Sanctuary of Fortuna Primigenia**, the largest Greek temple in all of Italy. This vast complex was built many years before it was first sacked in 80 BC. Throughout the town there are traces of great monuments and various temples and sacred shrines. The mosaic in the **Temple of Serapis**, is a prime example of its kind and the town's 5th century cathedral stands over the **Temple of Jupiter**. Cyclopean polygonal walls of the ancient city can be seen in places, as can traces of the early Forum.

At the upper level of the town, built as a series of terraces, evidence of the complex design of the **Sanctuary of Fortune** can be seen, some of the terracing restored in 1640. The crowning glory is the **Palace of Colonna-Barbarini**, now the **Archaeological Museum**. This houses the breathtaking mosaic of the Nile, created by Helenistic artisans in the 2nd century BC. Down to one side of the Museum is the 1660 **Church of**

Theatre of Marcello and the Temple of Apollo.

Santa Rosalia and a path leading up to the ruins of the **San Pietro Castle**. To another side of the museum, the **Terrazza degli Emicicli** (hemicycles) containing the celebrated **Oracle of Fortuna**, where the prophetess **Sibyl** offered her predictions.

Frascati

East of Palestrina is **Frascati**, a name that will be familiar to wine drinkers. The Etruscan city of **Tusculum** was originally sited here until its destruction in

Chestnut vendor by Piazza Santa Maria della Rotunda.

1191. Today's town is medieval and most of the major sites are of Renaissance origin. The **Villa Aldobrandini**, for example, was built in the 1590's, and its main claim to fame is its grandiose **Theatre of Waters**, built and added to by Giacomo della Porta, Giovanni Fontana and Carlo Maderno. The nearby **Villa Torlonia** also has a Theatre of Waters. Other villas in Frascati include the **Villa Lancelloti** which was constructed on the site of a 1st century farmhouse, and the **Villa Falconieri**, and **Villa Tuscolana**, originally built in 1580.

Albano

On the southern shores of Lake Albano, **Albano Laziale** is an important town situated opposite Frascati. The roundish lake itself is surrounded by numerous sites from classical times, as is **Lake Nemi**, a little further south. Ruins and vestiges of temples, civil buildings, and tombs abound in the area around both lakes and in the towns of Albano Laziale and **Genzano di Roma**, on the shores of Lake Nemi. In classical times, on the site of Albano, Septimus Severus established his 2nd Legion and the 6th century **Church of San Pietro** was built over the garrison's baths.

Passing the remains of the camp's gateway, the **Porta Praetoria**, another church, the 14th century **Church of Santa Maria della Rotonda** was built on the ruins of the **Nymphaeenum of Domitian**. Behind the church the traces of the **Amphitheatre** can be seen and nearby is the garrison's cistern, or **Cisternone**.

Castel Gandolfo

Although founded in the 12th century by the **Gandolfo** family who built a castle here, a recently discovered 9th - 7th century BC necropolis found on the site provides evidence that the hilltop location must have been occupied millenniums before.

Evidence of Roman occupation can be seen by visiting the **Emissarium**, a great tunnel carved out of the rock in 397 BC in order to drain the lake. The structure is still employed to regulate the lake's level. On the site of the original **Gandolfo Castle**, the **Papal Palace** was erected in 1624, and the Pope regularly gives audiences in the palace courtyard, when he uses Gandolfo as a summer residence.

Velletri

South, past Genzano di Roma and Lake Nemi, is **Velletri**, the ancient and largest of the many Castelli towns which surround Rome. Velletri was once a Roman town, remnants of which are revealed in the **Basilica** over which the Cathedral has been built. The site dates back to ancient **Volcia**, and there are a number of **Volscian sarcophagi** in the museum. The major edifice in this town is its campanile, or bell tower, the **Torre del Trivio**, which like the Pisa, completed around the same time, leans at an angle. It dates back to 1353 and is 45 metres in height.

Castel Gandolfo, the Pope's residence.

Lazio is divided into five provinces including Rome, all of which are steeped in history and set in rich scenery. North of Rome, Lazio offers a mixed attraction of inland lakes and scattered hills. Here, there are almost 30 Etruscan archaeological sites to visit and many monasteries and countryside chapels and churches of interest.

In the south part of the region some of the oldest inhabited towns of Europe can be visited, also some of the newest, founded by Mussolini. There are many charming hilltop abbey towns and Lazio's only national park, plus the vast, reclaimed **Pontine** marshes.

The **Tyrrhenian** coastline's best beaches are down south towards **Naples** and north of **Civitavecchia**, the main ferry port of the coast for sailings to and from **Sardinia**.

In the Lazio region, there are three large lake systems. **Lake Bracciano**, ringed by the **Sabatini Mountains**, lies just north of Rome; on the way is **Veio**, and near this village is the 7th century tomb of **Campana** and the **Etruscan Sodo Bridge**. On the last leg to Lake Bracciano are the ruins of **Galeria Castle**. The 15th century **Castello degli Orsini** stands sentinel by the shore side near the town of **Bracciano** where there is the **Italian Air Force Museum**. North

Isle of Bisentina, Bolsena.

Lazio

173

Villa Farnese, an opulent Renaissance palace, Caprarola.

Ruins of an Etruscan temple in Tarquinia.

of Lake Bracciano is **Lake Vico**. On the way there, one could visit the ancient site of **Sutri** which sports an amphitheatre and interesting duomo. Near the lake, in **Caprarola**, is the opulent Renaissance palace, **Villa Farnese** and the smaller **Palazzina del Piacere**. South-east of here is the town of **Civita Castellana** with its ruined ancient temples, a 1210 AD duomo, and an interesting archaeological museum. The third lake, in the north-west of the region, is **Lake Bolsena**, the fifth largest of Italy's lakes, and subject of many a famous

The fortress-like lake castle at Santa Severa.

Mysterious thermal springs at Viterbo.

landscape painting.

The **Castle Mondaleschi** in **Bolsena** should be visited, as should the archaeological area and the 15th century **church of Santa Cristina**. On the southern shore are the towns of **Montefiascone** and **Capodimonte**.

Etruscan exuberance

A little west of Rome is **Cerveteri**, site of one of the best examples of Etruscan necropolises and a national museum, housed in a small castle. The

a small ancient necropolis nearby. North-west of Rome, to the west of the Rome-Siena highway, is the medieval walled city of Tuscania.

Outside the city walls are many Etruscan ruins and tombs near the ravine, which drains Lake Bolsena via the **River Marta**. Inside the walls are two magnificent churches, the Romanesque twins of **Saint Peter** and **Saint Mary Maggiore**, and both were begun in the 7th century. There is a good museum in the town.

East of Tuscania is the large town of **Viterbo**, the seat of popes for much of the 13th century, as the architectural styles belie. There is the **Palazzo del Plebiscito** and that of **Priori**, the Pope's Palace, the **Palazzetto of San Tommaso**, and the **Papal Palace**, begun in the 1260's. There is a Romanesque cathedral here, the well preserved medieval **church of Santa Maria Nova**, the 11th century **Gesu Church** and the **church of San Sisto** which was begun in the 8th century. There are many interesting ancient houses here and four museums to visit. Outside the town are the **Spa of Bulicame**, the **Castle of Asso**, Etruscan tombs and a Roman amphitheatre. Just outisde **Bomarzo**, towards the motorway, is an amazing **Monster Park**.

East again is **Orte**, which should be visited for the artistic treasures in the **church museum of San Silvestro**. South of Orte is **Magliano Sabino** which has a magnificent cathedral and a 12th century church, **San Pietro**. East again is

Banditaccia Necropolis should be visited before moving on to more tombs and another excellent museum at **Tarquinia**, further to the north, on the coast, past **Civitavecchia**. Continuing north, are the two towns of **Vulci** and **Tuscania**.

The **Castello dell'Abbadia** in Vulci dates from the 13th century, and there is

Interior of an Etruscan tomb of the Monterozzi necropolis, Tarquinia.

Rolling hillsides around Viterbo.

the town of **Rieti** with its 12th century **Cathedral of Santa Maria Assunta** and the elegant **Palazzo Vecchiarelli**. The plains around Rieti are dotted with many convents and abbeys associated with **Saint Assisi**.

Roads here circle an area of the 'Land of the Sabines' which includes **Monte Sabini**. Within this region there are numerous hilltop abbey towns and many churches to visit like the 13th century **San Paolo** at **Poggio Mirteto** and the **Abbazia di Santa Maria di Fara**, founded in the 6th century.

Ancient walled cities

Due south of Rieti is the exquisitely pre-

served fortress village of **Roccsa Sinibalda**, dominating the surrounding countryside. South of Rome, Lazio offers even more scenic delights such as towards the coast. **Pomezia**, near ancient **Lavinium** where a hundred life-size Roman terracotta statues were found in 1977 could prove interesting.

Further south, and on the coast, are the twin sites of **Anzio** and **Nettuno**. Both are resort areas and the region is well known for being synonymous with events from World War II. The largest American military cemetery is located near **Nettuno** which boasts an ancient castle. Hydrofoils sail to the distant **Pontine Islands** from Anzio.

East of the promontory are the lands of **Latina**, around the town of the same

Ancient walls in deserted countryside of Ninfa.

name. Latina was founded in 1932 and is near to the site of **Cori**, with its remains of the **Roman Cyclopean** polygonal city walls, **Temple of Hercules** and other ruins.

More polygonal walls surround **Norba**; nearby is the deserted town of **Ninfa**, not far from the **Abbey di Valvisciolo**, well worth a visit. South of **Norma**, the town 'suspended twin heaven and earth', is the medieval town of **Sermoneta** with a 13th century **Castello Caetani**. **Sezze**, just to the south, is also walled in the same style as Norba and these walls date from the 4th century BC.

South-east lies **Priverno** and the **Abbey of Fossonova**. The cathedral of Priverno dates from the 1280's, while the Abbey's cloisters of **French Cistercian** design is a rarity in Italy. Right on the southern promontory is the long strip of the **Circero National Park**, Italy's smallest nature reserve but a haven for migratory wildlife and a variety of hawks.

A little further south along the coast is the large town of **Terracina** and the highway which leads past the beach resort of **Sperlonga**. A visit to the **Grotto of Tiberius** sea cave is worthwhile and the small museum should not be missed. Medieval **Gaeta** has an impressive cathedral with a 12th century *camponile*, a 13th century castle and the **church of San Giovanni a Mare**, built in the 9th century.

From here the Gaeta promontory is

An emerald forest cover in Ponza.

passed and the road leads to the town of **Formia**. The area around Formia is steeped in history; we know that Cicero was dispatched here after Caesar's assassination by Mark Anthony's men. Ferries sail to the **Pontine** islands from the port of Formia.

Abbeys and Citadels

Continuing inland, and north of Formia, is the town of **Cassino**. Here stands the famous **Abbey of Montecassino** lying around 80 kilometres north of **Naples**,

Both the abbey and the small town of Cassino, below the abbey, were the target of considerable bombing during the last war. There is a museum at the abbey with some interesting exhibits including many ancient manuscripts.

Also to the east of the main 207 motorway, and further south, is the **Abbey of Casamari**. Consecrated in 1217, the Abbey of Casamari is of French Cistercian origin and continues today to operate as a monastery. A visit to the little hamlets in the area makes an interesting tour and, apart from the spectacular scenery, tiny **Veroli**'s cathedral remains contain treasures dating from the 14th century. **Bovile Ernica** has an impressive medieval wall and **Monte San Giovanni Campano** its imposing castle.

West of Casamari is **Altari**, a 2,400 year-old town with a double circle of 6th century Cyclopean walls. Apart from its Roman remains, Altari has a magnificent 12th century church, **Santa Maria Maggiore**. Nearby, is **Ferentino** and its Cistercian Gothic **church of Santa Maria Maggiore**, built in 1150. There are also remains of Roman villas and Roman markets. Just north of Ferentino is **Anagni**. Last of our visits is to the '**City of Popes**', Anagni. **Boniface VIII's Palace** is a spectacular complex and contains the marvellous 11th century cathedral built in the Romanesque style.

The town is a gem of medieval architecture and its walls encapsulate the ancient towers, the 13th century **Casa Barnekow** and **Palazzo Comunale**.

and just to the right of the Route 207. The impressively situated Abbey of Montecassino was founded in 529 AD by **Saint Benedict**. The abbey has been rebuilt by monks after it was bombed in 1944 during the second World War. Its strategic position, set high on a mountain between Rome and Naples, led to the destruction of this abbey numerous times over its almost 1500 year history.

Lazio's coastline is not extensive, but remains rugged and pristine.

Molise

This is a small, mountainous, rugged rural region, almost centrally located on the Adriatic coastline. Around 350,000 people, mostly farmers, inhabit the region. The agricultural produce includes wheat, vegetables, vines, sheep and goats. This area is the backwater of Italy and rarely attracts the tourist as there is of little significance to see, and even less to do. The region's best claim to fame is that it has been provisionally established, by the evidence of fossils, that Stone Age man first set up home in Europe at **Iserna** a million years ago.

The often rural and rugged countryside of Molise.

Isernia

Isernia is the provincial capital, located far inland, on the region's western fringes. Few visitors pass through Isernia, and if they do, it is for the new **Museo Nazionale della Pentria** to see Isernia's exhibits of prehistoric life, one million years BC. These, excavated from the **Paleolithic** village nearby, include the remains of **Stone Age** man and the remnants of his dinners, elephant, rhinoceros, hippopotami, bison, bears etc. and prehistoric use of fire. The ancient **Fontana Fraterna** in the capital, is a 14th century jigsaw of bits of Roman stonework put together.

Ancient sites

North-east of Isernia is the '**Athens of the Samnites**' – **Agnone**. Its **Marinelli Pontifical** bell foundry claims to be the oldest in the country and was here in the year 1300. There is also a little museum here and souvenirs consist of copper ornaments and almond sweets.

High enough in the mountains to qualify, in 1914, as Italy's first ski club, **Capracotta**, nearby, overlooks the **Sangro Valley**, part of the border between **Molise** and **Abruzzi**. The town of 'Abandoned Stones', **Pietrabbondante**, is an isolated Samnite religious centre with a second century temple ruin, south of Agnone. Its semi-circular amphitheatre is Greek and also dates from the second century AD.

Campobasso is located in the south-central part of the Molise and is famous for its curious 'Mysteries' or **Corpus Domini** processions with children acting as angels and cherubs, 'flying' around the thirteen floats. Originally instigated in the 1600's, the parades were banned until 1740 as the performances and antics of the children made the onlookers laugh! Dominated by a turretted castle, **Monteforte**, built in the 16th century, Campobasso has two main Romanesque churches, that of **San Leonardo** and **San Giorgio**. This is an ancient Samnite area and the town has the **Museo Sannitico**, containing weaponry exhibits and gold and silver treasures of earlier days.

South of Campobasso is the ancient Samnite city of **Saipins**, now carrying the Roman name of **Saepinum**, with the remains of Roman walls, best preserved near the theatre, a forum, *basilica*, baths, houses, shops and marketplace. Highlights are the **Griffon Fountain**, a funereal monument, and the ruins of the **house of Impluvio Sannitico**. These are not the remains of an opulent Roman town, but a functional, administrative centre. A museum exhibits the progress of various excavations at the site.

Curving in an arc across the southern borders of Molise, providing a background to Isernia and Campobasso, are a ridge of mountains shown as the

Termoli, the fishing port on the Molise coast.

Matese. Lakes, streams and pretty, almost Alpine villages hide in seclusion in the folds of this rarely visited area.

Boiano is the largest of the villages of the Matese and boasts a Lombardic castle ruin and a prehistoric wall. From the summit of **Monte la Gallinola**, it is sometimes possible to view the tantalising Bay of Naples far to the south-west. Heading for the fishing port of **Termoli**, on the Molise coast, **Santa Maria della Strada**, a magnificent Romanesque church is passed before continuing down to **Larino**. Larino was the Samnite town of **Larinum** and the **Ara**

Fretana, or cylindrical altar in the town testifies to the fact. Also, artifacts from the age are on exhibit in the **Palazzo Comunale**, near the 1319 cathedral. The **church of San Fransisco** here has some beautiful 18th century frescoes.

Just on the town's outskirts are the ancient remains of the old city, walls, villa ruins and an amphitheatre. The Molise coastline is of little consequence apart from the **Campomarino** resorts and the endearing port of Termoli with its castle built by Frederick II. For the traveller seeking the rural and rugged, Molise will surely suffice.

Thi s almost circular region lies right in the centre of Italy's long peninsula and between the Apennine spine and the Adriatic Sea. Mountainous, but with a flatish coastline sporting some long, fine sandy beaches, this land was once wealthy and popular with the ancient Romans (Ovid was born here) even though it appears to be cut off from the rest of Italy by mountain ranges like those of **Laga** in the north, the **Gran Sasso d'Italia** and **Maiella Massif** in the centre and those of the **Molise** to the south.

Festival of the Snakes, a ceremony that dates back to pagan times.

Abruzzi

193

Abruzzi is an important area of antiquity. There are more than 25 important ancient ruin sites spread across the region and the same number of castle ruins and almost 30 major castles still standing. Ancient towers abound and the region can boast half a dozen major palaces. Mostly highland, the mountains are only recently being developed for tourists, with climbing, skiing and hunting resorts,

Hunting is a popular past-time around Caccia.

while its coastal beaches are similarly being revitalised. The highest point in the Apennine Range is in Arbuzzi at 2,912 metres (9554 ft). Handicrafts abound in the region, from embroidery to carpet and blanket weaving, copper and marquetry workmanship, ceramics and wrought ironwork.

L'Aquila

In the inland part of Abruzzi, the region has a population of about 70,000 and stands under the shadow of the Gran Sasso, or 'Big Stone' range to the north and east. **L'Aquila**, which means 'The Eagle', was founded by the Emperor Frederick II in 1240. There are around 60 churches in L'Aquila, surrounded by, as legend has it, 99 hamlets and castles. The city's symbol, the **Fontana delle 99 Cannelle**, meaning a fountain with 99 spouts, was built in 1272 and underscores the legend.

A massive, square-fronted facade with round windows and three decorative porticos introduces the region's greatest Romanesque church, the **Santa Maria di Collemaggio**, built in 1270 and housing the tomb of Celestine V, crowned in 1249. Around the **Piazza Duomo** the 12th century **churches of Santa Giusta** and **San Giuseppe** stand among some interesting old buildings which include the **Palazzo Franchi** and the **Palazzo di Giustizia**.

The bell tower of the Guistizia Palace chimes 99 strokes every day at dusk. In the **church of San Bernadino** is the saint's mausoleum. The **National Museum** contains a wide variety of treasures and exhibits from fossils to paintings and statues. Just to the west of L'Aquila, near **San Vittorino**, is ancient **Amiternum**, a Sabine city, mentioned in the Aeneid. Here, many Roman remains have been unearthed, including a theatre, amphitheatre and several decorated houses.

A coastal tour

Starting from the north and working down the coastline, a shoreline road and highway run parallel past a series of small and large beach resorts, begin-

Kiting in the summer on the Gran Sasso mountain range.

ning with **Martinsecuro**, on the regional border, past **Villa Rosa** and **Tortoreto Lido**, to ancient **Giulianova** with its Romanesque church of **Santa Maria a Mare** and museum.

From the coastal road, **Teramo** can be visited. Once a Roman centre, there are the remains of a Roman theatre here and the original cathedral, **Sant' Maria Aprutiensis**, dates from the 6th century. The current cathedral is medieval and the **church of Maria Santissima Grazie** is **Franciscan**. An interesting, ancient building in the town is the **Casa dei Melatini**, built during the Angevin period. Teramo is famous for its **Majolica Castelli** pottery vessels and numerous fascinating examples can be seen in the **Museo della Ceramica**.

Now the road runs past **Roseto degli Abruzzo** to **Pineto**, which sports the **Carolean Torre di Cerrano**. Between these last two, and inland a little way, is **Atri**, an ancient Roman town with a magnificent 13th century Romanesque cathedral, a 14th century ducal palace and museum of antiquities.

Campli, a short drive away, has a good archaeological museum housed in the convent of the Romanesque **church of San Francisco**. Many of the exhibits here come from the excavations of **Campovalano** nearby. In Campovalano, the **San Pietro** church was founded in the 6th century.

The next coastal resort is **Silvi**, and then the **Citta Sant Angelo Marina**, just before the road enters the vast 16 kilometre beach area and fishing port of

Pescara. This is the region's coastal jewel as far as seaside tourism is concerned, but the town has little of historic interest except the birthplace of **Gabriele D'Annunzio**, born here in 1864.

The main Rome highway heads west from Pescara, cutting right across the Apennines, and dividing the country and the region of Abruzzi in half. The town of **Chieti** can be visited from Pescara. Just up the **Aterno River** valley, this ancient Roman centre has a fascinating museum of archaeology and antiquity and a Roman *thermae*, or baths and a lone Romano gateway stands at **Casalincontrada** just a short distance west of Chieti.

After Pescara, the small resort of **Francavilla al Mare**, with a small museum and pretty church, stands halfway to **Orotona**, a town with a castle and the Canadian war cemetery. From Orotana several interesting places like **Guardiagrele** can be visited by the narrow-gauge railway. The marinas of **San Vito** and **Rocca** follow on the southbound road until it reaches the **Sangro River** and the resort of **Fossacesia**. The **Church of San Giovani** in **Venere**, in the resort of **Fossacesia Marina**, dates from the 8th century although it was rebuilt in 1015. This church was erected in a spectacular position overlooking the sea and on the site of the **Temple of Venus**.

Across the Sangro River is the British war cemetery. Two more resorts follow as the coast turns south-east, **Torino** and the **Casalbordino Lido**. The town

L'Aquila, a small town with 60 churches.

of **Vasto**, further south, has a resort area called the **Vasto Marina** and this is Abruzzo's most southerly port and beach area apart from the **San Salvo Marina** which stands on the coast at the border with the Molise Province. A ferry runs from the port of Vasto to the **Islands of Tremiti**, out in the Adriatic.

Sites of inland Abruzzi

Inland from Pescara, to the south of the Rome highway, and in the centre of the southern part of Abruzzi, lies **Sulmona**, birthplace of Ovid (43BC - 17AD). Here, the ancient church and palace of **Santa Maria Annunziata**, was founded in the early 14th century. The first stories of the church have been converted into a museum. A 1256 Gothic aquaduct runs through the town and, in the **Piazza Garibaldi** is the **Fontana del Veccio**. The ruins of a **Temple of Hercules** stands outside the town.

West of Sulmona

West of Sulmona is the village of **Cocullo**, famed for its 'Procession of Snakes' ceremony dating back to pagan times, but adopted by the church, and held on the first Thursday of May.

In the **Maiella Mountains** to the south-east of Sulmona are the natural wonders of the **Grotto of Cavallone** and the **Tavola Rotonda**, or 'Round

The Abruzzo National Park

Lying in the far south of Abruzzi and falling between both the region it is named after and neighbouring region of Molise, the national park was founded in 1923. This move has protected some very rare European mammals from almost inevitable extinction, such as the Marsican bear (only around 150 remain), the Abruzzo chamois, roe deer, the Apennine wolf, the Apennine lynx, boar, foxes, badgers, wild cat, pine martens, beech martens and red squirrel. Bird life includes golden eagles, hawks, the rare Dalmatian woodpecker and black grouse. The rare flora here consists mainly of black pine, beech and European Turkey oak. This is Italy's second largest park, at 400 square kilometres and is very mountainous.

In the Molise region **Mount Petroso** rises to 2,247 metres, and the highest region in the Abruzzi part is around **Monte Marsicano** (2,242 metres), **Monte della Corte** (2,186 metres), and **Monte Campitello** (2,026 metres), in the north-east. Another very popular region is the resort area around **Monte Tranquillo** (1,830 metres), **Monte Pietroso** (1,880 metres) and **Monte la Rocca** (1,925 metres), all in the east central part of the park.

There is one large lake, the long, narrow **Barrea**, in the east of the park with the towns of Barrea and **Villetta** at either end and the hill resort on the west side of the lake, **Civitella Alfedina**. Only one other town, **Pescasseroli**, is located in the park itself, although there is the village of **Opi**, in the middle of the reserve and **Alfendena, Montenero, Pizzone, Castel San Vincenzo** and **Rocchetta** villages in the area of scenic beauty which skirts the park on east and south side down into the Molise. There are around 20 camping sites, tourist sites and refuge huts throughout the National Park area. Apart from ideal opportunities for horse riding around Pescasserolli, and mountaineering, there are a number of grottoes in the park for exploration, like the **Grota di Ladri**, the **Chiatra del Re** and the **Grotto dele Fate**. On the edge of the park region, there is the **Grotta Valle d. Vacche**, and the **Grotta del Banditi**, in the south-east. In the **Maiella Mountains**, east of the Abruzzi National Park, there is a small nature reserve with its famous **Grotta San Giovanni**, and surrounded by beauty spots, or **Vallone**, like the **Blockhaus**, the **Bocca di Valle**, the **Ugni** and the **Vallone Fara San Martino**.

Table', just north of **Campo di Giove**. **Scanno** can be reached south and west of Sulmona and stands high above the **Scanno Lake** just north of the **National Park**. Here, in this pretty old village, the women still wear traditional dress, contrasting with the bright Lycra ski suits of the holiday-makers who come to revel on the snowy slopes of **Monte Rotondo**.

Along the coast

South of the port of Orotona, is the town of **Lanciano**, famous for its 11th century cathedral, built on a Roman bridge.

The town also has a Gothic church, **Santa Maria Maggiore**, and a medieval gateway, the **Porta San Biagio**.

Inland from Vasto

Inland from Vasto, in an area bordered by the regional boundary and the Sangro River, are the remains of ancient walls at **Paglieta, Pollutri, Archi** and **Tornareccio** – Roman walls like these are only found here. South-west of Vasto, far up-country, is the village of **Carunchio**, which has examples of Roman walls, but also a Roman gateway.

Uncrowded coves and beaches on Abruzzi's Adriatic coast.

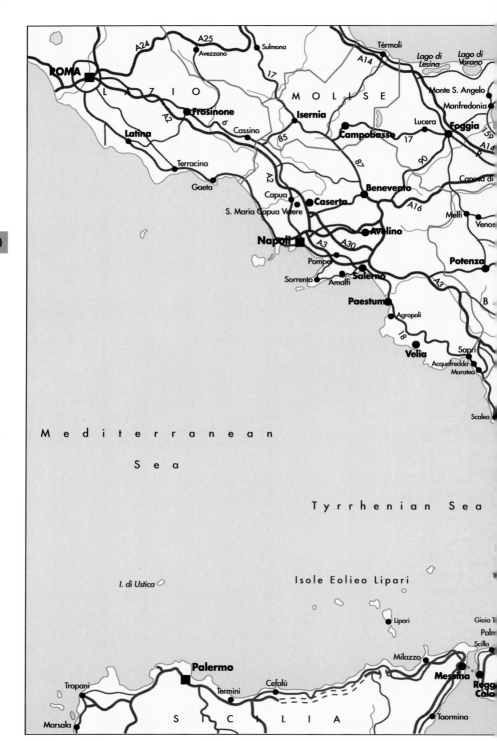

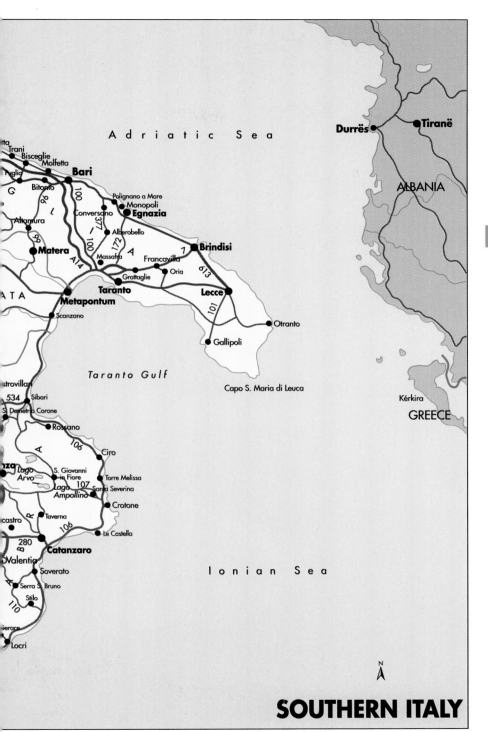

Adriatic Sea

Durrës

Tiranë

ALBANIA

ta
Trani
Bisceglie
Molfetta
ugli
Bari
G
Bitonto
96
Altamura
L
377
100
Polignano a Mare
Monopoli
Conversano
Egnazia
100
172
Alberobello
Matera
99
A14
A
Massafra
Francavilla
7
Brindisi
Grottaglie
Oria
613
Taranto
Metapontum
Lecce
ATA
Scanzano
101
Otranto
strovillari
Gallipoli
534
Sibari
Taranto Gulf
S. Demetrio Corone
Capo S. Maria di Leuca
Rossano
Kérkira
106
Ciro
GREECE
za
Lago
Arvo
S. Giovanni
in Fiore
Torre Melissa
Lago
107
Santa Severina
Ampollino
Crotone
castro
Taverna
106
Le Castella
280
Catanzaro
Valentia
Soverato
Ionian Sea
Serra S. Bruno
Stilo
110
erace
Locri

N

SOUTHERN ITALY

Naples

Dramatically positioned at the foot of **Mount Vesuvius** and overlooking the magnificent **Bay of Naples**, the narrow streets of this striking city sprawl over the coastal hills. Naples rates as one of Italy's top five tourist resorts and is one of the country's oldest cities. Apart from its own many attractions and lovely setting, **Naples** is surrounded by the beauty spots and sites of **Capri** and **Ischia islands**, nearby **Pompeii**, the **Phlaegrean Fields** and **Herculaneum**.

Castel dell' Ovo (Egg Castle) seen against the city of Naples from the bay.

In Grecian times, around 600 BC, the city was the capital of **Magna Graecia** and was known as Palaeopolis. In Roman times Naples was called Neapolis, and the ruins of this ancient city still lie undisturbed under the wheels of the frantic traffic in the *centro storico*, or old city. However, not even the noise and bustle of this most Mediterranean and third largest of Italy's cities penetrates Naples' six main museums. The **Capodimonte National Gallery and Museum**, north of the city on the continuation of Via Roma holds Botticelli, Bellini, Caravaggio, Masaccio, Brueghel and Titian paintings amongst others, plus ceramic and armoury collections. The **Archaeological Museum**, in the north-west corner of the city centre, west end of Via Foria, has Graeco-Roman

203

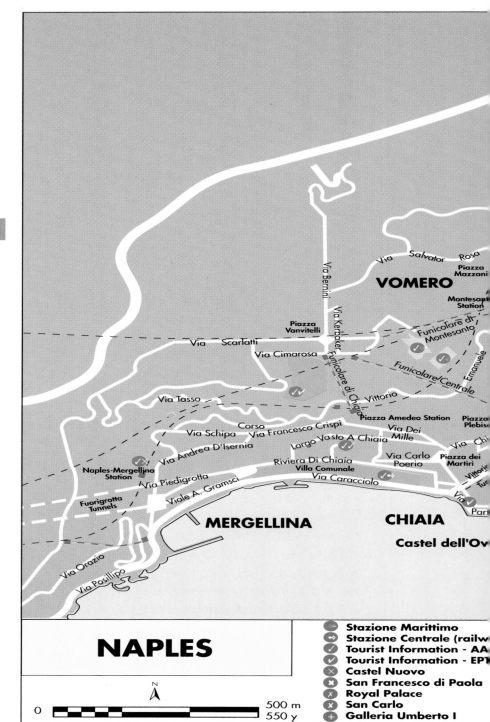

VOMERO

Via Salvator Rosa
Piazza Mazzani

Montesant Station

Piazza Vanvitelli

Via Bernini

Via Kerbaker

Funicolare di Montesanto

Via Scarlatti

Via Cimarosa

Funicolare di Chiai

Funicolare Centrale

Emanuele

Via Tasso

Vittorio

Piazza Amedeo Station

Piazza Plebisc

Corso

Via Schipa Via Francesco Crispi

Via Dei Mille

Via Andrea D'Isernia

Largo Vasto A Chiaia

Via Chi

Naples-Mergellina Station

Via Piedigrotta

Riviera Di Chiaia
Villa Comunale

Via Carlo Poerio

Piazza dei Martiri

Via

Fuorigrotta Tunnels

Viale A. Gramsci

Via Caracciolo

Vittori

Tur

Par

Via Orazio

MERGELLINA

CHIAIA

Castel dell'Ov

Via Posillipo

NAPLES

N

0 _____ 500 m
          550 y

- Stazione Marittimo
- Stazione Centrale (railw
- Tourist Information - AA
- Tourist Information - EP1
- Castel Nuovo
- San Francesco di Paola
- Royal Palace
- San Carlo
- Galleria Umberto I

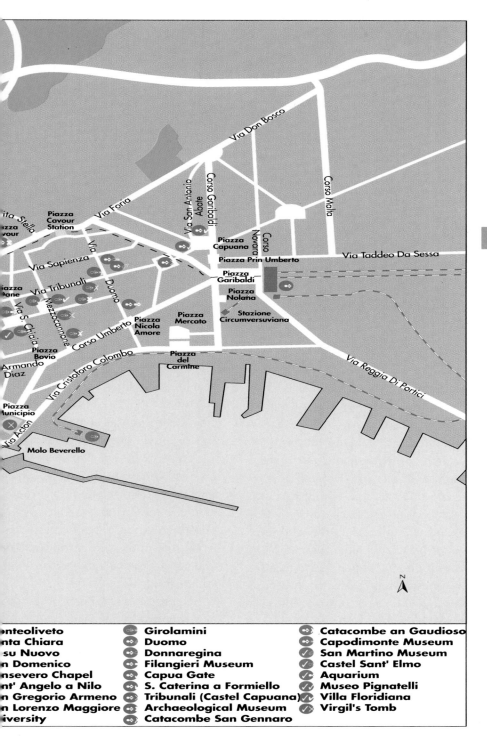

Via Don Bosco

Corso Garibaldi

Via San Antonio Abate

Corso Malta

ita Stella

Piazza Cavour Station

azza vour

Via Foria

Corso Novara

Corso

Via Taddeo Da Sessa

Piazza Capuana

Piazza Prin Umberto

Via Sapienza

Via

Piazza Garibaldi

Via Tribunali

Duomo

azza ane

Piazza Nolana

Mezzocannone

Stazione Circumversuviana

Via S. Chiara

Piazza Nicola Amore

Piazza Mercato

nt

Corso Umberto

Piazza Bovio

Via Cristoforo Colombo

Piazza del Carmine

Via Reggia Di Portici

Armando Diaz

Piazza Municipio

Via Acton

Molo Beverello

N

nteoliveto

Girolamini

Catacombe an Gaudioso

nta Chiara

Duomo

Capodimonte Museum

su Nuovo

Donnaregina

San Martino Museum

n Domenico

Filangieri Museum

Castel Sant' Elmo

nsevero Chapel

Capua Gate

Aquarium

nt' Angelo a Nilo

S. Caterina a Formiello

Museo Pignatelli

n Gregorio Armeno

Tribunali (Castel Capuana)

Villa Floridiana

n Lorenzo Maggiore

Archaeological Museum

Virgil's Tomb

iversity

Catacombe San Gennaro

Galleria San Carlo, a shopping arcade.

sculptures, wonderful mosaics, frescoes, paintings and treasures from Pompeii and Herculaneum; the **Museo Filangieri**, in the **Cuomo Palace** on Via Duomo, down towards the port from the **Cathedral**, one can see paintings by Ribera and Giordano plus others and collections of porcelain. The **Prince of Aragona Pignatelli Cortes Museum**, off the Riviera di Chiaia, near the **Villa Comunale**, has stately home furnishings and paintings. In the **National Ceramic Museum (Museo Duca di Martino)**, in grounds of **Villa Floridiana**, north of Villa Comunale, there are porcelain and ceramics from Italy and across the world; and the **Museo Nazionale di San Martino**, in **Certosa San Martino**, the monastery

near the **Sant'Elmo Castle**, has exhibits of historic Naples, costumes, folkloric art and craft, and the lavishly decorated church contains baroque paintings.

The museums of Naples contain a priceless variety of antiquities which trace the history of Naples from Graeco-Romanic times, through the days of Phoenician and Carthaginian traders, Byzantine rule, the Normans, the Swabian and Spanish kingdoms to modern times.

Naples is also the home of Europe's oldest **aquarium**, established in the year 1800, and located to the south-west of the city in the gardens of the Villa Comune. Even further out west of Naples is **Virgil's tomb** and, to the north-west of the city, lies the city's attractive

Many of the old castles have been converted into museums.

botanical gardens, another sanctuary from the bustling, overcrowded and noisy city.

Naples is also a city of many fine churches. The Gothic cathedral or duomo was constructed in 1315, and it conceals the head and two phials of the blood of **Gennaro,** the patron saint of Naples, which is a treasured relic of the cathedral. The Saint's 16th century old coagulated blood is said to liquify every year on December 16th, September 19th and the first Sunday in May, ever since the Saint's body was brought to Naples after his martyrdom. The duomo stands on Via Duomo in the north-west part of the city. Robert the Wise, king of the city in the early 14th century, begun the construction of the **Church of Santa** **Chiara** on Via B. Croce. The king's tomb behind the altar and the richly decorated cloister of the Order of Clares should not be missed. Near the centrally located **Church of San Domenico Maggiore** is the **Sansevero Chapel** which houses a remarkable collection of 18th century sculptures and the painting, 'The Veiled Christ', by Sammartino. In the **Spaccanapoli** section of the city, is the **Gusu Nuovo Jesuit Church** dating from the 16th century with its curiously patterned facade. Almost central in the old city is Naples' most beautiful Gothic church, the **San Lorenzo Maggiore,** founded under the auspices of King Charles I of Anjou.

Finally, a visit can be paid to a two storey subterranean cemetery, the **Cata-**

Pompeii

Villa of the Faun, the largest house in the city.

Whilst the AD 79 volcanic eruption of Vesuvius had the tragic effect of wiping out much of the population of this large Roman city, it resulted in preserving the entire spectrum of life as it was nineteen centuries ago.

Unfortunately, the disaster also killed the famous Roman naturalist **Pliny the Elder**, after whom a certain type of volcano is named.

More than 60 per cent of the streets and villas of this important Roman centre has been excavated from the volcanic dust and lava that once entombed it. Cobbled streets are followed to view the many structures in various states of repair and preservation. Not only have houses and civic buildings been preserved in minute detail, but the inhabitants, going about their daily business, were caught in the choking clouds of sulphur and encapsulated in the solidifying volcanic ash.

Most celebrated of Pompeii's many mansions which can be visited on tours of the ancient ruins is the **House of Vettii** where erotic paintings decorated the villa's walls and its **Etruscan courtyard** is embellished by statuary of various dieties. Near the **Herculaneum Gate** is the **Villa of Mysteries** which contains some of the most exquisite Roman frescoes ever found. More was learned about the Roman way of life (and sex and death) from excavations at Pompeii than from those at any other Roman city. An emperor's resort, just 24 kilometres away, has a magnificient basilica and temples to the gods **Apollo** and **Jupiter**, all three of which were grouped around the **Forum**. The **Villa of the Surgeon** contains a large selection of early doctor's and dentist's implements and in the **Antiquatium** there is a collection of kitchen

Ancient Roman inscriptions found on many of the ruins.

House of Vettii which is known for its erotic wall paintings

Exquisite frescoes at the Villa of Mysteries.

house in the city) so called after the bronze statue found there. Other important sites to visit include the **Amphitheatre**, the large and small theatres, the wine shop with amphorae still intact, and the house of **Loreius Tibertinus**. In a house off the Stabian Way, a woman's remains were found still clutching her jewellery in a vain attempt to salvage her valuables. Her house sports a magnificient mosaic of a bounding hound.

utensils and everyday items. A particularly grue-some exhibit is the ash cast of a dog, frozen in the holocaust of Vesuvius' wrath. In the **Stabian Thermae**, or **Roman baths**, skeletons of the bathers can be seen in plaster casts and guides direct (more usually) the male visitors from here to the erotic frescoes on the walls of the **Lupoanare**. Roman graffiti can be seen on many of the walls of Pompeii's ancient houses, shops and public monuments.

Discovered initially in 1600, excavations in Pompeii only begun in the mid-18th century and work was undertaken under the direction of the Italian Government in 1860.

Many of the artifacts and more important discoveries from the site can now be seen in the nearby **Archaeological Museum** in Naples, like the **Battle of Alexander the Great mosaic**, removed from the **Villa of the Faun** (the largest

The Odeon which used to be a 800-seat covered theatre.

Statue of Diana at the Apollo Temple.

The garden and portico of the Villa Giulia Felice.

Inside the magnificent Teatro San Carlo, Naples.

The local menfolk of Naples.

is the **Church of San Fransisco** and nearby is the **Galleria Umberto 1** shopping arcades.

Next to the palace stands the **San Carlo Opera House**, built in 1737, which is one of the most striking in Europe and from here it is a short walk to the **Castel Nuovo**, the 13th century castle of King Charles I of Anjou. Work of the designer Francesco Laurana, the 15th century triumphal arch curves over the towered entrance to the castle, which is unfortunately not open to visitors. The **Carthusian monastery of San Martino** next door, however, is a museum of the history of the city. Many of the old houses in this area, with its narrow alleyways and rabbit-warren streets leading towards the docks, were destroyed in an earthquake in 1980.

South of here is the old **Santa Lucia** district of Naples and, linked to the mainland by a small causeway, is the so called 'Egg Castle' or **Castel dell'Ovo** set on its tiny island and said to have been built over an egg placed here by Virgil. This castle, built by King Frederick II, is also closed to the public.

In Santa Lucia district, one can take a romantic horse-drawn carriage ride through the city's avenues, along the promenade or through the **Villa Comunale**.

From Santa Lucia village, stretching west along the promenade is the Villa Comunale park with an aquarium set in the centre and several cafes. A pleasant suburb, **Mergellina**, lies just west of the park and this is where the

combs of **San Gennaro**, which date from the 2nd century and are only open on Saturdays.

Kings and Capodimonte

Another favourite tourist respite from the noise of Naples is a visit to the 17th century **Royal Palace of Capodimonte**, or **Palazzo Reale**, on the dramatic Piazza Plebiscito near the **San Carlo Theatre**, by the port's main jetty. Eight kings' statues guard the palace facade and the fascinating, lavishly decorated and furnished royal apartments of past kings of Naples can be seen here.

The Palace was designed in 1600 by Domenico Fantana. Facing the palace

The Smoking Peak

Walking the crater rim, an
exercise to be undertaken
with caution.

typical of the respect, but resignation, the local workers have for the potentially lethal landscape.

After the fertile vineyards, the ground gives way to cinders and black lava before the summit and some of the most spectacular panoramas in the world are reached. Scaling the cone from the west might take around four hours for a return hike and, from the south, the steeper walk might be an hour's climb to the crater rim and back. The crater itself is half a mile in diameter and, until the volcano blew the top off its crater ring in 1906, it was 350 feet deep.

There is an admission charge of L3000 at the rim and one can walk, with caution, almost right around the smoking tinderbox of its crater. In ancient Roman times, Spartacus once hid in the tree-covered hollow of the volcano about 100 years before the Pompeii eruption. Since that eruption there has been over one hundred recorded. Many thousands were killed in the 1631 explosion and the last rumblings were heard in 1944, when extensive damage was caused by the eruption, but there were no fatalities.

Standing 12 kilometres south-east of Naples, **Vesuvius**, or **Vesuvio**, is the only live volcano on the mainland of Europe - the others are on islands. Major eruptions were in 1631, 1794 and 1906, and its last eruption occurred in 1944. On August 24th, 79 AD, its eruptions wiped out several of the Roman communities for miles around, including Pompeii, Stabiae and Heraculaneum. The purple peak stands 1280 metres high. It is best to travel to Vesuvius from the town of **Ercolano**, or by the road from **Torre del Greco** and **Boscotrecase**.

A cable car could once be taken from a point almost halfway up to the crater's lip. In summer, visitors can take a bus up the volcano slopes to the footpath from near **Herculano** station. It is about a half-hour walk from where the bus drops passengers to the crater rim. Fruit orchards and vineyards abound on the volcano's slopes and the wine made here is known as **Lacrimae Christi**, or the **Tears of Christ**, possibly relating to the many thousands of lives which the mountain's eruptions have claimed over the centuries. The growing of grapes on the slopes of this monster is

The fertile volcanic soil
hosts many vineyards,
whose wines are known as
the Tears of Christ.

hydrofoil services leave for island visits. Up above Mergellina, to the west, is the site of **Virgil's Tomb**. Even further on is the plush promontory district of **Posillipo**, with exotic trees, salubrious villas and marvellous views down across the Bay.

Inland from the long, narrow Comunale Park is another extent of gardens surrounding the National Ceramic Museum, this is known as the **Villa Floriana**.

Just to the east and standing on the highest point of the city, alongside the Carthusian Monastery of San Martino, is the 14th century **Castle of Saint Elmo** unfortunately not open to the public. The fortress dominates this residential area of Naples which is known as the **Vomero** district.

Via Roma divides western Naples from the **Spaccanapoli**, or ancient part of the city. Across to the eastern part of the city, and past the massive **Naples University** building on Corso Umberto 1, there is another castle, **Castel Capuana**, once the resident of the Norman king, Willian I. The **Porta Capuano** is a preserved remnant of the ancient Aragonese walls which defended the city from 1490.

Between the university and the castle is the **Museo Filanieri** and the open air city market quarter of **Forcella**.

Naples has many excellent restaurants and roadside cafes, some claiming to serve Italy's finest foods. Do try the local specialities of Neopolitan pizza baked over a wood fire, mussel soup

(zuppa di cozze), swordfish, octopus (polpo), numerous fish dishes, spaghetti alla Pescatore (which is actually spaghetti with a mixed fish-sauce, but the direct translation being "Spaghetti of the fisherman's wife"), Spaghetti alla mozzarella, mozzarella e prosciutto (not for dieters!), baked mozzarella and fried

Children at play.

mozzarella, all of which delicious.

The city is served by an efficient rail service; there are three funiculars which climb the hills, and there is the Metropolitana which is an underground rail network. Passenger ferries sail from the centrally located main port to Sar-dinia, Sicily, Capri, Ischia and Procida and a hydrofoil links Capri, Ischia and Procidia with the marina to the west of the city.

Nightlife in Naples is well provided for and clubs and discos are not neces-sarily located just in one area of the city.

Campania

The Bay of Naples, Vesuvius-Pozzuoli, Campi Flegrei, Ercolano, Sorrento, Amalfi Coast, Salerno, Cilento, Castera, Capua, Benevento... in the heart of the Mediterranean.

217

The Bay of Naples

Cicero called this the 'Bay of Luxury' and the Isle of Capri its 'Divine Pearl'. In Roman times, this region was an up-market resort with emperor's holiday villas dotted along the coastline and the three resort towns of **Herculaneum**, **Stabiae** and **Pompeii**, all constructed unwisely close to the active volcano of Vesuvius.

Temple ruins at Paestum.

To the north and south of Naples the **Golfo di Napoli** extends its arms towards the island of **Ischia** in the north, and isle of **Capri** to the south. Behind Naples lies the wide, flat plain which the Romans called **Campania Felix** – the happy, or fortunate plain, and the A3 motorway gives access to both promontories.

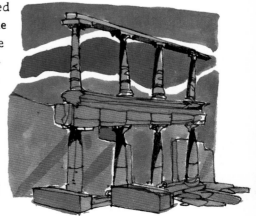

Hercules' City

South from the city of

An excavated street of homes and shops at Herculaneum.

Naples, on the far arm of the bay, lies **Sorrento**. Sorrento can be reached by the highway which passes the ancient Roman town of **Ercolano**, or Herculaneum, buried in the AD 79 eruption of Vesuvius and unearthed in the 18th century. On the way to **Pompeii** one cannot miss the great Vesuvio.

Land of the Sirens

To the south of Pompeii a range of high mountains fill the Sorrentine promontory and after the town of **Castellammare di Stabia**, the road becomes narrow and winding as it hugs the coast heading south and west towards **Sorrento**. Now on the Route 145

road, **Vico Equense** and **Meta** are small resort towns just before Sorrento. It is famed for being the eyrie of the legendary **Sirens** who attempted to lure Ulysses and his sailors onto the rocks around the cave known as the "**Baths of Diana**" at the base of the imposing cliffs of Sorrento. This pretty town is located on a terrace overlooking the 'Sea of Sirens' and a modern-day siren, Sophia Loren had a villa on a promontory facing this historic stretch of water.

Sorrento is the largest resort on the **Amalfi** promontory. It stands on a line of 150 feet cliffs looking north across the Bay of Naples to Naples itself, Mount Vesuvius and the island of Capri. The best hotels are located on the cliff edges with exceptional views and the town

Typical colourful pottery of the area.

has excellent facilities for shopping.

Sites to visit include the shady **Piazza Tasso**, the town square, constructed over a deep ravine with the ruins of an old watermill below. The museum at **Villa Correale di Terranova** has a good collection of paintings and marquetry, or tarsia. A summer festival is held in the marble, Moorish style cloisters of the 14th century **Francis of Assisi church** and the 13th century cathedral is worth a visit. Take an evening Carrozzella, or horse-drawn buggy around the cobbled streets of Sorrento for nostalgia and romance.

From Sorrento, ferries sail from the **Marina Piccola** to the islands of Capri and Ischia (see Italian Isles on page 253) and a favourite excursion east from the

town is a trip to the **Emerald Grotto** on the south coast of the promontory near Amalfi. This route is most tortuous and runs around the base of **Sant Angelo** mountain, through the leather-making village of **Positano**.

The Amalfi Coast

Positano was a favourite resort of John Steinbeck. Its pretty pink and peach-coloured houses seem to tumble in a riot of ice-cream shades down the almost vertical cliffside to the sea. The round, green and gold-tiled dome of the **Church of Santa Maria Assunta** stands out above the cube-shaped houses which fill the hillsides. There are good shops and a fine beach with a smaller beach at **Fornillo**.

Amalfi itself is a fine ancient town and a very pretty resort. It is built up the side of **Monte Lattari**. The town has suffered numerous tidal waves which destroyed a good part of the town. Subsequent tidal waves hit Amalfi in 1343 and 1924. The town center is the **Piazza Duomo** with its brightly mosaiced 9th century cathedral whose bronze doors came from Constantinople in 1066. **Saint Andrew** is the patron saint and his body was brought here from Constantinople in the 13th century. Saint Andrew's remains lie under the cathedral's altar. The cloisters are in the Arabic style, and are known as the **Cloisters of Paradise**. The cathedral also has echoes of Greek, Lombard, Norman and Gothic styles. There is an amusing fountain in the middle of the piazza.

Amalfi is the port from where the **Tavole Amalfitane** (Amalfi Maritime Tables) originated. These were in force in the Mediterranean until 1570 and they are on view in the town hall. West of Amalfi is the Emerald Grotto, reached by an elevator. The cave is flooded and draped with stalagtites and stalagmites which can be admired on the obligatory boat ride.

Another terraced town, **Ravello**, favoured by the wealthy and famous, including the late Greta Garbo, Richard Wagner, Ingrid Bergman, Humphrey Bogart and a wide selection of nobilities, lies east of Amalfi at the mouth of the **Valley of the Dragone**. The **Palazzo**

Rufolo in Ravello dates from the 11th century and this one time royal palace was the setting for an act in Wagner's 'Parsifal'. The cathedral was constructed in the 16th century. Lord Grimthorpe built the **Villa Cimbrone** with its statues and manicured gardens; this should not be missed. There is a bronze copy of the statue of David in the gardens. The **Hotel Palumbo**, perched on the 1,000

14th century Moorish-style basilica at the Francis of Assisi Church at dusk.

foot clifftop in Ravello, was once a palace, built in the 12th century and is favoured by the famous and wealthy.

From Ravello, the Amalfi coast curves around the **Gulf of Salerno** taking in several small towns and villages. The Moorish-style town of **Atrani** is one of Italy's smallest and its church also sports bronze doors made in 1086 from Constantinople similar to those in Amalfi's Duomo. Houses range up the rocky cliffs amphitheatre-like, around a small beach. Further east is the village of **Minori** which is almost twinned with

Houses cling to the almost vertical hillsides at Amalfi.

nearby **Maiori**. Minori is much prettier and has the ruins of an impressively located Roman villa. The village center is quiet and flagstoned and was built around the **Church of San Fransisco**. There is a small beach at Minori which is better than the larger one – almost a

half mile – at Maiori.

Salerno

Located on the great sweep of the bay of the same name, **Salerno** is the capital of

The local population have become accustomed to the visitors to Campania.

Campania's southernmost province. The town suffered substantial damage in the landing of the Allies in 1943. The cathedral, whose construction begun in 1076 led by Robert Guiscard, is a massive structure and has the third set of bronze doors from Constantinople (the others are in Amalfi and Atrani). The great campanile dates from the 12th century and the two mosaic pulpits date from 1173. The Duomo's cloisters surround a fountain and are embellished by pillars ransacked from nearby Roman Paestum. **Saint Matthew's remains**, brought here by knights from the Holy Land are said to lie in the cathedral's crypt.

The cathedral museum houses an altar front with carved ivory panels said to be the largest example of its kind in the world. In the old town some buildings date from the Middle Ages, when Salerno's Benedictine medical school was the most acclaimed in Europe. A Norman fortress stands on a mound towards the outskirts of the town. Salerno is the best base for visits to the Roman remains at **Paestum**, about one hour's ride south.

Paestum

The ancient city of roses and violets, visited and enthused over by Shelley, is the site of three of the best preserved **Doric temples** in Italy or Greece. There is the **Temple of Neptune**, dating from around 450 - 420 BC, and the **Basilica of Hera**, which features pillars five feet in diameter and numbering eighteen each side, and nine in the front make a most imposing monument. Thirty-four of the pillars of the **Temple of Caeres** remain standing and this structure was once used as a Christian church.

The ancient line of the city walls can also be traced. Paestum was built just 20 years after the Parthenon in 600 BC and is the old Sybarite city of **Poseidonia**. The Romans took the city in AD 173. Near the site is the **museum of Paestum**, containing some interesting Greek paintings and ceramics.

Cilento

The southern section of Campania is known as **The Cilento** and, although it represents a good quarter of the region, is comparatively unknown to the foreign visitor. Most of the larger settlements lie along the coastline, which is described basically by the line running south from Salerno, right around the Salerno Gulf, to Sapri, on the Gulf of Policastro.

Driving south from Salerno, the road hugs the coast in an almost straight line north to south. Almost at the end of this straight coast one comes to the Hellenistic remains of Paestum. After this the main road winds across the hills, inland, towards the coastal town of **Sapri**. This road passes through the towns of **Lucania** and **Laurito**.

A Roman statue at the Museo di Baia, near which there are many hot springs.

However, many visitors to Paestum take a detour out to the coast as the main route heads over the hills. In this corner of Cilento are the resorts and marinas of **Agropoli, Ogliastro, San Marco** and that of **Santa Maria di Castellebate**. From the main south road it is possible to turn off to the coast before **Vallo d. Lucania** to view the remains of ancient Greek **Elea**. Built around 540 BC, this site has an unusual archway, an acropolis, a temple and an amphitheatre. Overlooking the site is an imposing Norman tower.

There are a couple more resort beaches along this coastline like those near **Pisciotta, Palinuro** and the **Marina di Camerota**. On, then, to Sapri, which stands at the head of a long,

The ruined complex at Degli Scavi.

straight coastline which runs down almost to the point of the toe of Italy through a short coast which is **Basilicata** to the long coast of **Calabria**.

West from Naples to Cuma

Route 80 leaves Naples and heads up into the hill villages. The first important site on this route is the former Roman town of **Pozzuoli** where the amphitheatre, built in the 1st century, is one of the largest in Italy and holds an audience of over 40,000, or did, when the Romans put on one of their, usually gruesome, spectacles!

Not far from the amphitheatre, near the coastal road, is the so called **Temple**

of **Serpis**, or **Serapeum**. A good excursion from Pozzuoli, is a visit to the lava craters, hot springs and hot mud pools at **Solfatara**. Almost indiscernable earthquakes are a phenomenon of this region. A ferry sails from Pozzuoli to the island of Ischia (see Italian Isles on page 253).

In Greek and Roman times, the hot springs at **Baia**, out on the promontory, were Italy's busiest spa attractions. The thermae, or hot baths built by the Romans can be visited and here temples were erected to Venus, Mercury and Diana. Nearby is a vapourous lake known as the **Lago d'Averno** and dubbed the **"Gateway to Hades"** by the ancients. The **Temple of Apollo** guarding the lake is said by some to be the

A lookout from the Temple of Apollo at Cuma.

cave of the prophetess Sybil. **Bacoli**, next on the itinerary, is the site of an enormous Roman well and, from here, one can reach the tip of the promontory and, from the lighthouse, look out over the islet of **Procida** towards the isle of Ischia.

North, the road runs up to one of the earliest Greek settlements in Italy, **Cuma**. In the 5th century, the Greeks dug a sacred cavern into the hillside here. Cuma was dedicated to the god Apollo and the Romans built temples to their gods, Jupiter and Apollo on the hill above the town. In this temple was stored the documented predictions of the aged soothsayer, **Sibyl**; these were the famed **Sibyline Oracles** offered to King Tarquin the Proud of Rome.

On the road back to Naples is the **Arco Felice**, a triumphal arch, 64 feet high, built in the 3rd century by the Emperor Domitian. From here the road runs east, out over the region known as the **Campi Felgri**, or **Phlaegrean Fields**. This is the volcanic region of lakes and fire, the Greek's field of Heaven and Hell. Gas and steam are emitted from various vents and fissures in the crusty soil. The entrance to the ancient's underworld was identified as **Lake Avernus**, which Emperor Agrippa used as a naval harbour.

Caserta

North of Naples is the industrialised

The cave of Sybil, the prophetess, the site of an enormous Roman well, in Cuma.

township of **Caserta** and its older sister village of **Caserta Veccia**, which is a little to the north of the town, with its fine 12th century Norman cathedral. The attraction of the region is its dominating building, the 18th century royal palace.

The magnificient **Palace of Caserta**, the **Reggia**, was constructed under the auspices of the Bourbon King of Naples, Charles III (1734 - 59), by his favourite architect Luigi Vanvitelli.

It is the largest palace in Italy with a massive facade, four courtyards and 1200 rooms. Inside, the decorations are opulent with rich stucco and baroque embellishments especially in the grand state apartments, reached by a superb carved staircase.

The sumptuous royal apartments are stupendous celebrations of the art, decor and interior design of the period. The lavishness of the interior and its Bourbon richness is offset by the glorious gardens, like the exceptionally pretty English garden, and several ornate fountains and waterfalls, including the grand **Fountain of Diana** with its marvellous sculptures of the god and her attendants.

Capua

Directly north of Naples, on the main highway, is **Capua**, which attracts visitors because it is the home of the **Campania Museum**. The museum

The Royal Park and Grotto of the Winds at the Caserta Palace, the largest in Italy with 1,200 rooms.

shows the entire gamut of life in the district, from the remains of the ancient city and its grand buildings, to those of another of Frederick II's 1239 castle. The fortress at Capua is Norman and the bell tower of the cathedral dates from the 9th century.

Benevento

About an hour and a half's drive inland from Naples is another important Roman city located on the Appian Way surrounded by a ring of hills. This large town has a chequered past leading up to the vanquishing of Pyrrus of Epirus in 275 BC by the Romans. **Benevento** (Beneventum) was founded here in 278 BC and its main monument of those times is the great **Arch of Trajan** built in 117 AD, as the Emperor's triumphal entrance to the town.

This is decorated with lively panels and friezes showing Trajan in various munificent roles. The only other important relic of Roman occupation is the remnants of the Theatre constructed during the reign of Hadrian. Built to seat 20,000 spectators, the theatre is located in the town's old quarter.

Other Roman remains in this region include the 1st century BC Egyptian sculpture of a bull from the **Temple of Isis**, known as the Blue Apis, and the **Triggio**, or the town's old quarter which displays evidence of its numerous bits of Roman stonework and ancient masonry.

Santa Sofia

The **Ponte Leproso** here is an ancient Roman bridge. The **Museo Sannio** contains some magnificient ancient sculptures and terracottas, and is located on Corso Garabaldi in the 12th century cloisters at the back of the 8th century **church of Santa Sofia**, which is built in the shape of a six-pointed star. The cloister's pillars are of some note themselves, being decorated with animals and monstrous figures.

The sculpture of Benevento's famous witches in the museum should not be missed, and there is an interesting story behind the cult of local witchcraft (ask the locals). The city's art collection is also housed in this museum.

Near the museum is the town hall fronted by an obelisk from the Temple of Isis and, in the other direction from the museum is the 14th century fort of the **Rocca de' Rettori** or Castle of the Rectors, built by the popes of the ancient city. Benevento's cathedral, is a late reconstruction of the Romanesque duomo built in the 13th century. This cathedral, as with several in and around the Naples region, had great bronze Byzantine doors, brought probably, from Constantinople. These doors are now stored inside the cathedral.

Details of fountain statuary at Caserta Palace.

T

he Gargano Promontory, Vieste, Manfredonia, The Tavoliere, Foggia, Lucera, Barletta, Monopoli, Martina Franca, Alberobello, Truilli, Castellana Grotte, the Salentine Peninsula, Brindisi, Lecce, Santa Chesarea Therme, Taranto all make up the flat heel of the area of the so-called Italian "boot".

Puglia

231

Bari

A grotto on the Adriatic coast of Puglia.

Bari is the capital city of the **Apulia**, or **Puglia** region. Facing north across the Adriatic Sea, and the port of Dubrovnik, Bari is of Roman and medieval origins and southern Italy's 'Gateway to the East'. Around the ancient city, a modern sprawl evolved over the 19th century. The city has a Byzantine cathedral and the **Church of San Nicola** contains the remains of St. Nicolas of Bari, Patron Saint of Children and the original Father Christmas, brought back from Asia Minor by sailors in 1087. The bishop's throne in the cathedral is a masterpiece of carving. There

Typical cone-shaped trulli houses in Bari.

is a good archaeological museum in Bari with Neolithic, Greek and Roman artifacts, and the **Provincial Art Gallery** contains many important treasures of Apulian artworks.

The Gargano Promontory

Tourism has only recently discovered this wild, craggy, forested and beautiful 'spur' on the 'heel' of Italy. Rising up above the great plain to the south and west, this promontory has its own microgeological makeup of sandy coves and rocky grottoes around its coast and the beach and oak woods of the ancient **Foresta Umbra** inland. Fishing complements the tourism business which, in turn, has replaced the lucrative pilgrimage industry which centred around the **Sanctuary of Saint Michael.**

Of Phoenician origin, the giant fishing machines seen dotted around the coastline, are known as *trabucco* and is an ingenious device designed to catch the local mullet. A live mullet on a line lures other fish from the sea over a giant net which is then lifted by great winches. These fishing machines are a common sight on the rocky **Gargano** coast.

Vieste

Built on two promontories, the main attraction of **Vieste** is its fine beaches. The old town with its **Church of San**

A town jutting out to sea.

Francesco and extraordinary fishing machine, is located on the eastern promontory. Also in the old town is the **Chianca Amara**, or bitter stone, site of the beheading of 5,000 inhabitants by the raiding Turks in 1554. The city's cathedral dates from the 11th century and the earlier castle, also on the promontory, is another of the Emperor Frederick's imposing fortifications. Visits by boat can be made to the nearby **Tremiti Islands** (see Italian Isles on page 253), or to the many grottos along this coastline.

Manfredonia

Many of the ports along the south-east-ern coast were crammed with sailing ships taking Crusaders to the Holy Land in days gone by, and **Manfredonia** was one of these ports of departure. The main feature of this town is its fine castle. Apart from that, the port is generally a stopover between Vieste and Barletta.

Manfredonia is the centre from where to visit the **Monte Sant'Angelo**, a site of pilgrimage for millions since the Crusades. In the 11th century, knights returning from the Holy Land were said to have had a visitation from the Archangel and subsequently a Gothic chapel and shrine were built 86 steps down inside a great natural cave. It is guarded by doors supposed to have been taken from Constantinople. The maze of white-

Sunflower fields in Puglia.

washed buildings around the **Sanctuary of Saint Michael** is the medieval town of **Junno** which has a **Folk Museum** for the region. A huge eight-sided **Anjouesque** castle dominates the crest of the ridge inside which the shrine was built.

Near the Saint Michael Sanctuary are the churches of **San Pietro**, with its enigmatic 'Tomb of Rotari' and the **church of Santa Maria Maggiore**, built in 1198, and decorated with fascinating carvings and frescoes.

The Tavoliere

This is the great wheat bowl of southern Italy and the **Tavoliere Plain** spreads out east from the foot of Italy's spine to the coast in a great pocket of fertile soil patchworked by rich fields. The agricultural heritage of this region goes back well into Roman times and the wheat produced here is now the source of much of the country's pasta.

Foggia

This town is of little interest to the traveller apart from being a place to stop over en route between Pescara to the north and Bari in the south. **Foggia** is an important rail junction for trains from all points in Italy.

Lying inland from the coast and the Gulf of Manferdonia, Foggia stands

An elderly lady with a bunch of freshly picked poppies.

about halfway between the above mentioned cities and on the opposite side of Italy from Naples. The town, which is the main centre on the wide and long Tavoliere Plain, was badly bombed during the second World War following previous damage by the French in the early 16th century, and subsequent earthquakes.

The baroque/Romanesque, 12th century cathedral once held the remains of Charles I of Anjou and King Frederick II's heart – Foggia was one of Fredrick's favourite cities - and now displays the

The Trulli

The low hills of the **Murge**, particularly around Alberobello, are home to the unique *trulli* dwellers. Of all Italian architecture, the *trulli* houses must be the most extraordinary and create a fantasy landscape of their own. The *trulli*, of which there are more than a thousand, are primitive buildings, often round but varying in shape and size and generally of whitewashed limestone. Like the caps of gnomes, the *trulli* usually sport conical red or grey tiled roofs over the domed interior, sometimes surmounted with a whitewashed peak and a cross, and all are practically windowless. Most *trulli* start off as a one roomed dwelling, and many have expanded into a conglomerate of several *trulli* jumbled together in odd shapes and sizes to form a large home, or, as in the case of the **Supreme Trullo**, a second storey is added. Land is divided by a network of drystone walls which lend a Cumbrian look to the fascinating landscape dotted with the charmingly picturesque *trulli*.

city's symbol, a Byzantine icon, on which three flames was said to have burned in a stream when discovered by shepherds in the 11th century. Another church worth a visit is the five-domed **Church of the Cross**, built at the turn of the 17th century. Nearby, on **Piazza Nigri** is the **Civil Museum** which houses a collection of ancient artifacts and some folkloric and craft exhibits.

Lucera

A short distance north-west of Foggia just off the road to **Campobasso**, is **Lucera**, once the important Roman colony of Luceria. The amphitheatre standing outside the town is all that remains of the ancient Roman town although the Fransiscan **Church of San Francesco** is partly constructed from Roman rubble.

With the demise of Rome, Luceria was abandoned until Frederick II adopted it and imported thousands of Sicilian Arabs into the region as a political policy. Few vestiges remain of this one-time Muslim stronghold but, as soon as the Angevins had dealt with the Saracens, Charles II began building Lucera's cathedral in 1300. The **Civil Museum** contains a good collection of Greek artifacts and sculptures and is located not far from the **Duomo**.

Overlooking the town and commanding spectacular views over the Tavoliere Plain and with the backdrop of the Apennines, are the ruins one of Italy's largest castles built by the Emperor Frederick in 1233.

Barletta

Located on the coast between Manfredonia and Bari, this busy township's main claim to fame is the **Colossus** statue. Over 5 metres high, this is a giant bronze statue more than 1,500 years old and moulded in the image of a Byzantium Emperor, is said to have been part of the loot after the sacking of Constantinople in 1204. There is a small civil museum here, celebrating the works of the painter Nittis. The **Basilica of San Sepolcro** in the town dates from the 13th century.

Like caps of gnomes, the trulli in Alberobello are whitewashed, windowless, peaked, with a cross.

Monopoli

This is a small port town on the road from Bari to Brindisi and is really no more than a stopover but, should one take time out to visit, there is a 10th century reliquary, among other treasures in the **Cathedral Museum** and the town's **Santa Maria Amalfitana** was built in the 12th century. At the end of July, annually, the town celebrates one of the largest festivals held in Apulia.

However, **Monopoli** is the kicking off point for visiting the ruins of the ancient city of **Egnazia**, a short distance south, on the coast. Both a Greek and a Roman town, this centre prospered during the 5th century and its remains consist of an amphitheatre, temples, a forum and public buildings. The museum houses some fascinating artifacts from the excavations here.

Martina Franca

From Eganazia, inland, via the town of **Fasano**, one comes to the open-air museum of baroque architecture that is **Martina Franca**. The Duke's Palace, dating from 1688, fits in well with the wrought iron balconies and stuccoed fronts of townhouses in the main streets and the town's baroque churches. The palace is said to have been designed by Bernini and contains some excellent frescoes and murals. This town hosts one of Italy's most important musical festivals annually in July-August.

Alberobello

The main tourist attraction and features of this area, and particularly from the town of **Alberobello** and the region around **Locorotondo**, are the *trulli*, or rough, one-roomed drystone dwellings with cone-shaped roofs with a vent for the cooking fire smoke to escape. There is an excellent hotel in Alberobello, the accomodation of which is a group of *trulli*. It is otherwise uneventful.

Castellana Grotte

Inland, and south-east of Bari is **Castellana Grotte**, said to be the most beautiful of all grottoes in the whole of Italy. Indeed, the variety of underground wonderlands like the magical 'Milan Cathedral' and the mysterious 'White Grotto', are marvels of nature bedecked with alabaster stalactites and stalagmites formed from the easily-dissolved limestone of the area. Rivers and streams appear and disappear in the caverns and caves of the karst-type country.

The Salentine Peninsula

Stiletto in shape, the 'heel' of Italy, is a rather flat and overlooked peninsula located between the Adriatic and Io-

nian Seas. The nearest point of land from the southernmost tip is the Greek island of **Corfu** just over 100 miles to the south-east. Ancient neolithic ruins, caves, early watchtowers and cliffs dot the coastline and inland, the landscape, as with the agricultural crops, could well be Greek.

Brindisi

Overlooking the **Strait of Otranto**, part of the Adriatic Sea, **Brindisi** is Italy's

Evening view of Bari, the capital of Puglia.

'Gateway to Greece' and is located on the north-eastern side of the country's 'heel'. Ferries sail from the maritime station at the end of **Corso Garibaldi** to Corfu and several other Greek destinations. This route has been well sailed since the times of the Romans – Marc Anthony, Augustus, Cicero and Virgil all passed through here - and then the Crusaders whose pilgrimages departed Europe from here towards the Holy Land.

There are several sites of importance in the city which really is not much more than a seaport to be passed through rather than a place to spend much time sightseeing. Just a short walk north from the ferry jetties is the 1st century **Roman Column** which is 19th metres high and once sported the effigy of an emperor. This column marks the top of the flight of stairs known as **Virgil's steps** and indicates the southernmost terminus of the ancient Appian Way which runs from Porta Capena in Rome. In 19 BC Virgil is said to have died in a house nearby, now marked by a plaque. From the harbour, a short walk north, ferries link the city with a suburb fronted by the 52-metre high **Memorial to Italian Sailors**. A lift takes sightseers to the top of the monument for the spectacular views of the city and its surroundings.

Walking away from the promenade location of the column, past several imposing 17th and 18th century mansions, the next site is the city's cathedral which dates from the 11th century. Across the piazza is the **Archaeological Museum** which contains relics found along the Via Appia and artifacts from the **Egnazia** excavations. The facade on the square is all that remains of the **Crusader Temple**. Proceeding into the heart of the city, off the Via Tarentini, the little round church with its small square is the 11th century Crusader Church of **San Giovanni al Sepolcro** which contains some fine 13th century frescoes. Towards the post office, which marks the centre of Brindisi, and crossing the **Cosos Roma** and **Garabaldi**, the **Church of Santa Lucia** is decorated with frescoes from the 12th century.

To the north-west of the city is the ancient fortress of the **Castello Svevo** and, nearby, the **Tancredi Fountain** built by the Norman warlord, Tancred, and at which the Crusaders watered their mounts. A short bus ride from the city centre is the **Church of Santa Maria** **di Borgo Casale**, built by Philip of Anjou in 1320, and containing some important 14th century Byzantinesque frescoes including the startling 'Day of the Last Judgement'.

Lecce

Located in the centre of Italy's 'heel'. Constructed in the 16th and 17th century, **Lecce** has many ancient monuments like the cathedral on the **Piazza del Duomo**, dating from 1670, and the **Bishop's Palace**, built in 1632. The nearby **Seminary** dates from 1709, and the **Governor's Palace** from 1695. Also 16th century in origin, are the two fine churches, **Santa Croce** and **Sant' Irene**.

Santa Cesarea Therme

Facing east, on the sole of Italy's 'heel', the weird rocks and cliffs around this coastal spa have suffered sea and weather change, and have turned into something very strange, almost resembling a ruined town in themselves. Pillars and arches strike up from the sea in grotesque and fantastic shapes.

Taranto

This is the **City of Two Seas**, the **Mare Grande** and the **Mare Piccolo**. **Taranto** is built on a strip of land which divides these two vast lagoons. Located at the

Basilica di Santa Croce in Lecce.

head of the Gulf of Taranto built on a peninsular right up inside the 'heel' of Italy, Taranto is an ancient Spartan town mostly rebuilt in the 19th century. To the Greeks it was known as **Taras**, after Poseidon's son, and to the Romans, **Tarentum**. The giant bronze statue of **Poseidon** which once stood in the Acropolis, was one of the wonders of the ancient world but sadly little now remains of the grand temples and villas of the ancients. The ancient city was once famous for the imperial purple dye obtained from the murex shell and the special variety of oysters harvested here.

Near the Aragonese castle there are several Doric columns from early Greek times and there is a museum in the town which contains a vast collection of Greek terracotta and the Tarantine Collection, 15 rooms of Greek sculptures, sarcophagi and a collection of ancient gold artifacts. A 7th century Irish monk, Cataldo, patron saint of Taranto, is buried in the small chapel of the 11th century cathedral. Another church worth viewing is the 14th century **Church of San Domenico Maggiore**, not far from the cathedral and near to the fish market.

Taranto is the city of the **Tarantella** and of the tarantula. Ancient Greeks ritual dances, the Medieval Dance of Death and other mystical dances combined to form the modern day tarantella which is a wild, whirling dance, once believed to have the power to cure the bite of the infamous spider whose bite is far from fatal.

T

he Tyrrhenian Coast, Praia a Mare, Cosenza, Scilla, the Sila Massif, Ionian Coast, Crotone, Catanzaro, Stilo, and the Gulf of Taranto Coast make up this region.

Reggio di Calabria

Also known as **Reggio**, the capital of the district of **Calabria** is located on the western tip of the 'toe' of Italy. It faces Messina in Sicily across the Straits of Messina. Reggio is the terminus of the main motorway which runs from Rome down the western edge of the country to the very tip of Italy. It was founded by settlers from Chalchis in Greece, in about 750 BC as Rhegium. 5th century Greek remains can still be seen in the city walls and along the **Lungomare**, or promenade. Roman baths from the 2nd century can also be seen here.

However, because of the numerous earthquakes in the area over the past 2,000 years, little remains of the ancient city and the town was really rebuilt in its entirety

A farmer on his donkey in Calabria.

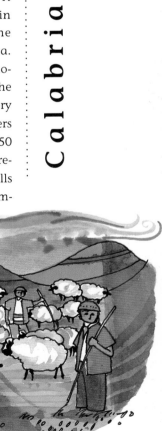

Capa Vaticano, Calabria.

after the devastation of the 1783 earthquake and again after the 1908 earthquake.

The provincial capital is built alongside the straight shore of the Straits of Messina with the museum at one end of the town and the duomo and castle at the southern end. The **National Museum of Magna Graecia** contains many fascinating prehistoric archaeological exhibits and some of the best examples of Greek art to be seen. Most celebrated of all its exhibits is the museum's two bronzes, slightly larger than life, sculptures known as the 'Warriors of Riace', found by divers off **Riace** on the east coast of the 'toe' in 1972. Other treasures include the terracotta plaques from the **Magna Graecia temples**, Greek ce-

ramics and a mosaic of a dragon. A rare optical illusion, sometimes experienced by looking out over the straits when atmospheric conditions are exactly right, is the **Fata Morgana**, a phenomenon which reveals an image of the city of Messina, across the straits, inverted and transformed into a magical, Disney-like turreted mirage.

The Tyrrhenian Coast

Almost describing a straight line from north to south, for 150 miles, from the border with Basilicata province on the Gulf of Policastro, to the Gulf of Saint Eufemia, Calabria's northern part of its Tyrrhenian coast is still undeveloped

An ancient Calabrian Catholic church.

and offers many secluded beaches and coves with grey sand and clear waters. Both the Tyrrhenian and the Ionian coasts have some of the broadest, least polluted beaches anywhere in Italy.

The airport of **Lamezia** is near the coast, just south of the inland town of **Nicastro**, and on the curve in the 'toe' formed by the Gulf of Sant Eufemia, halfway down this coastline. From the airport, east, this region forms the narrowest 'neck' of the Calabrian Peninsula, and roads link the coastal highways across the mountains.

beaches of this pleasant and uncrowded resort of **Praia a Mare**, which is one of many dotted along this coastline. Like all other towns here each has its ancient church or fortress as the main attraction. On the Isola di Dino, a short boat ride from Praia a Mare, is the **Blue Grotto** which can be visited with the assistance of boatmen. Travelling down the coast from here the main town on the coast is **Paola**, where the road from inland **Cosenza** meets the coastal road and the southern Calabrian Riviera really begins.

Praia a Mare

A 14th century castle overlooks the sandy

Cosenza

Halfway up the 'toe' of Italy, Cosenza is

A small Byzantine church ruin at Stilo.

located just to the east of the main motorway to **Reggio di Calabria**, on the Busento and Crati Rivers. This is a pre-Roman town with many ancient architectural jewels. Legend has it that in 410 AD, Alaric, King of the Goths, was buried at the base of the **Pancrazio Hill** in the town.

The castle here is Norman but mostly built by King Frederick II, and the cathedral, a Gothic structure dating from 1222, contains the remains of Isabella of Aragon. A jewelled crucifix in the cathedral was given to the church by Frederick II in the 12th century. An early copy of a famous 13th century Byzantine icon, the Maddona del Pilerio, is housed in the nearby **Palazzo Archivescovile**.

The **Museo Civico** has a collection of paintings and artifacts and is on **Piazza XV Marzo**. A number of alleyways lead up from the duomo to the 13th century **Church** and **Convent of San Francesco** and up to the eerie-like castle. Cosenza's claim of fame is its celebrated son, Bernardino Telesio, a philosopher and early scientist.

Scilla

This pretty little village nestles in a deep cleft in the towering cliffs and promontories just a short distance north of Reggio. A medieval castle, stands out on its own headland, commanding magnificient views of the rugged coast-

The veduta at Scilla.

line and its powerful seascapes. **Scilla** is one of the nearest mainland village to Sicily, just a couple of miles to the west.

The Sila Massif

Set behind the city of Cosenza, to the east, between it and the Ionian Sea, is the great 1,000 metre plateau of the **Sila Massif**. Its three divisions are the **Sila Grande**, the **Sila Picola** and the **Sila Greca**. Peaks like the **Monte Botte Donato** rise to nearly 2,000 metres. Densely wooded mountains make up the landscape, interspersed with many lakes and pretty hill villages. The Sila regions offer skiing as an alternative to summertime hiking. In 1968, the **Na-**

tional Park of Calabria was founded embracing the Sila Grande, the Sila Piccola and the **Aspromonte mountains**. Wildlife abound and include both the Apennine wolf, deer and wild boar.

The Ionian Coast

The S106 route follows the Ionian coastline of Calabria from Reggio, more than 300 miles north to the Basilicata border near **Rocca Imperiale**. Several great sweeps of bays form this shore, dotted with little fishing villages and several resorts like the **Bova Marina**, on the base of the 'toe', and **Catanzaro Lido** on the **Gulf of Squillace**. The mainland's southernmost point is generally accepted to be **Capo Spartivento**, less than 5 miles east of Bova. Further north is **Locri**, which has an interesting museum exhibiting remnants and artefacts of the Greek city which once stood here.

North again, inland from the **Monasterace Marina** is the Greek village of **Stilo** which attracts tourist for its 10th century church with Byzantine frescoes and nine striking cupolas. The town has a medieval cathedral and many other interesting old buildings.

Catanzaro

Located about midway along the base of Italy's 'toe', **Catanzaro**, the regional capital of Calabria, is a Byzantine town founded in the 9th century, and now its coastal namesake, a few miles south, is a popular resort and lido. A Norman castle is set in a dominating position in the clifftop town and there is a fine cathedral here, the 18th century baroque **Church of the Immacolata**. Inside are four works by the Neapolitan waxworker Caterina de Iuliani. The two main churches are that of the **Rosario** and the **Church del l'Osservanze**. The **Provincial Museum** has a good prehistoric collection, a coin collection and some ancient artifacts from the region. Nearby is the municipal gardens, the **Villa Trieste**.

This area, between the mountains and the sea, is one of the most fertile in Italy and produces jasmine and berga-

mot for perfume production. Stromboli volcano, on Sicily can be clearly seen from most of this part of the Calabria coastline.

Crotone

From being the home of Pythagoras, familiar to schoolboys around the world for his Pythagorean Theory, the Greek city of **Croton** grew into the large industrial town of modern day **Crotone**. By far the largest town on this part of the Ionian Coast, Cortone stands on the north side of the easternmost peninsula about halfway up the 'toe'.

All that now remains of this famous Greek city, apart from the exhibits and terracotta collection in the Archaeological Museum in the town, is the single column on a nearby promontory, which is all that remains of the ancient **Temple of Hera**.

Gulf of Taranto Coast

The only settlement of any real significance to the traveller on Calabrian is that of **Sibari**. Once this site, Sybaris, was the richest city of the Greek region known as Magna Graecia. The word 'sybarite' come from the decadant way of life led in the ancient city. In 510 BC victorious Crotonites razed the city and diverted the Crati River over the ruins which have recently been located by modern archaeologists.

The remains of the Tavole Palatine, a Doric temple, in Metaponto.

BASILICATA

Little goes on here except the idyllic rural life. Its culture remains Greek influenced and its landscape pockmarked by relics of an ancient history. It covers The Tyrrhenian Coast, The Ionian Coast, Metaponto, and Matera.

Known as **The Basilicata**, this is a virtual backwater of Italy when it comes to travellers and tourists. It covers mountains and rolling hills which divide isolated villages; rivers and valleys score the landscape and numerous rivers run down to the great sweeping coast of the Gulf of Taranto.

The region's eastern coastline lies on part of this bay from near **Metaponto** in the north, to just south of **Policoro** a highway and railway run along this coast through both these towns. In the west, Basilicata has a small coast between Campania and Calabria.

Potenza

Potenza is the modern provincial capital of Basilicata and has little to offer the visitor in terms of historic or interesting sights except for its **Archaeological Museum** on via Cicotto and the **Church of San Fransesco** which contains the **Madonna del Terremoto** icon.

The city is high up in the mountain folds, inland from Salerno, on the road to Bari, and is Italy's highest provincial

The coastline at Maratea.

capital. Most travellers pass through Potenza in order to view the sites of the surrounding countryside and the unusual landscape varieties typical of this region.

Maratea

Basilicata has a short coastline to the west which lies on the Gulf of Policastro, between the Campania coast to the north and that of Calabria to the south. The part of this seaside that belongs to Basilicata is the beautiful riviera of **Maratea**.

This resort has a fine marina, an ancient medieval town and a pretty beach, popular among Italians.

The southern coastline

Basilicata's southern coastline is also short and has little to offer in the way of places of interest to visit although there is the **Marina of Ginosa** and the **Lido of Metaponto**. Most travellers drive along the coastal road here from Taranto in Puglia, down the wide curve of the Gulf of Taranto, into Calabria province and towards the 'toe' of Italy and the Calabrian resorts.

Metaponto

Founded around the 7th century BC, the ancient city of Metapontum, inland from

Typical dolls and baskets for sale at Maratea.

Tramontano Fortress. The **Ridola Archaeological Museum** is located in the baroque convent building of **Santa Chiara** and the town's 18th century church is known as the **Purgatorio**. Apart from its other interesting churches, the attraction of Matera is its rock dwellings, cavern-carved places of worship and cliffside village.

The two ravines in which these cave-dwellings appear are known as the **Sassi**. Built into the living rock of a deep gorge, connected by a maze of stairs and alleys, this collection of troglodyte houses are now mainly abandoned but provide a fascinating insight into life as it was here many centuries ago. There are more than 125 rock-hewn churches in this ravine and several date from the 11th and 12th centuries.

the coast, has all but disappeared but the remains of the **Tavole Palatine**, a Doric temple, another smaller temple and a theatre can be seen and there are artifacts from excavations in the museum. Pythagoras, who lived in Crotone, to the south, is said to have died in **Metaponto**. There is a small lido resort on the coast here.

Matera

Inland from Metaponto is the extraordinary city of **Matera** which has a Romanesque cathedral and the Gothic **Church of San Francesco** housing a beautiful Venetian painting. The 15th century castle is known as the

A peasant lady outside a church in Maratea.

Italian Isles

Italy's largest and best known islands are of course, **Sicily** and **Sardinia**, but there are scores of other, smaller islands and islets, some teeming with tourists, others virtually undiscovered.

Elba, just off the Tuscany coast between Livorno and Grosseto, is probably best known as the exile home of Napoleon Bonaparte, although he resided here for less than a year between 1814 and 1815. It was also a favourite haven of the Barbary pirates (and in particular Barbarossa and Dragut). With its 90 miles of unspoilt coastline and over 50 beautiful undeveloped beaches, the island is a warm, sunny and calm sanctuary for those willing to make the effort to get there. Just far enough off the coast to deter hordes of package tourists, Elba is only crowded between July and August, mainly with Italians. Other, smaller Islands in this region are **Capraja**, **Pianosa**, **Montecristo**, and **Giglio**.

Ischia, to the north-west of the Bay of Naples, is a favourite among Italians, who prefer it to the more crowded **Capri**, and appears to be increasingly patronised by German visitors. A mountainous, volcanic island (its peak, Monte Epomeo, stands at 2,590 feet), it is blessed with sandy, golden beaches and crystal-clear waters. Often referred to as the **Emerald Isle**, it is known for its vine-

The azure waters of Tremiti Islands in the Adriatic Sea.

253

Underwater sanctuaries of the Italian isles.

yards, citrus groves and pine forests.

Described as "the most beautiful operetta stage in the world" by Noel Coward, the Island of Capri in the Bay of Naples is a wonderful mixture of jet-set playground and escapists' retreat. Only four miles long by two miles across, it still allows the jaded traveller to wander off into a hinterland of craggy solitude. Be warned, however - Capri is one of the most expensive places in Italy!

Sicily, hanging off the toe of the "boot" of Italy, is an extension of the Apennine chain, which is reflected in the mountainous nature of the north and east. The largest of the mediterranean islands, Sicily has always been a prize in the skirmishes of the area, occupying as it does the geo-graphical centre of the mediterranean. A rich cultural heritage of Eastern and Western invasions has left it with a legacy of baroque churches, Norman castles, Moorish cupolas and Hellenic temples. Today Sicily is remembered mainly (thanks to Hollywood and the media) as the home of the Mafia – they do exist and are powerful, exerting pressure on the political and economic status quo of the region, but this is not unduly apparent and should not alarm or deter the prospective tourist from visiting and enjoying Sicily.

Off the north-east coast of Sicily are the **Eolie** or **Lipari Islands: Lipari, Vulcano, Salina, Panarea, Stromboli, Filicudi** and **Alicudi**. Remote (they are the product of volcanic activity in this,

Panorama of the rather uninhabited Tremiti isles rising from the Adriatic.

the deepest part of the Tyrrhenian Sea) and primitive (there is no electricity apart from that provided by private generators), the islands are a haven of seclusion, and offer the visitor beaches of volcanic sand and clear blue waters, famed for their diving and fishing. Seafood is, not surprisingly, a speciality!

Sardinia, about 116 miles from the mainland and equidistant between Italy and North Africa, is separated from its northern (and French-owned) neighbour Corsica by the Straits of Boniface. It lies at the centre of the mediterranean trade routes, a fact which has left it open to successive invasions from Greeks, Romans, Phoenecians, Vandals, Byzantines, Arabs, Spanish and Austrians, quite apart from the doorstep claims of Pisa and Genoa! Despite (or perhaps because of) this, the Sardinians are a hardy, extremely independent people, speaking their own language, Sardo, and maintaining their own traditions and customs.

From Naples or Sorrento

Three islets are within a day's visit of either Naples and Sorrento, the most famous and crowded trip being that to **Capri**, south of Naples. West of the city is another island which is becoming increasingly popular with tourists, the **Isola D'Ischia**. However, there is a tiny islet between the mainland and Ischia called **Procida**. Few visitors to Italy will

Capri is dominated by the twin peaks of Monte Solaro and Monte Tiberio, where 850 species of flowers bloom in spring.

have the time to visit all three islands.

Elba is more usually reached by ferries out of the port of **Piombino**, about 4 miles from the island, however, a ferry does link Elba with **Livorno** in the north.

The **Tremiti Islands** lie off the **Molise** coast to the east. They can be reached by ferry from the more equi-distant (20 miles) ports of **Termoli** or **Rodi Garganico**. A ferry also runs from **Manfredonia** on the Gargano penin-sula, about 50 miles distance.

Capri

Not only did Capri inspire a song, but many writers have written books about it. D.H. Lawrence, Graham Greene, Shaw, Handel, Dumas, Mendelssohn and many others favoured Capri. The late Gracie Fields favoured the island and haunted the restaurant La Canzonne del Mare, and Compton Mackenzie had a house here. However, it was the Phoenicians, followed by the Greeks, who first discovered its charms (and its wild boars, after which the Greeks named the island). The Greeks built the **Scala Fenicia**, 777 mountainside steps leading up from the harbour of **Marina Grande**. The Emperor Tiberius spent a pleasant exile on Capri and many wealthy Romans built their vacation villas around the island. On **Monte Tiberio**, a good walk from the centre of Capri itself, is Tiberius' own villa, **Villa**

Jovis, dating from AD 27.

In those ancient days tourism was probably just becoming a popular pastime but today the streets, lanes and paths of Capri are regularly swamped by a sea of gawking visitors. Daily, boats crammed with tourists queue to tie up and disgorge their multi-national passengers. Calm only reigns when the boats sail away and darkness falls on its spectacular sights.

Most visitors come to Capri on a day's trip by boat or hydrofoil from Naples or Sorrento. Three miles of sparkling blue-green water separate the island from the mainland. Capri's main harbour is known as Marina Grande and it is from here that one can walk, or take the funicular up to **Capri town** itself which sits on a saddle between the

The Blue Grotto so named for the brilliance of the light reflection through the waters.

island's two main mountain peaks. There is a ruined 14th century Carthusian monastery called the **Certosa San Giacomo** near the town centre, and the meeting place, under the clock in **Piazza Umberto**, is nicknamed the 'drawing room of the world'. Sandy beaches can be found down on the **Marina Piccola** facing out to the rocky pinnacle known as the **Faraglioni**, or the 'Siren's Rocks'.

However, instead of visiting the town of Capri, most tourists immediately embark on a boat trip from the harbour to the famous **Blue Grotto**. This is just one of the many grottos which ring the island which is surrounded by steep cliffs and weirdly formed rocks. The Blue Grotto used to be

Shopping in Capri, a pleasant exercise for the feet and wallet.

Tourists are entirely dependent on the assistance of serenading boatmen to enter the Blue Grotto.

the haunt of the hooded seal or bove marino, around 75 years ago. The Blue Grotto can also be reached from Capri's other main settlement, **Anacapri**. Other grottos on Capri include the **Green**, **Pink** and **White** grottos, and the cave called the **Matromonia Cavern** which was converted into a temple by the Romans. The wily 'Count' Fersen's villa stands empty on a clifftop on the promontory of the island thus commanding fantastic views of the strangely contorted limestone coastline.

Inland, the countryside, dominated by the twin peaks of **Monte Solaro** (586 metres) and **Monte Tiberio** (305 metres), can be a wonderland of colour in spring, when 850 species of flowers come into bloom.

Anacapri is higher up than Capri and a chairlift takes visitors up to **Monte Solaro** for the excellent views. Built on the site of another of Tiberius' villas, **Villa San Michele**, former home of Swedish author and doctor Axel Munthe, can be visited from Anacapri.

Ischia – the green isle

Covered in green pinewoods, 18 square mile **Ischia** is a volcanic island and has some radioactive springs and beaches of volcanic origin. Warm mineral springs gush from flowered hillsides overlooking a clear sea washing against sandy beaches protected by towering headlands. Many hotels divert the beneficial spa water into pools which complement the ubiqitious swimming pools.

The island is crowned by a dormant volcano, **Epomeo**. A mule trip leaving from the old town of **Fontana** can be taken to view the sights of Vesuvius, Capri and Sorrento from its summit. Epomeo last erupted in 1320. There are four main settlements on Ischia. An ancient fort, the **Castello Aragonese**, also known as **Sant'Angelo**, dominates the main town and port of Ischia. A castle has stood on the same spot since 475 BC, and the existing structure dates from the 14th century. It is said that a widowed princess who lived here once took the eye of Michelangelo. A little bridge links the castle to the town. The second attraction on the island must be the spa resort of **Lacco Ameno** which is generally very busy compared with the other spa on this north west part of the island, **Casamicciola Terme**.

On the west coast are the sandy beaches of **Forio**, on the Gulf of Gaeta, where, it is reputed, the famous 'green flash' occurs at the very moment of sunset. The **Church of Santa Maria del Soccorso** stands on an outcrop of rock near the town. The only other centre is the pretty fishing village of Sant'Angelo linked to the island by a long causeway.

Procida Isle

The least likely excursion which visitors would make out from Naples and Sorrento would be to **Procida**. Most tourists head out past this tiny island to

The port of Ischia, an island of green pines.

Procida's neighbour, Ischia. In the port of **Marina Grande**, gaily painted houses line the harbour beneath a clifftop fortress. It is worth the climb up the narrow streets to the fort, part of which is a prison, for the spectacular view across the Bay of Naples. There is not much to see on this volcanic rock but the **church of San Michele** in the main port town of Marina Grande, is decorated with some interesting paintings.

Apart from the church, the major attractions are the island's clean and comparatively deserted beaches.

The Tremiti Isles

This pretty little archipelago which has a chequered history, consists of the isles of **San Dominico** and **San Nicola**, plus the uninhabited islets of **Pianosa**, **Caprara** and **Grottone**. Isolated coves and beaches and several stupendous grottoes can be visited on the first and largest island. A daunting castle/monastery and ancient church can be viewed on **San Nicola**.

Elba, Napoleon's retreat

Elba is the largest in a string of islands off the Tuscany coast and between Italy and Corsica. It is the third largest of the Italian isles after Sicily and Sardinia. The island is surrounded by clear waters and good beaches and coves around its 90-mile coastline which makes it a very popular resort. The Greeks and Etruscans mined iron on Elba but it was the Romans who appreciated the island's natural attributes and built many villas there. Most notable of the island's later visitors was Napoleon who ruled the island in exile for less than a year between 1814 and 1815. The capital of Elba is **Portoferraio** which is divided into the main centre for shops, ferry terminal, and the ancient walled town with its market, old houses and **Palazzina dei Mulini**, a Medici fortress and one of Napoleon's retreats. This palace houses a most interesting museum, and another museum of **Napoleonica** is in the **Misericordia** on the route to the palace. The town has a tiny cove and beach below the walled old quarter known as **La Viste**.

About three miles out of Portoferraio is the island's most famous historic site, Napoleon's summer villa at **San Martino**. A neo-classical palace stands in front of the villa, which houses Napoleonic memorabilia and, on the road out to the villa is yet another Napoloenic museum – the **Museo delle Ceramiche**.

Travelling west out of Portoferraio, two of the most attractive white sanded beach resorts on the island are **Biodola** and **Procchio**. The former is more of a campsite, while Prochhio has some excellent hotels.

The next resort sports a 12th-century Pisan tower and a shingly beach, but is an attractive fishing port. One of the island's most popular long white beaches is the **Marina di Campo** and

A view of Chiessi on the island of Elba, Napoleon's retreat.

most of the best hotels and good restaurants and nightspots are located here. For campers, there is a large campsite at **Lacona**, between Marina di Campo and Porto Azzurro.

Porto Azzurro is a fortified harbour town and its fortress dates from the days of King Philip III of Spain, 1603. The fort itself is now a prison. The old part of the town is most attractive with cobbled streets and good restaurants, but the main accommodation on this part of the coast are down south where the beaches are. Another fortified town, **Capoliveri**, lies south of Porto Azzurro and is constructed on a peninsula. From here there are several new resort hotels within easy reach.

Montecristo's Isle

This island is now a bird sanctuary and nature reserve and lies south of Elba. Alexander Dumas probably did not visit this rocky outcrop but made it famous by writing his book 'The Count of Monte Cristo'. There are day trips to the island from Marina di Campo and Porto Azzurro, Elba, and visitors are restricted to the sandy beach of **Cala Maestra**. There are three other islands around Elba and these are **Pianosa**, **Gorgona** and **Capria**, which now serves as a prison. **Giglio Island** lies between Montecristo and the ferry port of San Stefano, north of Civitavecchia.

Sicily

A great region for its stupendous beauties – (Lucretius) This quote from the Roman poet, written about 50 BC, was echoed in the 12th century by an Arab geographer, whom King Roger II commissioned to write the first ever geographical treatise on Sicily.

Italy's largest island and the largest isle in the Mediterranean Sea, Sicily covers almost 1,000 square miles (more than 25,000 square kilometres). Crossed by a mountain chain in the north, the east is dominated by Europe's largest active volcano, **Mount Etna**. Also in the northeast, the peak of the volcano **Stromboli** forms the island of the same name in the **Eolie** or **Lipari Islands** just offshore. Off the westernmost tip of Sicily are the **Egadi Islands**, and Malta lies off the southernmost point. Tunisia, on the North African coast, lies 230 kilometres (140 miles) south-west of the island.

The ancient Siculi tribe (after whom the island was named), were succeeded by the Greeks in the 7th and 8th centuries. To the following Romans, Sicily be-

Business is brisk at a market in Catania.

263

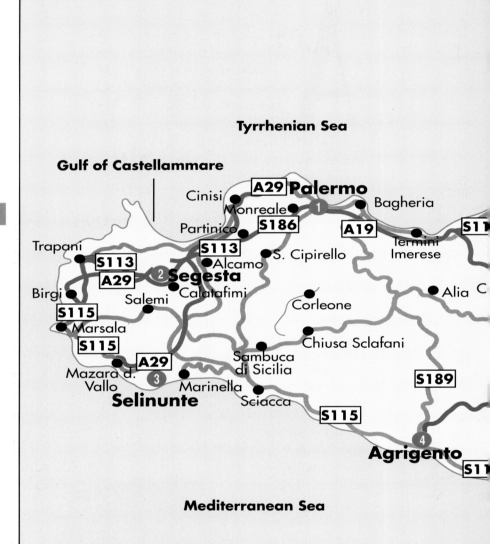

Tyrrhenian Sea

Gulf of Castellammare

Cinisi

A29 **Palermo**

Monreale ● Bagheria

Partinico **S186**

A19

Trapani **S113** **S113**

Alcamo ● S. Cipirello

Termini Imerese

A29 **Segesta**

Birgi Salemi Calatafimi

Corleone ● Alia

S115

Marsala

Chiusa Sclafani

S115

Mazara d. Vallo **A29**

Sambuca di Sicilia

S189

Marinella

Selinunte Sciacca

S115

Agrigento

Mediterranean Sea

| ① Palermo | ③ Selinunte | ⑤ Syra |
| ② Segesta | ④ Agrigento | ⑥ Taor |

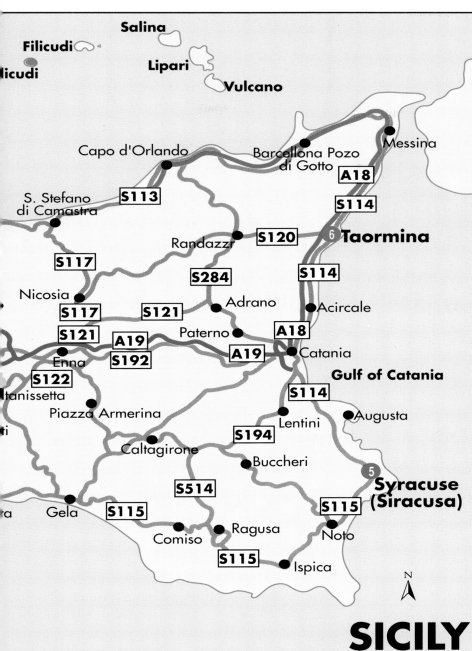

Salina

Filicudi

licudi

Lipari

Vulcano

Capo d'Orlando

Barcellona Pozo di Gotto

Messina

A18

S. Stefano di Camastra

S113

S114

Randazzr

S120

6 **Taormina**

S117

S284

S114

Nicosia

Adrano

Acircale

S117

S121

Paterno

A18

S121

A19

A19

Catania

Enna

S192

Gulf of Catania

S122

tanissetta

S114

ti

Piazza Armerina

Lentini

Augusta

S194

Caltagirone

Buccheri

5 **Syracuse (Siracusa)**

S514

Gela

S115

S115

a

Comiso

Ragusa

Noto

S115

Ispica

N

SICILY

The island is dotted with ruins and archaeological sites such as Temple "E" in Selinunte.

came a breadbasket, olive oil lake and wine cellar. The Arabs established an important Islamic centre in **Palermo**. Byzantine evidence exists in the grand Norman architecture of the island's many churches of the 11th and 12th centuries, and, in the 15th century, the Spanish Catalans introduced the Gothic style of architecture.

Today Sicily has a population of over 5 million, even though many of its inhabitants have been drawn to the attractions of the USA and the modern world. Agriculture is the mainstay of the island; fishing, too is important, and tourism is on the increase. The notorious Mafia organisation demonstrates its presence throughout the island, as it does on the Italian mainland, although

extraordinary attempts are being made to eradicate the movement. Tourists need not worry though.

Sicily is a land of great scenic beauty, rugged mountains and rolling hills surrounded by a sea teaming with fish and fringed by idyllic bays and rocky covers. The island is dotted with many well-preserved archaeological sites dating from classical times and its cathedrals and castles are spectacular and incorporate unusual architectural styles, reflecting Byzantine and Spanish influence.

Music and folklore is jealously Sicilian and has developed as a unique subculture to that of the mainland. Decoration and craftwork is often overtly ornate and colourful, as is the national dress. Puppetry is part of the ancient

Mosaics in a Norman palace in Palermo.

Sicilian tradition and employs intricate typical craftwork in wood, metal and cloth.

Sicilian food varies greatly from region to region and even Socrates waxed lyrical about the island's culinary temptations. Some of the traditional recipes are Catalan in origin, others stem from North Africa. One of the island's most famous treats is the excellent Sicilian cassata is made of candied fruit, cake and liquer-flavoured ice cream.

As far as the delights of the island, its countryside, its beaches, resorts, archaeological sites and excursions are concerned, the following is a brief glimpse of Sicily's major centres and their major tourist sites.

Palermo

The main port and capital of Sicily is a beautiful city built around the centre, known as the **Quattro Canti**, or 'four corners'. Surrounded by a fertile plain of orange and lemon groves, it stands on the north coast, but is sheltered from the north by the peak of **Mount Pellegrino** at 1,988 feet (606 metres). The city's name comes from 'Panormus', or 'all port'. Palermo airport is three miles (4.8 kilometres) south-west of the city.

Palermo's population is around 720,000 and it was founded by Phoenicians in the 8th century BC. Palermo blossomed during the period of Arab occupation from 831 - 1072 AD. As

View of the smouldering Etna, one of the world's most active, and Europe's largest volcano (3,323 metres).

11th century Church of San Cataldo in Palermo.

a reminder of those times, elegant gardens surround palaces and magnificent villas, whilst the old quarter is a maze of picturesque alleys and ancient narrow streets packed with tiny shops. After Norman occupation the city deteriorated, but with the advent of the Spanish, in the 17th and 18th centuries a baroque form of architecture was adopted and the Spanish founded a university in the city. Typical of the villas on the city outskirts of that period is **Villa Palagonia** built in 1715.

Sites which must be seen in Palermo include the Norman **Palatine** chapel, built in 1132; it contains some fine mosaics. Also the churches of **San Giovanni degli Ermeiti**, with its pink-tiled domes, **San Francesco**, the **San Lorenzo Ora-**

tory, and the **church of Santa Maria della Catena**.

The cathedral is quite unusual in its crenellated exterior and ornate campanile. Curious also are the three pink domes of the 11th century **San Cataldo Church** and, next door, is the lone Martorana bell tower. Sicily's background is well documented in the **Pitre Museum of Ethnography**, founded in 1909 and located in the **Parco della Favorita**. Other museums are those of archaeology and the **Gallery of Modern Art**, and the mosaics at **La Lisa** should be seen.

A more macabre visit is that of the catacombs of **Capuchin**, where the dry air has preserved more than 8,000 corpses. The fascinating necropolis of

Byzantine mosaics under the roof of the San Cataldo in Palermo.

Pantalica, with its 5,000 tomb niches should also be seen.

Catania

Catania, Sicily's second city stands under the shadow of Mt. Etna and is a large port. As if defying the rumblings of the volcano which destroyed the city in 1169 and 1669, many buildings are built from the black lava.

The original 1092 cathedral was reconstructed in 1693 and other churches which date from the 17th and 18th centuries include **San Nicolo** and **Santa Maria di Gesu**. Once a castle, the Ursino fort, built in 1232 by the Holy Roman Emperor Frederick II, is now a tower

housing a museum of archaeology. The composer Vincenzo Bellini was born and is buried here and the botanical gardens are named after him. There are the remains of two Greek theatres and one Roman amphitheatre in the centre of the city.

Syracuse

Sometimes spelled '**Siracusa**', this is an attractive and ancient town. Located on the island's south coast, this port was founded by the Corinthians in 734 BC and became the most important Hellenistic city outside Greece. Archimedes was born here in 287 BC and killed by Roman invaders in 212 BC. On the site of

Mount Etna

Once this volcano was seen as the home of the god Vulcan and the location of the workshops of the Cyclops. The ancients revered the mountain, Homer and Strabo, amongst other classical writers, wrote copiously about it. The volcano of Etna is classified as of the Strombolian type; it is one of the world's most active and Europe's largest volcano. Located in eastern Sicily, its base is 200 kilometres (125 miles) in circumference and rises to an average height of 3,323 metres (10,902 feet), which is changeable as the volcano is in an almost permanent state of eruption. Despite the more than 140 recorded eruptions dating from 1329, and the 200 cones scattered around its base, the lower slopes are farmed with vines, citrus and fruit,

The Etna with its fiery fits.

and some upper slopes developed for skiing. One of the highest inhabited dwellings in Europe, at 9,075 feet is the **Observatory**, founded in 1880.

There are roads and the **Circumetnea** narrow-gauge railway run around the base of the mountain and guide-accompanied excursions can be made from nearby **Catania**.

An example of the Capuchin friars in the catacombs in Palermo.

the Greek temple of **Athena** on the island of **Ortygia** is the Baroque Cathedral. There are many other classical remains in the city. The **San Nicolo church** dates from the 11th century and that of **Santa Lucia** from the 14th century. There are several grand palaces in the city including the 14th century **Palazzo Montalto**, the **Lanza**, the **Comunale** and the **Palazzo Beneventano**. **Palazzo Bellomo**, now a museum, dates from the 13th century. The **Maniace Castle**, 1239, was partially rebuilt in Gothic sytle. Pre-Hellenic and Greek artifacts can be seen in the **Archaeological Museum**. For curious sound effects and rock formations, the '**Ear of Dionysius**' cavern is quite spectacular.

Architectural details of the Cathedral in Palermo.

Messina

This seaport faces Italy across the Straits of Messina and is the main ferry port between Sicily and the mainland. Founded in the 8th century BC, earthquakes have destroyed many of the city's ancient buildings and the oldest surviving is the 12th century **church of Annunziata dei Catalani**. The city's cathedral is a reconstruction around the original Norman building of 1160 and it has an ornate campanile and clock tower.

The 16th century **Fountain of Orion** is by Montorsoli, and stands in the **Piazza dell'Unita d'Italia**. The Museum contains a great collection of archaeo-

logical exhibits from Egyptian to Roman and Byzantine.

Agrigento

Famed throughout the world as one of the most important archaeological sites of classical antiquity, this was once a

The Fountain of Pretoria illuminated in Palermo.

reat city, founded in 581 BC as **Akragas**. he city thrived under Greek rule and vas home to the philosopher mpedocles. Although Romans colo- ised the city, most classical remains re Greek, as in the spectacular **Valley f Temples**.

The city's cathedral was founded in the 11th century and the convent dates from the late 13th century. The two main museums contain fascinating collections of Doric artifacts plus the 2nd century BC Phaedra Sarcophagus in the **Museo Diocesano**.

The ruined Castle of Lombardia in Enna.

The ancient quarries in Syracuse.

Ragusa

This provinical city is now mainly industrial but was an important centre dating from prehistoric through to Arab and Norman times.

Its major sites now are mainly 18th century, like the Sicilian Gothic **Church of San Giorgio Nuovo** and the **San Giovani cathedral**. However, the portal of **San Giorgio Vecchio** was built in the 15th century.

Trapani

An important port under Carthaginian, Roman, Moorish and Spanish colonisa-

The island of Taormina has a number of ruins of churches, palaces, forts and archaeological sites.

tion, this small town is famed for its wine, tuna fish and macaroni. The magnificient Greek temples at **Selinunte** are some of the best preserved of the period. Later sites of interest include the 14th century **Annunziata Sanctuary** and the **Sant'Agostino church**. Other churches date from the 17th century, and the **Casa Ciambra** was built in the 15th century. The abandoned ancient saltworks outside the town is quite eerie with its sentinal windmills.

Enna

Known as the 'Navel of Sicily', this city lies south-east of Palermo and stands on a high plateau. It is a centre for the rock salts and sulphur trades, and is also a popular resort. The 14th century church and frescoes by Bruno of **San Francesco d'Assisi**, the **San Tommaso church** and the cathedral are well worth a visit, as is the 24 metres high **Pisan tower** in the turretted **Lombardia Castle**.

In the countryside

There are a host of spectacular archaeological sites, churches, palaces and forts to visit outside the main cities and towns. The Greek theatre at **Taormina** plus numerous other classical monuments and the 1372 **Corvasia palace**; the **cathedrals of Monreale** (1174), **Caltanissetta** (16-17th centuries), **Noto** (17th century), were well worth visiting.

erodetus said that **Sardinia** was the greatest of the isles of the seas. However, what is certain is that Sardinia is the second largest of Italy's islands and the second largest in the Mediterranean Sea, covering an area of 24,090 square kilometres (9,301 square miles). Its highest point is the **Punta La Marmora**, in the **Gennargentu** massif, reaching a height of around 1,835 metres (6,016 feet). The island is mostly gaunt, with craggy mountain pines and some wood-covered verdant valleys. The coast is rimmed by long sandy beaches, intimate rockbound coves, towering cliffs and wide, natural harbours and bays, all trimmed with seas ranging in colour from deep ultramarine to bottle-glass green and peacock blue. This emerald island has 1 , 8 5 0

Sardinia

281

Typical costumes and lovely Sardinians in Cagliari at a local festival.

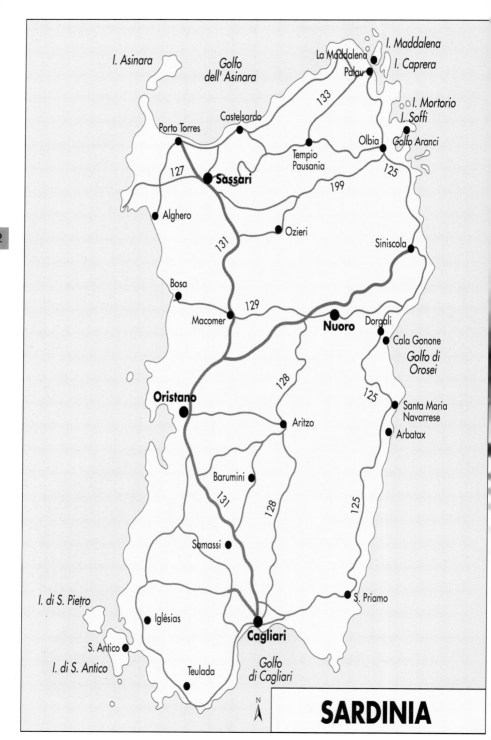

SARDINIA

The Saracen fortress tower, Torre Pelosa in Stintino.

The vineyards at Oliena lie beside rugged mountains.

kilometres (more than 800 miles) of coastline, much of which is undiscovered by tourists even though many of its beaches are coated with fine white sand.

Its history dates back to prehistoric times as can be witnessed in the plethora of massive megalithic sites found all over Sardinia. The original culture lived around 2,000 BC. Typical of these are necropoli dotted with curious '*domus de janas*' (fairy houses) tombs, which are oblong-shaped hollows carved deep into the living rock. Among other monuments are the '*tombas de gigantes*', or **Giant's Tombs**, with their great megalithic slabs and altars, the '*perdas fittas*' and the '*pozzi sacri*', or sacred wells, all evidence of this mysterious ancient island culture. The Nuraghic Culture

lasted from the Bronze to the Iron Age. The Nuraghi, or fortified settlements which they built around 1,500 BC were constructed of great blocks of stone. There are more than 7,000 Nuraghi buildings throughout Sardinia, many in a surprisingly good state of preservation, like that at **Barumini**.

The Nuraghi were constructed until around 500 BC even though, in the 9th century BC, the Phoenecians invaded the island. The Romans, Barbarians, Arabs and Spanish, amongst others, all settled on Sardinia and created a unique and fascinating culture, each leaving their mark on the landscape in the form of a wonderful selection of architectural styles. Mostly sheep and goat farmers, the population of Sardinia is almost one

A curious stone relic of the Nuraghic age.

and three-quarter million. There are many traditional crafts including carpet weaving which is done on a vertical loom and the designs hark back to those of Moorish Spain.

Cagliari

This city of almost a quarter of a million inhabitants was originally

The Sards number one and three quarter million and are mostly a farming society.

founded by the Phoenicians. It was the site of an ancient Cartheginian settlement. The Romans arrived on the island in 238 BC, and artifacts from its Roman occupation can be seen in the **Museo Nazionale Archeologico**. To the north and west of the ancient city walls is a Roman amphitheatre; also of Roman origin is the huge **Grotta della Vipera**, or **Grotto of the Vipers**, known as such for the twin serpents above the tomb entrance. The oldest standing Christian building on Sardinia is the 5th century church of **Santi Cosma e Damiano**, or **San Saturnino**. Raids by the Saracens frequently disrupted the city between the 8th and 11th centuries.

During the occupation of the Pisans, several grandiose medieval structures were built in the capital including the Romanesque **Santa Cecilia cathedral** (1312), the **Elephant Tower**, built in 1307, and the **Tower of San Pancrazio** constructed in 1305. An important structure from baroque times is the **church of San Michele**. The **Royal Palace** of the **House of Savoy**, now the Gover-

The Church of San Michele in Alghero.

nor's Palace, was built in the 18th century.

For sights of the city there can be no better viewpoints than those of the bastions of **San Remy** (the Terrazza Umberto 1) reached by walking up Via Lamamora, through the **Torre dell'Aquila** gateway and up the marble steps known as the **Passeggiata Coperta**, and that of the **Bastion of Santa Catarina**.

Sassari

The 12th century old town's major sites are its cathedral, the castle, now only a memory in the name **Piazza Castello**, and the university. The **University of** **Sassari** was founded by King Carlo V's secretary, Alessio Fontana in 1588, and is famous for its library stocked with more than 10,000 volumes.

Vittorini called the 13th century **San Niccolo cathedral** an 'immense flower in stone'– Remnants of the Aragonese castle, on the edge of the medieval town were still to be seen on the palm-lined 'Castle Square'. The cathedral is not often open to the public but contains a carved stone font from Piedmont. Little remains of the 13th century building as the cathedral was re-built in the 15th century, and its baroque facade was added in the 1700's. The town also has a notable music conservatory.

The **Palazzeto Usini** in the town

centre, was built in the 16th century. There are two remaining 15th century houses, Nos 42 and 47, on Vittorio Emanuele. The famous, opulently carved **Fonte del Rosello**, where the well-house dates from 1605, should also not be missed. The Duke of Asinara's 18th century **Ducal Palace** now houses an artwork museum.

Alghero

There is more evidence here than anywhere on the island of Spanish occupation during the 14th century. The people here still speak Catalan and the cathedral and old city fortifications, including numerous Gothic buildings, date from those times. **Alghero**'s cathedral is early but much of the remaining building is from the 16th century construction, showing Spanish influences.

Near the cathedral is the **Palazzo d'Albis** where the Emperor Charles V stayed in the mid-1500's. The **church of San Francisco** dates from the 14th century and has a Gothic presbytery. Another fine church is the **San Michele** on Via Carlo Alberto, built in the 17th century. It sports a dome made of coloured tiles. Other religious treasures include the font in the 16th century **Casa Doria** on Principe Umberto, which was carved for the Genoese Doria family.

The main round fortress tower of the five remaining, overlooking the harbour, was constructed during the Aragonese occupation. Other towers are

The Cathedral in Sassari.

of Saracen origin. The northernmost tower is the **Torre dello Sperone**, or **Torre di Sulis**, as Sulis, the locally celebrated revolutionary was once imprisoned there. The city's ancient gateway is marked by the **Torre di Porta Terra** and this leads to the botanical gardens known as the **Giardino**.

Oristano

When Tharros declined as capital of the region, in the early 11th century, **Oristano** was founded. Of the ancient 13th century city walls and fortifications, only a few crumbling remains stand, including two towers, the **Porta Mannu**, or **Saint Christopher**'s tower

The masked costume of Oristano.

and the **Portixeddu**, or "**Little Turret**" on Piazza Mariano. Queen Eleonora's reign is celebrated in several monuments in Oristano, the statue of her outside the municipio, an Avenue Eleonaro and a 16th century house, the **Casa do Eleonora**, which is located at No. 4 Via Parpaglia. She lies buried in the church of Santa Chiara.

The **Museum Antiquarian Arborense** has bronze and pottery exhibits from Neolithic times, Punic glassware, Roman objects and medieval artifacts. 15th and 16th century Catalan paintings decorate the walls. The cathedral, initially built in the 11th century, dates mostly from the 1700's and has an octagonal campanile. Inside there are some interesting paintings, wooden

sculptures and tapestries. The **Seminary**, dating from the 18th century, stands across the square from the cathedral. The **church of San Francesco**, rebuilt in 1838, contains a 14th century Spanish wooden Crucifix of Nicodemus and artworks including 'St. Francis Receiving the Stigmata', a polyptych painted in the 16th century. A balustrade in the right transept is fashioned from an 11th century pulpit. Probably the oldest surviving structure in this area is the 12th century Pisan Romanesque **church of Santa Giusta** which sports a wooden vaulted roof.

Olbia

This is the gateway to the **Costa**

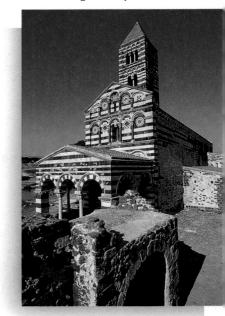

Church of della San Trinita, in Codrongianus.

Slick cruisers, villas, sunshine and the jet-set – the popular international
image of Sardinia.

Smeralda and one of Sardinia's most important ports. The town is situated at the head of a deep long, arm founded by the Cartheginians and served as a commercial port in the 4th century BC, although it is said to have a Greek history. The Romanesque, grey, granite-built **church of San Simplicio** was constructed in the Pisan style and dates from the 11th century.

Inside are a number of Roman tombs, milestones and a decorated sarcophagus lid. **Olbia** is dominated in the north by **Monte sa Curi** on which is the prehistoric site and **castle of Sant Nuragico Cabu'Abbas** reached from town by a steep track, obviously for the more energetic. Olbia's major feature is the great **Bianca jetty**.

Nuoro

Nuoro is the capital of the province of the same name with a population of around 30,000 and a growing industrial centre.

Nuoro's history dates from the 15th century although there is little to see from those times. The town became a bishopric in the 18th century but even its cathedral, the **Santa Maria della Neve**, restored in 1980, only dates from the 19th century. A reminder that this region was one of brigands and family feuds, of bandits and the vendetta, can be seen in one of the city's most prominent buildings, the prison. Nuoro also has an attractive older quarter although

Sardinian Panoply of Festivals

Costumed Sards at the Mamoiada Carnival.

animal world, with masks of wood and the skins of beasts, mainly symbolising the bull, and who imitate the magical elements of the natural world.

Sassari's festivities are legendary and few spectaculars can match the vast celebrations of the **Sardinian Cavalcade** in May. A morning procession is followed by a 'Palio' or horse race through the town in the afternoon. Also not to be missed is the city's feast and procession of "Il Candereri", the **Candlestick Festival** where giant candles are paraded through the town by members of the Gremi, or farm guilds in a ceremony dating back almost 400 years.

Another famed horse race is that of the 'seven circlings' of Ardia's church, a celebration of Emperor Constantine's conquests at the bridge of Milivan in 312 AD. Also a famous horse racing spectacle, the **Sa Sartiglia** at **Oristano**, is a Spanish-influenced ritual which involves riders jousting at silver stars hung from ribbons, with lances. The intention is to impale as many stars as possible. The riders dress in a costume adorned with red ribbons, the horses are highly decorated, and the challengers wear white, wooden female masks surmounted by an odd form of top hat.

Steeped in a history which goes back more than 5000 years, and which has absorbed influences from most of the ancient civilizations and religions, Sardinia has a unique panoply of festivals, fairs and celebrations which attract thousands of tourists.

The darker side of life, hidden in the mists of time and harking back to pagan gods of prehistoric ancestors, is celebrated at the **Mamoiada Carnival** where "**Mamuthone**" frightening wooden masks are worn to represent strange creatures from prehistory, their bodies covered with black sheep skins sporting lots of heavy bells. As they cavort through the streets, their acolytes, the 'issocadores' skilfully lasso members of the audience. Eventually the Mamuthones are driven from the city. The Mamuthone's performances are said to come from the pagan ritual of the ancient Romans who used to drive a man dressed in skins, impersonating Mars, the god of agriculture, before he became the God of War, out of the city gates. Just as ancient are the events in **Ottana** in central north Sardinia. This is the eerie celebration where players emerge on the streets representing the ancient clans of the **Merdules** and the **Boes**, who wear the dress of characters from the

Depictions of the ancient Merdules clans.

Marinas at Palau, berthed with luxury craft.

nowadays much of the town is quite modern.

The tiny quarter of **San Pietro** is where Grazia Deladda the poet was born, but Nuoro's important claim to fame is its museum. The **Museum of Sardinian Life** and **Popular Traditions** is on the hill of **Sant' Onofrio** on the southern edge of the city.

The museum houses a wide and colourful collection of traditional and festive costumes, jewellery, handicrafts and architectural styles from all over Sardinia. The **Handicraft Museum** on Corso Garibaldi also contains some fascinating exhibits among which are carvings, tapestries, ceramics and local craftswork. Nuoro is a good place for souvenirs, for variety and good prices.

The Costa Smeralda

The "**Emerald Coast**", since the advent of the Aga Khan, has long been favoured by royalty, the rich and the famous, not only from Italy, but among the internatinal jet-set.

This 50 kilometres (30 miles) coastline has long been praised for its natural beauty and clear green seas. The main resorts along the Costa Smeralda are **Baja Sardinia**, **Porto Cervo** and **Cala di Volpe**. All around these areas can be seen many villas, luxury hotels and developments. In addition its marinas harbour some of the sleek and slick cruisers, and a perpetual stream of well-heeled sunseekers.

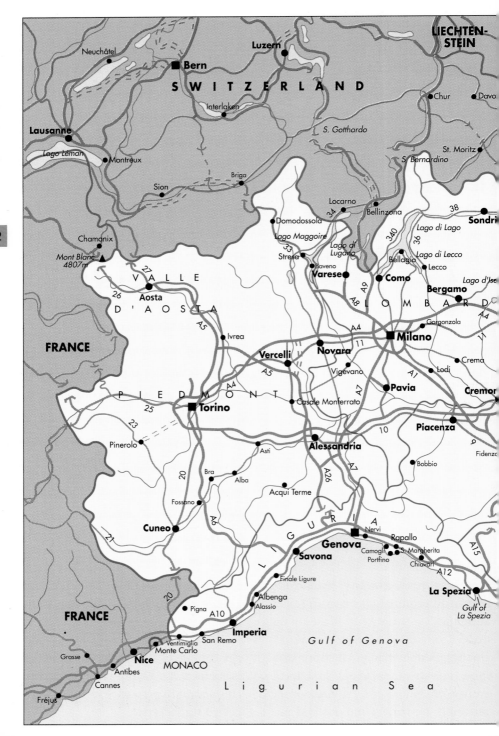

LIECHTEN-
STEIN

Neuchâtel

Luzern

Bern

S W I T Z E R L A N D

Chur   Davo

Interlaken

Lausanne   S. Gotthardo

Lago Leman   Montreux   St. Moritz

Sion   Briga   S. Bernardino

Locarno   Bellinzona   38

Domodossola   34   *Lago di Lago*   **Sondri**

Lago Maggoire   36

Chamonix   33   *Lago di Lugano*   *Lago di Lecco*

Mont Blanc   Stresa   Bellagio   Lecco

4807m   Baveno   **Como**   *Lago d'Ise*

V A L L E   **Varese**   **Bergamo**

27   A9   L O M B A R D

26   **Aosta**   A8   Gorgonzola   A4

D ' A O S T A   A5   11   **Milano**   11

Ivrea   A4   Crema

FRANCE   **Vercelli**   **Novara**   Lodi

A5   Vigevano   A1   **Cremor**

P I E D M O N T   A7   **Pavia**

25   Casale Monferrato   A1

23   **Torino**   10   **Piacenza**

Pinerolo   Asti   A26   Bobbio   Fidenzo

Bra   9

20   Alba   **Alessandria**

Fossano   Acqui Terme   A26

21   **Cuneo**   L I G U R I A   Nervi   Rapallo

Genova   Camogli   S. Margherita

Savona   Portfino   Chiavari   A12

20   Finale Ligure   A15

Pigna   Albenga   **La Spezia**

FRANCE   A10   Alassio   *Gulf of La Spezia*

Imperia

Ventimiglia   San Remo   *Gulf of Genova*

Grasse   Monte Carlo

Nice   MONACO

Antibes

Cannes   *L i g u r i a n   S e a*

Fréjus

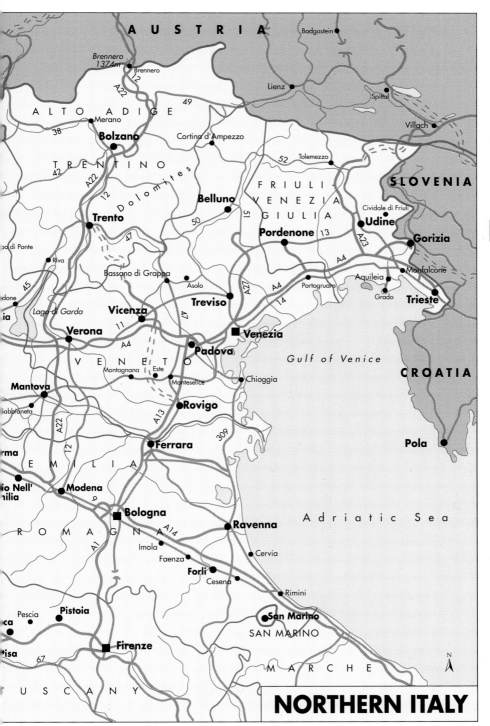

NORTHERN ITALY

M

ilan or Milano as the Italians call it, is the capital of the region of Lombardy. Milan ranks as one of Europe's most dynamic metropolis, and is the second most populous and second largest city in Italy, spreading out 182 square kilometres. Milan is a city that promises action, work, money; it takes a toll on the strongest nerves, and it attracts talents of all kinds, artistic and entrepreneurial. The city has been trading as early as around 100 AD.

The facade of the Duomo dominates the large Piazza del Duomo, Milan.

The history of Milan goes way back. The Cisalpine Gauls came in the 6th century BC and called a sacred spot of the swampy lowland, Mitta-land or "middle place". That spot is now under **Piazza della Scala** or **Piazza del Duomo**. Interesting enough, their most important god was a god of business! One of the oldest neighbourhoods in the Old Town or centro storico, the **Quadrilatero d'Oro** is near where Etruscans, Ligurians, and an Italic tribe called

Milan & Lombardy

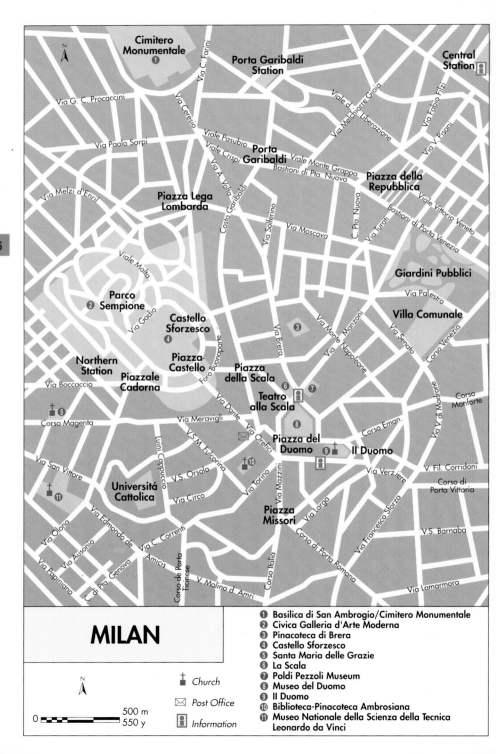

Feeding the pigeons in the Piazza dell Duomo.

Shopping in Milan is a never-ending exercise, especially in fashion goods.

the Insubres inhabited in succession. Around 222 BC, after 26 years of war, the Romans took Mitta-land and created Mediolanum, a military stronghold and centre of trade between Rome and Central Europe. It grew to become one of the largest cities of the Roman Empire. Milan was invaded during the late 4th century by the Huns, and she subsequently fell to the Visigoths, the Lombards, the Spanish in 1535, the French led by Napoleon in 1797, the Austrians in 1714 and again in 1815, the Fascists from 1919 to 1943, and most recently to the Allied Forces during World War II (1939-1945) when 60 percent of the city was flattened by bombs. Milan has always resurrected herself, attended to her wounds and grown larger.

There are two major airports in Milan, **Linate** and **Malpensa**. The city is a nerve centre for important roads railways. Unlike other Roman cities that were built on an efficient grid-block arrangement, Milan has a circle-within-a-circle design, expanding in concentric rings from the **Duomo**. The circular roadways in Milan are known as the Cerchia dei Navigli and the Circonvallazione Interna and Esterna. This probably partially accounts for some of the worst traffic jams in Europe which occur along with the seeming directionless movement of vehicles on the roads in Milan.

Different from other pretty Italian towns, much of Milan has a modern sombre appearance with many eyesores

- a cityscape of dirty brown and grey buildings floating in a sea of smog, pollution and noise. However, some changes have been made and more have been promised. New urban "pedestrian islands" and "green spaces" have been set up in more than 20 areas. Recently the historic centre has been limited only to cars with permits, and restoration work is being done on historical buildings and sites.

Milan earns almost a third of Italy's national income; this is the headquarters of the major banks, financial centres, international trading and Italy's stock market. Publishing, advertising, art, design and fashion houses, manufacturing plants, and thousands of small to medium-sized factories are based here, specializing in chemical, textiles, transportation equipment, tyres and electrical appliances. The people of Milan are called Milanese, with a reputation for being enterprising, ambitious and professional. They are mostly Roman Catholics. Most Milanese arrived only one or two generations ago, which is very unusual in Italy where people usually stay in their ancestral towns. Even Milan's famous personalities, from the past and from the present, such as Leonardo da Vinci, Bramante, Stendhal, Feltrinelli, Armani, Strehler, Aulenti, de Benedetti, were foreigners who came and made it big in Milan. Milanese like to occupy their afternoons by sitting at a cafe in the city, a favourite being in the **Galleria Vittoro Emanuele II**, also known as the "living-room of Milan", where they so-

The Milanese are reputed to be enterprising, ambitious and professional.

cialise or close business deals.

To explore Milan, to be honest, you have to like to walk. Take my word for it, you do not want to drive through the clogged streets where everyone seems to think they need to get onto any other lane but the one they are on, while you are trying hard to read seemingly unmarked streets and all cars behind yours are honking irritatingly at you. Finally, it is also close to impossible to find a parking space. Taxis are expensive and will invariably tend to join the quagmire on the roads. If you are in a hurry, there is the subway or Metropolitana Milanese, or you may like to try the old electric trams and have your bones rattled. For just running around, take numbers 29 and 30, and for getting across

One of the well-preserved castles in Milan.

the centre of town, take numbers 1, 4, 8, 13 and 15.

In Milan you will be able to find some of Italy's most magnificent early Christian and Romanesque monuments, this is because Milan played a large role in the spread of Christianity. From 286 to 402 AD, Emperor Constantine lived in Milan and heralded the Edict of Milan which allowed Christians to worship openly.

The best place to begin a tour of Milan is from the **Duomo** (open to the public year-round). This cathedral was begun in 1385 and it was not finished until 500 years later under the command of Napoleon I. This is the third largest cathedral in the world, after St. Peter's of Rome and the Cathedral of Seville, at a height of 112 metres, length of 158 metres and width of 62 metres. It can accommodate 40,000 people. It is built of white carrara marble and shares Late-Gothic, Renaissance and neo-classical styles. An organization called La Divina Fabbrica del Duomo di Milano is in charge of daily operation of the Duomo, including its maintenance, repairs, and cleaning which is a never ending job because of its massive size. More than 3000 statues decorate the inside and outside of the cathedral. The exterior is covered with marble spires, each balancing a life-sized statue of a saint, Biblical character, or historical figure. On the highest spire stands the shining Madonnina covered in 3500 layers of gold. The interior is enormous, with five aisles running from the entrances to the altar. Take time to study and savour the myriad colours of the intricate stained glass windows created by Nicolas de Bonaventura. The central window depicts the shield of the Visconti, who were the ruling family of Milan in the 13th and 14th centuries, and the family of the founder of the Duomo, Duke Gian Visconti. At the left transept stands a statue of Saint Bartholomew carrying his skin (he was martyred by flaying).

Notice the exceptional understanding of the anatomy by the sculptor Marco d'Agrate in 1562. The Duomo also holds the tomb of the 16th century Counter Reformation saint and Archbishop of Milan, St. Charles Borromeo (1538-1584), mummified, wearing neat white

The Galleria Vittoro Emanuele II shopping mall.

lace gloves and lying in a crystal casket which can be viewed. He was severely abstinent and tried to ban dancing, drama and sports, hence he often came into conflict with lay authorities. Many historical V.I.P.s of Milan are buried in this cathedral.

To get a better perspective of Milan and its surroundings, climb to the top of the cathedral. On a clear day you will be able to see the Alps in the north, the Po River and the Apennines to the south. To the north of the city, you will be able to see one of the world's biggest covered train stations, the grandiose **Stazione Centrale** with its stone eagles, reminiscent of the Fascist Empire. To the northwest is the 14th century **Castello Sforzesco** in the midst of the very green

Parco Sempiore. It was destroyed three times and rebuilt. Now it holds several excellent museums. Next to the Duomo you can clearly see the 36-storey **Pirelli Tower**, one of Italy's tallest business structures and one of the most important symbols of modern Milan.

Milan has several neighbourhoods, each with their own distinct character and essence: the aesthetically pleasing and fashionable **Brera**, with its Academy of Fine Arts, excellent art galleries, antique shops and trendy clubs; **Ticinese**, with its uncovered **Navigli** or canals; **Porta Romana**, with its **Universita Statale** or state university and the city's best theatres; **Magenta**, with **Cinque Vie** and **Sant' Ambrogio**; **Venezia**, with its elegant public gar-

The ceiling of the Galleria is a glass-roofed dome complex, with exquisite frescoes on the upper reaches of the walls.

dens; and sophisticated **Quadrilatero d'Oro**, with its chic shopping and exceptional restaurants. Quadrilatero d'Oro or Golden Rectangle lies between **Via Monte Napoleone** and **Via della Spiga**.

We descend onto the **Piazza del Duomo** and on its two sides are porticoes; this is where you may be able to watch the natives in all their attractive styles parade themselves. The large statue you will see at one end is of Italy's first king, Victor Emmanuele II. Going north will take you to the Galleria Vittorio Emanuele, built in the Unification era (1865); it is the world's most luxurious and oldest shopping arcades. It is four-storeys of boutiques, restaurants, cafes and offices, but needless to

say, the prices are high. You may like to pay a visit to the popular Camparino cafe, where you may sample the traditions of the Milanese cafe society. Nearby is **Savini**, one of Milan's most famous restaurants. If you have a passion for books, have a browse through **Rizzoli**, **Bocca** and **Cearzanti**. For your additional information there is a telephone office (SIP) and a major travel agency, (CIT) here.

By the Galleria is **Piazza della Scala** and the ornament of Milan, the **Teatro alla Scala**. It was built in 1778 in neoclassical style by Giuseppe Piermarini, and it seats 3000. The inside is like some scene from a fairy-tale: crystal chandeliers casting golden light on scarlet walls adorn with gilded details. La Scala re-

Rossini, one of Italy's master composers whose works are often staged at La Scala.

ceives many thousands of glamorous opera devotees each year, but unless you reserve years in advance, you have little chance of finding a ticket. However, you can try a ticket tout where you naturally will pay black market prices, or try to buy standing-room ticket on the actual day of the performance, or try C.I.T. (there is one at the Galleria Vittorio Emanuele II), at last resort, you may try certain consulates who sometimes hold tickets just in case a dignitary dropped by unexpectedly. Next door is the **Museo Teatrale alla Scale**, a definite for opera addicts; there are Verdi and Liszt's original compositions, portraits of past primadonnas and tenors, and much more.

Go up Via Verdi to the **Pinacoteca di Brera**, designed by Richini in 1651 and remodelled by Piermarini in 1780. It holds an excellent collection of predominantly 15th and 18th century paintings, for example, Caravaggio's 'Supper at Emmaus', Raphael's 'Marriage of the Virgin', Mantegna's 'Dead Christ' and Pierodella Francesca's 'Duke of Montefeltro'.

Sandwiched between Brera and the Quadrilatero d'Oro is the neighbourhood of **Borgo Nuovo** which was called Contrada di Sciori or "rich noblemen's neighbourhood" in Milanese dialect. If you have time, you may like to have a look at the many huge stone palazzi that boast beautiful porticoed courtyards with famous columns that survived the Allies' bombs. Take a stroll along Borgo

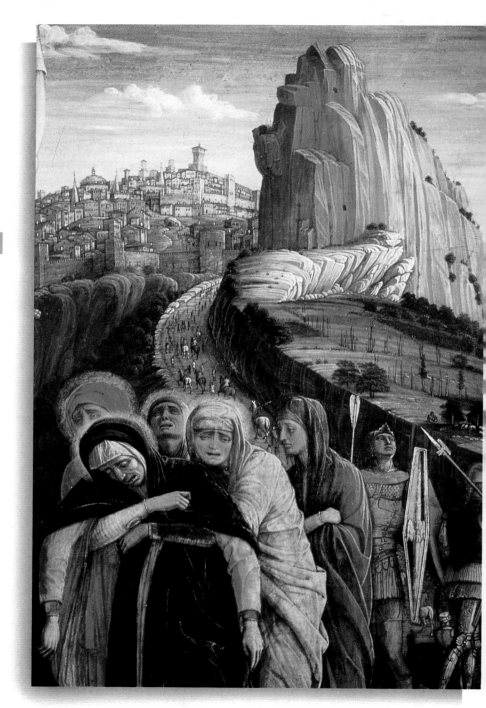

The Pinacoteca di Brera, holds excellent collections, including Mantegna's "Dead Christ".

Nuovo, the Brera, Corso Monforte and Via Cappuccio. The exact number of columns are not clear, Stendhal in June 1800, recorded that there were 20,000. From the Piazza del Duomo, off Via Mercanto is **Castello Sforzesco** on Via Dante. From here, during the 15th century, the Sforza family ruled Milan. In the **Corte Ducale**, there is a superb collection of sculptures which include Michelangelo's `Rondanini Pieta' and Mantegna's `Virgin and Child in Glory'.

In the **Magenta** neighbourhood, three blocks west from the Castello is the **Basilica of Sant' Ambrogio** on Via Carducci. This is a good place to start a tour of this neighbourhood. It is the first medieval building in Milan, founded by St. Ambrose and built in 379 AD, then he was bishop of Milan but later became patron saint of Milan. Over the years, it has been enlarged, altered and repaired. It is typically Lombard. There is a 4th century chapel of **San Vittore**, 5th century mosaics and don't miss the sarcophagus. Go down into the crypt and visit the skeletons of St. Ambrose and two early Christian martyrs. Walk down Via San Vittore and you will come to the **Museo Nazionale della Sienza e Tecnica**, the most interesting part of this museum to the non-physicist would be the massive room holding wooden models of Leonardo da Vinci's inventions of machines. Close to Sant' Ambrogio is the **Bar Magenta** also on Via Carducci, known to be frequented by fashion-models. Next to this is the huge **Catholic University**; there are two

cloisters dating from 1498 that are the last works of Bramante in Milan, truly worth seeing. Nearby is the **Santa Maria delle Grazie**, built in 1466. Bramante constructed the cloister and expanded the church in 1492, this being one of his greatest works in Milan. The structure next door, **Cenacolo Vinciano** was once a refectory for Dominican monks. Bramante's friend Leonardo da Vinci's 'Last Supper' (1495-1497) is sheltered there. Despite futile attempts at restoration, it is distressingly faded with time and water damage, but still worth visiting simply because it remains a stirring and inspirational experience to see that masterpiece – 4.5 metres by 9 metres.

In the **Ticinese** neighbourhood, it is said that the bones of the Magi are kept in the 11th century **Sant' Eustorgio**. Do visit the Sant' Eustorgio's Renaissance style **Portinari Chapi**, designed by Michelozzo in 1462. Milan's oldest church, nearby on Corso di Porta Ticinese is **San Lorenzo Maggiore**. Octagonal shaped, it was first built in the 4th century, rebuilt in 1103 and again between 1574 and 1588 by Bartino Bassi. There are exceptional 5th century mosaics, many original, that are worth seeing. It was built over a Roman amphitheatre, and to see it you have to go behind the altar of the church. In front of the church across the road you will see the 16 newly restored Corinthian columns of a 3rd century Roman bath, now an area for "alternative" restaurants and clubs such as the Pois, Le Scimmie and La Pasticceria. Going in the direction of the

Milan is known for many great restaurants and bars.

Duomo, you will find the library, **Biblioteca Ambrosiana**. It was constructed by Lelio Buzzi (1607-1609) and founded by Cardinal Federico Borromeo. It holds pieces painted during the 15th to 17th centuries. Have a look at Leonardo da Vinci's `Portrait of a Musician' and Caravaggio's `Basket of Fruit'. Nearby you may visit the **San Satiro** on Via Torino, constructed between 1478 and 1480 by Bramante who skilfully used stucco and created the illusion of spaciousness in the church.

Finally, what Milanese life is all about – the most fashionable and alluring streets of Milan is that of Corso Vittorio Emanuele, Corso Europa, Piazza San Babila and Via Monte Napoleon. There are rows upon rows of cin-

emas, boutiques, discos, clubs including the largest department store, La Rinascente. The lively young and old Milanese crowd the streets in all their glamour, doing their *passeggiata*, spilling into the vicinity's sculpture garden where sometimes the shapely sculptures are conveniently used as seats.

LOMBARDY

Lombardy is a region in northern Italy that stretches from the Alps to the fertile plains of the **Po Valley**. It is an area that has very diverse characteristics and aspects. A visitor can see romantic villas and botanical gardens skirting dramatic and thriving lakes shimmering among rugged mountains and sheer cliffs, blooming wilderness and fruitful farmlands complementing beautiful cities.

The region was named after the Lombards, a tribe that once lived there around the 6th century. Lombardy contains the provinces of **Bergamo**, **Brescia**, **Como**, **Cremona**, **Mantova**, **Milano**, **Pavia**, **Sondrio** and **Varese**. This is Italy's main industrial region, and it produces mainly wine, silk and cheese. **Milan** is the capital.

Pavia

Pavia used to be the capital of the Lombards from the 6th to the 8th century. Today, it is famous for its university that was founded in 1361.

From Milan, one should take a day trip to see Pavia. A good place to start would be the **Certosa**, a very famous church, mausoleum and monastery founded in 1396. It holds resplendent life-size effigies of Ludovico Visconti and his child-bride Beatrice d'Este. The cathedral itself is a masterpiece of Lombard-Renaissance architecture, the design of the structure is Gothic, but there are magnificent Renaissance and baroque features, notice the details of the relief sculptures and beautiful inlaid marbling.

Just behind the Certosa is the **Great Cloister** with an elegant courtyard lined with two-storeyed cottages where the Carthusian monks once lived in seclusion and isolation because they made vows of silence. The old centre is situ-

The town of Nesso, by one of the many scenic Lombardian lakes.

Inside the Duomo at Bergamo.

ated on Via Diacono where you can visit the **Church of San Michele**, consecrated in 1155. Take some time to study the detailed decorations on the columns and the scenes of the battle between good and evil above the three doorways. It was in this church that the Lombard king Federick Barbarossa was crowned.

Go along the Strada Nuova, you will arrive at the Duomo which presents to the eye a stange mixture of architectural styles: the cupola was created in the late 19th century and the facade in 1933, the clear Renaissance period works are by Bramante and da Vinci. Continue along the Stada Nuova and you will come to the Universita, one of its most famous graduates is the physicist Volta who discovered volts. The univer-

sity has a statue of him.

At the end of Strada Nuova is the stately citadel of **Castello Visconteo** built in 1360. Here you can visit the **Museo Civio** which contains relics from Pavia of Roman times as well as Lombard-Romanesque sculptures. **San Pietro**, a Lombard-Romanesque church is west of the citadel; it holds relics of Saint Augustine and has a beautiful Gothic arch.

Before you depart from Pavia, try a bowl of the local speciality, zuppa alla pavese. It was supposed to have been formulated by a peasant woman in 1525 for the king, Francis I of France who stopped for food at her cottage when he was about to lose the Battle of Pavia to the Spanish. She added eggs, cheese and toast to her minestrone for a more extravagant dish.

Cremona

Cremona is a two hour drive from Pavia, and lies on the shores of the Po River. This town is famous the world over for making violins. Cremona's most well-known son is Antonio Stradivari (1644-1737). It is said that his secret formula for violin varnish gives the Stradivari violin its exquisite sound. If you are a music enthusiast, you may like to pay a visit to the **International School of Violin–making** and the musical instruments exhibition in the 13th century **Palazzo del Comune** on Corso Vittorio Emanuele.

The beautiful 1190 Duomo in the town is worth a visit; it is made of pink marble in the Lombard-Romanesque style. Take some time to examine the columns in the Duomo depicting the life of Samson, the rose window above the entrance which dates from 1274 and the 17th century tapestries housed there.

Mantua

Mantua or **Mantova** was featured in Verdi's 'Rigoletto'. It sits on a peninsular on the Mincio River and is sometimes called piccolo Venezia. The town's history can be traced to a time before the Renaissance, when Mantua was just a small village. A woman living there

Violin-making in Cremona, home of the famous Stadivaris.

dreamt that she would give birth to a laurel branch; she delivered Virgil and gave the Roman world its greatest poet. From 1328, for 379 years, Mantua was ruled by the enlightened Gonzaga family. During the Renaissance under the blessings of the Marchioness Isabella D'Este, knowledge and culture flourished. She presented the literary genius Castiglione with a palace in Mantua and she commissioned Raphael, Mantegna and Giulio Romano to decorate the Reggia dei Gonzaga (Palazzo Ducale) where there are more than 500 rooms you can see. The **Appartamento degli Arazzi** is particularly worth visiting to see its nine tapestries which were produced from designs drawn by Raphael. In the matrimonial suite or

Details of a column outside the Duomo at Bergamo.

the **Camera degli Sposi**, you can see frescoes created by Mantegna portraying some events from the lives of the Marquess Ludovico Gonzaga and his wife, Barbara of Brandenburg.

A travel across town is worthwhile to see the **Palazzo del Te** which is where the Gonzaga family stayed during the summer. Sadly the linden (*tigli*) trees that the palace was named after have long since disappeared, but it contains many delicately decorated rooms adorned with charming frescoes depicting scenes of summer. This palace was constructed by Giulio Romano in 1525.

Also a must is the **Duomo** with the **Reggia** of Renaissance design. It has an exquisite baroque facade and stucco by Giulio Romano, and the **Basilica di**

Sant' Andrea in Piazza Mantegna. It was almost completed by L.B. Alberti from Florence in 1472 except for the dome which was added on about 300 years later. Inside there are frescoes designed by Mantegna and developed by his pupils, one of them being Correggio.

Mantua is lovely to wander in with its medieval air and cobblestone streets. Try to take a stroll around town in the moonlight, it makes one feel as if they were dropped back in time and part of a Shakespearean play.

Bergamo

Bergamo is a beautiful and picturesque town made of two cities: Bergamo Bassa

A cafe sign in the main piazza of Bergamo, one of the more picturesque cities of Lombardy.

and Bergamo Alta. **Bergamo Bassa** is the more modern of the two. Take a walk down Via Pignola with its grand 16th to 18th century palaces and then spend some time in the **Accademia Carrara** which hold paintings of such calibre, they could be called treasures. This is all due to the extreme good taste of the Count Giacomo Carrara, who lived in Bergamo Bassa in the 18th century. There are paintings by Lotto, Carpaccio, Bellini, Pisanello and Mantegna. An added point is that the museum is generally empty.

Bergamo Alta is balanced dramatically on a rocky ledge. Take a ride on the funicular, up the mountain to the town, unless you feel like mountain climbing. The town is beautiful and ancient, but kept in a strikingly wonderful condition. A good place for a drink or some food is at the **Piazza Vecchia**; you can try the local speciality polenta con gli uccelli. From the Piazza Vecchia, you can admire the 12th century **Palazzo della Ragione** and the 17th century **Palazzo Nuovo,** then proceed leisurely to **Piazza del Duomo** where you should visit the **San Maria Maggiore**, built in Romanesque style, the Renaissance, **Colleoni Chapel,** designed by G.A. Amadeo and dedicated to the Bergamesque condotierre, Bartolomeo Colleoni whom the Venetians (Bergamo at the time was under Venetian control) honoured with a mansion. The **Instituto Musicale Donizetti** is worth a visit; he died in 1848 at the age of 51, completely

Lake Superior and Mantua once a small village, grown into a cultured town during the Renaissance.

insane. In his lifetime he wrote and composed almost 70 operas!

The Italian lakes

The Italian lakes of Lombardy are for romantics (perfect for honeymooners), the rich, and for anyone who loves natural beauty. Hundreds of thousands of tourists have flocked to their shores and through centuries, they have attracted inspiration-seekers such as artists, writers and lovers.

Bella and named it after his wife **Isabella**. He commissioned the architect Angelo Crivelli Charles to build exclusive palaces and elegant gardens on that island. **Isola Madre** too has a palace and botanical gardens. While the third, **Isola dei Pescatori** is just a fishing village.

Stresa is Lago Maggiore's most vivacious and celebrated town. It is filled with exquisite villas within the town and on its outskirts. **Villa Pallavicino** is famous for its graceful gardens, and **Villa Ducale** is known as the residence of the philosopher, Antonio Rosmini (1797-1855). Take a short drive from Stresa to the top of **Monte Mottarone** for a gorgeous view of the Alps, the lake and the town. The next town is the small, peaceful town of **Baveno**, northwest of Stresa. Many rich people built villas here. One of them, **Castello Bianca** is well-known for its visitor, Queen Victoria who spent the spring of 1879 here. South from Stresa to **Arona** is a very beautiful drive, with its tree-lined roads and breathtaking views of dazzling lakes and islands. Arona itself is unexciting with a few nice 15th century buildings.

Lago di Como has sheer cliffs rising from its shores and Alps forming a wall at one end, it is truly the most impressive lake. The town **Como** specialises and thrives on silk weaving. Go first to see the gardens or the **Giardini Pubblici** commanding a fabulous view of the lake. In the centre of the garden you will find an archetypal rotunda, the **Tempio Voltiamo**. It has an exhibition of

The most special thing about **Lago Maggiore**, the westernmost lake is its three **Borromean Islands**. They were named after a leading Milanese family who owned the lake. One member of that family became a cardinal, another became a bishop, and a third became a saint! In the 16th century, Count Charles Borromeo III tamed and refined **Isola**

the instruments Volta used in his experiments. Take a relaxing stroll to see the beautifully carved 14th century marble cathedral **Santa Maria Maggiore**, with its statues of the two Plinys who were one of the earliest people who were attracted to Lago di Como. It is well worth your time to see the 11th century **Sant' Abbondio** situated just outside Como, it shelters stunningly stirring frescoes depicting the life of Jesus.

Instead of using the winding roads to get to **Bellagio** (its short distance will take you about one hour), a trip by boat from Como's pier is much more enjoyable and memorable. Bellagio's panoramic view of the entire lake and the Alps in the distance is sensational. Take another trip across the lake to **Villa Carlotta**. Its magnificent gardens are too perfect.

At the south-east end of the lake is the town of **Lecco**. It is renown as the backdrop to the 19th century Italian classic 'I promessi sposi' or 'The Bethrothed' by Alessandro Manzoni. In **Villa Manzoni** you will find his childhood home which is open to the public. He was also an important personage in Italian history and played a vital role in bringing about the unification of Italy. Also you can visit the **Basilica**, a sanctuary for 14th century frescoes showing scenes from the life of San Antonio, the Annunciation and Deposition. The oldest monument constructed in 1336-38 is the bridge called the **Ponte Azzone Visconti**, it is over the **Adda** river.

The largest lake is **Lago di Guarda**,

it is also the most clear. Many Northern Europeans come to relax and swim, and it has good sporting facilities like boating and water-skiing. In the **Gardone Riviera**, there is the vulgar home, or rather, shrine, to Gabriele D'Annunzio's dreams of imperial Italy. It is called **Il Vittoriale**, clearly left over from the fascist era. He was a poet and a very close adviser of Mussolini. In his house

A villa beside the placid waters of Lake Maggiore.

you can see his collection which includes the prow of the warship, Puglia, built into a hillside, and hanging from the ceiling, the plane he flew in World War I. The town of **Sirmione** surrounded on three sides by the waters of the lake was built on a small piece of land that juts out into the lake. At one end are the remains of a villa which dates back to Roman times, and at the other is the **Rocca Scaligera Castle**, which used to be owned by the Scaliger family who ruled over Verona. It is said that they used to invite the poet Dante to stay.

Piedmont or **Piemonte** and **Valle D'Aosta** is a north-western Italian region, they share very lengthy borders with Switzerland and France, hence the feel of this expansive region is a comfortable mix of influences from all three countries. The spectacular natural setting of the Alpine panorama in the distance makes Piedmont and Valle D'Aosta an inspirational region to visit in the summer as well as in the winter.

Piedmont & Valle D'Aosta

The sharp peaks of Mont Blanc.

Turin

Turin, the capital of Piedmont is also known as **Torino**. It has ties with France that go centuries back; it was the capital of the French province of Savoy in the 16th century and only in 1861 until 1865, did Turin become the capital of the United Italy following the Risorgimento. Still today the connections can be clearly seen. For example, visit the **Parco del Valentino** with its vast territory of gardens on the shores of the Po River. The

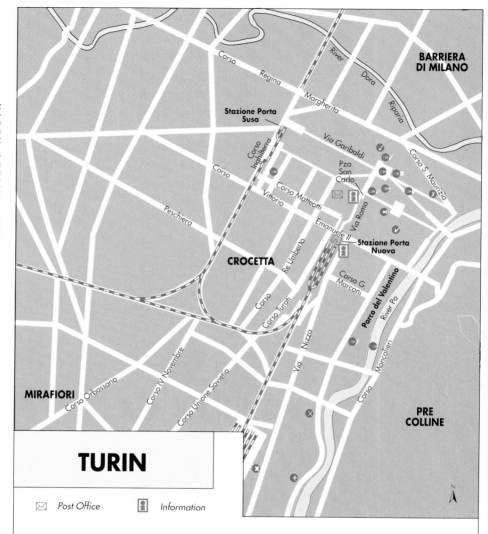

TURIN

BARRIERA
DI MILANO

MIRAFIORI

CROCETTA

PRE
COLLINE

⊠ Post Office   🛈 Information

- Borgo Medioevale
- Camera di Commercio
- Duomo
  Egyptian Museum (Building 10)
  Galleria Subauda (Building 10)
- Hospital (San Giovanni)
- Hospital (Maggiore di San Giovanni Battista)
- Lingotto
- Mole Antonelliana
- Municipio

- Museo dell' Automobile
  Museo Civico del Arte Antica (Building 12)
- Palazzo dell' Accademia delle Scienze
- Palazzo Carignano
- Palazzo Madama
- Palazzo Reale
- Palazzo dell' Universita
- Police
- Teatre Regio
- Torino Esposizioni

The elegant facade of Piazza San Carlo, Turin.

park contains the 17th century **Castello del Valentino** which looks very similar to a French chateau, and there is also a copy of a medieval town called the **Borgo Medioevale**, built in 1884 for an international exhibition.

Turin is well-known in the business world for its industries. Its particular strength is in its car industries; the most successful being the manufacturing of Fiat and Lancia cars. It has strong candy industries, metal indus-

tries and chemical industries, and it is especially famous for industrial design. If you are interested in cars, there is an outstanding automobile museum, the **Carlo Biscaretti di Ruffia Museo dell'Automobile**. Among its admirable collection, they have the first Fiat that was ever made, a gorgeous collectors' item - the Rolls-Royce Silver Ghost, and the Itala that won the world's longest car race held in 1907 from – Paris to Peking.

But for an industrial town, it is unusu-

Ski camps at Sestiere, Piedmont attract many holiday makers from Europe.

The Mole Antonelliana
illuminated.

ally pretty; it has many beautiful gardens, elegant parks and broad streets for relaxing strolls. If you like shopping, take a walk on the street **Via Roma**, which is Turin's main shopping arcade running from the main railway station to the Renaissance period **Piazza Castello**. While in the centre, do visit the 15th century castle **Palazzo Madama** which holds the **Museo Civio di Arte Anchio** or Museum of Ancient Art. Also in the centre is a baroque **church of San Lorenzo**, and in the nearby **Piazza Reale** is the **Palazzo Reale** built in the 17th century. Surprisingly, Turin is also the centre for the study of Egyptian art. There is an excellent **Egyptian museum** off Via Roma, at the **Palazzo dell' Accademia delle**

Scienze. Also in that palazzo is the **Galleria Sabauda** holding some delightful paintings by Piedmontese, Flemish and Dutch master painters.

Turin is also famous for the '**Turin Shroud**' , said to be the actual shroud that Jesus wore. Many pilgrims from all over the world have travelled here to visit this shroud, but note that it can only be viewed on rare occasions. It is said that it is kept in an urn on the altar in the **Capella della Si Sidone** or Chapel of the Holy Shroud by Guarino Guarini.

The whole of the south-east of Turin is a grape-growing and wine-making valley. To try the region's specialities, use the autostrada going in the direction of Alba. Ten kilometres (or 6 miles) from Bra is the town of **La Morra**. This is where Barolo, one of Italy's best wines

Costumed festival in Valle D'aosta.

Tasting grapes in a Vendemmia vineyard, Valle D'aosta.

are made. **Alba** is where gourmets come especially (in October) for white truffles. After you try the truffles, before you move on, you can visit Alba's late 15th century **Gothic cathedral**. The same autostrada will bring you to **Asti**. This is the home of the famous wine, Asti Spumante, and there are many other great wines to try. Between bottles, you may like to see the town's ornate Gothic cathedral and the medieval **Baptistery of San Pietro**.

For an unforgettable view of the Alps, cross the Po and take a bus or train to **Superga** and visit the **Basilica di Superga** by Juvarra, which is on top of a steep hill. The Basilica holds the crypts of various kings of Sardinia and a succession of princes of Savoy.

Valle D'aosta

In the Alpine environs Valle D'Aosta, you can find Europe's highest peaks of **Monte Rosa**, **Mont Blanc** and **Cervino** or the **Matterhorn**. During the winter there are very good ski facilities and ski runs, including glacier skiing, whilst during the summer, there are hiking trails that go by crystalline mountain lakes and rivers, glaciers that date from the ice age, fresh pine forests and meadows, and castles literally in the clouds. The capital of this region is the very Roman **Aosta**. You can visit ancient ruins and walls like the **Roman Theatre** with the particularly intact stage. Another intriguing structure is the 12th

Free-climbing in the summer in the mountain areas of Valgrisenche,
Valle D'aosta.

Town centre of Chatillon, Valle D'aosta.

Mountain goats in Valle D'aosta.

Castle of Chatelard, Valdigne,
Valle D'aosta.

century **church of Sant' Orso**, constructed in an awkward mixture of
Gothic and Romanesque styles. It is situated outside the Roman wall or **Via
Sant' Orso**. The church was named after Saint Orso who was the first to bring
some of the people of Valle D'Aosta to
Christianity. He remains buried under
the altar. Study the carvings on the
pillars in the cloister - each scene depicts
an era from the history of Christianity.

You may like to visit the castles
south-east of Aosta. You can see the
rooms with their elaborate tapestries,
furnitures and collections of jewellery. it
has been said that the most appealing
castles are at **Issogue** and **Fenis**, especially the one built by Giorgio de
Challant, the Lord of Verres in 1497.

Of all the north-eastern regions of Italy, **Trentino-Alto Adige** displays the dichotomy of contrasting cultures to the fullest effect. Bordered to the north by Austria, to the west by Lombardy, and to the east by Veneto, it is split into two distinct areas: **Trentino**, the southern and predominantly Italian speaking part, and the northern **Alto Adige**, actually part of the **Tyrol** (it is known also as the Sud Tirol) which is overwhelmingly Austrian in culture, language and appearance.

Politically and socially the two elements could not be further apart, and this has resulted in friction which occasionally flares into violence. In the sixties and again in the eighties, spates of bombings by political activists brought head-on confrontation with, and military intervention by the Italian Government; therefore unwanted publicity for a region as reliant as this on the

Young Tyrolean woman in typical regional dress.

Trentino-Alto Adige

A view of the Alto Adige Dolomites, with the little chapel of
St. Cipriano in the foreground.

Castle Selva gardens in Alto Adige.

fickle, yet lucrative, tourist trade. The two regional centres are **Trento** in the south, and **Bolzano** (or Bozen in Austrian) in the north.

The physical landscape is dominated by the ranges of the **Dolomites**, which, as part of the eastern Alps, extend from here across the northern parts of Veneto and Friuli-Venezia Giulia. Characterised by their jaggedness and the pinkish colour of the limestone and porphyry rock formations, the Dolomites stretch out on both sides of the Adige valley, in which both Trento and Bolzano lie.

The western Dolomites are best known for the **Marmolade** with its attendant glacier; the **Pale di San Martino**, the **Catinaccio** (Rosengarten) range, and the **Gruppa di Sella**. Further west, the **Dolomiti di Brenta** can be found overlooking the **Valle Rendena**.

To the east, beyond **Passo di Campolongo** and **Corvara**, the eastern range stretches into Veneto. As well as the attraction to walkers, hikers and mountaineers in summer, the Dolomites provide a superb challenge to winter sports thrill-seekers. With many peaks exceeding 10,000 feet, it is a skier's paradise, and it is of little surprise that one of the annual World Cup ski circuit races is held at **Val Gardenia** near Bolzano.

Trento

Trento, the capital of Trentino, was a

Castle of St. Antonio, Bolzano, the capital of Alto Adige.

strategically important (due to its position, like Bolzano, on the approach to the Brenner Pass) Roman town known as Tridentum.

In the Middle Ages it was ruled over by the Prince-Bishops of Trent, and in the 16th century it was notable for its Council, which attempted to put a halt to the Protestant Reformation sweeping the northern regions.

As with all the north-eastern regions, it fell to Napoleon before a long period under Austrian rule, although unlike its northern neighbour Bolzano, Trento has always been strongly Italian in character.

Many of the medieval and 16th century buildings still exist, most notable being the **Duomo** (12th/13th cen-tury; Romanesque and Gothic styles), the **Castello del Buonconsiglio** (in reality two castles: The **Castello Vecchio**, a 13th century fort, and the **Renaissance Palazzo Magni**), and the **Venetian Palazzi** (Renaissance) along the Via Belenzani. A small provincial town, Trento is not a lively city, with restaurants, bars and late-night entertainment decidedly thin on the ground.

Bolzano

The capital of Alto Adige, **Bolzano**, or Bozen (depending on your national and linguistic allegiances) lies in the northern part of the region, acting as the gateway to Austria via the Brenner Pass.

Young farm boys from Sud Tirol.

Trentino's people are predominantly Italian speaking, even though close to the Germanic influenced Tyrolean region.

This is truly an outpost of Austria, a "Little Austria" if you like, holding out against the Italian cultural influences to be found in the south. The stamping ground of both the Italian right-wing MSI and the Austrian secessionist SVP, this area has for decades seen various degrees of partisan infighting, not always in the best interests of the region as a whole.

This northern area, also known as the Southern Tyrol, or **Sud Tirol**, is typified by its Austro-Germanic atmosphere, particularly emphasised by the bilingual street signs and direction indicators. Visitors will usually fare better speaking German than Italian (Mussolini's nationalistic efforts in this area are still remembered, but not fondly!).

Lying at the juncture of the **Talvera** (Talfer) and **Isarco** (Eisack) rivers, just before they join the Adige, Bolzano has the typical Germanic appearance of most settlements in the Alto Adige.

Like Trento, Bolzano was an important Roman settlement, acting as a stepping-off point for the armies marching north into Europe via Austria. The Middle Ages were a time of turbulence for the city as it was passed to and fro in the power play of the twin antagonists of the Bishops of Trento and the Tyrolean Counts, while the vicissitudes of the 19th century were enlivened by the involvement of Bavaria in the Venetian/Napoleonic/Hapsburg struggles.

Mainly Tyrolean in architecture, with some interesting Gothic and ba-

Horse-back riding in the mountain farms.

The church tower of the former
submerged village in Lake Resla,
Alto Adige.

roque examples, Bolzano's central
square is the **Piazza Walther**
(Waltherplatz), dominated by the 14th
century Duomo (more of a parish church
really) with its mosaic roof and intri-
cately carved spire, and the nearby
Chiesa dei Domenicani. It is around
this piazza that most of the interesting
cafes and bars are to be found, most
overlooking the statue of the *minnesinger*
or troubadour, Walther von der
Vogelweide, after whom the piazza is
named.

For those who like crowds, a splendid open-air fruit market is held daily in
the **Piazza della Erbe** (where else?!),
while a flea market is held every Saturdays for those whose love to rummage.

On the outskirts is **Gries**, once a
resort town, now swallowed up into
Bolzano itself. Noted for its church with
carved alterpiece by the Tyrolean painter
and sculptor Michael Pacher, it also
boasts various interesting Gothic buildings. Not a town that likes to stay up
late, Bolzano is a quiet, restful town,

Winter serenity at Lake Garda, Trentino.

more of a resting place for the traveller to recharge before taking on the challenge of the high Dolomites beyond.

Throughout the region there are many small and charming inns and hotels where those who enjoy scenic holidays and quiet walks can park themselves, where the people are friendly, but without the temperament and the colour of the South.

Summertime sailing on Lake Caldaro, Alto Adige.

Bordered to the north by Austria, to the east by the former Yugoslavian state of Slovenia, and to the west by the Veneto, **Friuli-Venezia Giulia** is a small region which cannot help but be heavily influenced by its surroundings.

Mountainous in the north, where the Dolomites become the Giulian (or Julian) Alps, further south-east the Julian foothills open out into the Friuli region, a highly-independent area with a strong sense of regional identity. In the extreme south-east, the foothills give way to the **Carso**, a limestone plateau rich in swallow holes, dolines and caverns, and which is of such immense speleological importance that it has given its name to the karst phenomenon found in many limestone areas in other parts of the world.

The culture of this region is a potpourri of historical and geographical influences. As with all the north-eastern Alpine regions of Italy, the north is Austrian in

A crypt of frescoes in the Basilica at Aquileia in Friuli.

343

Trieste & Friuli-Venetia Giulia

After the Dolomitic north the Giulian Alps open out into the Friulian foothills and fields.

aspect, due both to the proximity of the border and the Hapsburg rule in the 19th century. The eastern and coastal areas reveal, in varying degrees, Roman, Venetian, Napoleonic and Slovenian influences.

These cultural influences are reflected, as always, in the food and drink and customs of the region. In equal parts Italian, Austrian, Hungarian, Slovenian and Greek, the food especially, varies dramatically from area to area, and sometimes with eccentric contrasts in taste and style. The blindfolded traveller would be forgiven for not knowing what country he was in!

The wines of Friuli-Venezia Giulia come mostly from the southern half, the three most important areas being **Grave del Friuli** (between **Pordenone** and **Udine**), **Collio** (around **Gorizia**) and **Colli Orientali** (along the eastern border with Slovenia). Until recently, most wine production has been of white, simply labelled as Tocai, with a smaller amount of red Merlot slipping through.

All that is changing, with some excellent varietal whites being grown, and a growing number of quality reds. New viticulture areas are establishing themselves, including the Carso, on the extreme south-eastern edge.

Beer drinking is becoming more popular amongst Italians, and **Udine** has established itself as the brewing capital of Italy, producing beer for both the home and export market.

The major earthquake of 1976 caused extensive damage, and in many areas rebuilding work is still ongoing (it is worth noting that many buildings of historical interest still remain closed to the public).

The Friulians are a hardy, resolute people, and the daunting task of rebuilding does not appear to have discouraged them.

Trieste

Trieste, the capital of Friuli Venezia Giulia, is found at the easternmost tip of the region, by the Slovenian border. The drive down the coast from **Monfalcone** is spectacular, bringing you down from the coastal plateau to the winding coast stretching along the **Golfe di Trieste**.

The views from the coastal road as it winds its way along the white limestone cliffs, and through innumerable tunnels, offering glimpses of the azure and turquoise Adriatic, take one's breath away. In many ways the panoramas beggar those of the Ligurian coast, or the Corniches outside Monte Carlo.

Trieste itself is the smallest capital of a region with a winding coastline

that stretches for fifteen kilometers along the gulf. As you travel along the coastal road you pass the **castle of Duino**, a double fortress (the **Castello Vecchio** and the **Castello Nuovo**) overlooking the Bay of Sistiana, while further down the coast you find **Miramare Castle**, an imposing Hapsburg residence marking the eastern end of the **Riviera di Barcola**.

The last few kilometers of your approach is along the sea fronts of Trieste. With its expansive coastline running down into the blue waters of the Adriatic, framed by the backdrop of the city and port, this area has long been a familiar port amongst Europeans.

Finally, as the approach road brings you alongside the train station (which, incidentally, houses one of the most comprehensive and helpful ENIT tourist offices to be found in Italy), the city centre opens up, dominated by **San Giusto Hill** with its cathedral, castle and Roman basilica.

History

Trieste has had a checkered history, primarily due to its proximity to several hostile city-states and countries.

It was originally a Roman city, Tergestum, and many Roman ruins still exist, or have been incorporated into later architectural styles. In the Middle Ages it suffered repeated attacks from Venice (at that time the dominant power in the region), and eventually placed itself under the protection of the Austro-

Castle of Mirimare, Trieste.

Hungarian Empire, where it was to remain for over 500 years. It was not until the early 18th century that it began to flourish under its new status as a free port. It was at this time that the city's current appearance was created, mostly at the instigation of the Hapsburg Empress Maria Theresa, who expanded the seaport and docks, and laid the basis for the grid pattern of streets in the **Borgo Teresiano**. This influx of development attracted other Europeans investors, and Trieste soon became the major trade centre in the Adriatic, eclipsing the waning influence of Venice.

Commerce, banking and finance houses established themselves here, and just as Venice had given the world the

further hardships lay in store.

Following World War II, the surrounding areas of the Istrian peninsula and most of the Carso were handed over to the former Yugoslavia. Ownership of Trieste was also in dispute, and in 1947 it was declared a free territory by the United Nations. It was not until 1954 that it was returned to Italy, and not before 1964 that it became the capital of the region.

Since then, problems imposed by the Belgrade government in the form of tax penalties in the early 1980s, and more recently the breakup of the Yugoslavian states and resultant warfare, have cut off the income and commerce so long enjoyed with the neighbouring state of Slovenia. Modern Trieste is a quiet, sedate city – more than half the inhabitants are retired, the young having moved out to the more cosmopolitan and industrial centres of **Udine** and **Padova**, with the exception of those involved in banking, insurance, and the fledgling electronics industry.

Courted, fought over, and finally dispossessed, Trieste today has the air of an ageing dowager, a once-proud beauty fallen on hard times, with only her glorious past to look back on.

Out and about

Despite the sprawling seafront, Trieste is not at all a large city, and a day should be more than enough to see the major sights in the city. Most of the buildings

concept of banking, so Trieste became the birthplace of modern insurance.

The reunification with Italy in 1918 was to prove Trieste's downfall, as she was cut off from her Slavic and Austro-Hungarian neighbours, the traditional hinterland of the region. Badly damaged in the first World War, and German occupation during World War II (and the establishment of a concentration camp, now a Resistance memorial)

to be seen date from the late 18th and 19th centuries, and this is amply illustrated in the **Piazza dell'Unita d'Italia** and surrounding streets. Overlooking the sea between **Molo Audace** and **Molo Bersaglieri**, the Piazza's main structure is the **Palazzo Communale** (Town Hall), designed by Giuseppe Bruni in 1877. Flanking the Piazza are several 19th century buildings of interest, including the **Palazzo Modello** (also by Bruni), the **Casa Stratti** and its famous **Caffe degli Specchi**, and the **Palazzo Pitteri**, Trieste's best example of baroque architecture. Opposite the Palazzo Pitteri is the **Mazzoleni fountain**, incorporating a representation of the four continents known at the time (1750).

Southwards along the waterfront is the **Stazione Marittima** (now a conference centre), and by it, the **Pescheria Centrale** (fish market). Abutting it is an interesting aquarium, with an impressive array of sea flora and fauna (not, as far as can be ascertained, part of the fish market's stock!).

Behind the town hall, a few hundred metres north, is the **Teatro Romano**. Only discovered and excavated in 1938, it was built in the latter half of the first century AD, and lies on the lower slope of San Giusto Hill, overlooking the sea.

On the hill itself, you find the ruins of the Roman Forum, with its Civil Basilica, lying between the Cathedral and the Castle (it was discovered under the Cathedral courtyard). The **Cattedrale di San Giusto** was built in the 14th

century by linking two existing basilicas, and is itself built on the ruins of a Roman Propylaeum.

The **Castle of San Giusto** is an imposing structure, not least for the numerous styles on display, hardly surprising when one discovers it took almost two centuries to build on the ruins of earlier fortresses (see "Quattro Castelli" page 351). The ivy-covered round ramparts seem to grow from the hill itself, and the view from here encompasses the entire city, sea, and Carso. The Castle is open daily, as are certain rooms which have been turned into a civic museum (open mornings only, with an admission charge), and the garden of **Orto Lapidario**, where Roman and medieval archeological finds excavated in Trieste and the surrounding region are on display.

The other great feature of San Giusto Hill is the **Scalinata dei Giganti**, or Giants' Staircase, which links the top of the hill with the **Piazza Carlo Goldoni**. The base of the staircase (steps flanking ornate terraced gardens) spans the mouth of a road tunnel (the Galleria Sandrinelli), connecting the Piazza to the southern side of the hill. The Piazza, an important road intersection for the city, was originally the site of a medieval leper hospital, but since the 17th century has hosted a bustling market!

For longer stays, half-day and full-day trips are recommended to the Carso region with its awe-inspiring rock formations and underground caverns. The **Grotta Gigante**, the largest natural cave

The wooded northern Alpine tracks are occasionally dotted with small altars.

known to man (it could happily accommodate St. Peter's cathedral) is an absolute must. Other places of interest are the surrounding castles of **Duino** and **Miramare**, and the delightful little fishing port of **Muggia** (also with a castle).

For those planning a longer stopover, ferries are available (both from Trieste and Venice) to a variety of destinations in the Adriatic and Mediterranean, including Ancona, Bari, Brindisi, Corfu, Piraeus (Athens), Heraklion, and Alexandria (Egypt)!

Bars and cafes

Despite the sedate and 'laid-back' atmosphere, the social scene in Trieste is varied, and diverse cafes, bars and restaurants abound (but don't expect bars and restaurants to stay open too late!). The cafes are worthy of note, in that they are meeting points for artists, writers and poets, as well as bankers, financiers and market-makers. Many have reading rooms with newspapers and magazines on display. Of the better known, the Caffe San Marco in Via Battista, the Caffe degli Specchi in Piazza del'Unita del Italia, and the Stella Polare in front of the Chiesa di Sant'Antonio are well worth a visit.

Food and drink

The food, and to an extent the wine of

The Carso

The **Carso** is a massive limestone plateau, formed over millions of years, which forms the basis of the geology of the Trieste area, and extends well into modern Slovenia.

The permeability of the rock means that surface water is rarely found (with the exception of a few ponds and lakes, found in the basins of dolines) - the percolation of water through the limestone strata has led to the creation of the typical rock formations now described as karst phenomena. Swallow holes, dolines and caverns abound, with the caves and grottoes being of particular interest from the historical as well as geological point of view, as early prehistoric human settlements having been unearthed throughout the region.

The most famous (and accessible) of these caverns is the **Grotta Gigante** (Giant Grotto) about 16 kilometres north of Trieste near **Opicina**. The largest natural cavern known to man, it is over 100 meters high, 65 meters wide and 280 meters long.

Now fitted out with staircases, walkways and lighting, the cave is open to the public (except Mondays) and guided trips are available, highlighting the many rock formations typical of karstian limestone areas, including stalagmites and stalagtites. There is an adjacent speleological and archaeological museum.

From the center of Trieste, the most picturesque (if not the quickest) way to reach the Grotta Gigante and the rest of the Carso is to take the tram from Piazza Oberdan to the village of Opicina.

Aside from the geological aspects of the area, there are several Bronze-Age settlements to be visited (known as the **Castellieri**), as well as the charming villages of the Carso, in the ethnic Slovenian style and preserving many of the centuries-old folklore traditions.

The fauna of the area is plentiful and diverse, but it is the flora which bring botanists from near and far, exhibiting as it does a curious blend of Mediterranean, Balkan, Illyrian and sub-Alpine features.

Hardly surprisingly considering the terrain, the Carso is also a favorite stamping ground for walkers and ramblers, as well as a Mecca for mountaineers (the national mountaineering school, the Rifugio Premuda, is based here).

Trieste is, not surprisingly, decidedly multi-ethnic. The cheapest and most convenient way of sampling the local cuisine is to visit one of the many buffets to be found, where one eats (and drinks) at a counter.

One local favourite is Rebechin, a combination of dishes usually comprising porzina (pork with mustard), sausages, Prague ham, goulash and tripe! Other popular snacks include salami, Tafelspitz (strips of boiled beef) and Jota (tepid bean soup served with sauerkraut). Desserts and cakes owe little to any Italian heritage – strudels, Krapfen and Sacher tortes from Austria; Dobos and Rigojanci from Hungary; Putizza and Presniz from Slovenia, all of which not lacking in variety or deliciousness.

The Trieste region is a well respected wine growing area, producing good Pinot Grigio, Tocai and Merlot, although it has to be said that the whites are the region's speciality. Wines from the Carso are now commonplace and improving in quality.

While wine is still the regional drink, beers of all descriptions are drunk - the ever-increasing local beers of Udine, as well as Austrian, German, and Slovenian imports can be found to cater to the Tyrolean taste for beer.

Muggia

Wedged between the sprawling industrial zones of Trieste and the Slovenian border, sits the medieval walled town of **Muggia**. This is a charming fishing port, little known to tourists and Italians alike, which boasts a castle, a cathedral, and famous walled fortifications. The small piazzas and cobbled streets conceal picturesque bars and restaurants, where the local fare (mainly seafood, excellent as always in this corner of Italy) has definite elements of both Venetian and Istrian cuisine.

Overlooking the dock is the small **Basilica dell'Assunta**, a pretty 10th century church, where many local works of art are housed, including bas-reliefs, sculptures and frescoes.

Gorizia

To the north-west is the ancient town of **Gorizia**, with its formidable castle, home to the Dukes of Gorizia, who ruled the area for four centuries before the Venetians, after whom Austro-Hungarians came to prominence. Subject to the same disruptions as the rest of this part of Italy during the last four hundred years, Gorizia was particularly affected by the border changes following World War II – the eastern part of the town was ceded to the former Yugoslavia! A "new Gorizia", Nova Gorica, was built up around this.

The appearance of Gorizia today owes much to the forces which shaped Trieste, in particular to Empress Maria Theresa of the Hapsburg Empire. Neo-classical and Romanesque buildings predominate, and one well worth a look at (from the exterior only, as it is closed for restoration) is the **Palazzo Attems** in the **Piazza de Amicis**.

Udine

Udine, further north-west, is the capital of the Friulian area. A hill town, it was originally a Roman garrison, and is rumoured to have been Attila the Hun's resting place while he watched the burning of Aquileia. The city's long Venetian heritage is evident in its buildings, as well as in the many canals which crisscross the town.

Modern Udine is an industrial centre, renowned for its metalworks, clothmaking, and increasingly for its brewing (Udine is fast becoming the beer capital of Italy, with such fine examples as Peroni Nastro Azzuri and Sans Souci).

Sights worthy of note include the **Piazza Liberta**, with its buildings and monuments clearly evincing the Venetian influence (the **Palazzo del Comune** and the **Torre dell'Orologio** echoing the Doges' Palace and the Clock Tower in Saint Mark's Square), the Castello on the hill, and the Duomo. North of Udine is the small town of **San Daniele del Friulli**, a picturesque settle-

Elaborate floor mosaic in the Basilica at Aquileia, Friuli.

ment made famous by its prosciutto di San Daniele, reputed to be the finest smoked ham in all of Italy, the greater quantity of which exported elsewhere in Europe.

The Carnia

Further north is the area known as the **Carnia**, which encompasses the Giulian Alps and their foothills. The capital of the area is **Gemona**, which was devastated by the 1976 earthquake (300 inhabitants lost their lives).

Tucked away in the extreme northeastern corner is the **Alpie Giulie National Park** with the twin lakes of the **Laghi di Fusine**.

The Southern flatlands

Palmanove, to the south of Udine, is a stunning Venetian fortress designed around a nine-pointed star, converging on the large central hexagonal piazza. Continue south along the flatlands (the alluvial plains of the **Isonzo** and **Tagliamento** rivers) and you will come across the ancient Roman city of **Aquileia**, and the resort and spa town of **Grado** on the coast.

Pordenone to the west is the third largest town of Friuli Venezia Giulia, and the most industrialised, specialising in electronics (like Trieste), textiles (as does Udine), and ceramics. There are various art and folklore museums to

The Quattro Castelli

Standing on the white clifftops of the Trieste Riviera, with the panorama of the Carso and the blue Adriatic beyond, who could blame anyone for building a palace or fortress to claim that spot for themselves? This is exactly what people of vision, be they romantics or strategists, have been doing for centuries. Castles abound along this coast, but it is the Quattro Castelli, the castles of **Duino**, **Miramare**, **San Giusto**, and **Muggia** which dominate.

Just south-east of where the Timavo river emerges from its underground course and flows into the Adriatic, the small village of Duino juts out into the sea. As a natural vantage-point, a fortified presence has been maintained here since Roman times, when two lookout towers were built (one of which is incorporated into part of the current buildings).

The castle as it stands today is actually two fortresses: the **Castello Vecchio**, the ancient keep, older of the two and whose age is not known; and the **Castello Nuovo**, built in the late 14th century on a high promontory.

Legends abound about the castle of Duino, most famous of which is the story of the Dama Bianca (White Lady), who was hurled from the ramparts by her husband and was turned to stone by her own screams before reaching the sea below.

Beyond the Bay of Sistiana, and further down the coast, is the Castle of Miramare, a Hapsburg residence commissioned by Maximillian, younger brother of the Hapsburg Emperor Franz Joseph, in 1856. A dazzling white building along the neo-Renaissance style, it was not completed until 1870, three years after Maximillian's death at the hands of Mexican rebels (he had accepted the Mexican crown in 1863). The rooms of the castle are exquisitely appointed, each in their own style (Rococo, Gothic, Japanese, etc) as was the 19th century custom.

The castle boasts an extensive park (22 hectares) again divided into themed areas - a swan lake, alpine pavillions and eldritch caves among others. Today the castle is a heritage museum, and regularly holds "Son et Lumiere" spectacles.

The Castle of San Giusto stands proud atop San Giusto Hill, a massive fortress overlooking Trieste and its bay. Originally the site of a Roman forum and basilica, later walled in, it is likely there was an earlier prehistoric settlement.

Various castles and fortresses were built in the Dark Ages, of which few traces remain, and it was not until 1470 that work on the current structure commenced. It took nearly two hundred years to complete the castle as it stands today, due to conflicts, wars, and financial crises, which explain the wide variety of styles implemented. Frederick III's original rectangular building with squared battlements, the later Venetian round rampart (1508-9), the Hoyos-Lalio rampart (1553-61), and the Pomis (flowered) rampart of 1630, all come together to form a incongruous, but imposing, spectacle.

In the centre of a pretty little medieval fishing port to the east of Trieste, the Castle of Muggia was built in the 14th century on earlier Roman and Dark Ages fortifications. Together with the ancient walls of the town, this fort formed an integral part of the town's defences.

Much of the castle as seen today only dates from the beginning of this century, when considerable rebuilding work was undertaken.

Little is known of the castle's original appearance, as contemporary drawings and descriptions have proved contradictory. Unfortunately, although once communal property, the Castle is now privately owned.

visit (including the **Museo Civico Ricchieri** and the **Museo Provinciale della Vita Contadina**), but many of the exhibits (particularly paintings and santuary) have been removed following the earthquake. Except perhaps for business visits, it is not an area which attracts many visitors and tourists.

Venice & Veneto

Venice, often described as "the most beautiful city in the world", has both its admirers and detractors. D.H. Lawrence once referred to it as "an abhorrent, green, slippery city"! Whether one loves it or hates it, **Venice** cannot help but impress the first-time visitor. With its pervasive atmosphere of faded elegance (many of the beautiful buildings and edifices along the **Grand Canal** are in a sad state of disrepair) and aura of centuries-old decadence, **La Serenissima**, as Venice is known to its inhabitants, leaves one with indelible memories that will haunt forever. Little wonder, then, that film directors have made a bee-line for this waterbound "city of wraiths" to create some of the most evocative of cinematic oeuvres, such as the adaptation of Mann's 'Death in Venice' and Roeg's 'Don't Look Now'. It has always attracted creative genius: Browning, Lord Byron, Henry James, and Wagner all came here for in-

Mask souvenirs make brisk sales in the St. Mark's area of Venice.

355

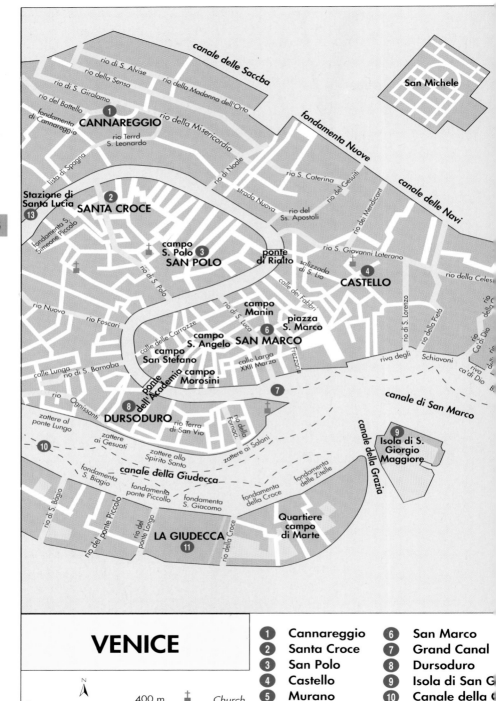

canale delle Saccba

San Michele

rio di S. Alvise
rio della Sensa
rio di S. Girolamo
rio del Battello
rio della Madonna dell'Orto
fondamenta
di Cannareggio

CANNAREGGIO ❶

rio Terrd
S. Leonardo

rio della Misericordia

fondamenta Nuove

canale delle Navi

lista di Spagna

rio di Noale

strada Nuova

rio S. Caterina

rio del Gesuiti

rio dei Mendicanti

Stazione di
Santa Lucia

❶❸ **SANTA CROCE** ❷

fondamenta S.
Simeone Piccolo

rio del
Ss. Apostoli

rio S. Giovanni Laterano

campo
S. Polo ❸

SAN POLO

ponte
di Rialto

salizzada
di S. Lio

CASTELLO ❹

rio della Celes

rio di S. Polo

rio Nuovo

rio Foscari

colle dei Fabbri

rio di S. Luca

campo
Manin

piazza
S. Marco

rio S. Lorenzo

rio della Pietà

riva Ca di Dio

calle delle Carrozze

campo
S. Angelo

SAN MARCO ❻

riva degli Schiavoni

ca di Dio

campo
San Stefano

calle Larga
XXII Marzo

Frezzaria

calle Lunga

rio di S. Barnaba

ponte
dell'Academia

campo
Morosini

❼

canale di San Marco

rio
Ognissanti

DURSODURO ❽

rio Terra
di San Vio

rio della
Fornaci

canale della Grazia

**Isola di S.
Giorgio
Maggiore** ❾

zattere al
ponte Lungo

zattere
ai Gesuati

zattere allo
Spirito Santo

zattere ai Saloni

❿

canale della Giudecca

fondamenta
S. Biagio

fondamenta
ponte Piccollo

fondamenta
S. Giacomo

fondamenta
della Croce

fondamenta
delle Zitelle

rio di S. Biagio

rio del
ponte Piccolo

rio del
ponte Longo

LA GIUDECCA ⓫

rio della Croce

Quartiere
campo
di Marte

VENICE

❶ Cannareggio	❻ San Marco
❷ Santa Croce	❼ Grand Canal
❸ San Polo	❽ Dursoduro
❹ Castello	❾ Isola di San G
❺ Murano	❿ Canale della (

N

0 — 400 m
440 y

✝ Church

spiration. A city of the Arts, it was here that the Bellini family established the Venetian school of painting, nurturing such talents as Giovanni, Titian, Tintoretto, Veronese and Giorgione; and later Tiepolo, Guardi and Canaletto.

Venice is a collection of 117 islets and islands, criss-crossed by 177 canals and interlinked by innumerable bridges. This "floating city", a complex "cats-cradle" of streets, alleyways, canals and bridges, relies on water as its lifeline, yet is paradoxically threatened by that same source (see "Venice in Peril?" page 374). The myriad tributary canals feed into the **Grand Canal**, the arterial thoroughfare of the city, and provide the only practical methods of transport, haulage, drainage and waste disposal. The city is protected from the sea by the natural breakwater of the **Lido**, a long, narrow sandbar which separates the lagoon from the Adriatic.

The centre, where most of the famous sights are to be found, is clustered on a closely-knit group of islands known as the **Rialto**. Off across the bay are the Lido, and the islands (or Isola) of **Murano** (the home of Venetian coloured glass blowing), **Burano** (famous for its lace), and **Torcello** (eclipsed by Venice, now only of real interest for its Byzantine architecture).

The Venetian year

Venice is inundated with visitors dur-

The famous Rialto Bridge over the Grand Canal.

ber, and, naturally enough, it is at this time that most people see it.

During the autumn and winter months, Venice is pretty much a ghost town, with a large proportion of the commerce houses and hotels closing up, with the exception of Christmas week and the time of the Feste. The two main winter festivals are the **Festa della Madonna della Salute**, on November 21st, celebrating the deliverance of the city from the plague of 1630, and of course, the **Carnivale**, held in mid-February, the legendary masked and costumed extravaganza made famous in the centuries heralding the height of the city's power. This is the best time to visit Venice (or make a return trip if you've been before in summer) – the pearlescent winter light and fog rolling in from the Adriatic give the city a moribund appearance, and make a dramatic backdrop to the pageantry being enacted before you. Two other festivals are held during the summer months – the **Feste del Redentore** in July (celebrating the end of another plague!), and **La Regatta Storica** (September), a regatta starting with a gala procession of boats along the Grand Canal and culminating in gondola races.

History

Venice was first settled in the first century by refugees from the Italian mainland, fleeing the armies of Attila the

Masquerade time during Carnevale in Venice.

Hun and other barbarian invaders. Over the next couple of centuries, this industrious people built a thriving community, connecting the islands by bridges, dredging the sea channels, and even diverting the course of the River Brenta. Venice soon established itself as a seaport of immense importance to the Mediterranean trade routes, serving the ascendant Byzantine Empire.

In the early centuries, the Venetians were ruled by Maritime Tribunes, but as the Byzantine Empire's influence took hold, administrative government transferred to the Doge, a democratically-elected official. Thus was born one of the world's first true democracies. But this state of affairs was not to last. By the end of the 12th century, the right of election of the Doge had passed to the powerful Venetian families, who had formed themselves into the "Great Council", and the former democracy became, by stages, an aristocracy.

Venice's Golden Age dawned in the 13th century, when, as the power of Byzantium declined, the Venetians saw an opportunity to break away from the Empire. In 1215, the Doge, Enrico Dandolo, amazingly persuaded the Fourth Crusade (who had chartered his fleet) to forestall its mission and assist in the sacking of Byzantium (Constantinople, now Istanbul). The spoils of war were brought triumphantly back to Venice, and to this day one can see the four bronze horses of Byzantium in the Basilica di San Marco.

The glass-blowers of Murano have mastered the art of making impossible-looking shapes.

Venice was now the world's foremost seaport, providing the gateway to the East and the silk and spice routes. The world's trade channelled through Venice. Commerce flourished, and the concept of banking as we know it today was born. The stock exchange, letters of credit and commercial contracts all originated in Venice at this time.

One of Venice's most famous sons was **Marco Polo**, but ironically, it was another great sea explorer who spelled Venice's downfall. As Constantinople (as it was then known) fell to the Ottoman Empire, Vasco de Gama, a Portuguese explorer, discovered a sea route to India, obviating the need for Western European trades to use Venice as an important staging post.

Venice declined steadily until 1797, when, in the first defeat of her history, she was conquered by Napoleon Bonaparte's army, and in the Treaty of Campoformio, bartered to the Austrian-Hapsburg Empire. It was not until the plebiscite of 1866 that the city was restored to the newly-unified Italy.

How to get there

Although there are regular ferry services from **Chioggia**, most visitors approach Venice from the land, crossing the three-mile bridge across the lagoon from **Mestre**, an unprepossessing little town whose claim to fame, apart from servicing the docks (Venice is still Italy's

The Regatta Storica, a colourful event in the Grand Canal.

second largest shipping port), is as the gateway to Venice.

Although tourists are often advised to part or alight from the train at Mestre (there are plentiful supervised car parks and regular bus services to Venice), the most direct route is to proceed all the way to the terminus at **Tronchetto** (car or bus) or the **Stazione San Lucia** (rail). Water buses (vaporetti) serve the entire Venice area from these points. There are three classes of service: "accelerato", "diretto", and "direttissimo" (don't be fooled: "accelerato" is the slowest service, making all local stops;"direttissimo" the quickest).

Thus the visitor's first view of Venice is from a vaporetto, and this will be the cheapest and most worthwhile ex-

pense of your visit. A one-way trip to **Piazza San Marco** on Linie 34 will cost about L2000, last about 35 minutes, and combine the best elements of an efficient public transport service and a sightseeing tour.

The Grand Canal

Moments after leaving Tronchetto, you pass under the **Ponte di Scalzi**, an impressive wooden bridge which, surprisingly enough, was only erected in 1934. Next to the bridge, on the left bank, is the **Church (Chiesa) of the Scalzi**, a beautiful example among the many baroque facades to be found along the **Grand Canal**.

Canaletto's magnificent Renaissance painting, "Dipinto di Venezia".

A regatta galley and crew in full regalia.

Along the banks, filling the space between the baroque churches and Gothic palaces (many with ornate friezes at first floor level), are the more modest residences, with their shuttered windows and trelliswork balconies. A wild palette of colours have been used: reds, greens, browns, blues, ochres, all reflecting off the murky waters below. Fleeting glimpses are caught of side canals; dark and shadowy they reveal little - a fairytale bridge perhaps, or a forgotten chapel.

As you turn into a tight, blind, right-hand bend, you pass under the arch of the **Ponte di Rialto**, surely one of the best-known of Venetian landmarks. Erected in the 16th century, it replaced an earlier, wooden structure, and was designed to allow a war galley in full sail to pass under its arch.

As you pass, you will notice the character of the canal change – pavement cafes and smart restaurants appear, gondolas bob around everywhere, and motoscafi ply their trade along this watery highway. The streets and sidewalks are thronged with people. This, then, is the heart of Venice, bounded by the twin bastions of the daytripper armies: the Ponte di Rialto here, and the **Piazza San Marco** half a mile or so downstream. Further down, as you pass the **Ponte dell' Accademia**, the canal widens and becomes the **Canale di San Marco**. On the right, you see the **Church of Santa Maria della Salute**, and next to it, the 17th century maritime customs

Piazza San Marco, the Companile, and Doge's Palace on the Grand Canal.

building of **Punta della Dogana**. Away across the **Bacino di San Marco**, the **Isola di San Giorgio Maggiore** and its splendid church by **Palladio** can be seen.

At the landing stage of **San Zaccaria**, you fight to get off as hordes stream on board for the onward journey to the **Lido**, with its beaches, bars, restaurants, and of course, the **Casino**!

Piazza San Marco and environs

The **Piazza San Marco** is now some two hundred metres back the way you have come. Don't be in too much of a hurry to dash there, for there is plenty to see on the casual stroll. The **Ponte dei Suspiri** (**Bridge of Sighs**) is easy to miss, tucked away between the **Doges' Palace** and the prisons. Allegedly named after the lamentations of convicted prisoners catching their final glimpses of the Bacino di San Marco through the tiny windows, it is in effect an ornate covered walkway linking the Offices of the **State Inquisitors Offices** in the **Palazzo Ducale** with the **Prigioni Nuove** (New Prison) at first floor level. One of it most famous inmates (and indeed escapees) was **Casanova**, imprisoned for sorcery and irreverence!

The Palazzo Ducale, or Doges' Palace, is probably the finest example of the Gothic architecture in Europe remaining today. First built in the ninth

The exquisitely painted ceilings of the basilica of San Marco.

century, the current facade dates back to about 1400, and apart from the Gothic portico and double loggia, is most noticeable for the pink and white marble geometric designs on its upper sections. Inside, the Grand Council Chamber (**Sala del Maggiore Consiglio**) and the Doge's private chambers are well worth a visit. Fine works of art are on display, including works by Tintoretto, Veronese, Giovane, Rizzi, Bandini and even Heironymus Bosch! The Palace is open daily to the public, and there is an admission charge.

Along the Piazzetta is the magnificent **Basilica di San Marco**, an intricately-decorated Byzantine edifice crowned with Gothic additions. Designed around the shape of a Greek cross, with

five cupolas or domes, the present structure dates from the 11th century, although this was added to continuously until the mid-1500s. The facade comprises five portals, the central one being an enormous elaborately worked structure of three concentric arches flanked by four marble columns. Above this, copies of the four bronze horses of San Marco prance. The originals, removed in 1980, are on display inside the Basilica, protected from weather risks.

Inside the Basilica, a veritable treasure trove is unveiled, testimony to the Venetians' talent for commerce, and indeed warfare over the centuries. Fabulous works of art and sculpture brought back from the Orient by traders and merchants stand cheek-by-jowl with the loot and booty from innumerable voyages of conquest. The flooring is a wonderful variegated marble carpet (it was very uneven due to subsidence until recently, when a restoration project involving the injection of massive amounts of pre-stressed concrete was undertaken), while the walls and cupolas are covered with intricate mosaics. Within the sanctuary (open daily, with a charge for admission), you will find the main altar, built over the burial place of Saint Mark, and above it is what must be the finest example of the goldsmith's art, the fabulous altarpiece, the **Pala d'Oro**.

The **Treasury** (also open daily with an admission charge) contains much of the pillage from the sack of Constantinople, and other subjects including the **Ortorphoron** (an 11th century silver casket for holding the sacrement), and the throne of Saint Mark, which is believed to have been made in the 6th or 7th century. The four bronze horses of Saint Mark can be found in the **Marciano Museum**, a small room on the first floor with galleries offering unparalleled views of the rich, often ornate mosaics of the Basilica.

Leaving the Basilica, with the Piazzetta to your left, the Piazza San Marco (St. Mark's Square) opens out in front of you. Across the way to your left is the **Campanile** (Belltower of St. Mark's). The original belltower collapsed on the morning of July 30th, 1902, without any (human) injuries as the Venetians are not noted for their early rising (the only fatality was the sexton's

Domes and facades of San Marco.

cat!). The current building, an exact replica, was erected in 1912, and from the top offers spectacular views of Venice, the Adriatic beyond the Lido, and on a clear day, the foothills of the Alps.

To the right of the square, you will see the **Torre dell'Orologio**, or Clock tower, an elegant Renaissance structure where the hours have been struck for the past five centuries by the two magnificient bronze Moors.

St. Mark's Square itself is probably the most photographed public square in the world. It is bounded on its north side by the **Procuratie Vecchie** (Old Procuratie), built in the 16th century.

On the south side is the **Procuratie Nuove**, a 17th century building famous for its columns in the classic Corinthian,

The strategically located Cafe Florian on St. Mark's Square.

Doric and Ionian orders. Spanning the two lateral sides, and opposite the Basilica, is the **Fabbrica Nuova**, commissioned by Napoleon in 1810 to complete the Square's classical balance. The building boasts a facade crowned by the statues of 14 Roman emperors, although the centrepiece, a statue of Napoleon himself, has since been taken down!

Around the Square

During daylight hours, the square is always packed with tourists. The air teems with wheeling pigeons, and the ground bristles with them. Photographers selling bags of seed try to encourage you to pose with one on your outstretched palm, or on your head (it is always advisable, upon leaving the square, to get a friend to check your hair and clothing for tell-tale streaks!).

Under the arches of the surrounding facades, countless shops and boutiques can be found, as well as restaurants and cafes, the most famous of which, the **Cafe Florian** (a beautiful cafe with decor executed in the Louis and Philippe styles) and the **Quadri**, will probably set you back most on the allowance for your trip for a cafe espresso or cappuccino, especially if you sit out in the terrace areas listening to the orchestras. Rest assured that here (and anywhere in Venice within a stones' throw of a national monument), you will be paying a 35-75% premium of

Venetians love their once-a-year make belief at Carnevale.

any consummables.

Out and about

Despite the emphasis on water transport, and the excellent value of the water bus services, the best way to see Venice is on foot. With its rabbits' warren of cobbled streets, alleyways and cul-de-sacs (many ending with a sudden drop into a canal, so be warned), the visitor can spend many happy hours exploring some of the lesser-frequented parts of the city.

This is the area that the more reasonably priced cafes or restaurants can be found. Look for the Tavola Calda, eateries which sell hot food and beverages to be consumed sitting at a stool at the counter – usually excellent in quality, and a fifth of the price you would expect to pay in one of the major squares or on the canalside. A good example of this sort of establishment is the cafe adjoining the **Chat Qui Rit** to the northwest of St. Mark's Square.

From St. Mark's Square, the best direction to take is north, passing through the arch of the clock tower and making your way down **Mercerie**, a narrow winding street effectively cutting the bend of the Grand Canal and leading back to the Ponte di Rialto. Countless shops proliferate, selling souvenirs (who can resist a "Venezia" straw boater!), millinery (if you don't like the boaters, then how about a genuine

Church of Santa Maria della Salute.

panama?), designer fashions and leather goods (very good value, even here in the land of the tourist trap), jewellery, Venetian glasswork, lace, and even electrical and electronic goods.

Off in the sidestreets, you will find plenty of beautiful churches and chapels, including the **Chiesa di San Salvatore**, an imposing 16th century building with later baroque facade, containing statues by Falcone, and paintings by Titian and Giovanni Bellini. It is easy for the uninitiated to get lost in these streets and alleys, for they often look similar, as do the canals you cross. The building numbers do not really help, as they are arranged according to districts, **Sestiere**, rather than by streets or blocks (or canals).

There are directional signs, however, posted on the buildings, leading to the major attractions (in this case San Marco, Accademia and Rialto). Following directions, you eventually come to the Rialto landing stage on the edge of the Grand Canal, with the Rialto bridge off to your right, a good opportunity for a pre-prandial drink at one of the many canalside bars and cafes (but watch out for the prices), before sauntering over the bridge to enjoy an excellent meal at a seafood restaurant on the far bank. Wonderful arrangements of crab, lobster, gambero (prawn), gamberetto (shrimp), oysters and other shellfish adorn the entrances to these establishments, making it impossible to pass them by.

Window boxes of homes fronting the canals of Venice.

On the bridge itself, you may like to investigate the various stalls and boutiques, particularly the one selling traditional dolls, mannequins and carnival masks. Made of papier mache over plaster casts, the traditional Venetian masks are back in vogue again (as a result of the resurgent popularity of the Feste and the Carnivale), and examples of formal carnival masks can be found, as well as the more grotesque commedi dell'arte versions (look out for Arlecchino, Panaleone, and Punchinello).

At this point, most daytrippers will be calling it a day, and be boarding the vaporetti for their onward journey back to Tronchetto. Most will have found their trip merely an appetiser, and will be vowing to return for a more in-depth study of Venice and its environs.

Where to stay

Those more fortunate souls who are staying in Venice for a while will have already made arrangements for accommodation. Those with an upscale budget will be staying either at the **Cipriani** (the most luxurious and expensive hotel in Venice, on the **Isola della Guidecca**, with its exquisite gardens and swimming pool, and 24-hour private motoscafi shuttle service from St. Mark's Square), the **Danieli** (on the Riva degli Schavioni, by the Doges' Palace and the prison, an old, romantic hotel once the residence of one of the 14th century doges), or the **Gritti Palace** (Hemingway's favourite European hotel, a Renaissance building, again a former Doge's residence, facing onto the Grand Canal).

Around St. Mark's

For those of more modest means, there are countless good hotels in the area bounded by St. Mark's Square, the Accademia, and the Ponte di Rialto, many moderately priced.

Night Rambling

Once checked into your hotel, and now fully relaxed, you may like to sample some of the nightlife of Venice. The choice is yours – walk in any direction and you are bound to find a cafe, bar or restaurant to your taste.

Again, it is best to avoid the central piazzas, with their correspondingly higher prices, but the establishments to be found in the backstreets (often offering splendid views of lesser-known canals) will be of high quality and offer good value. Should you choose a bar or restaurant overlooking the Grand Canal, watch out for the bizarre sight of five gondolas in formation working their way slowly upstream, an audience of enraptured tourists (usually Japanese) listening to gondoliers singing Venetian folk songs accompanied on an accor-

Gondola parking posts, famous symbols of Venice.

dion by a veritable gymnast leaping expertly from boat to boat!

Harry's Bar

No overnight stay in Venice is complete without a visit to **Harry's Bar**, that legendary watering hole of the rich and famous. This, the original Harry's Bar, was opened in 1931, its most famous guest being Ernest Hemingway, who created the Montgomery (15 parts Gin to 1 part Martini Rosso!). More modestly, the Bellini Cocktail (Champagne and peach juice) was invented here. There is also a restaurant (very expensive) with a menu reknown for its excellence. Harry's Bar can be found in Calle

O Sole Mio!

This, the most famous of the gondoliers' barcaroles, or songs, must grate on the ears of many of them, to judge by (some of) their demeanours! The ubiquitous gondola is undoubtedly the universally-acknowledged symbol of Venice, its sleek sombre lines, reminiscent of a waterborne hearse with its gloss black colour and brass fittings, recognised the world over from Helsinki to Hyderabad.

A large, flat-bottomed boat, the gondola is descended from the boats used by fishermen in the early days of the colonisation of the islands. It is asymmetrical in shape, which explains how the gondoliers steer them using a single oar on the starboard side. The distinctive metal "comb" on the prow is said to denote the **Sestiere**, or districts, of Venice.

The solemn appearance only dates back to 1562, when a Ducal edict was issued proclaiming that thenceforth, all gondolas were to be painted black, a measure undertaken to halt the (perceived) alarming trend of decorating them with ever more garish and opulent livery! The profession of gondolier is a highly-esteemed one, and you will often see, in the early morning or late afternoon, gondolas being scrubbed and polished meticulously by their attentive and proud owners.

This being surely the most romantic way on earth to travel, and a must for all visitors, the fares are correspondingly extortionate! Gondoliers are licensed by the city, and have fixed tariffs, so haggling may only work at slack periods (ie first thing in the morning - even then there is a fixed minimum charge of L70,000)! The cost can be shared, however, as a gondola may carry five passengers (although the romantic effect may well be lost when sharing the trip with a family of bickering strangers!).

Whichever way you do it, try to pick a jolly gondolier (and if you want to keep him that way, don't ask for a rendition of "O Sole Mio"!).

Gondoliers are extremely familiar with the twists and turns of the canals.

Venice in Peril?

Much has been made in recent years of the rising sea level and the resultant threat to Venice. "A new Atlantis!" and "Venice sinks!" shriek the headlines. While the twin menaces of 'global warming' and unseasonal tides do threaten the city, and the gradual erosion of the soil and silt supporting the buildings' pilings due to passing water traffic contribute to subsidence and the increased risk of flood, there is evidence that the severity of the situation has been, to a certain extent, exaggerated.

The floods of recent decades, notably those of 1966, 1968, 1969 and 1979, have done nothing to reassure the inhabitants of this maritime city. Recent studies by UNESCO, however, have shown that Venice has suffered almost total flooding on no less than fifty different occasions between its founding in the 5th century and the present day! This is not to say that a problem does not exist, but modern engineering and restoration methods should be up to the task of halting, if not reversing, the trend. One project under consideration is the UNESCO proposal to install floor barriers in the lagoon's three outlets which would activate automatically in times of high water. Various projects have already been carried out to halt the subsidence of individual buildings (including the Ba-

silica), by the use of cement injection and pre-stressed concrete.

Of more immediate concern is the effect of damp and pollutants on the building facades themselves. At greatest risk are the beautiful frescoes which adorn the many splendid Palazzi and churches along the canal. Prone naturally to the humidity and accompanying bacteria, the threat to the buildings is exacerbated by the effects of the industrialisation, during the 19th and 20th centuries, of the surrounding areas. The docks and industrial areas of nearby Mestre and Porto Marghera pump pollutants into the air and sea by the ton, while domestic heating and local boat traffic have have made their own, not insignificant contribution. Even the pigeons cause considerable damage to the buildings!

Steps are underway to remedy the situation: domestic diesel-burning systems are now banned, while pollution controls have been introduced across the lagoon. Various research institutes have been set up to study the problem, while restoration projects are being financed to preserve, and where applicable, restore Venice's countless works of art. An immense undertaking, it is to be hoped that these measures have been instigated in good time to remedy the situation.

Vallaresso, 1323, just West of Saint Mark's Square on the Grand Canal. Harry's Bar shuts at 11:00 in the evenings (in common with many of Venice's bars and cafes - although Venice is a city of late risers, they tend to retire early too). So where to next? Why not try a flutter at the tables of the **Casino** – a short vaporetto ride on the Linie 2 to the Lido. You approach the Casino along a private canal, a faerie brook overhung with greenery, forming a natural tunnel, which suddenly opens in front of the Casino. Soon after you have paid

the L15,000 admission fee, the scales fall from your eyes. Decorated in late 1950s and early 1960s, the establishment is dated and the staff at times surly, the food and drink extortionate, and the stakes high (minimum stake L10,000). This lack of attention to detail, particularly in the areas of food, drink and service, is surprising only until one discovers that this is only one of four casinos allowed by law in Italy. It is, effectively, a sellers' market.

Jaded and disillusioned, you leave the casino to find a little gem just next

The Orient Express

"The Train of Kings, the King of Trains" - host to royalty, statesmen, millionaires and spies, the **Orient Express** is undoubtedly the best known and most romantic rail journey in the world. The embodiment of stylish travel from a bygone age, with sumptuously ornate surroundings, gourmet food and wine, and solicitous personal service, a journey on the Orient Express is surely the voyage of a lifetime.

The brainchild of a Belgian, Georges Nagelmackers, who was inspired by the revolutionary "sleeping cars" pioneered by the American George Pullman, The Orient Express first ran on October 4th 1883, from Paris to Budapest. Although its passengers' final destination was Constantinople, it was not until the turn of the century that a through service was possible. With the extension of the service to the channel ports of Calais and Ostend, this new service soon became the ultimate luxury in international travel, serving Paris, Vienna, Budapest, Bucharest and Constantinople. The opening in 1906 of the Simplon Tunnel under the Alps linking Switzerland and Italy gave access to Milan, Venice, and later, Trieste.

The first World War brought a sudden (but happily temporary) end to rail travel in Europe (it is interesting to note the curious role played by the Orient Express in European warfare of this century – wagon-lit 2419 was used to accept the German surrender at Compiegne in 1918; in 1940 Hitler accepted the French surrender in the same carriage; but in 1945 it was blown up by an SS unit to prevent the allies exploiting its propaganda value!).

It was in the 1920s and 1930s that the Orient Express first gained its reputation for intrigue, mystery, and even murder! Countless novels and short stories have used the Orient Express as their setting (the most famous of which must be Agatha Christie's "Murder On The Orient Express"); but reality was somewhat more mundane! While there certainly were kings, queens, courtiers and beautiful contessas from time to time, the average passengers were, in the main, officials, businessmen, touring theatre companies, and tourists. Even Agatha Christie's masterpiece was originally entitled "Murder in the Calais Coach" until the publishers decided on a racier title!

Most damning to the inveterate romantic must be the admission by the late NKVD defector, Peter Deriabin, that contrary to his long-held claim that he escaped from Vienna in 1954 disguised as an Austrian on the Orient Express, he was actually smuggled out in a packing case on an American military freight train, and was almost discovered when he lit a cigarette near a Soviet checkpoint!

The social and economic privations following the second World War, and the increasing popularity of air travel all contributed to the general demise of rail travel, and despite several misguided cost-cutting excercises, the Orient Express fell into decline, and the service was discontinued in 1977.

Fortunately, the ideal and romance lived on in the minds of people with a love of rail travel and its "Golden Age", and later the same year the president of Sea Containers, James Sherwood, was able to buy two of the wagons-lits at auction in Monte Carlo. So began the slow process of location, aquisition, fitting-out and restoration of rolling stock for this, the most famous of trains. The new Venice Simplon-Orient-Express made its maiden run from London's Victoria Station to Venice on May 25th 1982.

door. A small, pretty arbour houses a snack bar, serving snacks and refreshments at the most unbelievably cheap prices. Sitting here at a terrace table, you are likely to miss several vaporetti while enjoying the fare.

The journey home is unforgettable. Try and get a seat in the stern if you can. Chugging up the private canal, the vaporetto emerges into the lagoon. The far-off lights of Venice twinkle in the darkness. The vaporetto picks up a fair

Gondolier's boater hat.

VENETO

From the imposing **Dolomites** to the north, to the southern plains of the **River Po**; from the mist-shrouded shores of **Lake Garda** in the west to the golden shores of the Adriatic coast in the east, the **Veneto** offers a wealth of diversity - geographic, cultural and gastronomic - unsurpassed even in this land of contrasts. Venice, the pearl of the Adriatic; **Padua**, **Vicenza**, **Verona**, **Garda**, **Treviso**, **Belluno**, **Cortina**; all displaying various elements of their architectural heritage, be it Etruscan, Roman, Byzantine, Gothic or Renaissance.

This is a region characterised by water (although look out for the sight of dry river beds that scar the land in the

bit of speed, as it is in the open lagoon and there are no buildings near and no water-borne traffic.

Spray flies from the spluttering propellers, and the oily black waters churn past. The occasional gull is startled from its fitful sleep atop a mooring post. Soon the features of Venice become clear: The Basilica, the Bell Tower, the Doges' Palace, Santa Maria della Salute; all floodlit in the otherwise impenetrable darkness. Pure magic.

Disembarking at **Calle Vallaresso**, you drift back towards your hotel, stopping perhaps for a final nightcap at one of the extortionate cafes on the Piazzetta, but by this time you don't care anymore. You are already planning tomorrow's trips of discovery.

Veneto country greenery outside the city of Venice.

Venice canals are lined with stately homes, villas and palaces.

The Arena in Verona, Veneto.

summer droughts): the rivers **Po**, **Adige**, **Brenta**, **Piave**, **Sile** and **Livenze** all flow into the Adriatic through this area, while the eastern shore of Lake Garda (Italy's largest lake, and one of its largest holiday resort areas) forms the western boundary of Veneto. The food of the region reveal its chequered history and cultural influences: stodgy dumplings, stews, and incredibly rich desserts typify the fare of the northern Dolomites, while the Adriatic Riviera is noted for its excellent seafood (shellfish especially). Venetian wines are enjoyed throughout the world, from the dry Pinot biancos and grigios, to the Cabernets and Merlots. It has to be said that these wines have had a poor press over recent years, due to overplanting and a ten-

dency to sacrifice quality for quantity, but the situation has improved dramatically in the last decade. Who, after all, can resist the allure of the crisp dry Soave, the deep rich Bardolino, or the light, fruity Valpolicella?

Whether pandering to the sunseeker indulging in the sybaritic pleasures of the lidos of **Jesolo** and **Venice**, or challenging the adventurous skier or mountaineer in the high Dolomites, or just tempting the discerning palate of the true gourmet, the Veneto seems to have something to offer everyone!

Padua

Following the **Brenta** canal inland from

Villa Pisani and its large and beautiful expanse of gardens, ponds and statuary.

Venice, where rich Venetian families once maintained extravagant summer residences, you come to **Padua**, or Padova as it is now known. One of the largest industrial, commercial and agricultural towns in northern Italy, Padua presents a grim initial face to the visitor. It is only at its heart that it reveals its rich historic legacy.

Dating back to Trojan times, it bears strong Roman influences, although it was not until the 13th century that the famous walls first appeared. Feudal rule by powerful families followed, until conquest by Venice and the later cession to the Hapsburg Empire. An important University town (founded in 1200), Padua today has many interesting buildings and monuments from different epochs, including the Gothic **Basilica of the Santo**, named after **Saint Anthony** (patron Saint of lost objects), whose shrine it protects; the **Scrovegni Chapel** and its extensive frescoes by Giotto; and the neo-classical **Caffe Pedrocchi**, a 19th century edifice designed by Giuseppe Jappelli.

Vicenza

Northwest of Padua, Vicenza is a quiet town best known as the birthplace of Palladio, and where many of his finest architectural works still stand, most imposing of which is the basilica, a High Renaissance building which he converted from an existing palace in

Rugged Dolomitic peaks in North Veneto.

the Gothic style. Originally a Roman colony, Vicenza came close to destruction several times in the Middle Ages in clashes with neighbouring Padua and Verona, before enjoying a ressurgence as a satellite of Venice. The countryside around Vicenza is populated with villas

and palaces by Palladio or his students, and many are open to the public.

Verona

Verona, one Italy's oldest cities, and

The bell tower of the Cathedral at Caorle, Veneto.

one of the most visually stunning, has had a chequered past. Always a border town, it was known in pre-Roman Etruscan times. It grew to be one the most successful of Roman colonies, and over the centuries has been ruled in turn by the Goths, the Lombards, the Franks (under the leadership of Charlemagne), the Venetians, the armies of Napoleon, and finally the Hapsburgs! The times of greatest influence on Verona were during the rule of the Della Scala family (the Scaligeri), in the late 13th and 14th centuries, when many of the cities' finest buildings and monuments were built. It was at this time that the powerful Montecchi (Montague) and Capuletti families were supposedly tearing their hair out over the love-lives of their off-

spring! Shakespeare (who never visited Verona, nor any other Italian city for that matter) is supposed to have got the idea for his play from a popular 19th century story on the subject. Verona is a strange dichotomy of styles: there is the older, Roman presence, typified by the remains of the Arena, host to magnificent open-air operas (where backpackers rub shoulders with "Grand Dames"!), and there is the substantial medieval influence, seen in the architecture of the 12th century **Duomo**, and in the 14th century **Castelvecchio** and adjoining **Ponte dei Scaligeri** (both bombed in the last war, and reconstructed, as was the nearby **Ponte Pietra**, from salvage from the bottom of the River Adige).

The **Casa de Guiletta** (Juliet's House; open daily), at Via Cappello 23 with a medieval balcony and bronze statue of Juliet (observe her left breast; it has been polished to a shine by generations of grasping hands – a bringer of good luck, apparently!); and the **Casa di Romeo** on Via Arche Scaligere are worth visiting. The (supposed) tomb of Romeo and Juliet can be seen, at Via del Pontiere, and is open daily. An interesting note is the oft-expressed belief that the crenellated rampants on the Castelvecchio (and for that matter on many other medieval castles in this part of Veneto), forming a stylised 'M', are the family symbol of the Montagues. While this may be so, this writer finds it hard to credit as the fortresses in question were commissioned by and built for the Scaligeri family.

Genoa (Genova to the Italians) is the capital of **Liguria**, and the fifth largest city in Italy, stretching for 25 miles along the coast. The approach from the west is rather depressing, after the beauty of the Ligurian coastline, but nothing prepares you for the chaos as you come into the dock area and try to find a way into, and around, the city proper! The city appears to be built on different levels, with tunnels, overpasses and terraces everywhere, all dominated by the towering elevated section of the A12, whose pylons bring to mind the martian machines of H G Wells' "The War Of The Worlds"!

Although an industrial society, Genoa reveals a multitude of monuments, cathedrals, palaces, theatres, architecture and works of art.

There is nowhere to park (especially near the Columbus exhibition), and directions are poorly indicated.

At first sight, a nightmarish scene. Yet, when with a little patience, and on closer inspection, you peel away the superficial layers of a highly

Genoese live very close to the sea.

Stone lion outside the Basilica di San Lorenzo.

industrialised regional capital, a rich cultural heritage reveals itself, with a multitude of monuments, cathedrals, palaces, theatres and works of art and architecture awaiting the interested visitor.

History

Genoa, known as La "Superba", can trace its history as an important port back to pre-Christian times, when it was used as a harbour and safe haven by the Greeks and Etruscans. With its narrow coastal strip, and the defence of its mountain borders inland, it was in a perfect position to defend itself from attack - its only open border was the sea.

Unfortunately this was where attacks usually came from – attacks by barbarians, pirates and later, Saracens. Despite this, the Genoese always recovered, having by the 3rd century AD established strong connections with the Byzantine Empire, and continual predations were the main factor in Genoa establishing such a powerful naval fleet.

By the Middle Ages, Genoa was the main rival of Venice, having defeated the other main (and geographically close) contender, Pisa.

Genoa's **Golden Age** was between the 13th and 15th centuries, despite constant external political pressure. It was after Andrea Doria drew up the constitution of 1529 that Genoa entered an era of relative peace, safe under the protection of Spain which was to last for 200 years. This allowed Genoa to maintain trading settlements all over the Mediterranean and Middle East, dealing in all manner of commodities.

Paradoxically, it was Genoa's most famous son who was to spell her downfall as an important maritime power. After **Christopher Columbus** discovered the Americas for Spain in 1492, Genoa found itself increasingly cut off from the most profitable (western) trade routes, and slowly lost its political clout in European affairs, although its military and financial institutions were to maintain a significant involvement for the next couple of centuries.

Genoa's independence effectively ended with the Napoleonic annexation, but even after Italian unification, the Genoese have maintained a fierce sense of national identity.

Out and about

The **Cattedrale di San Lorenzo**, in the **Piazza San Lorenzo**, is in the heart of the old medieval city. Dating from the turn of the 11th century, its original Romanesque facade was replaced with a Gothic frontage in the 13th century. Decorated with frescoes depicting the saint's life, it is also reputed to house the ashes of Saint John the Baptist, as well as the plate which held his head, and the chalice used in the Last Supper.

A few minutes' walk from the

The Royal Palace of Genoa.

Cattedrale is the **Chiesa di San Donato**, also demonstrating the awkward transition between Romanesque and Gothic styles. To the north-west of the city, in contrast, can be found the baroque splendour of the **Chiesa di San Filippo Neri**, completed in 1700. It contains numerous masterpieces, including the "Virgin of the Immaculate Conception" by the sculptor Cacciatori, as well as the "Virgin" by Puget.

Most interesting of sights in Genoa is the **Via Garibaldi**, a street (the only one in Europe) composed entirely of palaces, created by the exodus in the 16th century of rich patrician families out of the cramped living conditions to be found within the walls of the old medieval city.

Exquisitely painted exterior walls of Palazzo St. Giorgio, Genoa.

Among the most notable are the **Palazzo Tursi**, the **Palazzo Carrega-Cataldi**, the **Palazzo Bianco**, the **Palazzo Rosso**, and the **Palazzo Spinola**.

Memories of Columbus' times

The **cloisters of Sant'Andrea**, where Columbus probably learned his Latin, still stand alongside the ancient gateway. Today they make a restful park. The **Olivella** gateway can be found to one corner of the **Piazza di Ferrari** near the **Ducal Palace**, which has a collection of paintings about Columbus' life, and also has car parking facilities. The

Palace contains paintings related to Columbus' life.

Near the city's main Principe railway station there is a spectacular monument to Columbus in the **Piazza Acquaverde**. The rail station is in the centre of Genoa.

A tour of the port of Genoa by boat can be taken from the **Calata Zingari** in front of the **Doria-Pamphily Palace** near the rail station. Here, the boatmen's cooperative guides point out the city's historic sites including the grand lighthouse, **'La Lanterna'** which still stands at the entrance to the harbour and was a major structure and feature of Genoa port before Columbus was born. However, the present building, standing 117 metres high, was re-erected

Genoa's Greatest Son

Probably the greatest name in exploration and discovery is **Christopher Columbus**. Every schoolboy knows how Columbus sailed from Spain 'Crossing the Ocean Blue in 1492', to discover the New World. Many claims have been made to Columbus' origin, but Italy has the most authentic claim to his birthplace.

The story of Christopher Columbus and his travels begins in the Italy of the early 15th century. In medieval times, the country was divided into several republics. At that time, there was no port more busy than that of Genoa. The great trading port of Genoa was then known as '**Genova la Superba**' or 'Genoa the Proud' for its maritime and trading reputation. Genoa was the capital of the Genoese Republic, (before modern Italy), and it is located on the Bay of Genoa, part of the Ligurian coast of the north-western Italian peninsula.

In July 1451, two residents, a Domenico and Susanna Colombo had their first son, Cristoforo or Christopher, 'The Christ Bearer'. He was named after the patron saint of travellers and ferry men, St. Christopher, as he was probably born on that Saint's Day, the 25th of July. Both Cristofro's Christian and family names have been anglicized to 'Christopher Columbus'. The Colombos had moved from the outskirts of Genoa to **Porta Sant' Andrea** in the city, to a small house just near the ancient **Olivella** gateway or 'The Olive Gate'.

The house still stands today. It is called '**La Casa Verde**' or the 'Green House', it is in the district of **Via Porta Soprano** near the **Piazza Dante** in old Genoa, known as such for the ivy which still clings to its portals and surrounding

Monument to Christopher Columbus, an explorer celebrated beyond his hometown.

walls. Above the doorway, now covered in green creepers, is the legend:

'*Nulla Titulo Diognior - Heia - Paternis in Colombo - Pueritiam - Primam Juventam Transegit*'. 'There is none more worthy of fame. In this, his native country, Colombus spent his boyhood and youth'.

on the site of the original in 1543 and is now the symbol of the city of Genoa.

In Columbus' day lighters from the great galleys would transfer various produce from across the known world to the five jetties. One of these, the **Ponti Spinola**, was just a few minute's walk from Columbus' home.

More mementos of the Columbian era in Genoa can be found in the **Collection of the Contessa d'Albertis**, where there are paintings of Columbus' exploits. Also in the **Castello d'Abertis**, a fine selection of contemporary artifacts, and several manuscripts written by the Admiral can be viewed in the **Sala**

An entrance to a building on Via Garibaldi, Genoa.

Columbiana, Palazzo Municipal. In the **Palacio Tursi**, on Via Garibaldi, are the ashes of some of the remains of Columbus which lie in state in a glass capsule exhibited in a golden urn. Here also is the impressive mosaic of the discoverer created by the Genoese artist Antonio Salviati.

In the **Naval Museum** at nearby **Pegli**, it is possible to see the large collection of contemporary maritime artifacts and some articles which are said to have belonged to Columbus himself. Today's Genoa is recognised as Europe's largest medieval centre.

Columbus himself would have been familiar with at least a dozen of the grand palaces, churches and monuments which now comprise the spec-tacular wealth of Genoa's architectural heritage.

LIGURIA

The Ligurian coast is Italy's Riviera, a narrow strip of land stretching for 220 miles from the French border at **Menton** to just beyond **La Spezia**, where Tuscany begins.

Behind the coast, the foothills of the Alps, and further east, the Apennines, begin. Liguria is a land of vibrant colours, deep greens on the backdrop of foothills and on the terraced clifftops, cutting into the azure blues of the sparkling Ligurian Sea.

Bright silver flashes bring to your

St. Fruttuoso Abbey, Liguria.

notice the thousands of glasshouses dotting the hills, their presence explained by the fact that Liguria is Italy's, and Europe's, largest producer of fresh flowers. Wine and olive oil are also produced here, and vineyards and olive groves carpet the hills. Not surprisingly, the seafood is excellent, considered by many to be the finest in Italy.

Liguria is split by its capital, **Genoa**; to the west is the **Riviera del Ponente**, while to the east is the **Riviera del Levante**.

Riviera del Ponente

As you leave the hustle and bustle of Nice, Monte Carlo and Menton on the French side of the border, the change of pace is evident. Life moves more sedately, even if the buildings may seem a little run-down in comparison. Armed with a roadmap, a booklet of petrol coupons and an autostrade toll card obtained from the ACI office at the border, you head east towards the A10, which starts at **Ventimiglia**. Do not fall for the trap of having to overnight without prior booking at this border town - in common with all frontier settlements, particularly close to more "ritzy" foreign resorts, Ventimiglia is there to rip you off.

Parking is impossible, hotel rooms, if available, are exhorbitant (I was only slightly amused, having been grudgingly offered the last available room,

Men enjoying a street game of petanque.

but how many other poor waifs were charged a hefty premium for the "last available room"!), and a couple of tepid drinks in the seediest cafe will set you back the price of an average meal elsewhere. Far better, if feasible, to push on to the equally expensive but more upmarket resorts of **Bordighera** or **San Remo**. Should you not be deterred by this, or if you are planning a day trip or just passing through, Ventimiglia offers some interesting diversions, particularly the sprawling food and clothes market (Fridays), and the various Roman ruins in the nearby foothills.

The prehistoric caves at **Balzi Rossi** (Paleolithic settlements, open daily except Mondays, admission charge) are well worth a visit, as are the botanical gardens at **La Mortola**.

Bordighera is a small, quiet *fin de siecle* winter resort, very popular with the British, famous for its palms (the town has an exclusive contract, dating back centuries, for supplying the Vatican with palm fronds for Holy Week), while San Remo further east is the capital of this area of coastline, known as the **Riviera di Fiori** (Riviera of Flowers). An imposing Edwardian resort, it somewhat of a playboy's paradise, as can be seen from the multitude of yachts in the marina.

One of the main attractions is the weekday flower market, the **Mercato dei Fiori** (open October to June), where countless varieties are on display – over 20,000 tons of blossoms are exported every year.

On a clear day, a trip on the funicular railway to the top of **Monte Bignone** to experience the view of the Ligurian and French Rivieras will be rewarding, while those of more sedentary habits might enjoy a flutter at one of Italy's only four casinos.

Continuing east, you run the gauntlet of the A10 once more, being passed on both sides by lunatic drivers who appear oblivious of velocity or spacial coordinates. Lane discipline seems alien to the Italian psyche, or perhaps just an interesting theoretical hypothesis for after-dinner conversation. This must be one of the most dangerous autostrade in all Italy, populated as it is with a deadly mix of speeding supercars, swaying articulated lorries, and confused, apoplectic tourists.

Add to this the pitch-black tunnels that you flash in and out of every few hundred yards, and you soon start trying to remember if there is a history of epilepsy in your family!

Soon, to your right, you look down on **Imperia**, the provincial capital created by Mussolini, and beyond it, **Cervo** and **Alassio**.

Albenga, a small market town situated in an alluvial plain, is worth a short detour for its medieval walled town and its cathedral.

Finally **Ligure** is a large tourist resort, a pleasant place for families to stay, and with some interesting diversions. The cliffs to the east are very popular among climbers, while the

A fisherman tending his boat in Portofino.

Grotte della Arena Candide are among the finest caves in Europe for prehistoric remains (closed to the public, although finds are displayed in the Museo Archeologico – Tuesday-Saturday 10:00-12:00; Sunday 9:00-12:00).

Continuing east, you pass the small fishing village of **Noli**, and the town of **Spotorno**, before curving round the bay to **Savona**, an unprepossessing industrial city, which prepares you somewhat for Genoa further around the gulf.

Riviera del Levante

Extending to the east of Genoa to Tuscany, the **Riviera del Levante** tends to be extremely crowded in the summer

Portofino, a picturesque port and marina, once a playground for the
international jet-set.

months, and not the place to come to get away from it all! Nevertheless, there are some interesting places to visit, particularly charming (despite the hordes of tourists) fishing ports, and spectacular scenery.

Should you find your way out of Genoa unscathed, you will, if you take the coast road rather than the A12, come across **Nervi**. While you might be forgiven for thinking that the sign is a solicitous enquiry on the part of the traffic department, it is in fact a quiet suburb of the city, a small harbourside

make a detour back around the headland down to **Santa Margherita Ligure**, a lovely little resort split into two sections – an old town clinging to the side of the headland, and a resort on the coast itself.

Doubling back westwards along the coast, you come to **Portofino** (if you have the time, it might be best to park in Santa Margherita and walk along the two or three kilometres of narrow, winding road – tailbacks are common and parking is limited at this small port). Portofino was once (back in the 1950's and 1960's) the playground of the international jet set, and is still finding it hard to live down its reputation as a millionaire's paradise.

The playboys are largely gone now, and the prices, while still expensive, are no different from other resorts along this coast. It is a charming little fishing village built on the slopes of the headland, opening out onto a picturesque port and marina.

The luxury yachts are still in evidence, but then, so too are the little fishing smacks, and the sight of an old fisherman mending his nets or painting his hull is not an uncommon one. The buildings surrounding the port are painted in glorious earth colours – yellow ochres, burnt ambers, the occasional vermillion and crimson – reminding one of some of the more colourful parts of Venice.

The shops and boutiques are of the typical tourist variety, selling souvenirs and mementoes, chandlers' items such

settlement among the orange groves and villas. This might make a good place to unwind with a cool drink at one of the quayside bars.

Just further on is **Recco** – not much to see since it was rather unsympathetically rebuilt after being flattened in the war, but the area is reputed to have some of the best restaurants in Liguria.

After **Ruta**, and just before **Rapallo**,

Inside the grotto of Basura at Toirano, Liguria.

as framed knot arrangements and decorative lanyards, while there are an inordinate number of art galleries and craft stalls. Portofino lace seems to be a major seller, with every other stall offering lots of these pretty souvenirs.

A couple of hours spent at a pavement cafe, watching the world go by while you sip at a cold Peroni, soon restores the spirit, perhaps even enough to scale **Monte Portofino**, an undemanding hike at 610 metres high. The view from the top is spectacular! Also overlooking the port is the Splendido Hotel, one of the Orient Express Hotels chain, and said to be the best hotel along the Riviera – not for those on a tight budget!

Returning to the top of the head-

land via Santa Margherita, you continue on to **Rapallo, Chiavari** and **Lavagna** in the broad, sweeping **Golfo di Tigullio**. Rapallo, in common with most of the settlements along the gulf, is a highly developed tourist resort, although there is a surviving old town, with cobbled streets, and also hosts a market on Thursdays. Chiavari and Lavagna are smaller resorts, also with medieval centres.

The next large town on the route is **Sestri Levante**, the largest and most commercialised resort on the Riviera del Levante. A town which spans two bays, the **Bay of Fables** and the **Bay of Silence**. As might be surmised, the Bay of Silence is the more sedate of the two, but the "silence" is often relative!

An old fort, Colle di Nava, Liguria.

Out of Sestri Levante, and past the shipyards of **Riva Trigosa**, the coastal road (and the accompanying railway tracks) enters a series of tunnels which obscure much of the view until reaching the town of **La Spezia**.

It would be easy to miss the five villages of the **Cinque Terre** – **Monterosso**, **Corniglia**, **Vernazza**, **Manarola**, and **Riomaggiore**. Remote fishing villages, they cling precariously to the cliffsides, and until recently were only accessible by boat or by foot (as it is, rail is the only sensible way to reach them – **Monterosso** is only accessible by car). It is worth spending a day or two exploring these wonderful villages and the clifftop paths, for apart from the seafood, they now also produce some excellent white wine (Sciacchetra) from the cliff terraces, and the regional food is spectacular.

Tourism, while on the increase, is still manageable, except in Monterosso, the largest and least interesting of the five villages.

La Spezia is an enormous mercantile shipping port, and Italy's largest naval base, the **Arsenale**. A modern, industrialised city, it was almost razed to the ground in World War II, hence there is a dearth of interesting architecture for the casual visitor. In fact, there is little here to attract the visitor at all, apart from the lure of cheap accommodation, providing a base from which to explore the surrounding region, and to continue on from, into Tuscany.

The region of **Emilia-Romagna** stretches across the fruitful soils of the Po Valley, so not surprisingly, this is Italy's main agricultural area. Even the pleasant climate of long hot summers and cold wet winters suit the crops well.

The history of this region dates back to Roman times; pretty towns that grew up beside the old Roman road, Via Emilia, which runs through the region, was founded by ancient Roman traders who built trade routes that reached into the interior of the country from the Adriatic Sea.

Impressive examples of Byzantine mosaics on the ceiling of the Battistero Neoniano in Ravenna.

Bologna

Bologna is the capital of **Emilia Romagna**, with a population of 456,000. It has important industries ranging from motor vehicles, farm machinery, velvets, silks and Bologna sausage.

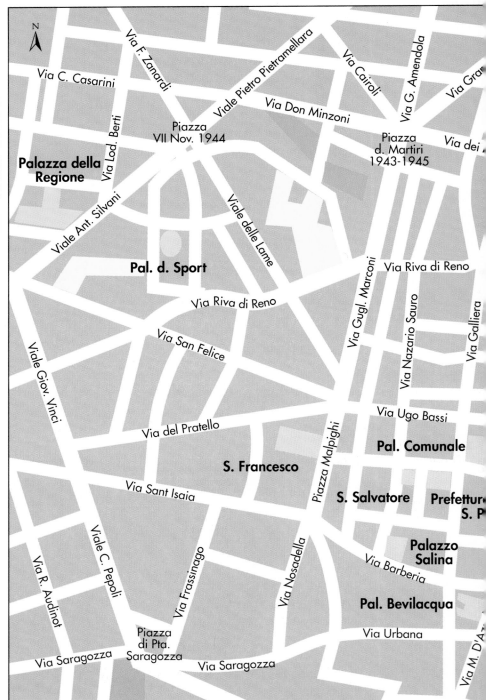

N

Via C. Casarini

Via F. Zanardi

Viale Pietro Pietramellara

Via Cairoli

Via G. Amendola

Via Gran

Via Don Minzoni

Via dei

Via Lod. Berti

Piazza
VII Nov. 1944

Piazza
d. Martiri
1943-1945

Palazza della
Regione

Viale Ant. Silvani

Viale delle Lame

Pal. d. Sport

Via Gugl. Marconi

Via Riva di Reno

Via Riva di Reno

Via Nazario Sauro

Via Galliera

Viale Giov. Vinci

Via San Felice

Via Ugo Bassi

Via del Pratello

Piazza Malpighi

Pal. Comunale

S. Francesco

S. Salvatore

Prefetture
S. P

Via Sant Isaia

Via Nosadella

Palazzo
Salina

Via Barberia

Viale C. Pepoli

Via Frassinago

Pal. Bevilacqua

Via R. Audinot

Via Urbana

Via M. D'A

Piazza
di Pta.
Saragozza

Via Saragozza

Via Saragozza

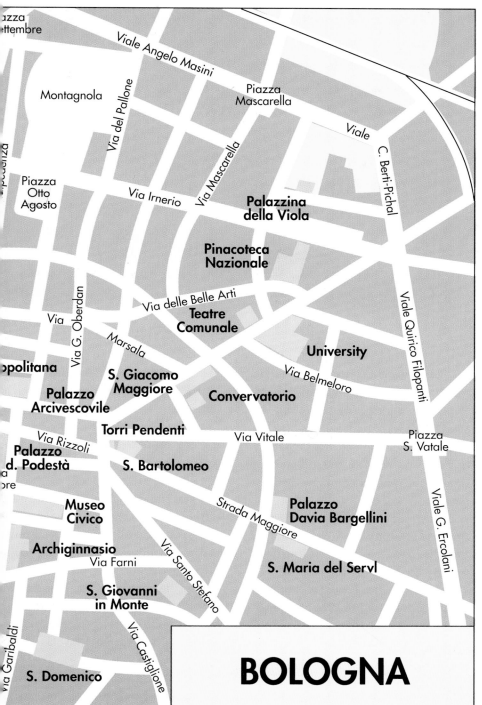

Piazza
·ttembre

Viale Angelo Masini

Montagnola

Via del Pallone

Piazza
Mascarella

Viale

C. Berti-Pichal

Piazza
Otto
Agosto

Via Irnerio

Via Mascarella

Palazzina
della Viola

Pinacoteca
Nazionale

Via delle Belle Arti

Via G. Oberdan

Via

Teatre
Comunale

Marsala

Viale Quirico Filopanti

·politana

S. Giacomo
Maggiore

University

Via Belmeloro

Palazzo
Arcivescovile

Convervatorio

Torri Pendenti

Via Vitale

Piazza
S. Vatale

Via Rizzoli

Palazzo
d. Podestà

S. Bartolomeo

·re

Museo
Civico

Strada Maggiore

Palazzo
Davia Bargellini

Viale G. Ercolani

Archiginnasio

Via Farni

Via Santo Stefano

S. Maria del Servl

S. Giovanni
in Monte

Via Castiglione

Via Garibaldi

S. Domenico

BOLOGNA

Fornovo di Taro region, Emilia Romagna.

The city has a very medieval feel to it, with its narrow, serpentine streets. Many of its streets have beautifully designed arcades or roofed walkways that are lined with shops, so that on a rainy day it is still possible to spoil yourself around the centre's boutiques and not get wet.

There are a number of interesting things to see and taste in Bologna. This town, for good reasons, has earned the names "La Dotta" or The Learned, "La Turritta" or The Towered and "La Grassa" or The Fat (it will become obvious to the visitor as to the reason for this last epithet). It is a treasure chest historically, artistically, scholarly and especially gastronomically.

The art collections that can be found in Bologna are world-famous. It has one of the world's oldest universities which dates from 1100. It has 130 churches that date from 1200, and Bologna used to have 180 towers during the Middle Ages, but today, only a few remain dating from around 1110.

Remember to indulge yourself with all these phenomenons at the same time; while your eyes luxuriate in the beauty of the town, allow your taste-buds equal pleasure! Savour the sausage masterpieces, the rapture of the Mortadella, which is the ingenious preparation of shredded and perfectly spiced pork, energetically packed into a flawless casing of suckling pig skin.

Try the unforgettable way the Bolognese prepare the charming

Entrance to hot mineral baths in Emilia.

tortellini and tagliatelle. There is a delightful story behind the tortellini's origin: an extremely rich Bolognese merchant was married to one of Italy's most beautiful women. He was also a very jealous man and he hid his wife away from all eyes.

One day the merchant's young cook accidentally entered the room of the beautiful woman while she was asleep and beheld her naked body. He was immediately besotted. He wanted to pay his compliments to her without directly revealing how intimately he knew her and hence risking his life, so he created the tortellini, the pasta in the shape of her navel.

The Bolognese fish dishes are also marvellous, as can be expected with their access to the Adriatic Sea which is constantly cleaned and diluted by pure Alpine streams. It would be a crime to miss the Rombo and the Gobies.

Another amusing story surrounds how the Gobies got their Latin name, *Gobius Pagenellus* or little pagans. Legend has it that in 1221, St. Anthony came and preached a sermon. All the fishes of the sea were elevated out of the waters, except for the Gobie!

An ideal place to start taking in all these wonders is at the **Piazza Maggiore**, where you can visit the largest church in the city, the huge **San Petronio**. Because they ran out of money (they had planned to build it larger than Saint Peter's cathedral in Rome!), the church is still unfinished; the museum within

Teatro Comunale in Bologna.

the church holds architectural sketches
showing what it was supposed to look
like when completed.

It was begun in 1390 and designed
by Antonio di Vincenzo. Some of the
completed parts of the facade, made of

the university had no permanent spot, and today the university's different faculties are spread out, but the recognised centre is at the **Palazzo Poggi**, constructed in the 16th century.

Near the university is the **Pinacoteca Nazionale** which shelters paintings mostly by local artists from the Middle Ages to the 18th century; there are some paintings by outsiders: you must see Raphael's 'Ecstasy of Saint Cecilia'. The Bologna university is Italy's oldest university, founded in the 11th century and renown for the study of Roman law. It had many famous students, including Petrarch and Copernicus. The university gave the world's first lessons of medical science in human anatomy, and the upper stories of the Archiginnasio was used in the 17th century as an anatomical theatre.

Today, it is used as a library. From the Archiginnasio, go down Via Garibaldi, it will take you to **San Domenico** which holds the tomb of St. Dominic who founded the Dominican order.

Next to the Piazza Maggiore is the **Piazza Nettuno** with the grandiose **Palazzo Comunale**, showing medieval and Renaissance styles. The Renaissance designs were by Fieravante Fieravanti. There are two notable statues, one of Pope Gregory XIII in bronze above the gateway (he was from Bologna), and one made of terracotta of the Madonna by Nicolo dell'Arca. The **Fontana del Nettuno** or the Fountain of Neptune in

elegant red and white marble show historical scenes from Biblical times.

Near the church is the **Archiginnasio**, which used to be part of the Bologna university. For centuries

Inside the 6th century Church of San Vitale, Ravenna.

the centre of the piazza was constructed in the 16th century.

The connecting Via Rizzoli is a beautiful street with many cafes. At the end of which you will see the surprising twin leaning towers of Bologna or **Due Torri** at the **Piazza di Porta Ravegana**. It is said that during the medieval times there were 180 of them built by the city's nobles.

The two that remain are by Asinelli and Garisendi, two of the richest families. They made a contest to see who could build the more magnificent tower in height as well as in beauty. Today we can judge that the Asinellis won, as the Garisendi's tower had to be shortened in 1351 to 48 metres (157 feet) because it has a weak foundation. The **Torre Garisenda** leans more than 3 metres (10 feet) out of its perpendicular, while the **Torre degli Asinelli**, at its original height of 97 metres, leans at a little more than one metre.

Part of the old Roman road Via Emilia that runs east of the towers, now renamed **Strada Maggiore** will bring you to the **Basilica di San Bartomeo**, which holds an exquisite Madonna by Guido Reni. Follow the same road to the 14th century Gothic church, **Santa Maria dei Servi**.

From here you can cut down to Via Santo Stefano where you will see the **Basilica di Santo Stefano**, several churches all consecrated to the martyr St. Stephen. The oldest of the group is the 5th century **Santi Vitale e Agricola** with obvious Roman influence; in **San**

The people are mainly engaged in manufacturing of farm equipment, velvets, silks and sausages.

Sepolcro, the patron saint of Bologna, San Petronio was buried near the pulpit in similar practice with other cities and towns. The design of the pulpit is worth going in to have a look at; it is truly extraordinary, done in a Romanesque style. The San Sepolcro also features a 12th century courtyard called **Cortile di Pilato** or "Pilate's Courtyard" and a 13th century **church of the Trinita**.

Using Piazza Maggiore as a landmark, the road leading away from the piazza, going in the opposite direction of Via Rizzoli is Via Ugo Bassi. It will bring you to **Piazza Malpighi**. There you will see **San Francesco** constructed in the mid-13th century in French Gothic style. Take time to visit this beautiful church, and study the towers and the

Statue of Pope Gregorio XIII in Bologna.

decorations in terracotta by Antonio di Vincenzo.

Ravenna

Ravenna is an important port town of the Adriatic coast of about 101,000 people. Today it is famous for its art and architectural treasures, and it is also an agricultural and industrial area. A ten kilometre canal connects the town to the Adriatic Sea. It featured greatly in the centuries-long historical struggles for control over sea trade routes.

From 402 AD, the invading Barbarians made Ravenna capital of the Western Empire. Its status as capital remained when the Ostrogoths under Odoacer took over in 476 AD. Then when Theodoric murdered Odoacer and became king of the Ostrogoths, he continued to rule the vast empire from this town. From around 540 AD to the 8th century, Ravenna became a vital part of the Byzantine Empire with its direct sea links to Byzantium. Emperor Justinian took pains to make Ravenna the beautiful town it is today.

Its stunningly detailed mosaics, perhaps some of the most beautiful in the world, should not be missed by any visitor to Italy. One of many famous churches to start with is the 6th century San Vitale. Notice the startlingly bright colours, the characters, and animals portrayed by mosaics. Savour the intricate details and humorous expressions on many of the faces.

Try to spot Abraham and his wife Sarah; the sacrifice of Abraham's son Isaac; the story of Moses' life; Moses on Mount Sinai; Saint Vitalis and Bishop Ecclesius; Emperor Justinian with his wife Theodora, accompanied by their courtiers. There is the interesting scene with Jesus Christ giving a crown to Ravenna's patron saint, and the bishop who founded this church holding in his hands a prophesy of what this very basilica would look like many years after his death.

Nearby is the Mausoleo di Galla Placidia which holds the tomb of Galla Placidia. The wall, floor and ceiling decorations are simply gorgeous. Christ as the Good Shepherd floats above the door, Saint Lawrence stands guard op-

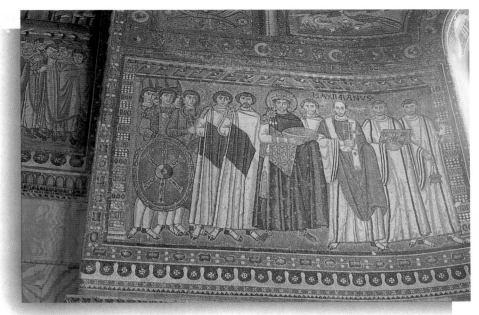

Religious themes are portrayed in the golden wall mosaics in the
San Vitale, Ravenna.

posite, and the apostles and many disciples encircle the room.

The ceiling reflects a sky full of twinkling stars embracing the cross of Christ. The woman whom this building was named after was very wily and lived a very intriguing life. **Galla Placidia** was a Roman princess who was taken prisoner by Goths. She shrewdly married the leader of the Goths, Athaulf and became co-leader. When he died, she cunningly married a Roman general and bore him a son, who consequently was made Emperor Valentinian III. With her connections at the highest levels of both peoples, she became extremely powerful politically.

In the Renaissance **Museo Nazionale** next door, there are more beautiful mosaics and interesting Ravenna artifacts. The 5th century Duomo on Via d'Azeglio was added to in the early 18th century, and so reflect some baroque tones. The 5th century baptistry, **Battistero Neoniano** next to the Duomo used to house a Roman bath. There are many impressive examples of Byzantine mosaics and show lovely use of marble.

From the Duomo, cross Piazza Cadutti to get to **Tomba di Dante**. Here you can see the sarcophagus which holds Dante's bones. The story behind how the Florentine's bones came to be in Ravenna is quite interesting: In 1317, Dante was given a safe haven in Ravenna, when he was exiled from his home in Florence for political reasons.

Sidewalk cafe in Piazza del Popolo, Ravenna.

Here, during the last four years of his life he finished his greatest work 'The Divine Comedy'. When he died, Florence demanded to have his body back, as they wanted very much to show how sorry they were by honouring him with a beautiful tomb. But of course Ravenna refused. A quarrel that lasted for centuries between the two cities ensued. The Florentines thought they had the winning card when in 1519, the representatives of the ruling Medicis of Florence came, armed with a direct order from the Pope. Dante's sarcophagus was opened and Lo! it was empty. The bones were so well hidden that they were found only in 1865!

On Via di Roma, the **Sant Apollinare Nuovo** is filled with beautiful mosaics. On the ceiling, you will find many exquisite mosaics detailing the life of Jesus Christ, and on the walls there are more depicting the processions of martyrs and virgins marching between palms to the altar.

Rimini

Rimini is famous for its beach resort which is only one mile from the city. It has huge modern hotels and it is mostly full of tourists from Northern Europe. Rimini the city, consists of the medieval town and the Renaissance town.

Rimini's most well-known personality is its ruler **Sigismondo Malatesta**. He did not get along with religious peo-

Bologna and the region of Emilia Romagna are best known for their culinary creations amongst which is the tortellini.

ple at all, especially not religious persons in positions of authority; most of all, made no attempt to hide this fact. He refurbished the 13th century Franciscan church and changed it into the extravagant **Tempio Malatestiano** – one of Italy's most ravishing Renaissance structures. It was obviously made as a tribute to Sigismondo's then mistress, and later third wife, Isotta degli Atti, and was never meant to resemble a church at all. Leon Battista Alberti created the exterior decorations and Matteo de Pasti the lavish interior.

Near the entrance is Sigismondo's tomb. The insignia you can see on the tomb, as well as everywhere in the church, is Sigismondo's and Isotta's initials entwined. He was excommunicated

by Pope Pius II, who sentenced him to hell publicly! He was a man who appreciated beautiful art as he patronised many artists, including Piero della Francesca and Leon Battista Alberti.

The Romans left two major structures: the **Roman forum** on the **Piazza Tre Martiri** and the 27 BC **Arco di Augusto** on **Corso di Augusto**, situated four blocks from the piazza. The Romans used this arch to mark the point where Via Flaminia joins Via Emilia. Via Flaminia comes all the way from Rome and reaches the Adriatic coast.

Ferrara

Ferrara sprang up by the Po River and

made its wealth as a market. This town has a medieval south and a Renaissance north. If you like, you can try to rent a bicycle – bicycling is a popular way for locals to get around this flat town. Through enlightened rule, the **Este family** who governed Ferrara from the late 13th century to the late 16th century, brought great prosperity and wealth to the town. They were patrons of many artists, poets and scholars, and converted Ferrara into a large trading and market place.

Make your way to the immense medieval castle, **Castello Estense**. It is equipped with fairy-tale towers, drawbridges, moats and even dungeons. Behind this is Ferrara's Duomo and museum. It holds beautiful paintings by famous artists, including Jacopo della Quercia and Cosimo Tura.

Do not miss Querica's 'Madonna della Melagrana' and Tura's 'San Giorgio'. Near the Duomo is a piazza with the medieval **Palazzo del Comune**. It is at present Ferrara's town hall. Take a look at its lovely Renaissance stairway. This piazza is where the natives do their daily *passagiata*, take a seat and watch the parade!

If you go north from the Duomo, you will come to the long broad avenues with their lovely Renaissance palaces and manicured gardens. The most beautiful avenue has to be the **Corso Ercole D'Este**. Stroll down to the **Palazzo dei Diamanti**, it was designed by Biagio Rossetti, one of Ferrara's most famous Renaissance architects. He used repeat-

edly the diamond emblem of the Este family and created an unusual facade for the palazzo.

Go south of the Duomo, and you will see many citadels, including the Este family's impressive summer house called the **Palazzo di Schifanoia**. Up the stairs to the **Salone dei Mesi**, take some time to study the beautifully coloured frescoes depicting the different months of the year. These paintings were done by several local masters from the Ferrarese school, one of then being Ercole de Roberti.

Nearby is another Este family residence, the Renaissance **Palazzo di Ludovico il Moro**. This ornate palace was designed by Biagio Rossetti.

Modena

Modena grew wealthy because it is surrounded by rich farmland. Today it has factories making cars for both Maserati and Ferrari.

Have a look at the late 11th century Romanesque Duomo in this town, it is an imposing and grandiose structure, designed by Lanfranco, the most respected architect of that time. It holds the remains of Saint Geminiano, who is the patron saint of Modena.

Here, you can also see the legendary **Torre Ghirlandina**. It is a part Gothic, part Romanesque bell tower which shelters a bucket! There is of course an even more peculiar story behind this curious phenomenon; in 1325, this very

This region is famous for Parmiggiano, more popularly known as
Parmesan cheese.

There are many restaurants throughout the region of Emilia Romagna.

ordinary bucket was stolen from Bologna and as a result, war broke out between the two cities! You would also want to see the **Palazzo dei Musei**, which holds a good art collection and a library you must not miss, called the **Biblioteca Estense**, which belongs to the Este family. It has many priceless manuscripts including a 1481 transcript of Dante's 'Divine Comedy', and also a beautiful Borso d'Este Bible.

Parma

Parma is about 120 kilometres southeast from Milan and it has a population of about 177,000. The town dates back to 509 BC, around the period of the Roman Republic. There are many art treasures to see here.

Parma's, and perhaps even one of the region's most breathtaking sight is her 11th century Lombard-Romanesque **Duomo** and its **baptistry**. Emilia's master painter, Correggio is also one of the greatest painters of the Italian Renaissance. Well-known for his delicate, graceful style, and exquisitely sensuous tones, he created the frescoes decorating the nave and dome. The dome's fresco is called 'Assumption of the Virgin'. It was said by Titian (recognised world over as one of the greatest master painters) that if the dome were to be turned upside down and filled with gold, it would not be as valuable as Correggio's masterpieces. Correggio's actual name is

Antonio Allegri, he took his name from his native Italian town. Correggio's works display a higher emotional quality and a more dramatic way of using light than even Raphael or Leonardo da Vinci. His invention of the spectacular illusion of ceilings that open up into sky with many divine beings that abide among the clouds influenced paintings of the baroque era during the late 16th and 17th centuries.

The adjoining baptistry was constructed by Benedetto Antelami. He lavished the whole structure with precious red Verona marble and he also created the reliefs that can be seen throughout the building. Another of Correggio's exquisite fresco can be seen in the dome of **San Giovanni Evangelista**. It portrays St. John looking up towards heaven, where Jesus Christ and the other apostles were supposed to be gathered.

The Viennese Marie Louise or to the locals **Maria Luigia**, is an interesting figure in this town's history. She was the second wife of Napoleon Bonaparte and the daughter of Emperor Francis I of Austria. She was not allowed to go with Napoleon when he was exiled, but then she remarried twice after Napoleon's death. In 1816, she received the Italian duchies of Parma, Piacenza and Guastalla. She did much to organize Parma's public works, for instance she built roads and bridges, and she set up orphanages. She also established an art gallery for paintings in the 16th century **Palazzo della Pilotta**. This art gallery boasts four large masterpieces by Emilia's famous Correggio.

Finally, this is where Parmiggiano or Parmesan cheese came from. Do try a slice; it is nothing like what you have known Parmesan cheese to be!

Piacenza

On the way to **Piacenza** from Parma, if you have the time, stop in the little town of **Roncole** to see where Giuseppe Verdi, one of the world's greatest operatic composer was born and the little cottage he lived in when he was a child.

Piacenza was built on the intersection of the Po River and the old Roman road, Via Emilia. Not surprisingly, Piacenza was a very successful trading town, and it has had a market for farm produce since 218 BC!

Have a look around Piacenza with its buildings that date from medieval and Renaissance periods. There are two structures in particular that are worth stopping for. There is the Romanesque **Duomo**, situated at the end of Via Venti Settembre. It has interesting frescoes of saints on columns near the entrance to the cathedral. They are supposed to give the illusion of saints mingling with the congregation. The **Palazzo del Commune** or **Il Gotico**, now used as the town hall, was started in 1280. The two huge baroque statues on horses at the front of the building is of Duke Alessandro Farnese and Duke Ranuccio, his son. They were rulers in Piacenza during the 16th century.

Florence & Tuscany

The rustic Tuscan countryside thrives with villages scattered about the lush landscape. Gentle hills overlook windy valleys and the air is scented and warm with languid breezes. Now and then the narrow country lanes will surprise you with the occasional shrine to the patron saint of the neighbouring hamlet.

Rural Tuscany is best enjoyed for the spacious scenery; the tranquil remoteness of Tuscany is found intact there. Spending days in the peaceful hills is a pleasant respite from the hustle bustle and intensity of the lively hearts of the Tuscan cities. If we look for romantic history, it is surely to be found in the traditions of the country. It is a myraid of greens in the height of summer, teeming with historical traditions. The bread baked in the distant hills is distinctive for its lack of salt and the communal life of the Tuscan is best observed by watching their festivals of saint days and religious feasts.

Florentine skyline with the Duomo and Palazzo Vecchio in the foreground.

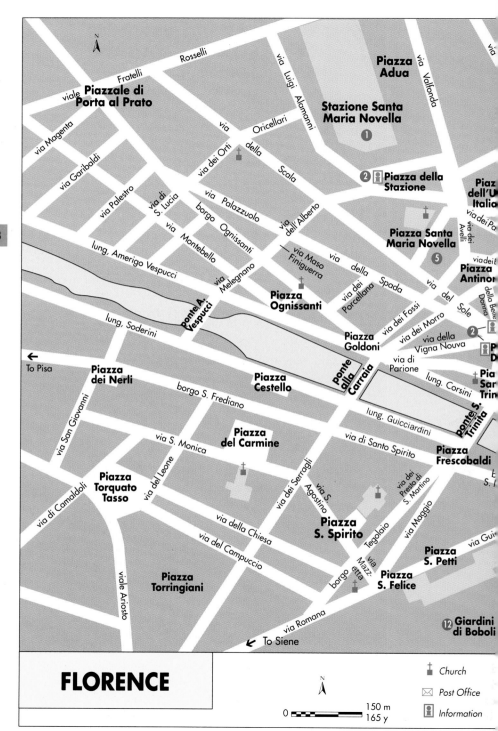

N

To Pisa

Rosselli

Fratelli

**Piazzale di
Porta al Prato**

viale

via Magenta

via Garibaldi

via Palestro

via di
S. Lucia

via

Montebello

borgo Ognissanti

via Palazzuolo

via dei Orti

della

Scala

Oricellari

via

via Luigi Alamanni

via
dell' Alberto

**Piazza
Adua**

via Vallonda

**Stazione Santa
Maria Novella**
❶

❷ 🛈 **Piazza della
Stazione**

**Piazza Santa
Maria Novella**
❺

**Piaz
dell'U
Italia**

via dei Pa

via dei
Avelli

via dei t

**Piazza
Antinor**

lung. Amerigo Vespucci

lung. Soderini

**Piazza
dei Nerli**

borgo S. Frediano

via San Giovanni

via di Camaldoli

viale Ariosto

**Piazza
Torquato
Tasso**

via del Leone

via S. Monica

via Maso
Finiguerra

**Piazza
Ognissanti**

Ponte A.
Vespucci

via
Melegnano

via dei
Porcellana

via

della

Spada

via dei Fossi

**Piazza
Goldoni**

via dei Morro

via della
Vigna Nouva

via di
Pariione

Ponte
alla
Carraia

**Piazza
Cestello**

**Piazza
del Carmine**

via dei Serragli

via della Chiesa

via del Campuccio

**Piazza
Torringiani**

via S.
Agostino

Tegolaio

**Piazza
S. Spirito**

lung. Corsini

lung. Guicciardini

via di Santo Spirito

della Belle
Donna

❷ 🛈

**P
D**

**Pia
Sar
Trin**

Ponte S.
Trinita

**Piazza
Frescobaldi**

via dei
Presto di
S. Martino

via S. Martino

via Maggio

**Piazza
S. Petti**

via Gui

b
S. l

via Gui

To Siene

borgo

Mazz-
etta

**Piazza
S. Felice**

via Romana

via del
Sole

⑫ **Giardini
di Boboli**

FLORENCE

N

0 ━━━━ 150 m
       165 y

† *Church*

✉ *Post Office*

🛈 *Information*

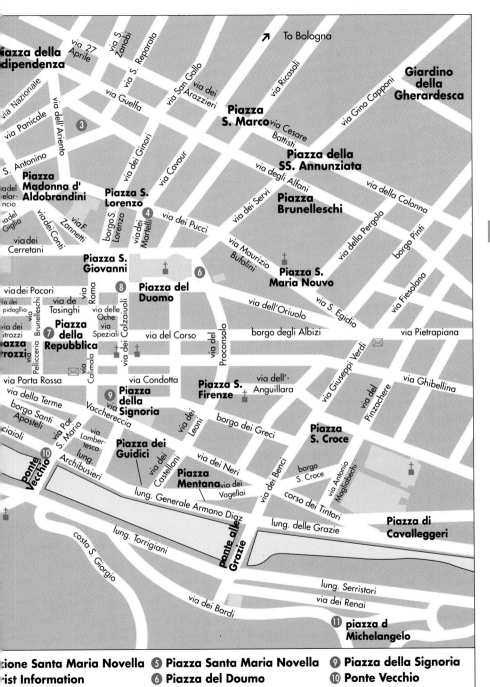

Piazza della
dipendenza

via 27 Aprile

via S. Zanobi

via S. Reparata

To Bologna

via Ricasoli

via Gino Capponi

Giardino
della
Gherardesca

via Nazionale

via Panicale

via dell'Ariento

via San Gallo

via dei Arazzieri

via Guelfa

via dei Ginori

via Cavour

Piazza
S. Marco

via Cesare Battisti

S. Antonino

Piazza
Madonna d'
Aldobrandini

via del elar- ncio

via del Giglio

via F. Zannetti

via del Conti

via dei Cerretani

Piazza S.
Lorenzo

borgo S. Lorenzo

via dei Martelli

via dei Pucci

Piazza della
SS. Annunziata

via degli Alfani

via dei Servi

Piazza
Brunelleschi

via della Colonna

via della Pergola

borgo Pinti

via Maurizio Bufalini

Piazza S.
Maria Nouvo

via Fiesolana

Piazza S.
Giovanni

via Roma

Piazza del
Duomo

via dell'Oriuolo

via S. Egidio

via Pietrapiana

via dei Pocori

ia dei pidoglio

via de Tosinghi

via dei Strozzi

via dei Brunelleschi

Pelicceria

Piazza
della
Repubblica

via delle Oche

via dei Calzaiuoli

via della Speziali

via del Corso

via del Procansolo

borgo degli Albizi

iazza rozzi

via Calimala

via Condotta

Piazza S.
Firenze

via dell'- Anguillara

via Giuseppi Verdi

via Ghibellina

via Porta Rossa

via della Terme

borgo Santi Apostoli

ciaioli

via Por. S. Maria

via Lamber- tesca

Piazza
della
Signoria

via Vaccherecia

via dei Leoni

borgo dei Greci

via del Pinzachere

Piazza
S. Croce

Ponte Vecchio

lung. Archibusieri

Piazza dei
Guidici

via dei Castellani

Piazza
Mentana

via dei Neri

via dei Vagellai

borgo S. Croce

via Antonio Magliabechi

via dei Benci

costa S. Giorgio

lung. Generale Armano Diaz

corso dei Tintori

Piazza di
Cavalleggeri

Ponte alle Grazie

lung. Torrigiani

lung. delle Grazie

lung. Serristori

via dei Bardi

via dei Renai

piazza d
Michelangelo

---

zione Santa Maria Novella   ⑤ Piazza Santa Maria Novella   ⑨ Piazza della Signoria

rist Information   ⑥ Piazza del Doumo   ⑩ Ponte Vecchio

cato Centrale   ⑦ Piazza della Repubblica   ⑪ Piazza Michelangelo

Lorenzo Marketplace   ⑧ Via Calzaiuoli   ⑫ Boboli Gardens

Cathedral of Santa Maria del Fiore built in 1436 AD.

The poetic beauty of Tuscany inspired many literary figures; some of the greatest include Dante, D.H. Lawrence, and Lord Byron. The literature is accompanied by the art that overflows from the best museums of the world.

Florence

The Renaissance bloomed out of **Florence** to revolutionise the rest of the known world. History was made out of the antiquity-laden streets and walkways of **Firenze**. Famed paintings, frescoes, sculpture and feats of architecture adorn this region.

There is harmony and grace in the city, it is filled with a sense of serenity and dignity which seems to come from the gentle course of the river **Arno**, through the city's umber-coloured buildings: a relic of the Renaissance. Also it is filled with the civil grace of gentlemen with full shop windows displaying luxury goods and handsome jewellery.

However, Florence's history is fraught with strife. The city was founded by the split of Tuscan tribes, when some members went to the area around the Arno from the Fiesole hill. A Roman camp followed, making the **Via Romana**, a Roman highway across the empire – it was the Romans who called the settlement **Florentia**. The next settlers were Goths, Byzantines and Lombards they were followed by the period of clashing Guelphs and

The Ponte Vecchio and the Arno as seen from a room with a view.

Ghibellines, the so-called blacks and whites, which caused the exile of many Florentines such as Dante. The city stood in the path of the dreaded Black Plague, which unmercifully wiped out half the population in the 14th century.

Florence surprises many visitors, in the **Piazza San Giovanni** in the heart of the city, the **Duomo** rises from the stern and defensive buildings. The Duomo is constructed out of marble from **Prato**, **Maremma**, and **Carrara** – it dates from the 19th century. It is accompanied by **Giotto's Campanile**. The **Baptistry** is octagonal and dates from the 9th century, its interior is glittering mosaic and it is famed for its glorious bronze doors – made out of a contest between Ghiberti and Brunelleschi.

Michelangelo called the east doors of Ghiberti "the Gates of Paradise". But it is Brunelleschi's dome of the **Duomo (Santa Maria del Fiori)** which magnificently overlooks the Baptistry: the interior of the Duomo is huge, 10,000 Florentines could have fitted into it.

The works of art from the Duomo are housed in the **Museo dell'Opera del Duomo** behind it. The greatest museums of Florence are the **Uffizi**, the **Pitti Palace**, and the **Barguello**, all of whom house the most immaculate collection of art of the Renaissance in the world.

In **San Marco**, north of the Duomo, the cloistered convent is remarkable; art is a part of everyday life. A fresco of Fra Angelico decorates every cell there. San Marco also houses the first library in

Renaissance frescoes in the Santa Maria Novella depict life in an era of refinement and elegance.

Europe. Near San Marco, there is the Renaissance's first outdoor architectural feat – the **Ospedale degli Innocenti**, built in the 1420s by Brunelleschi, has a loggia which is in graceful contrast to Michelangelo's famed statue of **'David'** in the **Galleria dell'Accedemia**. David rests in his rotunda in a long hallway with Michelangelo's unfinished **'Slaves'**. David shows the ideal Rennaissance man at his most splendid and noblest.

The **Medici** family dominated Rennaissance Florence, being rulers and art patrons until the 1700s. Their influence can still be seen in the **Palazzo Medici Riccardi** on **Via Cavour**. The commission intended for Brunelleschi was given to Michelozzo as Cosimo Medici feared a grand design would alienate the populace. In the small chapel, you can see the faces of the Medicis in Benozzo Gozzoli's fresco of the 'Journey of the Magi'.

The nearby **church of San Lorenzo** with an interior by Brunelleschi and Michelangelo's sculptures of **'Dawn'**, **'Dusk'**, **'Night'** and **'Day'** holds the Medici's chapel, crypt and library. The sweeping staircase of **Biblioteca Laurenziana** (1524-34) shows the splendid architecture of San Lorenzo. Outside, a bustling street market sells old and new clothes, leather goods and delightful little gifts. The street market grows busiest at the large cast iron **Mercato Centrale** where two storeys of wares include wild boar, fresh herbs, porcini mushrooms, tripe, tomatoes, and

The Duomo in Siena was imaginatively constructed with green, pink and white marble.

so on.

In west Florence, the **church of Santa Maria Novella** was the chapel of the powerful Strozzi and Rucellai families. It is near the grand **Palazzo Strozzi** and the **Palazzo Rucellai** (which was by Alberti). The Santa Maria Novella has frescoes in its Spaniards chapel showing catholic life. In the apse, there are frescoes by Domenico Ghirlandaio (1485-90). In their elegant refinement, they provide an insight into contemporary life in Renaissance Florence.

Fashion in Florence is found at its highest in **Via Tornabuoni** with great Italian fashion houses displayed there such as Ferragamo and Armani.

The 19th century **Piazza della Republica** nearby, is surrounded by outdoor bars. Close by, the **Piazza della Signoria** brings you back in history with the towers of **Palazzo della Signora** or the **Palazzo Vecchio** – the town hall. The atmostphere of the civil and political centre is majestic and awesome. There Savorgrola was burned at the stake, and the **Neptune fountain** of **Ammanati** borders the **Loggia dei Lanzi**. There are gruesome statues of rapes and beheadings standing as permanent witnesses to the scenes of blood and battle in the **Salone dei Cinquecento** within the Palazzo. The **Bargello**, a former prison towers behind the Palazzo; today it is the **National Sculpture Museum**.

Bells used to sound there when there were executions taking place. Masterpieces of sculpture are in the courtyard,

Donatello's David, together with St. John, St. George and Marzocco grace the Piazza della Signoria.

Michelangelo's "La Sacra Famiglia" in the Galleria Pitti.

Visiting Florence is not complete without a glimpse of Botticelli's
"La Primavera" at the Uffizi gallery.

Medieval Florence depicted in an old painting.

Donatello's marble David, and later bronze David, St. John, St. George and Marzocco – the lion herald of the city are all there. Next to the Bargello stands the **Uffizi Gallery** designed in 1544 by Vasari – it is the biggest and best collection of Renaissance art, with rooms of Raphael, Lippis, Titians and Botticelli. It includes Botticelli's well known 'Birth of Venus' and 'Primavera'. Michelangelo, Machiavelli and Galileo all have tombs in the east of the city in **Santa Groce**. Its interior is superb with a marble floor that makes up tombs. Its chapels are frescoed by Giotto and beside the cloister the **Pazzi chapel** by Brunelleschi shows off the small scale and purity of finest Renaissance design. It suffered some bomb damage in May 1993.

No visit to Florence is complete without walking along the **Ponte Vecchio**, the bridge which spans the Arno. It has

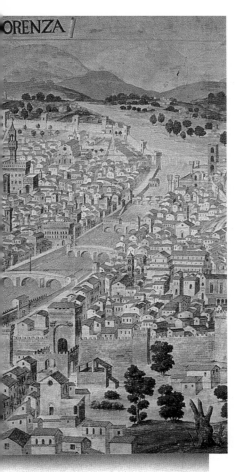

in his space – he painted the 'Tribute of Money', and 'Adam and Eve' there. Also in the Oltrano there is the 15th century art museum, the **Pitti Palace**. It is spectacular in its interior, with gilt and silk hangings surrounding the great paintings of the galleries. The collection spread about the former state palace is huge and ranges from Titians, Raphaels and Reubens to antique vases. It is filled with royal opulence and grandeur. The formal style of the Pitti enhances the simpler charms of the 11th century **San Miniato**, a church on a nearby hill. Its intricate sculpted pulpit on a zodiac laid floor with the **della Robbia** vaulted chapel make it one of the most popular chuches in Florence. Descending from the hill, go to the **Piazzale Michelangelo** and see the hills of **Fiesole** and

been lined with jewellers since 1593 and it is the only bridge which was not bombed and destroyed during the second World War. On the other bank of the Arno across the Ponte Vecchio, there is the **Oltrano** which is reminiscent of a country town rather than a city. The **Piazzo Santo Spirito** in front of Brunelleschi's church shows the relaxed style of the area with benches, trees and a small market. The **church of Santa Maria del Carmine** nearby has the revolutionary frescoes by Masaccio who was the first painter to show perspective

The University at Pisa.

The Baptistry in Florence is famed for its glorious bronze doors, constructed
as a result of a contest between Ghiberti and Brunelleschi.

Bellosguardo which surround the city and take in the breathtaking view of the treasures that make up Florence.

Prato, Pistoia & Fiesole

Prato, Pistoia and Fiesole are interesting places to visit near Florence. Prato contains much of the master Fra Filippo Lippi's frescoes. Lippi (1406-1469) fell in love with a novice nun, Lucrezia Buti, who was the model for many Salomes and Madonnas. Their son Filippino (1457 - 1504), also was an artist. Lippi's (senior) work can be seen at the Prato Duomo; some of his finest work includes the 'Banquet of Herod', 'Salome's Dance', scenes of Saint Steven and Saint John. The chapel of Cappella del Sacro Cingolo is said to contain the girdle of Mary. According to legend the Apostle Thomas received it from Mary in a vision, to prove her assumption and the ressurrection of Christ.

Pistoians used to have a reputation for violence, hence the first handguns to be introduced in Italy were named after the daggers they carried. There are remains of an impressive city wall, the Gothic Palazzo del Comme and the Duomo with della Robbia facades. Now, industry thrives in both Prato and Pistoia.

Fiesole in contrast is set on a former Roman city – you can visit the hill city and see Piazza Mino da Fiesole named for the artist Mino da Fiesole whose work is in the Duomo. Climb the hill left of the Duomo for a breathtaking view of

The Tuscan countryside which inspired many writers and poets.

the entire city of Florence. A little higher a small **church of Sant' Alessardro** rests on the site of a pagan temple to Bacchus, god of wine. On the summit is a monastery, **San Francesco**. Down the hill, there are lush public gardens to an archaeological site where **Etruscan** and **Roman relics** are to be found – an impressively restored amphitheatre, a ruined Roman bath and temple are accompanied by a small museum.

Arezzo

In the south-east of Florence, lies the walled city of **Arezzo**. Its position in the Apennines allowed it to control all the passes there. In the centre, the plain looking **church of San Francesco** offers delightful frescoes behind the altar. Painted by Piero della Francesca, they depict the legend of Christ's cross from Adam's tree of knowledge to its being founded by Saint Helena. The **Arezzo Duomo** next to the park of **Passeggio del Prato** (13th and16th centuries); it has beautiful stained glass windows by Marcillat, grand tombs and a fresco of Mary Magdelene by Piero della Francesca. There is also a side chapel with della Robbia terracottas. The church of **Piere d Santa Maria**, built about the 12th to 14th centuries, is between theDuomo and San Francesco. Easily identifiable because of a tall **campanile** (bell tower). The campanile has many bifora windows and the church has three-

Nature park of Maremma.

tiered loggias. On one side of Santa Maria, the **Piazza Grande** is a quiet square with medieval buildings and antique shops. An antiques fair is held there on the 1st Sunday of each month. In the 1st Sunday of September, a 12th century costume pageant is held. Arezzo is the hometown of Giorgio Vasari, whose house is on **Via Vente Settembre**. He built the loggia of the **Piazza Grande** and designed the Uffizi in Florence. Petrarch the poet, Pietro Arentino, the writer and Spinello Arentino the artist also lived here.

Siena

Siena lies on three hills, its **Campo** (square) is divided into nine sections – symbolic of the council of nine men who ruled Siena from 13th to the early 14th centuries. Traffic is barred from most of Siena, and twice a year the **Paleo Pageant** and horse race is held on July 2 and August 16th. It is a sumptuous celebration for the Sienese and the winner of the medieval race becomes a local hero.

At the bottom of the square is the **Palazzo Pubblico** dating from the 14th century. It has a tower called the **Mangia** and a long climb to the top offers a panoramic view of Siena. Part of the Palazzo is **Museo Civico** which contains the city's treasures. Up the winding streets from the Campo you find the huge green, pink and white marble of the **Duomo**. Its interior is filled with black and white

Men of Siena meeting and exchanging along the sidewalks.

geometric designs and its 15th and 16th century marble paving depicts biblical scenes. In the left nave there is the **Libreria Piccolomini** which was built to contain the papers and books of the Pope Pius II. It is frescoed by Pinturicchio and has a copy of the statue of the 'Three Graces'. Siena also has two important museums, the **Museo dell' Opera Metropolitana** (the Cathedral Museum, left of the Piazza del Duomo) and the **Pinacoteca Nazionale** on **Via San Pietro** near the Campo.

Pisa

Pisa was the city-state of greatest power in the 12th century, situated 12 kilome-

tres from the coast. Pisa was a major trading port but her power waned in the next century and by the 15th century, Pisa's harbour had become filled with silt. More recently Pisa was subject to massive destruction from bombs in the second World War. The **Piazza del Duomo** was not bombed and it is an impressive sight with the **Campo dei Miracoli** – together they constitute fine examples of Pisan architecture, which has eastern influences. The Pisan **Duomo** began the style that was copied in other regions' churches. It holds Pisaro's detailed pulpit and Andrea del Santo's Saint Agnes. The **Baptistry** is in front of the Duomo and it has Nicola Pisano's beautiful pulpit. The holy field on the left is the **Camposanto**, the earth

Procession of the Paleo di Siena, part of an event of costmes, flags, tournaments and jousts.

from Calvary brought back by crusaders, said to be in the burial ground. The famous Campanile which was begun in 1173, is the leaning tower. This is where Galileo disproved Aristotle's theories by dropping different mass balls from the top of the tower. It is now slanting 15 feet out of plumb.

Lucca

North of Pisa is **Lucca**, its 16th century walls re-designed in the 19th century to incorporate a promenade. It has diverse architectural styles such as medieval alleyways, orderly Roman passages, Renaissance loggias and even Rococo influences. Lucca used to be a banking centre in the Middle Ages and it was known for trading in silk; today it offers the finest olive oil. **Saint Michele in Foro** is an example of the architecture of the region. The **Palazzo Pretorio** government building was begun in 1492 by Matteo Civitali. On the **Via de Poggio** you can find the house of Giacomo Puccini. Follow Via Fiullungo, past the **Torre dell' Ore** clock tower, to find a Roman amphitheatre dating back to the second century. Nearby is the gilded mosaic of the **Church of San Frediano**. East of Lucca is **Villa Guinigi** the **Museo Nazionale di Villa Guinigi**. The **Palazzo Mansi** houses the **Pinacoteco** in the west. The **Villa Reale**, **Villa Torrigiani** and **Villa Garzoni** show off the culture and nobility here.

Landlocked, and located in the middle of central Italy, this region's landscape is comprised of a series of undulating rounded hills in the Apennine mountains north of Rome. The hills are green and olive with black oak woods, and the valleys are carefully cultivated, lakes, rivers and streams abound, and farming is the main industry. The population of the entire area does not exceed 100,000.

Famous sons and saints of **Umbria** include Perugino and Pinturicchio, and St. Benedict made his home here, as did St. Francis of Assisi.

An Umbrian man sporting a medieval costume at a festival occasion.

Perugia & Umbria

Perugia

Perugia is the capital city of the region of Umbria. This centrally located hillside Etruscan city overlooks the Tiber Valley. The National Gallery of Umbria is housed in the 13th century

Cultivated landscape of olive trees.

Scaling Mount Sibillini, near the town of Norcia in Umbria.

Palazzo dei Priori on the **Piazza IV Novembre**.

One of Italy's most opulent public buildings, the **Palace of the Priors** is medieval and adjacent buildings include the 13th century **Hall of Notaries** and the vast **Archbishop's Palace**. There are numerous old churches in the city and Perugia's oldest is the 5th - 6th century **Church of Saint Angelo**. The **Church of San Pietro** is originally 10th century and its sacristy houses beautifully painted panels by Perugiono, Caravaggio and Raphael. The cathedral is Gothic, it was begun in 1345 and was completed in 1490, and it was from the outside pulpit that St. Bernadino blessed the populace in 1425. The **Church of San Dominico** is also Gothic,

beside which is the **Archaeological and Prehistorical Museum** housed in the old monastery. The city's **Maggiore Fountain** dates from the 13th century and was decorated by Nicol and Giovani Pisano.

In the historic **Stock Exchange** dating from the 15th century are paintings by Raphael and Perugino. The city walls are Etruscan and the main relic of these is the basis of the **Estrucan Gate**. The gateway is now known as the **Porta della Mandora**, or the **Augustus Arch** as the Romans erected their gate above the Etruscan original. Apart from the Etruscan exhibits in the **Archaeological Museum**, there is the underground **Tomb of Volumni**, a family tomb, built like a Roman villa and located around

7 kilometres south-east of the city.

Citta di Castello

This former Roman township lies due north of Perugia and dates from medieval times. In the **Piazza Matteotti**, located at the centre of the town, is the baroque-cum-Gothic **Palazzo del Podesta**. Also in the same quarter is the **Palazzo Comunale** and the town's cathedral. The third palace houses the art gallery, or **Pinacoteca**. Built in the 16th century, the gallery houses magnificent works by Domenico Ghirlandaio, Raphael and Luca Signorelli.

The 14th century panels, painted by an unknown artist are among the finest treasures of their kind in the region, possibly in all Italy.

Gubbio

Nearer than **Citta di Castello**, and to the north-east of Perugia stands the exquisitely preserved and typically medieval town of **Gubbio**, where five terraced levels from the main streets are linked by almost vertical alley-ways.

The town is a time capsule, a living museum, crowned by the city centre known as the **Piazza della Signoria**, and constructed in 1322. It is a strange construction which forms a balcony-like platform high over the town. The piazza is dominated by the **Palazzo dei Consoli**, which has a small museum in

Details from the Church of San Francesco in Assisi.

which are exhibited the bronze plaques known as the **Gubbio Tables**. Even further up the hillside is the old ducal palace, built in the 15h century, which faces the town's Gothic cathedral.

Assisi

A short distance south-east of Perugia is the charming town of **Assisi**, home of St. Francis, the founder of the Franciscan Order of Friars in the 13th century. Assisi is a small town on the slopes of **Mount Subasio**. The basilica is constructed on two levels and contains some of the best examples of Italian frescoes including Cimabue's 'The Crucifixion'. Left of the altar in the basilica, is the

The old town of Assisi, on the slopes of Mount Subasia.

sacristy which contains a collection of the saint's relics including his sandals and grey habit.

The 2nd century Romanesque **cathedral** of **Saint Rufino** is worth a visit and it is at this cathedral's font that St. Francis and St. Clare, founder of the Poor Clares, women followers of St.

Francis, were both baptised. The Emperor Frederick II was also baptised here. The crypt of the 13th century **basilica of St. Clare** contains the remains of the saint and the crucifix here is the one in front of which St. Francis prayed and learned of his mission in life.

Relics of ancient Roman times in-

Medieval town of Gubbio where five terraced levels from the main streets are linked by virtually vertical alley-ways.

clude the **Temple of Minerva**. Saint Francis was buried, in 1226, in a miniscule church called the **Porzouncola**. This tiny chapel, where he founded his order, is now covered by the great cupola of the 16th century **basilica of Santa Maria degli Angeli**, a short distance south of Assisi itself.

Foligno

Located south of Assisi and on the long wide plain of **Teverone River**, is **Foligno**. Once an important Roman centre, it is now a fair-sized town with a 12th century cathedral. Just to the north-east of Foligno, near **Spello**, is the region's national park, around **Mount Pennino**.

Spello

This small town has survived since imperial Roman times and is located off the Perugia-Foligno road, just north of Foligno. Roman relics include the grand gateway at the town's entrance, the **Augustine Gate of Venus** and an amphitheatre. The **Church of San Severino** was built in the 12th century and the **Church of Santa Maria Maggiore** contains one of Pituricchio's most impressive masterpieces.

In the countryside around **Spello** are many small villages which can be visited. The **Church of San Silvestro** and that of **San Michele** both date from the late 12th century, and the **Consoli**

The Church of Santa Maria della Consolazione, Todi.

Palace was built in around 1290. In **Montefalco**, frescoes dating from the 14th - 16th centuries decorate the Gothic **Church of Sant'Agostino**.

Spoleto

South of the highway of **Terni** from Foligno, is **Spoleto**, a stunningly situated hill town located in deep woods. Spoleto is synomymous with its **Festival of Two Worlds**, held each August. The oldest monument in the town is the Cartheginian **Gate of Flight**, or **Porta Fuga**. This was so called because Hannibal was turned back by the Cartheginians at this point.

The Romans left some prime exam-

ples of their architecture here, especially the grand amphitheatre which is used during the festival, and the '**Bridge of Blood**'. This Roman bridge once spanned the flow of the **Tessino River**, and Romans are said to have thrown Christians from its ramparts into the gorge – hence its name. When the river changed its course, the redundant bridge was buried, and remains underground to this day, perfectly preserved. The **Roman House** is said to be the home of Emperor Vespasian's mother.

Near the Roman House is the 11th century **Sant'Eufemian Church** and the Romanesque 1198 cathedral. Its facade is unique with a mixture of medieval, Renaissance and Byzantine mosaic. It is said that 10,000 Christians are

Extruscan inscriptions found in a necropolis at Orvieto.

buried beneath the **Church of San Gregorio** which was constructed in 1079. Just on Spoleto's outskirts is the **Church of San Pietro** which originally dates from the 5th century. The decoration and reconstruction is typically imaginative of medieval craftsmen. In the 14th century, Cardinal Albornoz topped the town with a giant fortress and, to ensure an escape route and a supply of fresh water, he built the stunning **Bridge of Towers** behind it. This is one of the best examples of medieval construction engineering in Italy.

Norcia

East of Spoleto is the small town of **Norcia**. This settlement dates from pre-Roman times and its main claim to fame is that Saint Benedict and his twin sister Saint Scolastica were born in the first century Roman building now part of the crypt of the 14th century church named after the saint. The saint and his sister were born in the year 480 and an oratory was erected over the birthplace in the 6th century. It was Saint Benedict that founded Western monasticism.

Elsewhere in the town are the **Cathedral**, revamped in the 16th century, and the 14th century **Church of Sant'Agostino**, which contains some interesting murals. The other main building in Norcia is the smart **Palazzo Comunale**. Its porch dates from the 14th century.

An handsome Umbrian couple in medieval costume.

Todi

Across the mountains, west of Spoleto, is the walled medieval city of **Todi**, standing above the wide plain of the **Tevere River**.

The city walls date from Roman and Etruscan times and the majority of the buildings in this maze of alleys and passages, are medieval. The **Piazza del Popolo** is dominated by the **Priors' Palace**, constructed in 1337, and by the **Gothic Cathedral** which was started in the 12th century.

Behind the **Palazzo dei Priori** is the **Church of San Fortunato** with an elaborately carved door. Just outside the city is the Renaissance, 16th century **Church of Santa Maria**, which, according to some, was designed by the first architect of St. Peter's in Rome, Lazzari Bramante.

Terni

This is certainly not a city where the visitor will want to tarry. It was bombed during World War II as it was a munitions production centre.

What is left of the Old City is not really worth seeing and the only place of interest is the **Art Gallery** housed in a 17th century palace on Via Fratini. Terni is one of Italy's most important industrial centres and specialises in steel, chemicals, engineering and hydroelectricity.

Pastoral country in the Attigliano area, Umbria.

Just a short distance east of Terni is the famous waterfall, the **Cascata delle Marmore**. From the plateau, 165 metres. above, the fall thunders in three bounds, down the cliffside into the **Nera River** at the bottom of the valley.

So natural does the waterfall look that few tend to enquire of its origin. It is, in fact, a magnificent piece of Roman engineering. Built in 271 AD by the Consul Curius Dentatus, the fall was designed to drain the flat, swampy land fed by the **Velino River** on the high plateau.

Orvieto

Lying 75 miles north of Rome, on the Route 273, is the town of **Orvieto**. Orvieto is a spectacular hill town on a tributary of the river **Tiber**. The lovely cathedral and the adjacent papal palace are worth visiting for a few hours. Both date from the 13th century and the papal palace is now a fascinating Etruscan museum.

There are two other papal residencies in the town and both are interesting; the 11th century **Palazzo Vescovile** and the 12th century **Palazzo del Capitano del Popolo**. The 13th century **Church of Sant Andrea** has an unusual 12-sided campanile, or bell tower.

In 1527, the then pope, Pope Clement VII had a great deal constructed in the town; the **Well of Saint Patrick** was constructed to ensure a supply of water to Ovieto in case of seige.

T he Marches means the 'Frontier Lands' in the language of Charlemagne, this refers to the bare, rolling hills, lying in the swathe between the flat coast and the heights of the Apennine Cordillira. Most of the region is often overlooked by visitors as it is the beaches that attract the tourists. This region is also a land many travellers see only in passing, on their way to the more attractive areas of the south. A major agricultural region, it has well-tended plots of land growing olives, vines and cereals. Livestock farming is prevalent as is craftwork, including paper-making, shoe-making and crafting musical instruments.

Sant'Agata, Feltria, in winter.

Ancona

Located almost midway along the Marche coast, the capital of the region, **Ancona**, drives its name from the Greek for 'elbow'. Founded by the Greeks, it was taken by the Romans from which times many artifacts remain. It is an important seaport for ferries across the Adriatic Sea and a major fishing port, but has quite a small population of around 110,000. Among the remains of ancient classical occupation, the great **Arch of Trajan**, built in 115 AD, is

Marche

447

Ancona's port berths many ocean-going liners.

exquisitely preserved on the quayside.

A mixture of Byzantine, Gothic and Romanesque architecture, the 11th century cathedral of **Saint Ciriaco**, whose tomb is in the crypt, is built in the form of a Greek cross. The city's art gallery has an exceptional collection of superb paintings.

There are many more churches in the **Old Quarter** which dates from medieval times and one of its highlights is the **Palazzo**. The **Church of Santa Maria del Piazza** dates from the 5th and 6th century but was rebuilt in the 13th century. The **Logia dei Mercanti**, or **Tradesmens Hall**, was built in the 15th century. In the harbour is the **Mole Vanvitelliana fortress**, built in the 18th century in the shape of a pentagon.

The Adriatic Coast

Beginning in **Pesaro** in the north, this beach resort town is almost as populous as the region's capital. It was once a Roman fortress, dominated by a 15th century ducal palace where Lucrezia Borgia once lived, and it was also the birthplace of Rossini in 1792. The town boasts what is said to be the most extensive and one of the finest ceramic museums in the world.

The **Rossini Festival** is held between August and September in the 17th century theatre named after him.

Fano, just a short distance down the coast, is a major fishing port of the Adriatic seaboard of Italy. In 222 BC the

The Abbey of St. Vittore delle Chiuse in the peaceful setting of the countryside.

Romans opened a route to the coast to Fano from Rome. It is still a major highway and many ties with Rome remain, including the story of Julius Caesar installing a squadron in Fano. Built just a little before the 9th century BC, the grand **Arch of Augustus** is Fano's great claim to historic greatness.

The nearby church is built from the blocks blasted of the arch during a seige in 1463.

The Renaissance **Church of Santa Maria Nuova** houses two Peruginos and a painting from the school of Raphael. In the early 1400's the **Malatesta Palace** was built and also contains some treasured artworks. Re-enacted Roman chariot races are held on the dockside in Fano annually.

Further south is the beach resort of **Marotta** and the larger holiday centre of **Senigallia**, the first Roman colony on the Adriatic coast. A huge fortress dominated Senigallia and the town was a great trading centre between the 15th - 18th centuries. Pope Pius IX's birthplace can be viewed here.

Falconara Mar is another resort town just north of Ancona. From Ancona the coast turns sharply south in a straight line of brilliant white sandy beaches crammed with resorts of all kinds. The catalogue of beaches run from **Numana**, through **Porto Recanati** and **Porto Potenza Picena**, to the main town of **Civitanova Marche**.

It is from here that the inland town of **Macerata** is best visited.

Villa Bonaccorsi in Marche.

Macerata

Macerata is well-known world-wide as one of Italy's major operatic centres. During July and August everything centres around the spectaculars which are staged at the 1829 stadium, one built for tournaments of the 'arm-ball' game. Known as the **Sferisterio**, the open-air theatre is one of the best examples in the country. Aida was first staged here in 1921, and the stadium seats around 7,000 spectators. Dating from the Middle Ages, Macerata has a pretty central piazza with houses and buildings from the 16th, 17th, 18th and 19th centuries. One of these buildings has been converted into a carriage museum.

A short distance south-west of Macerata, and well worth a short detour, is the 12th century **Cistercian Abbadia di Fiastra**, founded by monks from Milan led by St. Bernard. It is built of stones purloined from the nearby site of Roman **Urbs Salvia** which was founded in the lst century BC. Although the classical site was destroyed by the barbarians in 410 AD, the little amphitheatre seems to have escaped vandalism more or less intact.

Back on the coast, after **Civitanova Marche**, are more stretches of beach extending south to **Porto San Giorgio**. This ancient harbour, dating from the 13th century, is the port of early Roman legacy. In **Fermo** is the vast freshwater reservoir, built to water the Roman garrisons and the fleet of Roman galleys which used Porto San Giorgio during the Second Punic War. Inside the cathedral there is a chasuble made in Almeria, Spain, in 1116 for Saint Thomas a Becket. The **Palazzo Comunale** dates from the 16th century and contains an art gallery and a library which boasts letters perportedly written by Christopher Columbus.

More small beach resorts dot the coast until the road comes to the largest of the Marche resorts, **San Benedetto del Tronto**. This is a large seaside town with a grand boulevard, promenade and avenues shaded by palm trees and crammed with hotels of all shapes and sizes. Traffic jams in the town are nothing to the 'people jams' on the crowded beaches!

It is from San Benedetto del Tronto that visitors can take the short journey inland to see the Roman town of **Ascoli Piceno** which boasts 94 churches. The vast and impressive city square is known as the **Salotto**, or **Drawing Room**, as it seems to be the meeting place of the town's entire population (around 56,000). The 4th century **cathedral of Saint Egidius** houses an impressive 1473 altar-piece by the master Crivelli. Adjacent to the square is the finest Franciscan church in the region, the part Gothic, part Romanesque **Church of San Fransisco**. In the medieval quarter is the 11th century **Church of Saint Vincent** and **Saint Anastasius** which has a rare, once frescoed, 14th century facade. Roman remains include the bridge over the **River Tronto**, built in Augustus' time and one of the largest examples of Roman bridges in Europe. After the burning out of rebels in 1535, a replacement palace was built in the city centre known as the **Palazzo of the People's Captain**.

From here, another string of small pretty beach resorts continue down the coastline to the border of Abruzzi and beyond.

Into the hinterland

Urbino is the largest town in the north of the Marches region, although it has a comparatively small population of just 9,000. The painter Raphael was born here but only one of his paintings is exhibited in the town's **National Gal-**

Raphael was born in Urbino, but only one of his paintings is exhibited in his hometown.

The town of Urbino has many ancient buildings of Gothic, Romanesque and Renaissance architecture.

lery. His birthplace contains another of his works, said to have been painted when Raphael was 13. The **Oratory of Giovanni Batista** is decorated with frescoes by the brothers Salimbeni, and completed in 1416. Dating from the 15th century, the **Ducal Palace** is predominantly Renaissance in architectural style. There is much to see in the Palazzo, the Throne Room, the Hall of the Late Nights, the Library, the Duke's Study, the Temple of Muses and the Chapel of Pardon. This may take a few hours.

South of Urbino is the much larger town of **Fabriano**, noted for being the place where the watermark was invented, and it is still an important paper-making centre. The 13th century **Palazzo del Podesa** on the **Piazza del Commune**, is Gothic-Romanesque and the Palazzo nearby dates from the 15th century. Seventeenth century architecture is represented in the 19-arched arcade on the square. The **Art Gallery**, also situated on the square, contains some of the most exquisite 13th century frescoes in existence.

A diversion from the town of Fabriano might be to visit the **caves of Frasassi**, one of the natural wonders of the region. From Fabriano, on the way east towards Ancona, is the ancient hilltop town of **Jesi**, once a Roman stronghold, but now a jumble of medieval alleys. Frederick II was born in Jesi in 1194 as was Pergolesi, whose name is given to the town's theatre, near the **Falconara Mar**.

The fountain and palace at Fabriano, a town famous for the
invention of the watermark.

Cuisine

Italian food and drink is, needless to say, as varied (both in style and quality) as the country it relates to. Who could expect a country with borders onto France, Switzerland, Austria and the Slovenic states to have a specific national cuisine? Add to that the legacy of centuries of settlements, invasions and cessions, plus the heritage of a seafaring and exploring nation, and you have the recipe for a gastronomic feast unequalled in its diversity as well as its scope.

Lasagna, pasta filled with promise of delicious fillings of meat and tomatoes.

Many people think of Italian food as being pasta, pizza and everything with tomatoes, while staple fare is the less adventurous food of the Trattoria Italiana found the world over (and also some of those found in the larger Italian cities and tourist traps). This picture is far from complete. Pasta does play a significant part in much of Italy's regional cuisine, but is normally an accompaniment to, or a starter before, a main dish, while the now ubiquitous pizza was originally a Neapolitan dish, served very

Cured meat delicatessen shop.

Wines, bread, cheese and meat – stuff of life for the Italians.

much as a convenient meal to the dockside workers (a true Italian pizza bears little resemblance to the limp, doughy pancakes served up at the franchise outlets throughout the rest of the world!). As for tomatoes, they were first introduced to Italy in the 16th century, along with rice, raisins and various spices. At first, the tomato, brought from Peru, was treated with suspicion (Peru was thought to be the site of the Garden of Eden, and the tomato the apple with which Eve tempted Adam), and only the Neapolitans would consider using it in food. However, this reticence was short-lived, and today tomatoes do form an important item in the ingredients list for much of the cuisine in central and south-ern parts.

Regional cuisine

Piemonte and the Valle d'Aosta owe a lot to the proximity of the French and Swiss borders, with butters, cheeses and cream used extensively in sauces – one of the most common dishes is fondata (fondue). In Piemonte, Alba is the home of the famous (and exorbitantly expen-sive) truffle.

If the above regions owe much to Gallic influence, then Alto Adige and Friuli-Venezia Giulia owe everything to their Austro-Germanic heritage! With everyday items on the menu such as speck, knodel and sauerkraut, and their famous sweet plum and apple-filled cakes and strudels, culinary origins are

Typical antipasta buffet in an Italian restaurant.

plain to see! Hungarian and Slovenian dishes also feature heavily in Friuli-Venezia Giulia, while the southern part of Trentino is more reminiscent of central Italy.

Lombardy spans a wide variety of terrains and cultures, from the Alpine foothills in the northwest to the plains of the Po Valley in the east (and not forgetting the lakes), so its cuisine can vary from commune to commune. Milanese specialities such as risotto alla milanese and ossobucco (veal shin) are world famous, while in more rural areas rice, pasta and polenta are widely used. Lombardy is also one of Italy's largest cheese-producing regions, with Gorgonzola and Bel Paese among the best known.

Liguria, with its mild mediterranean climate, enjoys a more southern-style cuisine than its geographical location would indicate. Seafood is an obvious speciality, considering Liguria's long coastline and narrow coastal plain, while pine nuts are used in many local dishes, particularly around Genoa (pesto sauce originated from here, as did pandolce, the soft, sweet breads of the region). Genoa's historic links with Sardinia have led to the adoption of Pecorino as the most favoured of the regions cheeses.

The Veneto is the land of the risotto, with the seafood risotto of Venice having pride of place. Another famous ingredient from here is the raddacchio leaf, while that most gorgeous of Italian desserts, tiramisu, also hails from the Veneto. Pork is heavily featured in many meat dishes.

Emilia-Romagna is generally regarded as the gastronomic capital of Italy, specialising in various egg pastas, cheese (notably Parmesan and ricotta), boiled meats and hams (Parma ham especially), as well as the production of wine vinegar.

Tuscan food has a straight-forward, no-nonsense quality - heavy, thick sauces do not make much of an appearance, and meat (such as bistecca alla Fiorentina) is usually simply grilled to taste. Beans and pulses are widely used, often in cold salad dishes, and mixed with the delicate olive oils of the region. Pasta is a firm favourite, and spinach is an unmistakeable hallmark of Tuscan cuisine. Siena is noted for its rich, sweet breads and pastries.

Sardinian sweets.

Lazio cooking means Roman cooking. Similar to Tuscan cuisine in its simplicity, it favours pork meats (cured hams and bacons) and regional vegetables (tomatoes, aubergines, courgettes and artichokes) in a variety of sauces served on pasta (penne is a firm favourite). Pizzas are also in evidence, particularly the simple, traditionally-cooked pizza rustica. Cheeses include Pecorino, Romano, ricotta and provatura.

Abruzzo and Molise are typified by their hot, fiery dishes, with chili, peppers and garlic finding their way into most meals. Scamorza is a cheese peculiar to this area. Umbria, like Piemonte, is noted for its truffles, used in most dishes. Very much a rural region, and noted for its hunting, wild boar,

gamebirds and the ever-present pork are the staple diets, with sausages, salamis, hams and the delicious stuffed roast suckling pig, la porchetta, being local specialities.

Campania, and Naples in particular, are the true home of both pizza and pasta. Garlic, onion and Parmesan are used generously, though rarely together, while olive oil is used throughout. This then, is the "tomatoes with everything" Italy you've heard so much about! Seafood is excellent, with mussels, clams, squid and octopus finding their way into many regional dishes (spaghetti alla vongole, zuppe di cozze). Calabria and Basilicata share much of the influences of Campanian cooking, with a certain amount of Greek influence in the ingredients (such as swordfish, figs, almonds and honey). Dishes are strong-flavoured, with many spices, peppers and ginger in evidence. Strong, smelly cheeses accompany these dishes. Puglia, to the north-east of these, and on the south Adriatic coast, is strong on seafood on the coastal strip, where it is usually eaten raw, and pork products (sau-sages, hams) further inland. Its location has led to a strong Greek and Arab feel to its cuisine, with preserved vegetables (sun-dried, salted, in oil etc) being a local phenomenon. Sicilian food is a real mish-mash of cultures due to the countless invaders and settlers which have come and gone over the centuries. Couscous and rice point to the Arab and North African influence, and seafood is, naturally enough, a major part of the fare on offer. But Sicily is probably best known for its fabulous desserts: cassata, a rich layered ice cream cake; and zabaglione, a whipped confection of egg yolks and Marsala wine.

Dining out

There are a wide variety of places to eat out at in Italy, with a bewildering number of descriptions.

Ristorante are the most expensive, upmarket restaurants which display a

menu, whereas at the humbler Tratto-ria and Osteria (or Locanda) there may be a blackboard up or maybe just a waiter to advise you of today's dishes. Tavola Calda and Tavola Fredda are basic eateries where you get your food from a counter and eat it there (some-times there are barstools pro-vided) and pay later at the coun-ter. Alcohol in the form of beer and wine is available, but generally no spirits or liqueurs. These Tavolas are usually excellent value, and provide a good lunch spot for the weary tourist (especially if there is seating avail-able!). Paninoteche come in at the low end of the market, being snackbars of-fering filled Italian bread – Panini. In between there are all manner of Pizzerie, Spaghetterie and bars.

Assuming that you are going to a Ristorante, and that you have decided to go either for lunch (pranzo) or dinner (cena), the first thing to do is to look at the menu (la lista). In Italy the first course is usually antipasto, comprising cold cuts of meat, seafood and vegeta-bles. Common antipasto dishes are pro-sciutto (sliced ham), carpaccio (thinly-sliced raw beef), diced vegetables, or vegetable or seafood salads.

The next course is il primo piatto, which, in conjunction with il secondo piatto comprises your main course. Il primo will typically be some pasta, or a soup, while il secondo will be your main meat or fish dish, with perhaps some garnish. Salads are available as side dishes, usually green (insalata verde) or mixed (insalata mista).

This will be followed up with fresh fruit (sometimes cheese first) and a selection of desserts, which will include the *gelato* (ice-cream) which is the basic type, but many others will be on offer as well: "semi-freddo", soft and rich; "granita", crushed ice with flavouring; "sorbet", similar, but softer; and "torta gelata", cake made with layers of ice cream, sponge, nuts etc – such as the Sicilian cassata. Coffee and a local liqueur round off your meal. When you get the bill (il contro) do not be surprised to see "panne e coperto" listed – it is the cover (and bread) charge, added to the bill with the service charge.

Drinks

Wine is traditionally served with every meal (except breakfast!) and there is nowhere better to try it than in this country which is the largest wine-exporter in Europe. You will be received better if you ask for a local wine to complement your meal . Beer (birra) is now widely drunk in Italy, usually as a piccolo (1/3 litre) or a grande (2/3 litre) bottle. Alternatively, draught beer ("alla spina") is usually available. The national brews (birra nazionale) are the cheapest (Peroni is a good example); but there are an increasing number of more expensive imported beers (usually from Germany).

As well as the standard imported spirits, and the local brandies and grappas, there are plenty of liqueurs to round off your meal with – Amaro, Amaretto, Sambuca, Strega and the like, as well as the traditional fortified wines like Martini, Cinzano, Campari and Marsala, as well as less well-known ones such as Cynar (artichoke sherry!).

Teetotallers and those wishing to slake a thirst are well-served with soft drinks – Spremute (freshly-squeezed fruit juice), lemonade, colas, mineral waters (still and sparkling) and tea, hot chocolate, and of course, coffee!

The Caffe tradition

While tea is widely available (either hot – te caldo, or cold, te freddo), coffee is the national hot drink. The Italian Caffe is the social meeting point of the nation, for chats, a read of the newspapers, or just quiet contemplation. People pop in and out throughout the day. The basic drink is plain black coffee (known as espresso, or just caffe), while white frothy coffee (with steamed milk) is cappuccino. Other variations abound – caffe lungo (watered down espresso), caffe macchiato (with a drop of plain milk), caffe con panna (with whipped cream), and caffe corretto (with a dash of the hard stuff – usually brandy or grappa – an ideal morning-after tonic!).

N

ightlife in Italy really depends on whether one is in the cities or in rural Italy or the small town centres and naturally also on what one is looking for in the way of evening entertainment. Generally, folk entertainment in the evening centers around the various festival activities (see Festival chapter) which often extend from religious functions. Music, dancing or evening feasting is well possible to watch or join in, if one is in the right town at the right time. For more cultured entertainment refer to the Literary and Performing Arts chapter.

If one is looking for active nightlife in Italian cities, then it may best to look at what the main cities of Rome, Milan, Venice, Naples and Florence have to offer.

Dare and flair, nightlife attractions.

Do as Romans do

The Romans from time immemorial have been reputed to be fun-loving – a pos-

Many hotels in Italy have been converted from former villas and old palaces, and now have restaurants, bars, discos, and casinos in elegant surroundings.

sible legacy from the decadent ancient days of wine, song and the good life, the dolce vita.

The "Golden Triangle" in Rome framed within the Piazza Navona, Piazza di Torre Argentina and the Pantheon offers much activity to the wee hours of the morning. The locale is peppered with bars, cabarets, discos, piano bars, jazz clubs and nightclubs with live entertainment. There is everything from the chaotic, the crowded to the elegant, slick and chic in this area, which is not short of effervescence. Action tends to start as a Roman unwinds after work.

But this is not to say that there are no other nightspots in the rest of the Eternal City. Indeed there are. Seek out discos, jazz clubs, nightclubs and piano bars for your Camparis, chianti or capuccinos in the Trastevere, Pariole and the Via Veneto districts. Trastevere is particularly known for its nightlife and has a small theatre called Pasquino.

A noteworthy observation that one will make in these places is that the ambience is as much created by the decoration than just the patrons. In most of the clubs and bars, one will find that the Romans have gone to great lengths to pose great decor which reflects the Italian flair for design and style, and love of great atmosphere.

The interiors could be fitted up as Anglo Saxon pubs, New York-style piano bars, belle epoque Parisian or South American style. A club crawl could turn out to be like a Roman theatre of different stage sets!

Intellectuals and artists may gather to explore and argue their views over aperitifs in some of the gorgeously decorated bars. 10pm is a good time for them and the more effervescent swinging set takes over at about midnight onwards.

Best known bars are the Bar belle Pace (via della Pace, 3), an absolutely elegant place; Le Cornacchie (via del Pozzo della Cornacchie, 53), slightly more American-style; and Hemingway (Piazza delle Coppelle, 46), a small but fashionable watering hole for the smart set. Cafe de Paris (via Vittorio Veneto, 90), where "la dolce vita" was reputed to spring eternal, still attracts, especially the well-heeled tourists out to make a point with a visit there.

Try also Sant' Eustachio, Parnaso, Othero, Oro Preto, Giardino Fassi, Gardenia and Tartarughino.

Discos can be very slick and chummy, among the noteworthy, Bella Blu (via Luciani, 21), Le Stelle (via Beccaria, 22) and Jackie O' (via Boncompagni, 11).

Alfellini's (via Cavallotti, 5) with its audience participation cabaret acts gives you the impression that this is where the Karaoke started. Try also the Acropolis (via Schiaparelli, 31), Cabala (via dei Soldati, 25) and Open Gate (via San Nicola da Tolentino, 4).

For jazz afficionados, Rome's the place, the time is around midnight. Try Mississippi Jazz Club (Borgo Angelico, 17), Saint Louis Music City (via del Cardello 13A), Big Mama (Vicolo San Francesco a Ripa, 18), the basement at Fonclea (via Crescenzio, 82A) and Alexanderplatz (via Ostia, 19). The repertoire to be enjoyed ranges from rock, blues, soul and classical jazz.

Milanese evenings

Milan's nightlife tends to live up to its big sisters in Rome, but patrons are cut from a more local profile, the business community to be more precise. Good times are still to be enjoyed in the bars, discos and nightclubs, whose activities and interiors range from art-nouveau to soda fountains to Paris bistro styles.

Try La Belle Aurore (via Castelmorrone), Berlin Cafe (via Giacomo Mora, 9), Bar Basso (via Plinio, 30), Bar Giamaica (via Brera, 32) and Al Teatro (via Corso Garibaldi, 16). Portnoy Cafe Lettarario is for the more literati-seeking and Cafe Milano. The Resentin Cafe attracts the artistic community of Milan who go for the Tsentino wines and Spumatis.

To experience Milan club and disco scene venture into Ca 'Bianca Club (via Lodovico il More, 117) or virtually next door the Capolinea. Then there are others like Tangram, Miro, Le Scimmie, Zelig, Prego, Plastic, Hollywood, Notorius and Agora.

Needless to say, Milan being fashion capital of the world, one would be dazzled by the amount of good looks not spared in all of these places. Fashion is big business in Milan, and business is business.

Evenings in wine bars and restaurants are best times to sample the great wines of Italy.

Neapolitan nights

Lifestyle in the south of Italy is very different from the northern lights and evening activities are not as effervescent as in Rome, the capital. However, a very late dinner is more what makes an evening's program, but that is not to say that there are insufficient nightspots to cater to the more restless.

Places to check out for entertainment are La Cachaca (via Petrarca, 29), Shaker Club (via Nazario Sauro, 24), Accademia (via Porta a Posillipo, 1), Airone (via Petrarca, 123), Il Gabbiano (via Partenope, 26), Il Gallo Nero (via Tasso, 466) and Villa Scipione (via Scipione Capece, 4). Try also 'A Fenestella, Bar dell 'Ovo, Le Grotte Risto-Club and Guinnes Club. The young are supplied with numerous modern discos all over the city.

Florentine style

Florentine formality and swinging clubs seem to be a contradiction in terms, but even in this cultured city of Renaissance splendour and classical art, there are some evening gems, cloistered though, among the old buildings.

The younger generation, the art students and the tourists will find some smart clubs with excellent ambience in Jackie O' (via dell 'Erta Canina, 24 Ar), Central Park (via del Fosso Macinante,

2/4r), Andromeda Club (via de' Cimatori, 13r) and Cappriccio (via delle Oche, 19r).

Others to try are Oberon, Yab Yum, Villa La Massa and Xenon. Manila is full of happenings featuring art, fashion and design shows if one likes that scene and on the other hand Paradise is preferred for a quiet drink.

Venetian labyrinths

There seems only room for Cocteau's pigeons to walk; his lions have to fly, therefore, how do rules apply, especially stomping at discos?

Watery labyrinths do house a few discos, casinos, nightclubs and piano bars to amuse the smart Venetian set and friends of Venice, a city which is itself an event.

The Palazzo Vendramin – Calergi is where the Il Casinò Municipale di Venezia is housed in 16th-century style, overlooking the Grand Canal. Incorporated is the Cassanova club where one can mull over one's winnings or losses over drinks. The casino's summer address is 4, Lido di Venezia, at Lungomare Marconi where fresh sea breezes attend the players, the change of location so reminiscent of a Shakespearean change of scene.

For the more lively try the Acropolis (Lungamare Marconi, 22), Club El Souk (Accademia 1056A), and Rouge et Noire (Casino di Venezia, Palazzo Vendramin - Calergi, Cannaregio 2040) for a drink

and dance amidst mirrors, marble pillars, statues and disco music.

In addition on the Piazza San Marco, there is the Caffè Florian, for summer evenings, when a small orchestra makes the drinks, light meals or ice cream go down more elegantly and when people-watch turns into entertainment.

There are few casinos in Italy, but wherever they are, they are in the grandest surroundings such as in Venice.

All in all, an Italian evening out, whichever is the city chosen, can be had, at times expensively, but on the other hand for a fair price, if one knows the places to seek. Some concierges could be helpful in directing one to the less touristy spots. Be it casual chic or with panache, there is always something going for anyone who is game to explore.

471

There are none better than the Italians to blend style, design and colours into a vast list of consumer products and to satisfy the eager shopper and discriminating gourmet. In fact one does not need to set standards very high without already enjoying the benefits of great quality in Italian goods from durables to perishables.

One of Italy's biggest industries lies in apparel and fashion goods. As a result, Italian designers, entrepreneurs and factories churn out wonderfully looking clothing in silk, cotton, linen or leather, shoes, handbags, belts, wallets, hats etc. Many have become multinational brand names, exported throughout the cities of the entire world. However, there's still nothing like having picked up something at source. In the upper scheme of things, there's great clothing and accessories from Valentino to Versace, Armani to Missoni, Gucci to Pucci – the entire list of designer names read off an alphabet list. Yet there are even much more, of lesser glamour status, but of no less quality, to be bought in the thousands of shops and

Coral necklaces make lovely souvenirs and they can be bought inexpensively in most resorts.

Fashion goods are well stocked in all the Italian towns, and much more in Milan, Florence, Rome, Venice and Naples.

boutiques in Rome, Milan, Florence, Napels, Venice and the other cities. The designers have all marketed their way into perfumery, wines, ceramics, household linens and a host of other product opportunities, so one should not be surprised to be able to purchase a set of Valentino dishes, or Gucci towels or Pucci wines.

One may shop in boutiques in Via Veneto and Via Condotti or the Spanish Steps area in Rome or Via Montenapoleone or the Duomo area in Milan, or Via Tornabuoni area in Flor-

Buccellati and many others.

Shoes are a great buy in any part of Italy, designer name or not, though for top of the range one is not far from always being recommended names like Rossetti, Ferragamo or Magli. Other types of leather goods, like shoes are always found to be superb in design and quality, though not necessarily cheap. In fact, nothing is really cheap.

Shopping should not be confined to apparel and leather goods only, for in Italy food and wine shopping can be enormous fun to buy and are wonderful as gifts. One can be in a state of pleasant confusion choosing wines ranging from Sicilian Marsalas to South Tyrolean Whites, or sorting out salami, or Bologna sausages or sniffing cheeses. Italian delicatessens are great fun. Food shopping is almost a cultural experience and a gastronomic exercise acquainting with the stomach of Italy (see Cuisine chapter for more). Food products are generally very well packed and good for travel. Do not forget to let the wines rest after a long trip.

With its grand and long cultural history it should not be a surprise to find a great industry in the more 'arty' purchases one can make. Objets d'art, antiques, furniture, painting, classical bric-a-brac may be bought from dealers, artshops and antiques stores. It is of course shopping at a more serious end, especially concerning money. One could classify this as investment rather than souvenir shopping.

Bookshops are plentiful in Italy and

ence. Even in Venice, boutiques are squeezed into crevices in a maze of canalsides and bridges. Florence and Venice have very renown shopping bridges, that is, the Ponte Vecchio bridge and the Rialto, both of which are famous for jewellery shops. Italian jewellery design is renown and the array is endless and exquisitely supplied by the artisans and the famed houses of Bulgari,

Imaginative and interesting paintings may be bought off the streets of Italy,
especially in artists' communities.

A summer favourite, the Venetian straw hat.

visitor. Vendors, pedd-lars, marketmen call out, strike out some-times, and make their deals. There is some fun to be had in driving a hard bargain and get-ting your price finally. Outdoors one can buy anything from matches to magazines, souvenirs, bric-a-brac to leather goods (genuine and the imita-tion branded goods).

you will find good ones in almost all the city centres amongst the smart shops and department stores. Look out of Remo Croce, Rizzoli, Antiquaria Scarpignato, Galleria Giulia and Librars & Antiquaria in Rome. In Milan there are many bookshops and many have become specialist e.g. travel, or art and architecture or English language. There is certainly no shortage of bookshops in Florence with Antiquaria Caldini, Feltrinelli, Franco Maria Ricci and Gonelli amongst many others. Natu-rally the other cities all have their staple list of book, magazine and stationery outlets.

Department stores are the way to go for safe purchasing – meaning you know what you want , what you are getting and what to pay for it. In Rome the main ones are La Rinascente, Coin, Standa and Upim which also have branches in Milan, Naples, Florence and some of the other cities and towns.

Lastly and not least, street-shop-ping. It has its pleasures and its risks, but there is too, its convenience to the

Whichever is one's preferences of purchases or locations, Italy has virtu-ally the best to offer for shopping.

Lacework from Burano make exquisite gifts.

W e all know that the Italians are an excitable, passionate people and there is no exception to this in their attitude towards sport. Italian spectators are volubly partisan and push their representatives hard both in regional and international tournaments. In this individualistic nation a sportsman might be booed and threatened or kissed and embraced depending on his performance. The competitive sportsman is therefore under enormous pressure, with a weight of great responsibility to his country but many still manage to produce outstanding results. In football, tennis and motor-racing the Italians perform consistently well and in numerous other sports including skiing they put in more than creditable international performances.

Recreation on the other hand is the art of enjoyment and the whole Italian lifestyle orientates around such pleasurable activities as: sitting in café, taking an evening stroll, watching TV or going to the beach. The

White-water rafting in Valle D'aosta. A vigorous and exciting sport, not for the tender.

477

Italians like to take their time with such activities relishing as always the taste of good food and involved conversation. Italy has for centuries been a wonderfully creative nation and for many of us who seek to do likewise it is worth spending time to sample the recreational pursuits of the Italian people.

Soccer

Soccer is the national passion, a weekend activity is or more popular than Roman Catholic Mass. The British first introduce the Italians to soccer, which was later encouraged by Mussolini who felt that the international victories of Italian teams – much like those of soldiers – could instil national pride. Mussolini built a number of stadia where sports and nationalistic rallies were field. One of these – the **Foro Italico Sports Complex** – became the Olympic stadium and in 1990 housed the World Cup tournament which sends fans the world over to all night or day long (depending on their position in the hemisphere) visits around the television screen.

The national football league is headed by 16 series A (first division) teams, and these teams compete in a series. A championship takes place between September to May each year. The team that emerges as champions from this tournament is forwarded to May in the European Championship Cup. The main teams of series A are Juventus FC from Turin, Fiorentino from Florence,

Lazio and Roma and Internazionale and AC Milan from Milan. Verona has also put in a few surprise performances. These teams have become household names throughout Europe and indeed the world. Matches are played on Sunday afternoons and so for most Italian men – Sunday afternoon in front of the

Being foremost in sports car manufacturing, grand prix formula races are followed by fans around the world.

television has become an institution.

Italian football like the character of her people tends to be on the flamboyant and stylish side. Like the Latin American countries this ensures fervent audience participation and thousand upon thousands of people–mostly men–

turn out each Sunday whatever the weather to watch a match.

The spectators however, like the players, are excitable and verbose sometimes to the point of being rabid. Players who are injured are often booed at venomously and as for the opposition

If one is in the right resort at the right season, sailing the Mediterranean seas makes a pleasant sport.

fans, things are frequently thrown at them. Even when the fans' team wins there is no sedate applause, but rather supporters flood on to the playing field and tear the shirts off their team play- ers, who when the final whistle sounds must be sharp enough not to get stranded in a sea of fans in the middle of the field. In 1986 when Italy were runners up in the World-Cup their team was met at the airport not to be congratulated but rather booed at; in this partisan nation second is just not good enough.

Unfortunately as in England, foot-

Skiing, especially in the northern mountains, is offered at many Italian resorts.

ball violence or hooliganism is increasing in Italy, though it has not reached the same appalling notoriety as of the infamous English fans. However, in the 1985 European Cup in Belgium, 39 fans were killed in an ugly brawl. Football is no longer family entertainment for the Italians, as with the increased violence, many people prefer to watch their local village or town's team, but it is definitely a male territory and frequent subject of café conversation and newspaper gossip. Over a 19,000 hours of soccer are shown on Italian TV in a year.

Motor-racing

Another sport close to the heart of an Italian man, is motor-racing, a sport to which many Italian drivers–especially in Rome– appear to aspire. However, the real thing is serious business and many Italians like to make a flutter on the stakes of the Italian Ferrari team. The old Caparelle track in Rome attracts an upper class crowd whereas less high-flyers meet at the Tordi Valle on the Via del Mare. Formula 1 races are international events but the two Grand Prix races in Imola and Monza bring out the Italian flags and cheers.

Baseball and basketball

Baseball and basketball are two American inheritances. Baseball is led by a number of US imported players. Italian fans are committed and follow their hero's fortunes either in Italy or the US. **Nethino** is the oldest baseball stadium but its crowd capacity at 1,000+ is rather a limitation and only at the larger, more modern stadiums do you have a real chance of obtaining tickets. Despite the crowds' enthusiasm, thankfully there is little violence, with the interest focused on events on the pitch. Baseball remains a purely amateur sport in Italy and thus ensures its participation in the Olympic games. Players are however well-salaried and commercially sponsored to encourage this sport public.

Other sports

For more accessible sports involving personal activity, Italy like most European countries, is well equipped. These sports include horse-riding, running, cycling, swimming, boating, tennis, skiing and bocce. The latter is an Italian version of classic lawn-bowling.

There are a number of horse-riding schools in Italy, for professional information about this contact the **Italian Federation of Equestrian Sports**, on the Viale Tiziano in Rome. There is also an **International Riding Show** every April at the Piazza di Siera in Rome.

Cycling is a well-followed sport in Italy, some of the stretches of the Tour de France, sometimes crossing its boundaries. Bicycles can be hired in many cities and country areas for your own exploration of the beauty of Italy. Leave the Alps however for those who are highly fit and experienced cyclists!

Sailing and boating are always possibilities along the extensive stretch of Italy's coastline and there are even inland watersports opportunities along the length of its rivers. Contact the **Nautic Co'op** in Piazza Amedo in Naples for information on sailing.

For all watersports including swimming and beach life, beware of the area around Naples since the beaches are clearer and the sea bluer the further south you go, towards the open and away from the environmental hazards of the big city areas. For information on fishing, contact the **Federazione Italiana Pesca Sportiva**.

Tennis as in most of Europe, is available both in private clubs and on public courts, which can be rented by the hour. The **Tennis Club Parioli** is one of Rome's most prestigious private clubs. Italy is not a big golfing nation, but there are as in most places a number of good courses available.

In Rome–where one would expect prices to be higher–visit the **Circolodel Golf Roma** or the new country club, the **Caskel Gardolf**. Out of Rome, the **Afsouth Golf Club** west of Naples is a nine hole course.

Cortina, site of the 1956 Winter Olympics is a well known and beautiful city for winter sports. The Olympic Ice stadium is the place of skating and ice hockey. Any of the smaller ski resorts in this area of Trentino Alto Adige, are ideal winter or summer retreats.

Recreation

A large part of Italian recreation involves talking and the best place to go for this is the nearest café. Cafés like their French counterparts may be anything from small smokey rooms to outdoor terraced restaurants. Either way both the young and old hang out here. The most touristy of these cafés are situated in a city's major Piazza (square), but prices here will be expensive. Italian cafés are not mere eating and/or drinking establishments but places to while away time, talk with the proprietor and meet your friends. There is no pressure to leave and you will often find patrons enjoying a good novel or writing a letter there.

An evening stroll is another time to meet your friends and catch up on the latest happenings. Even in the depths of winter you will see Italian men gathering in groups in the streets of towns and villages, smartly dressed in long coats and fashionable hats conversing seriously with one another. Italians dress up before going out, even if it is only to walk their dogs in the town square.

Other forms of recreation may be of cultural nature where you will find that the Italians are great opera, film and theatre lovers. If you are familiar with the Italian language, you will find that there are a whole host of newspapers which cater to a range of political sympathies but which tend to be almost arrogantly intellectually-oriented and opinionated. The Pink-coloured **Gazzetta dello sport**, is the paper to read about all forms of sport and sporting life.

Last but not least a classic Italian and international favourite, is of course the television. Here you will find many choices, Rome alone has 83 channels whilst Sicily has an incredible 123. Out of all these you might find a programme you like. The Italian film market even in this most creative country, is saturated by the Americans and you are more than likely to find a Hollywood hit dubbed into Italian.

TRAVEL TIPS

ACCOMMODATION

Although most of Italy provides a wide range of accommodation from the excessively expensive to the very cheap, in major city centres like Rome, Florence, Naples etc. it is becoming increasingly difficult to find clean and good economically priced lodgings. Accommodation ranges from rooms rented by the night, to a range of hotels and motels from five star deluxe hotels, to one star guest houses or inns; alternatives include rented villas, flats, chalets or apartments; self-catering in country houses, farmhouses or holiday clubs; or camping, caravan, camper and youth hostel or student's hostel accommodation. There is also the choice of staying in tourist villages, overnighting in mountain huts with Club Alpino Italiano, or Agriturismo holidays in farmhouses.

ACCIDENTS AND BREAKDOWNS

The emergency telephone number for accidents (incidentes), Police, Ambulance and Fire Brigade throughout Italy and its islands is 113. Should a breakdown (guasto) occur, assistance is available in English 24 hours a day on telephone number 116. The ACI,or Italian Automobile Association will be notified and their services are charged for, unless a tourist fuel card, which entitles the visitor to petrol discounts (available from the ACI and hire companies), is produced. The ACI will tow the breakdown to the nearest ACI office. ACI branches number over 100 and are located in most towns and cities.

AIR TRAVEL

Alitalia is the national airline and serves all the major international airports in Italy, linking with most main connections throughout the world. There are several domestic airlines, some of which offer attractive discounts for flying on domestic routes at certain times. There is an excellent domestic airline network and most large towns and the smaller cities are not far from an airport. There are a total of 33 airports throughout the Italian mainland and Sicily and Sardinia.

BUSINESS HOURS

Shops generally open from 8.30 am. - 1.00 pm. and from 3.30 pm. or 4.00 pm. to 7.30 pm. or 8.00 pm. Shops are normally closed on Sunday and one afternoon per week. Resort shops and supermarkets often open six days a week and their hours vary according to demand.

Museums can open at varying times and usually their ticket offices close around one hour before the museum's doors. Many museums close on Mondays and keep short hours during the week. Banks open on weekdays from 8.30 am. - 1.30 pm. & 2.45 pm. - 3.45 pm.

CHURCHES & RELIGION

With many thousand cathedrals, basilicas, churches, chapels, religious sanctuaries and other places of worship across the land, the Italians are generally a most devout people and they follow the Roman Catholic religion. For visitors, please observe the times of services and devotions. Most churches are closed for two hours for lunch time and open until around 7 pm. although major cathedrals and St. Peter's Basilica are open all day. Also take a number of 100-lire coins which are used to illuminate works of art etc. in the darker niches of churches. Decorations on windows, ceilings, towers etc. might be best seen with the aid of binoculars.

CLIMATE

Italy has a Mediterranean climate with warm summers all the year round, but more hot in the south. The winters are usually cold but milder the more southerly one travels. The hottest months are from July to August. The Alpine region is cold and dry, and during winter the coast and the south can be quite mild and in the summer, hot and dry. Rainfall is generally light. Sea temperatures are more often than not, warm and pleasant.

CLOTHING

Although the climate is mild or hot during the day, apart from in the northerly regions, the nights can grow cool and some shawl or light jacket is recommended for evenings. Shorts are not often worn in cities and most Italians expect smart dress. A raincoat is advisable for sudden short showers and comfortable walking shoes are best for day-; long sightseeing tours. Women should cover arms and the head, generally with a scarf, whilst visiting churches and religious monuments.

CURRENCY

Currency is the Italian Lire which is available in coinage; 5, 10, 20, 50, 100, 200 and 500 lire; and notes; 500, 1,000, 2,000, 5,000, 10,000, 20,000, 50,000 and 100,000 lire.

Most hotels, restaurants and shops take major credit cards but petrol stations generally only deal in cash (with tourist discount coupons). Although banking hours vary slightly from place to place, the usual hours are, Monday to Friday from 8.30 am - 1.30 pm & 2.45 pm - 3.45 pm Banks close on national holidays.Currency exchange bureaux often stay open until 7.00 or 8.00 pm.

CUSTOMS REGULATIONS

Most goods visitors usually take on holiday for personal use, like cameras, video camera, books, camping gear, skis, tennis rackets, tape recorder, fishing tackle, bicycle, portable radio, binoculars, personal jewellery etc. are exempt from duty. Duty is not levied on the import of EEC tax paid goods:- 300 cigarettes or 150 cigarillos or 75 cigars or 400g. of tobacco, alcoholic drinks over 22% vol. 1 1/2 litres, under 22% vol. 3 litres, fortified or sparkling wine or still table wine 5 litres. Perfume 75g. toilet water 375cc. Duty-free goods allowed: 200 cigarettes or 100 cigarillos or 50 cigars or 250g. of tobacco, alcoholic drinks over 22% vol. 1 litre, under 22% vol. 2 litres, fortified or sparkling wine or still table wine 2 litres. Perfume 50g. toilet water 250cc.

DISABLED TRAVELLERS

Several tour operators cater for holidays for the disabled in Italy and these can be reached through the relevant organisations or most travel agents. Those disabled travellers taking their own vehi-

cle, should display the orange badge prominently on their vehicles to benefit from special parking privileges.

In Rome, some monuments are accessible by the disabled such as St. Peter's, the Sistine Chapel and the Vatican museums but, generally in Italy, the provision for disabled travellers is poor.

Few hotels cater for the disabled although facilities are slowly being installed. Most monuments throughout Italy prevent access by the disabled either because of their location, or because of steps etc. Public transport is also not adapted for the disabled, nor are toilet facilities, telephones etc. However, the authorities are gradually adapting services to accommodate disabled visitors.

DRIVING HINTS

A car is essential for visitors travelling in Italy if one wishes to see the sights and points of interest located away from the beaches or main towns. Those not taking their own vehicle can hire from one of the many car hire companies (Maggiore Autonoleggi, or local companies, and international car hire firms), located in the major towns, airports, ports and resort areas. Cars normally available range from Fiat Pandas to Peugeot 205, from Ford Fiesta and Fiat Uno to Alfa 33 or Pel Kadett, to the larger Alfa's and Lancia's to minibuses.

A current driving licence with translation is required. The minimum age for drivers of cars with less than 112 mph/180 kph power, is 18 years,over that capacity the minimum age is 21. A Green Card insurance cover is recommended although most car hire conditions include breakdown cover, maintenance and basic insurance.

The speed limit is 31 mph/50 kph in built up areas, and 56 mph/90 kph on country roads. At certain times this maximum speed can be exceeded, but these times are specified by the local authorities and should be checked. The wearing of seat belts is compulsory and fines are exacted on the spot. Deferred payment of fines attract a third percentage surcharge.

Toll exists on almost all the 'A' motorways except route 'A2' and the Salerno - Reggio Calabria section of the A3; the Palermo - Catania A19; and the Palermo - Mazara del Vallo A29. Tolls also exist on most major motorway tunnels.

The ACI (Italian Automobile Club) and ENIT offer a "Tourist Supercoupon Booklet", available only to foreign nationals, which comprises petrol coupons and a motorway toll card. Supposedly offering discounts, this scheme does, at first sight, appear a rip-off (on the Italia booklet the discount on petrol worked out to be a measly 4%!), but the motorway toll card is good value, and the scheme is worthwhile if only for ease of use and convenience. The Booklets are available at ACI offices at all frontiers.

ELECTRICITY & WATER
Voltage varies from 125-160 and 220 AC, 50 cycles per second. An adaptor of the Continental two-pin type should be taken with electrical appliances and the voltage should be checked with the hotel etc. before use.

The water in Italy, apart from parts of some cities, is generally potable although one can always purchase noted brands of bottled water, particularly in the shops and supermarkets of holiday resort areas. In several regions the water is thermal and some springs have been designated health spas. Water from many of these spas is bottled for medical treatment.

HEALTH & HEALTH REGULATIONS
Italy is in the EEC and documents (No. SA30 for information, and form CM1 to complete) are available whereby members of the Community can claim free medical treatment under the Italian Social Security Service. Once completed, form CM1 should be presented to the home-based equivalent health service offices, where a E111 form should be obtained and presented to the offices of the Local Health Unit (Unita Sanitoria Locale) when treatment is required. The EEC arrangement may not cover all medical and dental costs and so a separate holiday insurance should be taken out.

The most common ailments visitors may require treatment for is sunburn and dehydration.

Salt pills and quantities of non-alcoholic liquids diminish the effects of too much sun and Calomine Lotion is a useful addition to a first aid kit. The sun is at its strongest between 11.00 am and 3.00 pm and some sort of head protection is advisable during these hours in the summer months. A good sun block lotion with the correct DEET content for the individual's complexion should be used.

Nausea, lethargy, increased heartbeat, headaches and cramps are signs of sunstroke and medical treatment should be sought immediately should these symptoms occur. Sunglasses are a must in the Sardinian summer sun. It is sensible to pack an antiseptic in case of scratches or cuts. A mild diarrhetic may be a useful addition to the per-

sonal first aid pack if one is unused to foreign foods. A standard charge is made for prescriptions.

Many proprietory brands of medication are available at chemists, or 'farmacias' which are usually open during shop hours and display a sign, if closed, of the nearest alternative chemist. Dial telephone No. 116 for information about medical services. The Italian word for doctor is 'medico'. No innoculations are needed for entering Italy.

HOTEL CHARGES
Throughout Italy there are around 37,000 hotels and many more accommodations from motels to chalets, villas, flats and self-catering establishments. Hotels are categorised into five star divisions and all have a fixed charge with a hotel tax of 10% for most hotels and 18% for deluxe hotels. Service charges are included in the per day price of the room and rooms are charged as single, double, or full board.

HOTEL RESERVATIONS
The following are hotel organisations through which bookings can be made. Most offer either 4 or 5 star accommodation.

ATA Hotels; Best Western Group; Brookeer (R.M.) Ltd; Choice Hotels International; Holiday Inn Worldwide; Erna Low Consultants; Expotel; Hilton International Co; Holiday Inns International Reservations Centre; Hotels in Italy; Hotels of Distinction; Hotel Promotions Services Ltd; Inter-Continental Forum Hotels; Italberghi; Interhome Ltd; Inter-Reps; Italian Grand Hotels Company (C.I.G.A.); Jolly Hotels; Keytel International; Leading Hotels of the World; Liasons Abroad; Pullman International Hotels; Quality International; Supereps International; S.R.S. Hotels; Trust House Forte Hotels; Utell International Ltd; Wasteel Travel.

When booking directly with a hotel, a specifically detailed letter or fax should be send well in advance to the hotel manager or booking desk. AGIP, the petrol, or gasoline company, have almost 40 motels located strategically for the motorist throughout the country.

PHOTOGRAPHY
As in any country, the photographing of airports and sensitive sites is forbidden and permission should be sought before photographing in museums, churches etc. Photographs are one way to share holiday experiences of the country and its

charms. Most makes of film are available in Italy in the cities, major towns and resort shops but check expiry dates. Processing film locally is quite expensive.

Always ask permission before taking a photograph of someone you do not know. Lighting conditions in these latitudes make Italy an excellent location for good, clear photographs during the day although every morning, late afternoon and days with slightly overcast skies are best to avoid strong light. Don't forget that sunrise, sunset, and even moonlight, can produce unusual and effective results. The intense reflection of white sandy beaches and the surface of water like pools and the sea, can ruin a good photograph. A skylight filter is useful, not only in cutting out glare, but to protect the lens.

POSTAL SERVICES

Post Offices open from 9.00 am - 1.00 pm and from 6.00 pm - 7.00 pm. Money can be telegraphed from abroad to Post Offices. The postal system is slow and there are few set rates on how many stamps will be required for cards, letters etc. Tobacconists, identified by a black 'T' sign, also sell stamps, as do some resort hotel receptions.

PUBLIC HOLIDAYS

Festivals, religious holidays and local celebrations can rate as public holidays as well as the Italian national holidays. With more than 100 national holidays, festivals, fair days, local religious observance days and carnivals, one could attend some sort of celebration almost twice every week of the year! Italy's major holidays include:

January 1	- New Year's Day
January 6	- Epiphany
April	- Good Friday
April	- Easter
April 25	- Liberation Day
May 1	- Labour Day
May	- Ascension Day
June 2	- Republic Day
August 15	- Assumption
November 1	- All Saints
December 8	- Immaculate Conception
December 25	- Christmas Day
December 26	- St. Stephen's Day

RADIO & TELEVISION & THE MEDIA

RAI-TV, Radiotelevision Italiana service is broadcast throughout the country. The national Italian newspapers like La Stampa, La Repubblica, I Mattiono (Naples), L'Europeo (Milan), and L'Espresso are available generally. International publications are stocked by many hotels and resort establishments and news stands, particularly during the summer months.

TELECOMMUNICATIONS

The two Italian telephone companies, AAST and SIP, have telephone offices in major towns and the token, or gettoni, telephone boxes accept 200-Lire tokens available in bars, tobacconist and at news stands.

The SIP system operates telephone credit card boxes and other boxes take coinage in 100, 200 and 500-Lire denominations.

For international calls dial 00, the country code, the city code, and then the number.

Credit card telephone booths are generally available at all major airports.

TIME

Italy is one hour ahead of Greenwich Mean Time and 16 hours ahead of New York time. Italian Summer Time adds another hour from late April to the end of September.

TIPPING

Although tipping is not normal in Italy, most good restaurants appreciate a gratuity of sorts as do hotel porters and taxi drivers who expect around 10% of the fare. The service charge on restaurant bills, (receipts must be obtained and retained), is known as the 'coperto'.

TRAINS & FARES

There are supplements charged on the 'Intercity' or 'Super-Rapido' express trains which work out to around 30% of the basic fare charged.

Eurail passes are valid, but check with your travel agency.

USEFUL PHRASES

Hospital	L'ospedale
Post Office	L'ufficio postale
Hotel	L'hotel
Telephone	Telephono
Left/right	A sinistra/a destra
I am ill	Sto male
Stop!	Alt!
Watch out!	Atenzione!
One	uno

Two	due
Three	tre
Four	quattro
Five	cinque
Six	sei
Seven	sette
Eight	otto
Nine	nove
Ten	diece
Yes/no	Si/No
Please	Per favore
Thank you	Grazie
Yes, Please	Si, grazie
Good morning/afternoon	Buon giorno
Good evening	Buona sera
Goodbye	Arrivederci
How are you?	Come sta?
I am fine, thank you	Bene, grazie
I do not speak Italian	Non parlo Italiano
I don't understand	Non capisco
What is your name?	Come si chiama?
Mr.	Signore
Mrs.	Signora
Ms.	Signorina
Excuse me	Scusi
Sorry!	Mi spiace!
How?	Come?
When?	Quando?
What?	Che cosa?
Slowly	Lentamente
I would like	Vorrei
I want to buy	Vorrei comprare
I want to book a room	Vorrei una camera
How much is it?	Quanto costa?
I am thirsty/hungry	Ho ste/fame
What time is it?	Che ore sono?
Where is?	Dov'e
Where is the toilet	Dov'e il bagno?
Is it far?	E lontano?
Train station	La stazione

VISAS

No Visa is required for American, EEC or Canadian travellers in Italy staying for up to three months. Other international passport holders should check with the Italian Embassy prior to travel.

WEIGHTS AND MEASURES

All Italy's weights and measures are in metric.

DIRECTORY

AIRPORTS
FLORENCE
Peretola
Tel: (055) 317123

MILAN
Linate and Malpensa
Tel: (02)74852200

NAPLES
Napoli Capodichino
Tel: (081) 7805763

Domestic flights
Tel: (081) 7092815

International flights
Tel: (081) 7803042

PISA
Galileo Galilei
Tel: (050) 40132

ROME
Ciampino
Tel: (06) 4684
Fiumicino
Tel: (06) 60121

Urbe
Tel: (06) 8120571

VENICE
Marco Polo
Tel: (041) 661111

AMBULANCE
FLORENCE
Tel: (055) 4976

MILAN
Tel: (02) 7733

NAPLES
Tel: (081) 7520696 / 476178

ROME
Tel: (06) 5100

VENICE
Tel: (041) 5230000

CAR RENTAL
BOLOGNA
AVIS
35 Via Pietramellara
Tel: (51) 551528

FLORENCE
AVIS
128r Borgo Ognissanti
Tel: (055) 289010 / 213629

BUDGET
134r Borgo Ognissanti
Tel: (055) 289010 / 213629
EUROPCAR
120r Borgo Ognissanti
Tel: (055) 294130

HERTZ
33r Via Maso Finiguerra
Tel: (055) 2398205

MILAN
AVIS
Tel: (02) 167863063

EUROPCAR
Tel: (02) 167868088

HERTZ
Tel: (02) 20483

MAGGIORE
Tel: (02) 57603846
All car rental agencies at
airport counters.

ROME
AVIS
Piazza Esquilino 1
Tel: (06) 4701
38a Via Sargegna
Tel: (06) 4701229

HERTZ
Via Sallustiana 28
Tel: (06) 463334

MAGGIORE
Via Po 8
Tel: (06) 869392

CITY POLICE DEPART-MENT
FLORENCE
Tel: (055) 352141

MILAN
Tel: (02) 77271

NAPLES
Tel: (O81) 7513177

ROME
Tel: (06) 67691

VENICE
Tel: (041) 5224063

CITY HALL
FLORENCE
Tel: (055) 27681

MILAN
Tel: (02) 6236

NAPLES
Tel: (081) 7951111

ROME
Tel: (06) 67101

VENICE
Tel: (041) 788111

CREDIT CARDS
American Express
FLORENCE
Via Guiciardini 49
Tel: (055) 288751

MILAN
Via Brera 3
Tel: (02) 809410

ROME
Piazza di Spagna 38
Tel: (06) 67641

VENICE
1471 San Moise (San Marco)
Tel: (041) 5200844

Diners
ROME
Piazza Cavour 25
Tel: (396) 35751

Visa
Any bank with a Visa sticker
display will handle your
requirements.

Mastercard
Office in-charge of Europe is
in Belgium. In Emergency call:
Tel: (322) 3525649

EMERGENCY AID
Tel: 113

FIRE DEPARTMENT
Tel: 115

HOTELS
ARITZO
Sa Muvara,
Via Fontana Rubia,
Aritzo.
Tel: 0784 629-336

Hotel Corte Rosada
Loc. Porto Conte
Alghero.
Tel: 079 942-038

ANCONA
The Grand Palace Hotel
Lungomare Vanvitelli 24
Ancona.
Tel: 071 20 18 13

ALGHERO
Carlos V Hotel
Lungomare Valencia 24
Alghero.
Tel: 079 979-501

BIMINI
The Grand Hotel
Via Ramusio 1
Rimini.
Tel: 0541 56000
Fax: 0541 56886

BRINDISI
Mediterraneo Hotel
Viale Aldo Moro 70
Brindisi.
Tel: 0831 82811
Fax: 0831 87858

BERGAMO
Excelsior San Marco
Piazza della Repubblica 6
Bergamo.
Tel: 035 23 21 32
Fax: 035 22 32 01

CAMPANA REGION
Qquality Hotels
Via S. Giacomo 32,
80133,
Napoli
Tel: (081) 551 8888
Fax: (081) 551 8989

Cabal Hotels
Albergo Terme La Reginella,
80076 Lacco,
Ameno Isola D'Ischia,
Tel: (010) 39 81 7961111
Fax: (010) 39 89 251844

Europa Palace Hotel
Via Capodimonte,
2b 80071 Anacapri,
Capri Isola

Grand Hotel Quisisana
Via Camarelle, 2
Capri
Tel: (081) 8370788

Punta Tragara
Via Tragara, 57
Capri
Tel: (081) 8370844

La Scalinatella
Via Tragara, 10
Capri
Tel: (081) 8370633

Marina Rivera Hotel
Via P. Comite 19,
84011 Amalfi

Santa Catarina
Via Nazionalee 9,
Amalfi,

Hotel Poseidon
Via Pasitea 148,
84017 POSITANO (SA),

COMO
Barchetta Excelsior
Piazza Cavour 1
Como.
Tel: 031 26 56 31

CATANIA
Jolly Hotel Triacria
Piazza Trento 13
Catania.
Tel: 095 31 69 33
Fax: 095 31 68 32

DIRECTORY

CORTINA D'APEZZO
Cristallo Hotel
Via R. Menardi 42,
Cortina.
Tel: 0436 4281
Fax: 0436 868058

COSTA SMERALDA (Porto Cervo)
Hotel Luci de la Muntagno
07020 Porto Cervo
Costa Smeralda.

Hotel Cervo
Costa Smeralda
Tel: 0789 92-003

COSTA SMERALDA (Cala di Volpe)
Cala di Volpe Hotel
Costa Smeralda.
Tel: 0789 96-083

DOLOMITE REGION BOLZANO
Schloss Korb
Missiano (outside the town),
Tel: 0471 633333

EMILIA-ROMAGNA REGION PARMA
Croce di MALTA
Borgo Palmia 39A
Parma.
Tel: 0521 233686

FLORENCE
Hotel Excelsior
Piazza Ognissanti 3
Florence.
Tel: (055) 26 42 01

Regency Hotel
Piazza Massimo D'Azeglio 3
Florence
Tel: (055) 24 52 47
Fax: (055) 234 2938

Astoria Pullman
Via del Giglio 9
Florence.
Tel: (055) 239 80 22
Fax: (055) 21 46 32

Loggiato dei Serviti
Piazza Santissima Annunziata 3,
Florence.
Tel: (055) 289 5292

La Residenza
Via Tornabuoni 8
Florence
Tel: (055) 284 197

Palazzo Vecchio
Via Cennini 4
Florence
Tel: (055) 212 182

Villa Cora
Viale Machiavelli 18
Florence
Tel: (055) 2298451

Savoy
Piazza della Repubblica, 7
Florence
Tel: (055) 283313

LOMBARDY/LAKES REGION MILAN
Antica Locanda Solferino
Via Castelfidardo, 2
Milan
Tel: 02 656905

Ascot
Via Lentasio, 3
Milan
Tel: 02 862946

Carlton Senato
Via Senato, 5
Milan
Tel: 02 798583

Cavour
Via Fatebenefratelli, 21
Milan
Tel: 02 650983

Centro
Via Broletto, 46
Milan
Tel: 02 8692821

Diana Majestic
Viale Piave, 42
Milan
Tel: 02 203404

Duca di Milano
Piazza della Repubblica, 13
Milan
Tel: 02 6284

Excelsior Gallia
Piazza Duca d'Aosta, 9
Milan
Tel: 02 6277

Grand Hotel et de Milan
Via Manzoni, 29
Milan
Tel: 02 8707575

Milano Hilton
Via Galvani, 12
Milan
Tel: 02 20124

Palace Milan
Piazza della Repubblica, 20
Milan
Tel: 02 6336

Principe di Savoia
Piazza della Repubblica, 17
Milan
Tel: 02 6230

Duomo Hotel,
Via San Raffaele 1
Milano,
Tel: 02 88 33
Fax: 02 872752

LIGURIA REGION GENOA
Agnello d'Oro
Vico delle Monachette 6
Tel: (010) 26 20 84

LATINA REGION
Maga Circe
Lungomare Circeo,
04017 San Felice Circeo
Latina

NAPLES
Brittanique
Corso Vittorio Emanuele, 133
Naples
Tel: (081) 660933

Excelsior
Via Partenope, 48
Naples
Tel: (081) 417111

Jolly Hotel
Via Medina, 70
Naples
Tel: (081) 416000

Miramare
Via Nazario Sauro, 24
Naples
Tel: (081) 427388

Vesurio
Via Partenope, 45
Naples
Tel: (081) 417044

OLBIA
Mediterraneo Hotel,
Via Montello 3,
07026
Olbia SS

PADUA
Europa Hotel
Largo Europa 9
Padua.
Tel: (049) 66 12 00

PUGLIA REGION
BARI
Sheraton Nicolaus
Viale Bari 11
Bari.
Tel: 080 504 2626
Fax: 080 504 2058

PORTOFINO
Splendido Hotel
1603 Portofino.
Tel: (0185) 26 95 51
Fax: (0185) 26 96 14

PIEDMONT/VALLE D'AOSTA
REGIONS
AOSTA
Vale D'Aosta
Corso Ivrea 146
Aosta.
Tel: (0165) 41845
Fax: (0165) 236660

ROME
Atlante Star Hotel
Via Vitelleschi 34,
00193
Roma
Tel: 081 446 0126

Bolivar Hotel
Via Delia Cordonata 6,
00187
Roma

The Charming Hotels
Via Bocca Di Leone 14
00187
Roma
Tel: (06) 672 161
Fax: (06) 684 0828

Colonna Plaza Hotel
Piazza Montecitorio 12
00186
Roma

Garden Hotel Atlante
Via Crescenzio 78
00193
Roma

Hotel Giolli
Via Nazionale 69
00184
Roma
Tel: (06) 4755928

Marcella Hotel
Via Flavia 106
00187
Roma

Ludovici Hotels
Traiano Hotel
Via IV Novembre 154
Roma
Tel: (06) 679 23 58
Fax: (06) 67 83 674

Aldrovandi Palace Hotel
Via Aldrovandi, 15
Roma
Tel: (06) 841091

Ambasciatori Palace
Via Vittorio Veneto, 70
Roma
Tel: (06) 47493

Bernini Bristol
Piazza Baberini, 23
Roma
Tel: (06) 463051

Cardinal
Via Giulia, 62
Roma
Tel: (06) 6542719

Cavalieri Hilton
Via Cadlolo, 101
Roma
Tel: (06) 3151

Condotti
Via Mario de' Fiori, 37
Roma
Tel: (06) 6794769

D' Inghilterra
Via Bocca di Leone, 14
Roma
Tel: (06) 672161

Eden
Via Ludovisi, 49
Roma
Tel: (06) 4743551

Excelsior
Via Vittorio Veneto, 125
Roma
Tel: (06) 4708

Hassler
Piazza Trinita dei Monti, 6
Roma
Tel: (06) 6792651

Lord Byron
Via Giuseppe de Notaris, 5
Roma
Tel: (06) 3609541

Savoy
Via Ludovisi, 15
Roma
Tel: (06) 4744141

SAN REMO
Royal Hotel
Corso Imperatrice 80
San Remo.
Tel: (0184) 799991
Fax: (0184) 61445

SANTA MARGHERITA
LIGURE
Imperial Palace
Via Pagana 19
Santa Margherita.
Tel: (0185) 28 89 91
Fax: (0185) 28 42 43

SICILY
PALERMO
Jolly del Foro Italico
Foro Italico 22
Palermo.
Tel: 091 54 37 44
Fax: 091 54 76 54

Grande Albergo e delle Palme
Via Roma 396
Palermo.
Tel: 091 58 39 33
Fax: 091 33 15 45

SYRACUSE
Motel Agip
Viale Teracati 30,
Syracuse.
Tel: 0931 66944
Fax: 0931 67115

Jolly Hotel
Corso Gelone 45,
Syracuse.
Tel: 0931 64744
Fax: 0931 21786

SARDINIA
Cagliari
Regina Margherita
Viale Regina Margherita 44
Cagliari.
Tel: 070 670-342.

Sardegna Hotel
Via Lunigiana 50/52
Cagliari.
Tel: 070 286-245

SPOLETO
Dei Duchi Hotel
Viale Matteotti 2
Spoleto.
Tel: 0743 44541

SIENA
Palazzo Ravizza
Via Pian dei Mantellini 34,
Siena
Tel: (0577) 28 04 62
Fax: (0577) 27 13 70

Minerva
Via Garibaldi 72
Siena
Tel: (0577) 284474
Fax: (0577) 284474

TAORMINA
Jolly Diodoro
Via Bagnoli Croce 75
Taormina.
Tel: 0942 23312
Fax: 0942 23391

TUSCANY REGION
PISA
Royal Victoria
Lungarno Pacinotti 12,
Pisa.
Tel: (050) 502 130

TRIESTE
Duchi d'Aosta
Piazza dell'Unita d'Italia 2
Trieste
Tel: (040) 73 51
Fax: (040) 36 60 92

TURIN
Turin Palace Hotel
Via Saachi 8
Turin.
Tel: (011) 51 55 11
Fax: (011) 56 12 87

TRENTO
Accademia Hotel
Vicolo Colico 4/6
Trento.
Tel: 0461 233600
Fax: 0461 230174

UMBRIA/THE MARCHES
REGIONS
PERUGIA
Locanda della Posta Hotel
Corso Vannucci 97
Perugia.
Tel: 075 61345
Fax: 075 61345

VERONA
Columba d'Oro
Via Cattaneo 10
Verona
Tel: (045) 595 300
Fax: (045) 594 974

VENETO REGION
VENICE
Danieli Hotel
Riva Degli Schiavoni 4196
Venice
Tel: (041) 522 64 80
Fax: (041) 520 02 08

Saturnia Internazaionale
Calle Larga XXII Marzo 2398
Venice
Tel: (041) 520 83 77
Fax: (041) 522 36 79

Accademia Hotel
Fondamenta Bollani 1058,
Venice
Tel: (041) 523 78 46
Fax: (041) 523 91 52

Fenice Hotel
Campiello Fenice 1936,
Venice
Tel: (041) 523 23 33
Fax: (041) 520 37 21

San Stefano
Campo San Stefano 2957,
Venice
Tel: (041) 520 01 66
Fax: (041) 522 44 66

La Residenza
Campo Bandiera e Moro
3608,
Venice
Tel: (041) 528 53 15

Cipriani
Giudecca, 10
Venice
Tel: (041) 5207744

Bauer Grunwald
Campo San Moise, 1459
Venice
Tel: (041) 5231520

Des Bains
Lido Di Venezia
Lungomare Marconi, 17
Venice
Tel: (041) 768800

Europa e Regina
Calle Larga XXII Marzo, 2159
Venice
Tel: (041) 5200477

Excelsior
Lido di Venezia
Lungomare Marconi, 41
Venice
Tel: (041) 5260201

Gritti Palace
Campo Santa Maria del Giglio,
2467
Venice
Tel: (041) 794611

MAJOR AIRLINES
Alitalia
Air France
American
Austrian Airlines
British Airways
KLM
Lufthansa
Qantas
SAS
Singapore Airlines
Swissair
TWA
United

MEDICAL EMERGENCY
FLORENCE
Tel: (055) 4976

NAPLES
Tel: (081) 7513177

ROME
Tel: (06) 4756741

VENICE
Tel: (041) 1662113

PHARMACY
FLORENCE
Tel: (055) 192

MILAN
Tel: (02) 192

NAPLES
Tel: (081) 192

ROME
Tel: (06) 1921 / 1922

VENICE
Tel: (041) 192

POLICE
Carabinieri (State Police)
Tel: 112

POST OFFICE & TEL-EGRAPH
FLORENCE
Tel: (055) 160
MILAN
Tel: (02) 160

NAPLES
Tel: (081) 5511456

ROME
Tel: (06) 160

VENICE
Tel: (041) 160

RADIO TAXI
FLORENCE
Tel: (055) 4390 / 4798

MILAN
Tel: (02) 8585 / 5251 / 8388 / 6767

NAPLES
Tel: (081) 364444 / 364340

ROME
Tel: (06) 3750 / 4994 / 3875

VENICE (Water Taxis):Rialto
Tel: (041) 5230575

San Marco
Tel: (041) 5222303

Santa Lucia (train station)
Tel: (041) 5216286

Airport
Tel: (041) 5415084

STATE RAILWAY INFORMATION
FLORENCE
Tel: (055) 278785

MILAN
Tel: (02)67500

NAPLES
Tel: (081) 264644

VENICE
Tel: (041) 715555

THEATRES
BOLOGNA
Teatro Dehon
59 Via Libia
Tel: (51) 344 772

Teatro Duse
42 Via Cartoleria
Tel: (51) 231836

Teatro Moline
1 Via delle Moilne
Tel: (51) 235288

Teatro Soffitta
41 Via D'Azeglio
Tel: (51) 331425

Teatro Testoni
2 Via Tiarini
Tel: (51) 368708

FLORENCE
Teatro Niccolini
5 Via Ricasoli
Tel: (055) 213282

Teatro della Pergola
32 Via della Pergola
Tel: (055) 2479652

Teatro Tenda
Lungarno Aldo Moro
Tel: (055) 676942

Teatro Variety
47 Via del Madonnone
Tel: (055) 660632

MILAN
The Manzoni
40 Via Manzoni
Tel: (02) 790543
Teatro Lirico
14 Via Larga
 Tel: (02) 866418

Piccolo Teatro
2 Via Rovello
Tel: (02) 8877663

Salone Pier Lombardo
14 Via Pierlombardo
Tel: (02) 584410

ROME
Teatro Eliseo
183 Via Nazionale
Tel: (06) 4882114

Teatro Quirino
73 Piazza dell'Oratorio

Teatro Sistina
129 Via Sistina
Tel: (06) 4826841

Teatro Valle
23 Via Teatro Valle
Tel: (06) 6543794

VENICE
Teatro Goldoni
4650b Calle Goldoni, San
Marco
Tel: (041) 5205422

Teatro Ridotto
Calle Vallaresso
Tel: (041) 5222939

TOURIST OFFICES
**ABRUZZI REGIONAL
TOURISM**
Assessorato Regionale
Tourismo
Piazza di Santa Maria di
Paganica 5,
L'Aquila
Tel: 0862 410808
Fax: 0862 22306

**ALTO ADIGE REGIONAL
TOURISM,**
Piazza Parrocchia 11-12,
Bolzano
Tel: 0471 993880
Fax: 0471 975448

**AOSTA VALLEY REGIONAL
TOURISM**
Piazza Chanoux 8,
AOSTA
Tel: 0165 35655
Fax: 0165 34657

BARI
Tel: 080 278111
Fax: 080 404 564

**BASILICATA REGIONAL
TOURISM**
Via Cavour 15,
Potenza
Tel: 0971 21839

**CAMPANIA REGIONAL
TOURISM**
Piazza dei Martiri 58
Napoli
Tel: 081 405311
Fax: 081 401961

**EMILIA ROMAGNA RE-
GIONAL TOURISM**
Via Marconi 45,
BOLOGNA
Tel: 051 239660
Fax: 051 261878

**LIGURIA REGIONAL
TOURISM**
Via Roma 11
GENOA
Tel: 010 581407
Fax: 010 581408

**LOMBARDY REGIONAL
TOURISM**
Via Marconi 1
MILANO
Tel: 02 809662
Fax: 02 72022432

**MOLISE REGIONAL TOUR-
ISM**
Piazza della Vittoria 14
CAMPOBASSO
Tel: (0874) 95662

**PIEDMONT REGIONAL
TOURISM**
Via C. Ferrucci
TURIN
Tel: (122) 3352440
Fax: (122) 3859785

**PUGLIA REGIONAL TOUR-
ISM**
Piazzqa Moro 33/a
Bari
Tel: (080) 5242361

**REGIONE CALABRIA
ASSESSORATO TURISM0**
Vico 3, Raffealli 88100
CANTANZARO,
Tel: 0961 741764
Fax: 0961 25595

**REGIONE LAZIO
ASSESSORATO TURISMO**
Via Parigi 11
ROMA
Tel: 06 4881851
Fax: 06 4819316

**REGIONE MARCHE –
SEREVIZIO TOURISMO**
Via Marcello Marini 14
ANCONA 1
Tel: (071) 201980
Fax: (071) 200313

**SICILIAN REGIONAL
TOURISM**
Assessorato Tourismo
Comunicazioni Transporti
della Regione Siciliana, Piazza
Castelnuovo 35/
Via E. Notarbartolo 9/11
90141 Palermo,
Sicily
Tel: (091) 586122
Fax: (091) 331854

**SARDINIA REGIONAL
TOURISM**
Piazza Deffenu 9
CAGLIARI
Tel: (070) 654811
Fax: (070) 663207

**TRENTINO REGIONAL
TOURISM**
Via Sighele 3
Trentino
Tel: (046) 1 980000
Fax: (046)1 231597

**TUSCANY REGIONAL
TOURISM**
Via Manzoni 6
Florence
Tel: (055) 2478141
Fax: (055) 2346286

**UMBRIA REGIONAL
TOURISM**
Corso Vannucci 30
Perugia
Tel: (075) 6061
Fax: (075) 5042483

**VENETO REGIONAL
TOURISM**
Castello 4421
VENICe
Tel: (041) 5298711
Fax: (041) 5230399

WAKE-UP CALL
Tel: 114

WEATHER SERVICE
Tel: 191

ROME
Tel: 1911

PHOTO CREDITS

498

PHOTO CREDITS

499

INDEX

A

Abano Terme, 46
Abbazia di Santa Maria di Fara, 182
Abbey di Valvisciolo, 183
Abbey of Casamari, 185
Abbey of Fossonova, 183
Abbey of Montecassino, 184
Abruzzi, 31, 43, 61, 193-168, 451, 459
Abruzzo National Park, 57, 60, 63, 198
abstract, 127
Academy of Fine Arts, 301
Accademia Carrara, 311
Accademia di San Luca, 154
Accademia, 370, 372
Accidents and Breakdowns, 486
Accommodation, 488
ACI, 391
Agnone, 190
Agrigento, 110, 274, 275
Agropoli, 224
Air Travel, 488
Alassio, 393
Alba, 322, 323, 457
Albano Laziale, 169
Albenga, 393
Alberobello, 236, 238
Alberti, L.B., 123, 125, 310, 411, 423
Alfendena, 198
Alghero, 287
Alicudi, 254
Allegri, Antonio, 415
Alpie Giulie National Park, 352
Altar of Augustan Peace, 160
Altari, 185
Alto Adige, 46, 329, 335, 457
Amadeo, G.A., 311
Amalfi, 218, 219, 223
Amaretto, 461

Amaro, 461
Amiternum, 194
Anacapri, 258
Anagni, 185
Ancona, 349, 447, 448, 449, 452
Angelico, Fra, 114, 123, 421
Angiolieri, Cecco, 98
Anjouesque castle, 234
Annunciation, 114
Annunziata Sanctuary, 279
Antelami, Benedetto, 415
Anticoli Corrado, 165
antiques stores, 473
Antonines, 15
Anzio, 182
Aosta, 52, 323
Appartamento degli Arazzi, 309
Appian Way, 12, 228, 240
Apulia, 13, 43, 231
Aquileia, 351, 352
Ara Fretana, 191
Aragonese castle, 241
Arch of Augustus, 163, 449
Arch of Constantine, 139
Arch of Constantine, 142
Arch of Septimus Severus, 163
Arch of Titus, 163
Arch of Trajan, 228, 447
Archaic Necropolis, 163
Archi, 198
Archiginnasio, 405
Arco di Augusto, 411
Arco Felice, 226
Ardia, 290
Arezzo, 89, 430, 431
Aris Pacis, 160
Arona, 313
Art nouveau, 127
artshops, 473
Ascoli Piceno, 89, 451
Asinelli, 407

Assisi, 90, 439-441
Associazione Ornitologica Italiana, 62
Asti Spumante, 323
Asti, 323
Atrani, 221, 223
Atri, 196
Augustine Gate of Venus, 441
Augustus Arch, 438
Augustus, 15, 101, 118, 160, 239, 451
Aurelian Wall, 146, 147
Aurora, 46

B

Bacino di San Marco, 365
Bacoli, 226
Baia, 225
Baja Sardinia, 291
Balzi Rossi, 392
Bandini, 366
Banditaccia Necropolis, 179
Baracci Trophy, 93
Bardolino, 378
Bareback Horse Race, 95
Bargello, 423, 426
Barguello, 421
Bari, 37, 90, 231, 234, 236, 237, 249, 349
Barletta, 233
Barolo, 322
baroque, 126, 127, 146, 154, 158, 206, 227, 235, 237, 248, 251, 254, 270, 273, 285, 286, 307, 310, 335, 348, 364, 370, 409, 415, 439
Barraco Museum, 157
Barrea, 198
Barumini, 284
Basilica Aemillia, 163
Basilica dell'Assunta, 351
Basilica di San Bartomeo, 407

Basilica di San Marco, 119, 359, 366
Basilica di Sant' Andrea, 310
Basilica di Santo Stefano, 407
Basilica di Superga, 323
Basilica Julia, 163
Basilica of Hera, 224
Basilica of Maxentius, 163
Basilica of San Sepolcro, 236
Basilica of Sant' Ambrogio, 305
Basilica of Santa Sabina, 145
Basilicata, 43, 225, 243, 244, 247, 249-251, 459
Bassi, Bartino, 305
Bastion of Santa Catarina, 286
Baths of Caracalla, 145, 146
Baths of Diana, 218
Baths of Diocletian, 147
Baths of the Imperial Palace, 162
baths, 196, 209, 243, 430
Battistero Neoniano, 409
battle of oranges, 94
Baveno, 313
Bay of Fables, 396
Bay of Genoa, 389
Bay of Naples, 76, 191, 203, 217, 218, 253, 260
Bay of Silence, 396
Bay of Sistiana, 353, 345
beach, 194, 196, 197, 221, 232, 250, 260, 410, 449, 451, 39, 173, 193, 194, 232, 245, 253, 257, 258, 259, 260, 261, 267, 281, 365, 449
Bel Paese, 458
Bellagio, 314
Bellini Cocktail, 372
Bellini, 107, 203, 271, 311, 357, 370
Bellosguardo, 427
Belluno, 376
Benedetto, 415
Benevento, 228, 229
Bergamo Alta, 311
Bergamo Bassa, 310, 311
Bergamo, 37, 93, 307, 310
Bernini, 126, 147, 154, 156, 161, 237
Bertolucci, Bernardo, 106
Bianca jetty, 289
Biblioteca Ambrosiana, 306
Biblioteca Estense, 414
Biblioteca Laurenziana, 422
Biella, 38

Biodola, 260
bistecca alla Fiorentina, 458
Blockhaus, 198
Blue Apis, 228
Blue Grotto, 245, 257, 258
Bocca di Valle, 198
Boiano, 191
Bologna sausage, 399
Bologna, 115, 399-408
Bolzano, 332, 333-339
Bomarzo, 179
Bordighera, 392
Borgia Apartment, 149
Borgo Medioevale, 319
Borgo Teresiano, 346
Borromean Islands, 313
Borromini, 126, 156
Borso d'Este Bible, 414
botanical gardens, 207, 271, 287, 392
Botticelli, 115, 123, 203, 426
Bova Marina, 247
Bova, 248
Bovile Ernica, 185
Bozen, 332, 333
Bra, 322
Bracciano, 173
Bracio Nuovo, 149
Bramante, 305, 306, 308, 125, 444
Brescia, 37, 307
Bridge of Blood, 442
Bridge of Sighs, 365
Bridge of Towers, 443
bridge of Milivan, 290
Brindisi, 12, 146, 237, 238, 240, 349
Brueghel, 203
Brundusium, 12
Brunelleschi, 114, 123, 125, 421, 422, 426, 427
Bruni, Giuseppe, 348
Bruno, 279
Burango, 62
Burano, 357
Buzzi, Lelio, 306
Byzantine, 83, 95, 119, 122, 123, 147, 206, 229, 231, 236, 246, 248, 266, 274, 357, 359, 366, 376, 386, 408, 409, 442, 448, 17, 240, 420, 255, 71
Byzantine, 131

C
'Count' Fersen, 258

C.I.T., 303
Cabernets, 378
Cacciatori, 387
Cagliari, 93, 285
Caius Cestius Pyramid, 146
Cala di Volpe, 291
Cala Maestra, 261
Calabria National Park, 64
Calabria, 31, 43, 49, 83, 225, 243-248, 249, 250
Calendimaggio, 90
Calergi, 468
Calvino, 100
Calvino, Italo, 100
Camera degli Sposi, 310
Campania, 12, 43, 217-229, 249, 250, 459
Campari, 461
Campi Felgri, 226
Campo dei Fiori, 158
Campo dei Miracoli, 432
Campo di Giove, 198
Campobasso, 190, 236
Campomarino, 191
Camposanto, 432
Campovalano, 196
Canale di San Marco, 364
Canaletto, 357
Cancelleria, 158
Candlestick Festival, 290
Capella della Si Sidone, 322
Capitoline Hill, 142, 143
Capitoline Museum, 142
Capitoline, 138
Capo Spartivento, 248
Capodimonte, 178
Capoliveri, 261
Cappella del Sacro Cingolo, 429
Capraja, 253
Caprara, 260
Caprarola, 175
Caprera, 31
Capri, 61, 203, 215, 218, 219, 253, 255, 256, 257, 259
Capria, 261
Capua, 227
Capuchin, 270
Caravaggio, 142, 159, 160, 203, 303, 306, 438
Carducci, 100
Carlo Biscaretti di Ruffia Museo dell'Automobile, 319
Carnia, 352
Carolean Torre di Cerrano, 196
Carpaccio, 311

carpaccio, 460
Carriage Museum, 148
Carrozzella, 219
Carso, 343, 345, 347, 348, 350, 353
Cartheginian Gate of Flight, 442
Carthusian monastery, 257, 212
Carunchio, 198
Casa Barnekow, 185
Casa Bianca, 31
Casa Ciambra, 279
Casa de Guiletta, 381
Casa dei Melatini, 196
Casa di Romeo, 381
Casa do Eleonora, 288
Casa Doria, 287
Casa Stratti, 348
Casalbordino Lido, 196
Casalincontrada, 196
Casamicciola Terme, 259
Casanova, 365
Caserta Veccia, 227
Caserta, 126, 227
cassata, 460
Cassino, 184
Castel Capuana, 214
Castel dell'Ovo, 212
Castel Gandolfo, 22, 169
Castel Nuovo, 212
Castel San Vincenzo, 198
Castel Sant'Angelo, 160, 161
Castellammare di Stabia, 218
Castellana Grotte, 238
Castellieri, 350
Castello Aragonese, 259
Castello Bianca, 313
Castello Caetani, 183
Castello d'Abertis, 389
Castello degli Orsini, 173
Castello del Buonconsiglio, 333
Castello del Valentino, 319
Castello dell'Abbadia, 179
Castello Estense, 412
Castello Nuovo, 345, 353
Castello Sforzesco, 301, 305
Castello Svevo, 240
Castello Vecchio, 333, 345, 353
Castello Visconteo, 308
Castelvecchio, 381
Castiglione, 309
Castle Mondaleschi, 178
Castle of Asso, 179
Castle of Saint Elmo, 214
Castle of San Giusto, 348
Castle of Sant'Angelo, 160

castle of Duino, 345
castle of Licenza, 165
castle of Sant Nuragico Cabu'Abbas, 289
Castroreale, 46
catacombs, 119, 270, 146, 207
catacombs, 131
Catania, 271, 273
Catanzaro Lido, 247
Catanzaro, 65, 248
Cathedral of Modena, 122
Cathedral of Santa Maria Assunta, 182
cathedral of Saint Egidius, 451
cathedrals of Monreale, 279
Catinaccio, 332
Cattedrale di San Giusto, 348
Cattedrale di San Lorenzo, 387
Cavallini, 122
caves of Frasassi, 452
Cenacolo Vinciano, 305
Centro Storico, 135, 138
Cerchia dei Navigli, 298
Ceri Race, 94
Certosa San Giacomo, 257
Certosa San Martino, 206
Certosa, 307
Cerveteri, 178
Cervino, 323
Cervo, 393
Cezanne, 159
Chapel of Nicholas V, 149
Chapel of Pardon, 452
Charles, Angelo Crivelli, 313
cheeses, 38, 457, 458, 460
Chianca Amara, 233
Chiatra del Re, 198
Chiavari, 396
Chiesa dei Domenicani, 338
Chiesa di San Donato, 387
Chiesa di San Filippo Neri, 387
Chiesa di San Salvatore, 370
Chiesa di Sant'Antonio, 349
Chieti, 196
Chigi Chapel, 159
Chioggia, 360
Christopher Columbus, 387, 389, 451
Church (Chiesa) of the Scalzi, 361
Church del l'Osservanze, 248
Church of Gesu, 158
Church of Saint Angelo, 438
Church of Saint Vincent, 451
Church of Saints Cosma and

Damiano, 163
Church of San Domenico Maggiore, 207, 241
Church of San Dominico, 438
Church of San Fortunato, 444
Church of San Francesca Romana, 163
Church of San Francesco, 99, 166, 232, 246, 288, 430
Church of San Fransesco, 249
Church of San Fransisco, 212, 222, 451, 191
Church of San Frediano, 433
Church of San Giorgio Nuovo, 277
Church of San Giovani, 196
Church of San Giovanni, 146, 114
Church of San Giuseppe, 194
Church of San Gregorio, 443
Church of San Michele, 308, 260, 285
Church of San Nicola, 231
Church of San Pietro, 161, 165, 169, 438, 443
Church of San Severino, 441
Church of San Silvestro, 441
Church of Sant Andrea, 445
Church of Sant'Agostino, 442, 443
Church of Sant'Andrea della Valle, 157
Church of Santa Chiara, 207, 288
Church of Santa Croce, 114
Church of Santa Domenico, 115
Church of Santa Lucia, 240
Church of Santa Maria Assunta, 219
Church of Santa Maria del Piazza, 448
Church of Santa Maria del Soccorso, 259
Church of Santa Maria della Rotonda, 169
Church of Santa Maria della Salute, 126, 364
Church of Santa Maria di Borgo Casale, 240
Church of Santa Maria Maggiore, 441, 147, 185, 234
Church of Santa Maria Nuova, 449
Church of Santa Maria, 143, 161, 444, 143

Church of Santa Rosalia, 166
Church of the Cross, 236
Church of the Immacolata, 248
church museum of San Silvestro, 179
church of Annunziata dei Catalan., 274
church of Maria Santissima Grazie, 196
church of San Bernadino, 194
church of San Clemente, 139
church of San Croce, 147
church of San Francisco, 196, 287
church of San Giovani e Paolo, 146
church of San Giovanni a Mare, 183
church of San Gregorio Magno, 146
church of San Lorenzo, 322, 422
church of San Simplicio, 289
church of San Sisto, 179
church of Sant' Agnese, 156
church of Sant' Alessandro, 430
church of Sant' Orso, 327
church of Santa Cristina, 178
church of Santa Maria degli Angeli, 147
church of Santa Maria del Carmine, 427
church of Santa Maria del Popolo, 159
church of Santa Maria della Catena, 270
church of Santa Maria Nova, 179
church of Santa Maria Novella, 423
church of Santa Maria Sopra Minerva, 156
church of Santa Sofia, 229
church of the Trinita, 407
church of Trinita dei Monti, 147
churches of San Giovanni degli Ermeiti, 270
churches of San Pietro, 234
churches of Santa Giusta, 194
Cianciano, 46
Ciaramonti Museum, 148
Cilento, 224
Cimabue, 122, 439
Cinzano, 461
Circe, 63, 166

Circero National Park, 183
Circus Maximus, 142
Cistercian Abbadia di Fiastra, 450
Cisternone, 169
CIT, 302
Citta di Castello, 439
Citta Sant Angelo Marina, 196
Civita Castellana, 175
Civitali, Matteo, 433
Civitanova Marche, 449, 450
Civitavecchia, 173, 179, 261
Civitella Alfedina, 198
climate, 489, 43
Cloisters of Paradise, 220
coastline, 253, 258, 260, 284, 345, 63
Cocullo, 93, 197
Col du Nivolet, 60
Colleoni Chapel, 311
Colli Orientali, 344
Collio, 344
Colosseum, 138, 139
Column of Phocas, 163
Como, 38, 307, 313, 314
Comunale, 273
conceptualism, 127
Consoli Palace, 441
Consul Curius Dentatus, 445
Convento di San Benedetto, 165
Convento di Santa Scholastica, 165
Corfu, 238, 239, 349
Cori, 183
Corniglia, 397
Corpus Domini processions, 190
Correggio, 159, 310, 414, 415
Corso Ercole D'Este, 412
Corso Europa, 306
Corso Garibaldi, 239
Corso Monforte, 305
Corso Vittorio Emanuele, 157, 158, 306
Corte Ducale, 305
Cortile di Pilato, 407
Cortina, 376, 483
Cortona, 115, 126
Corvara, 332
Corvasia palace, 279
Cosenza, 65, 245, 247
Cosmedin, 143
Costa Smeralda, 288, 291
Count Cavour, 21
Count Charles Borromeo III,

313
Count Giacomo Carrara, 311
coves, 260, 281
Craxi, Bettino, 30
Cremona, 307, 309
Crivelli, 451
Crotone, 248
Crucifix of Nicodemus, 288
Crusader Temple, 240
Cuma, 226
Cuomo Palace, 206
Curia, 163
Currency, 487
Customs & Regulations, 487
Cynar, 461

D
d'Agrate, Marco, 300
D'Annunzio, Gabriele, 196, 314
d'Este, Beatrice, 307
da Fiesole, Mino, 429
da Modena, Wiligelmo, 122
da Ponte, Lorenzo, 107
da Sangallo, Giuliano, 125
Dante, 97, 98, 315, 414, 420, 421, 99
De Chirico, 159
De Sica, 106
de Bonaventura, Nicolas, 300
de Ivliani, Caterina, 248
de Medici, Lorenzo, 98
de Pasti, Matteo, 411
de Roberti, Ercole, 412
del Santo, Andrea, 432
Deladda, Grazia, 291
Deladda, Grazia, 307
dell'Arca, Nicolo, 405
della Francesca, Piero, 303, 411, 430
della Quercia, Jacopo, 412
della Robbia, 427, 429, 430
di Lampedusa, Giuseppe tomasi, 100
di Vicenzo, Antonio, 404, 408
Dodecanese Islands, 23, 26
Doges' Palace, 122, 365, 371, 376
Dolomites, 51
Dolomiti di Brenta, 332
Domus Augustana, 142
Domus Aurea, 139
domus de janas, 284
Don Giovanni, 107
Donatello, 123, 426
Doria, Andrea, 386

Doria-Pamphily Palace, 388
Doric, 368, 223, 148
Drawing Room, 451
Driving hints, 488
Due Torri, 407
Duino, 349, 353
Duke Alessandro Farnese, 415
Duke Gian Visconti, 300
Duke of Asinara, 287
Duke of Montefeltro, 303
Duke Ranuccio, 415
Dukes of Gorizia, 351
Dumas, Alexander, 261

E
Ear of Dionysius, 273
Eco, Umberto, 100
Edward Trelawney, 145
Egadi Islands, 263
Eganazia, 237
Egnazia, 237, 240
Egyptian Museum, 148, 322
Egyptian obelisk, 148
Elba, 46, 253, 256, 260, 261
Elea, 224
Electricity & Water, 487
Elephant Tower, 285
Elephone Fountain, 156
Emerald Coast, 291
Emerald Grotto, 219, 220
Emerald Isle, 253
Emilia-Romagna, 43, 46, 399, 458, 399-415
Emissarium, 169
Empedocles, 275
Empress Maria Theresa, 351
ENIT, 345
Enna, 279
Ente Produttori Selvaggina, 64
Eolie Islands, 46, 254, 263
Epiphany, 95
Epomeo, 259
Ercolano, 218
Esquiline Hill, 147
Este family, 412
Estrucan Gate, 438
Ethnological Museum, 149
Etruscan, 98, 159, 160, 167, 173, 178, 179, 376, 430, 435, 438, 444, 445, 208, 149, 9, 10, 71, 101, 111, 295, 386, 260, 11
European Championship Cup, 478
European Cup, 481

F
Fabbrica Nuova, 368
Fabriano, 452
Falconara Mar, 449, 452
Falcone, 370
Fano, 448, 449
Fantana, Domenico, 212
Faraglioni, 257
Farmer's Horse Race, 94
Faro, 162
Fasano, 237
Fata Morgana, 244
Feast of St. Nicolas, 90
Federazione Italiana della Caccia, 64
Federazione Italiana Pesca Sportiva, 483
Federcaccia (Italian Hunting Federation), 64
Fellini, Federico, 154, 106, 161
Fenis, 327
Ferentino, 185
Fermo, 450
Ferrara, 411, 412
ferry, 173, 197, 225, 239, 256, 260, 261, 274, 360, 239, 215, 219, 256, 349, 447
Festa della Madonna della Salute, 358
Feste del Redentore, 358
Festival of St. Elisio, 93
Festival of the Redeemer, 94
Festival of Two Worlds, 442
Fieravanti, Fieravante, 405
Fiesole, 420, 427, 429, 430
Filarete, Antonio Averlino, 125
Filicudi, 254
Firenze, 420
fishing, 259, 260, 266, 313, 349, 353, 393, 394, 395, 397, 483
Flavian Palace, 142
flea market, 338
Florence, 18, 49, 93, 99, 102, 114, 115, 122, 125, 310, 417, 420-429, 431, 463, 472, 473, 475, 478
Florentine, 409, 467, 125, 74
Foggia, 234, 236
Foligno, 441, 442
Fontana del Nettuno, 405
Fontana del Veccio, 197
Fontana delle 99 Cannelle, 194
Fontana Fraterna, 189
Fontana, Alessio, 286
Fontana, Giovanni, 168

Fontane del Triton, 147
Fonte del Rosello, 287
Foresta Umbra, 232
Forio, 259
Formia, 184
Formula 1, 482
Fornillo, 220
Foro, 433
Forum of Augustus, 144
Forum of Nerva, 144
Forum of Vespasian, 144
Foscolo, 98
Fossacesia Marina, 196
Fountain of Diana, 227
Fountain of Orion, 274
Francavilla al Mare, 196
Frascati, 167
fresco, 147, 415, 421, 422, 430
frescoed, 426, 432, 451, 111, 139, 147, 160, 165, 166, 191, 206, 208, 209, 234, 237, 240, 279, 310, 314, 351, 379, 387, 412, 414, 423, 427, 429, 439, 442, 452, 420
Friuli, 343, 351
Friuli-Venezia Giulia, 43, 46, 457, 458, 332, 343-353
Futurism, 127
Futurist, 100

G
Gaeta, 183
Galeria Borghese, 159
Galeria Castle, 173
Galeria di Arte Antica, 147
Galeria Nazionale d'Arte Moderne, 159
Galleria dell'Accedemia, 422
Galleria Giulia, 475
Galleria Sabauda, 322
Galleria Sandrinelli, 348
Galleria Spada, 158
Galleria Umberto 1 shopping arcades, 212
Galleria Vittorio Emanuele, 302
Galleria Vittoro Emanuele II, 299
Gallery of Modern Art, 270
Gallery of Modern Religious Art, 149
Game of Calcio, 94
Garda, 376
gardens, 159, 220, 227, 248, 270, 313, 322, 392, 412, 430
Gardone Riviera, 314

Gargano coast, 232
Gargano peninsula, 256, 62
Garisendi, 407
Gateway to Hades, 225
Gemona, 352
Gennargentu, 281
Genoa, 18, 31, 37, 126, 255, 383-390, 391, 458, 74
Genzano di Roma, 169
German, 57, 335, 347, 350, 375
Gerusalemme, 147
Gesu Church, 179
Ghiberti, 123, 421
Ghirlandaio, Domenico, 423, 439
Giacomo della Porta, 168
Giardini Pubblici, 313
Giglio Island, 261
Giglio, 253
Giordano, 206
Giorgione, 125, 357
Giotto's Campanile, 421
Giotto, 122, 123, 147, 379, 426
Giovane, 366
Giovanni de' Bardi, 102
Giovanni, 357
Giulian Alps, 352, 343
Giulianova, 196
Golden House of the Emperor Nero, 139
Golfe di Trieste, 345
Golfo di Napoli, 217
Golfo di Tigullio, 396
gondolas, 364, 372, 373
Gonzaga family, 309, 310
Gorgona, 261
Gorgonzola, 458
Gorizia, 344, 351
Gothic, 114, 122, 207, 220, 233, 246, 266, 273, 287, 307, 308, 323, 327, 333, 335, 338, 353, 364, 365, 366, 376, 380, 387, 407, 412, 429, 438, 439, 442, 444, 448, 451, 197, 379, 323, 156, 198, 251, 452
Gounod, 148
Gozzoli, Benozzo, 422
Grado, 46, 352
Graie Alps, 52
Gran Paradiso National Park, 52, 60
Gran Sasso d'Italia, 193, 194
Grand Canal, 126, 355, 357, 358, 361, 369, 370, 372, 374
Grand Prix, 482

Gransci, 145
grappas, 461
Grave del Friuli, 344
Great Cloister, 307
Greece, 10, 25, 165, 223, 239, 243, 271
Greek, 10, 19, 83, 102, 109, 118, 142, 166, 220, 225, 226, 232, 237, 238, 241, 248, 249, 271, 273, 275, 279, 289, 344, 447, 448, 459, 460, 9, 71, 98, 101, 111, 255, 256, 260, 263, 386, 11
Green grottos, 258
green flash, 259
Greggio Nature Reserve, 60
Gregoriano Museum, 149
Gries, 338
Griffon Fountain, 190
grigios, 378
Grosseto, 253
Grota di Ladri, 198
Grotta del Banditi, 198
Grotta della Vipera, 285
Grotta Gigante, 348, 350
Grotta San Giovanni, 198
Grotta Valle d. Vacche, 198
Grotte della Arena Candide, 393
Grotto dele Fate, 198
Grotto of Cavallone, 197
Grotto of Tiberius, 183
grottoes, 198, 232, 238, 350, 233
Grottone, 260
Guardi, 357
Guardiagrele, 196
Guarini, Guarino, 322
Guarino Guarini, 322
Guastalla, 415
Gubbio Tables, 439
Gubbio, 94, 439
Guercino, 154
Guido di Pietro in Vicchio, 114
Guido Reni, 407
Guinnes Club, 467
Gulf of Gaeta, 259
Gulf of Manferdonia, 234
Gulf of Policastro, 224, 244, 250
Gulf of Saint Eufemia, 244
Gulf of Salerno, 221
Gulf of Sant Eufemia, 245
Gulf of Squillace, 247
Gulf of Taranto, 249, 250
Gulf of Venice, 47

Gusu Nuovo Jesuit Church, 207

H
Hadrian's Mausoleum, 160
Hadrian's Villa, 162, 165
Hadrian, 165, 228
Hall of Notaries, 438
Hall of the Late Nights, 452
Handel, 256
Handicraft Museum, 291
Harry's Bar, 372, 374
Health & Health Regulations, 487
Heironymus Bosch, 366
Herculaneum Gate, 208
Herculaneum, 110, 119, 203, 206, 217, 218
hot springs, 225, 162
Hotel Charges, 485
Hotel Reservations, 485
House of Savoy, 20
House of the Vestals, 163
House of Vettii, 208
house of Impluvio Sannitico, 190
hydrofoil, 214, 215

I
Il Candereri, 290
Il Gotico, 415
Il Vittoriale, 314
Imola, 482
Imperia, 393
Instituto Musicale Donizetti, 311
International Riding Show, 482
International School of Violin-making, 309
Ionian Coast, 248, 249, 247
Ionian Sea, 247, 238
Ischia islands, 203
Ischia, 46, 215, 217, 219, 226, 253, 258, 260
Isernia, 7, 189
island of Ortygia, 273
Islands of Tremiti, 197
islands, 219, 253, 214
Isle of Capri, 217
Isola Bella, 313
Isola D'Ischia, 255
Isola dei Pescatori, 313
Isola della Guidecca, 371
Isola di Dino, 245
Isola di San Giorgio Maggiore, 365

INDEX

505

Isola Madre, 313
Isola Tiberina, 143
Issogue, 327
Italia Nostra, 69
Italian Air Force Museum, 173
Italian Federation of Equestrian
    Sports, 482
Italian Isles, 253-261
Italian Lakes, 312-315
Italian Tourist Board, 93
Italian WWF, 69
Italo, 100
Ivrea Carnival, 94
Ivrea, 37

J
Jappelli, Giuseppe, 127, 379
Jesi, 452
Julius Caesar, 14, 158, 449
Junno, 234
Juvarra, 323

K
karst, 57, 238, 343, 350
Keats, 145
Keats-Shelly Memorial, 154
Kingdom of Italy, 19, 22, 31
Kingdom of Naples, 31
Kingdom of the Two Sicilies,
    31, 20
kingdom of Sardinia, 21

L
L'Aquila, 194
La Casa Verde, 389
La Fenice, 106
La Lanterna, 388
La Lisa, 270
La Morra, 322
La Mortola, 392
La Regatta Storica, 358
La Scala, 106, 107
La Spezia, 94, 390, 397
La Viste, 260
Lacco Ameno, 259
Lacona, 261
Laghi di Fusine, 352
Lago d'Averno, 225
Lago di Como, 313, 314
Lago di Guarda, 314
Lago Maggiore, 313
Lake Albano, 169
Lake Avernus, 226
Lake Bolsena, 179
Lake Bracciano, 173

Lake Garda, 376, 378
Lake Nemi, 169
Lake Vico, 175
Lamezia, 245
Lanciano, 198
Lanfranco, 412
Lanza, 273
Larino, 191
Larinum, 191
Laterano, 146
Latina, 182, 183
Latium, 10, 11, 43
Laurana, Francesco, 212
Laurito, 224
Lavagna, 396
Lavinium, 182
Lazio, 31, 63, 64, 459, 478,
    173-185
leaning tower, 433, 122
Lecce, 240
Lecco, 37, 314
Leonardo da Vinci, 19, 98, 109,
    115, 125, 305, 306, 415, 308
Leopardi, 98
Levi, Primo, 100
Levico, 46
Libreria Piccolomini, 432
Lido of Metaponto, 250
lido of Venice, 378
Lido, 357, 365, 367, 374, 248
lidos of Jesolo, 378
Ligure, 393
Liguria, 43, 49, 383, 390-397,
    458
Lipari Islands, 254, 263
Lippi, Fra Filippo, 429
Lippis, 426
Liszt, 303
Livia's House, 142
Livorno, 253, 256
Locorotondo, 238
Locri, 248
Loggia dei Lanzi, 423
Logia dei Mercanti, 448
Lombardia Castle, 279
Lombardy, 18, 20, 36, 43, 55,
    47, 64, 87, 295, 306-315, 329,
    458
Longhena, 126
Lord Grimthorpe, 220
Lotto, 311
Lucania, 224
Lucca, 433
Lucera, 236
Ludus Magnus, 139

Lupoanare, 209

M
Macerata, 449, 450, 451
Machiavelli, Niccolo, 98
Maderno, 126
Maderno, Carlo, 168
Maggiore Fountain, 438
Magliano Sabino, 179
Magna Graecia, 109, 111, 203,
    248, 244
Maiella Mountains, 197, 198
Maiori, 222
Majolica Castelli pottery, 196
Malatesta Palace, 449
Mameli, 100
Mamoiada Carnival, 290
Manarola, 397
Manfredonia, 233, 236, 256
Mangia, 431
Maniace Castle, 273
Mannerism, 126
Mantegna, 303, 305, 309, 310,
    311
Mantova, 307, 309
Mantua, 309, 310
Manzoni, 98
Map Room, 149
Maratea, 250
Marcellus Temple, 143
Marche, 447-452
Marches, 38, 43
Marchioness Isabella D'Este,
    309
Marciano Museum, 367
Marcillat, 430
Marco Polo, 360
Maremma, 64, 421, 34
Marina di Camerota, 224
Marina di Campo, 260, 261
Marina Grande, 256, 257, 260
Marina of Ginosa, 250
Marina Piccola, 219, 257
marina, 215, 250, 392, 395, 224
marinas of San Vito, 196
Maritime Alps, 49
Maritime Baths, 162
Maritime Theatre, 162
market, 214, 338, 348, 392, 393,
    396, 412, 422, 427
Marotta, 449
Marsala wine, 460
Martina Franca, 237
Martini Rosso, 372
Martini, 461

Martinsecuro, 196
Masaccio, 123, 203, 427
Masolino, 139
Matera, 62, 249, 251
Matromonia Cavern, 258
Mattatoio, 145
Mausoleo di Galla Placidia, 408
Mausoleum of Augustus, 160
Mazzoleni fountain, 348
Medeival Dance of Death, 241
Medicis, 125, 115, 422, 410
medieval crossbow competi-
    tion, 95
medieval, 146, 168, 198, 231,
    234, 248, 250, 286, 310, 348,
    351, 353, 387, 389, 390, 393,
    396, 402, 405, 412, 415, 431,
    433, 438, 442, 443, 444, 451,
    452, 323
Menton, 390
Merano, 46, 94
Mercato dei Fiori, 392
Mergellina, 212, 214
Merlot, 344, 350, 378
Messina, 43, 243, 274
Mestre, 360, 361, 374
Meta, 218
Metaponto, 249, 250, 251
Michelangelo, 19, 98, 115, 125,
    126, 142, 147, 148, 156, 158,
    259, 305, 421, 422, 426
Michelozzo, 125, 305, 422
Milan, 18, 36, 37, 38, 60, 107,
    115, 122, 125, 295-306, 375,
    414, 450, 463, 466, 472, 475,
    478, 307
Milanese, 458, 313
minimalism, 127
Minori, 221, 222
Miramare Castle, 345
Miramare, 349, 353
Misericordia, 260
Modena, 412, 414
Modigliani, 159
Mole Vanvitelliana fortress, 448
Mole Vanvitelliana, 448
Molise, 7, 43, 189-191, 193,
    256, 459
Molo Audace, 348
Molo Bersaglieri, 348
Monasterace Marina, 248
Mondrian, 159
Monfalcone, 345
Monopoli, 237
Monster Park, 179

Mont Blanc, 49, 323
Montale, Eugenio, 100
Monte Bignone, 393
Monte Botte Donato, 247
Monte Campitello, 198
Monte Carlo, 345, 375
Monte della Corte, 198
Monte Epomeo, 253
Monte la Gallinola, 191
Monte la Rocca, 198
Monte Lattari, 220
Monte Marsicano, 198
Monte Mottarone, 313
Monte Pietroso, 198
Monte Portofino, 396
Monte Rosa, 323
Monte Rotondo, 198
Monte sa Curi, 289
Monte Sabini, 182
Monte San Giovanni Campano,
    185
Monte Sant'Angelo, 233
Monte Solaro, 258
Monte Testaccio, 145
Monte Tiberio, 256, 258
Monte Tranquillo, 198
Montecatini, 46
Montecristo, 253, 261
Montefalco, 442
Montefiascone, 178
Monteforte, 190
Montenero, 198
Montepulciano, 46
Monterosso, 397
Monteverdi, 106
Montgomery, 372
Montorio, 161
Montorsoli, 274
Monza, 482
Moravia, Alberto, 100
Moro, Aldo, 29
Morrecone, Ennio, 102
Mortadella, 402
mosaic, 111, 119, 139, 145, 166,
    223, 244, 338, 390, 421, 433,
    220, 147, 206, 305, 367, 408,
    409, 410, 209
Mount Etna, 48, 263, 272
Mount Pellegrino, 267
Mount Pennino, 441
Mount Petroso, 198
Mount Subasio, 439
Mount Vesuvius, 203
mountaineering, 39, 198, 332
mountains, 247, 248, 249, 343,

    47, 281, 311, 323, 350, 378
Mouth of Truth, 143
Mozart, 107
Mt. Etna, 271
Mt. Ingino, 94
Muggia, 349, 351, 353
Murano, 357
Murge, 236
Museo Civico Ricchieri, 353
Museo Civico, 246, 431
Museo Civio di Arte Anchio,
    322
Museo Civio, 308
Museo dell' Opera
    Metropolitana, 432
Museo dell'Opera del Duomo,
    421
Museo della Ceramica, 196
Museo delle Ceramiche, 260
Museo Diocesano, 275
Museo Duca di Martino, 206
Museo Filangieri, 206
Museo Filanieri, 214
Museo Nazionale Archeologico,
    285
Museo Nazionale della Pentria,
    189
Museo Nazionale della Sienza e
    Tecnica, 305
Museo Nazionale di San
    Martino, 206
Museo Nazionale di Villa Giulia,
    159
Museo Nazionale di Villa
    Guinigi, 433
Museo Nazionale, 147
Museo Provinciale della Vita
    Contadina, 353
Museo Sannio, 229
Museo Sannitico, 190
Museo Teatrale alla Scale, 303
Museum Antiquarian
    Arborense, 288
Museum of Christian Art, 149
Museum of Rome, 156
Museum of Sardinian Life and
    Popular Traditions, 291
museum of Paestum, 224
Mussolini, Benito, 24
Mussolini, Benito, 25, 26, 63,
    100, 106, 173, 314, 335, 393,
    478, 24

N
Naples, 20, 31, 37, 48, 76, 94,

INDEX

508

107, 110, 126, 173, 184, 203-215, 217, 235, 255, 257, 259, 459, 463, 475, 482, 483
Napoleon Bonaparte, 253, 360, 415, 333, 368, 19, 20, 260, 298, 381
Napoleonica, 260
National Ceramic Museum, 206, 214
National Museum of Magna Graecia, 244
National Park of Calabria, 247
National Parks, 52-69, 173, 198, 441
National Zoo, 159
nature reserve, 261
Nautic Co'op, 482
Naval Museum, 390
Necropolis, 162
neo-classical, 260, 379, 127, 351
neo-realist, 106
neo-Renaissance,
Neopolitan pizza, 214
Neptune fountain, 423
Nervi, 394
Nettuno, 182
Nicol, 438
Nicola, 122
nightlife, 372, 463-469
Ninfa, 183
Nittis, 236
Noli, 393
Nora, 93
Norba, 183
Norcia, 443
Norma, 183
Norman, 122, 220, 223, 224, 227, 228, 240, 246, 254, 266, 270, 274, 248, 71, 206
Noto, 279
Numana, 449
Nuoro, 94, 289, 291
Nuraghi, 284
Nymphaeenum of Domitian, 169

O
Observatory, 273
Ogliastro, 224
Olbia, 288, 289
Olivella gateway, 389, 388
Oltrano, 427
Open City, 106
Open Gate, 466

Opera, 102
opera, 106, 145, 450, 483, 95, 147, 93, 102-107
Opi, 198
Opicina, 350
Oracle of Fortuna, 167
Oratory of Giovanni Batista, 452
Orbetello, 62
Oristano, 287, 288, 290
Orotona, 196
Orsini Palace, 142
Orte, 179
Orto Lapidario, 348
Orvieto, 445
Orvietto, 122
Ospedale degli Innocenti, 422
Ostia Antica, 161
Ostium, 161
Ottana, 290

P
Pacher, Michael, 338
Padova, 347, 379
Padua, 376, 378, 379, 380
Paestum, 110, 111, 127, 223, 224
Paganini, 107
Paglieta, 198
paintings, 147, 158, 159, 160, 166, 206, 219, 224, 246, 288, 322, 353, 412, 415, 420, 448
Pala d'Oro, 367
Palace of Barberini, 147
Palace of Caserta, 227
Palace of Colonna-Barbarini, 166
Palace of Justice, 160
Palace of Massimo, 157
Palace of Montecitorio, 154
Palace of Quirinale, 147
Palace of Spada, 158
Palace of the Conservatory, 142
Palace of the Priors, 438
Palace of Venezia, 159
palaces, 366, 197, 221, 227, 260, 310, 412, 439, 193, 270, 273, 279, 313, 380, 387
Palacio Tursi, 389
Palaeopolis, 203
Palatine chapel, 270
Palazzeto Usini, 286
Palazzetto of San Tommaso, 179
Palazzina dei Mulini, 260
Palazzina del Piacere, 175

Palazzo Archivescovile, 246
Palazzo Attems, 351
Palazzo Bellomo, 273
Palazzo Beneventano, 273
Palazzo Bianco, 388
Palazzo Carrega-Cataldi, 388
Palazzo Communale, 348
Palazzo Comunale, 185, 191, 405, 439, 443, 451
Palazzo d'Albis, 287
Palazzo dei Consoli, 439
Palazzo dei Diamanti, 412
Palazzo dei Musei, 414
Palazzo dei Priori, 438, 444
Palazzo del Capitano del Popolo, 445
Palazzo del Comme, 429
Palazzo del Commune, 415
Palazzo del Comune, 309, 351, 412
Palazzo del Plebiscito, 179
Palazzo del Podesa, 452
Palazzo del Podesta, 439
Palazzo del Te, 310
Palazzo dell' Accademia delle Scienze, 322
Palazzo della Pilotta, 415
Palazzo della Ragione, 311
Palazzo della Signora, 423
Palazzo di Giustizia, 194
Palazzo di Ludovico il Moro, 412
Palazzo di Schifanoia, 412
Palazzo Ducale, 309, 365
Palazzo Franchi, 194
Palazzo Madama, 322
Palazzo Mansi, 433
Palazzo Medici Riccardi, 422
Palazzo Modello, 348
Palazzo Montalto, 273
Palazzo Municipal, 390
Palazzo Nuovo, 311
Palazzo of the People's Captain, 451
Palazzo Pitteri, 348
Palazzo Poggi, 405
Palazzo Pretorio, 433
Palazzo Pubblico, 431
Palazzo Reale, 126, 212, 322
Palazzo Rosso, 388
Palazzo Rucellai, 423
Palazzo Rufolo, 220
Palazzo Spinola, 388
Palazzo Strozzi, 423
Palazzo Tursi, 388

Palazzo Vecchiarelli, 182
Palazzo Vecchio, 423
Palazzo Vendramin, 468
Palazzo Vescovile, 445
Paleo Pageant, 431
Palermo, 94, 266, 267, 270, 279
Palestrina, 166
Palinuro, 224
Palio, 290
Palladio, 365, 379, 380
Palladio, Andrea, 125
Palmanove, 352
Panarea, 254
Pantalica, 271
Pantheon, 154, 156, 465
Paola, 245
Papal Gardens, 148
Papal Palace, 158, 169, 179, 445
Parco del Valentino, 317
Parco della Favorita, 270
Parco Sempiore, 301
Parma ham, 38, 458
Parma, 38, 414, 415
Parmesan cheese, 415
Parmesan, 458, 459
Parmiggiano, 415
Passeggiata Coperta, 286
Passeggio del Prato, 430
Passo di Campolongo, 332
pasta, 34, 38, 234, 455, 458, 459, 461, 458
Pavia, 307
Pazzi chapel, 426
Pegli, 390
Peŀlico, 98
perdas fittas, 284
Pergolesi, 452
Perugia, 435-439
Perugino, 435, 438, 449
Peruzzi, Baldassare, 157
Pesaro, 448
Pescara, 196, 197, 234
Pescasseroli, 60, 198
Peter Deriabin, 375
Petriolo, 46
Phaedra Sarcophagus, 275
Phlaegrean Fields, 203, 226
Photography, 487
Piacenza, 415
Piana degli Albanesi, 94
Pianosa, 253, 260, 261
Piazza Acquaverde, 388
Piazza Amedo, 482
Piazza Barberini, 147

Piazza Bocca della Verita, 143
Piazza Carlo Goldoni, 348
Piazza Castello, 286, 322
Piazza Cavour, 160
Piazza Dante, 389
Piazza de Amicis, 351
Piazza del Commune, 452
Piazza del Duomo, 240, 295, 302, 311, 432
Piazza del Popolo, 159, 444
Piazza dell'Unita d'Italia, 274, 348
Piazza della Erbe, 338
Piazza della Republica, 147, 423
Piazza della Scala, 295, 302
Piazza della Signoria, 423, 439
Piazza di Ferrari, 388
Piazza di Porta Ravegana, 407
Piazza di Siera, 482
Piazza di Torre Argentina, 465
Piazza Duomo, 194, 220
Piazza Farnese, 158
Piazza Fiume, 159
Piazza Garibaldi, 197
Piazza Grande, 431
Piazza IV Novembre, 438
Piazza Liberta, 351
Piazza Maggiore, 403
Piazza Malpighi, 407
Piazza Matteotti, 439
Piazza Mino da Fiesole, 429
Piazza Navona, 156, 465
Piazza Nettuno, 405
Piazza Nigri, 236
Piazza Oberdan, 350
Piazza Plebiscito, 212
Piazza Reale, 322
Piazza San Babila, 306
Piazza San Giovanni, 421
Piazza San Lorenzo, 387
Piazza San Marco, 361, 364, 365, 468
Piazza San Pantaleo, 157, 158
Piazza San Pietro, 161
Piazza Tasso, 219
Piazza Tre Martiri, 411
Piazza Umberto, 257
Piazza Vecchia, 311
Piazza Venezia, 143, 158, 159
Piazza Walther, 338
Piazza XV Marzo, 246
Piazzale Michelangelo, 427
Piazzo Santo Spirito, 427
piccolo Venezia, 309
Piedigrotta, 94

Piedmont, 20, 36, 43, 87, 286, 317, 457, 459, 317-323
Piere d Santa Maria, 430
Piermarini, 303, 302
Pietrabbondante, 190
Pinacoteca di Brera, 303
Pinacoteca Nazionale, 405, 432
Pinacoteca, 149, 439
Pinacoteco, 433
Pineto, 196
Pink grottos, 258
Pinot biancos, 378
Pinot Grigio, 350
Pinturicchio, 435, 432, 160
Pio Clementino Museum, 149
Pio Cristiano Museum, 149
Piombino, 256
Pirandello, 100
Pirelli Tower, 301
Pisa, 18, 95, 122, 169, 255, 386, 432, 433
Pisan tower, 279
Pisanello, 311
Pisano, 122
Pisano, Giovani, 438
Pisano, Nicola, 432
Pisciotta, 224
Pistonia, 429
Pitre Museum of Ethnography, 270
Pitti Palace, 421, 427
Pituricchio, 441
pizza rustica, 459
Pizzetti, 107
Pizzone, 198
Po Valley, 33, 36, 47, 49, 306, 399, 458
Poggio Mirteto, 182
Policoro, 249
Pollutri, 198
Pomezia, 182
Pomis, 353
Pompeii, 119, 203, 206, 208, 217, 218, 209, 110
Pompey's Theatre, 158
Ponte Azzone Visconti, 314
Ponte Cavour, 160
Ponte dei Scaligeri, 381
Ponte dei Suspiri, 365
Ponte dell' Accademia, 364
Ponte di Rialto, 364, 369, 372
Ponte di Scalzi, 361
Ponte Leproso, 229
Ponte Pietra, 381
Ponte Vecchio, 426, 427, 473
INDEX

509

Ponti Spinola, 389
Pontine islands, 184, 182
Pontine marshes, 34, 173
Pordenone, 344, 352
port of Orotona, 198
port of Vasto, 197
port, 161, 256, 259, 260, 261, 289, 267, 271, 274, 277, 345, 394, 346, 349, 353, 361, 389, 395, 396, 397, 408, 432, 450, 233, 256
Porta Capena in Rome, 240
Porta Capuano, 214
Porta della Mandora, 438
Porta Fuga, 442
Porta Giovanni gate, 147
Porta Maggiore, 147
Porta Mannu, 287
Porta Praetoria, 169
Porta Romana, 301, 162
Porta San Biagio, 198
Porta Sant' Andrea, 389
Portinari Chapi, 305
Portinari, Beatrice, 99
Portixeddu, 288
Porto Azzurro, 261
Porto Cervo, 291
Porto Marghera, 374
Porto Potenza Picena, 449
Porto Recanati, 449
Porto San Giorgio, 450, 451
Porto Tolle, 47
Portoferraio, 260
Portofino, 395
porzina, 350
Porzouncola, 441
Positano, 219
Postal Services, 486
Potenza, 249
pozzi sacri, 284
Pozzuoli, 225
Prague ham, 350
Praia a Mare, 245
Prati, 100
Prato, 421, 429
Prince of Aragona Pignatelli Cortes Museum, 206
Priors' Palace, 444
Priverno, 183
Procchio, 260
Procession of the Snakes, 93, 197
Procida, 226, 255, 259, 215
Procuratie Nuove, 367
Procuratie Vecchie, 367

prosciutto di San Daniele, 352
Public Holidays, 486
Puccini, 107, 157
Puget, 387
Puglia, 64, 231-241, 250, 315, 460
Punic Wars, 12, 13, 451
Punta della Dogana, 365
Purgatorio, 251
Palatine Hills, 138
Parco Traiano, 139

Q

Quadrilatero d'Oro, 295, 302
Quasimodo, Salvatre, 100
Quattro Castelli, 353
Quintana Tournament, 90

R

Radio & Television & The Media, 486
Ragusa, 277
rail, 215, 234, 361, 388, 393, 397
Rapallo, 395, 396
Raphael, 19, 125, 126, 147, 159, 303, 309, 405, 415, 426, 438, 439, 449, 451, 154, 427
Ravello, 220
Ravenna, 99, 119, 408-410
Realism,
Recco, 395
Regatta, 95
Reggia dei Gonzaga, 309
Reggio di Calabria, 246, 65
Reggio, 243, 247
Renaissance, 19, 97, 98, 102, 109, 114, 115, 123, 135, 142, 157, 165, 168, 305, 309, 311, 322, 333, 372, 376, 379, 405, 410, 411, 412, 414, 415, 420, 421, 422, 423, 426, 433, 442, 367, 444, 449, 452, 409, 158
resort, 196, 217, 220, 248, 260, 261, 279, 338, 352, 392, 395, 396, 410, 448, 449, 224, 247, 267, 291, 392, 451
Respighi, 107
Reubens, 427, 142
Riace, 244
Rialto, 357, 370, 473
Ribera, 206
Richini, 303
Ridola Archaeological Museum, 251

Rieti, 182
Rimini, 410, 411
Riomaggiore, 397
risotto alla milanese, 458
Riviera del Levante, 391, 393-397
Riviera del Ponente, 391-393
Riviera di Barcola, 345
Rizzi, 366
Rocca de' Rettori, 229
Rocca Imperiale, 247
Rocca Scaligera Castle, 315
Rocca, 196
Rocchetta, 198
Roccsa Sinibalda, 182
rococo, 127, 353, 433
Rodi Garganico, 256
Roman Forum, 138
Roman, 11, 139, 144, 142, 19, 15, 101, 106, 163, 411, 126, 179, 223, 225, 231, 232, 236, 237, 271, 274, 277, 288, 289, 298, 315, 323, 327, 333, 335, 344, 345, 348, 351, 352, 353, 368, 376, 379, 380, 392, 399, 407, 409, 414, 420, 429, 430, 433, 439, 441, 442, 443, 444, 445, 448, 450, 451, 452, 459
Romanesque, 119, 122, 143, 179, 191, 194, 196, 229, 235, 251, 285, 300, 308, 311, 327, 333, 351, 387, 407, 412, 415, 442, 448, 451, 440, 288
Romano, Giulio, 309, 310
romanticism, 98
Rome's Environs, 161-169
Rome, 8, 9, 10, 11, 12, 13, 14, 21, 22, 24, 31, 60, 62, 64, 87, 95, 106, 114, 115, 118, 119, 125, 243, 298, 435, 449, 463, 465, 472, 475, 482, 483, 131-161
Roncole, 415
Rondo da Ponte, 107
Rosario, 248
Rosmini, Antonio, 313
Rossellini, 106
Rossetti, Biagio, 412
Rossini Festival, 448
Rossini, 107, 448
Rowing Race, 94
Royal Palace of Capodimonte, 212
Royal Palace of the House of Savoy, 285

5

Spanish Steps, 135
a Sartiglia, 290
Saepinum, 190
Saint Benedict's Holy Grotto, 165
Saint Christopher's tower, 287
Saint Mark's Square,
Saint Peter's Basilica, 126, 148
Saint Peter's Cathedral, 115
Saint Peter's Square, 148, 161
Saint-Vincent, 46
Sala Columbiana, 389
Sala del Maggiore Consiglio, 366
Salerno, 222, 223, 249, 224
Salimbeni, 452
Salina, 254
Salone dei Cinquecento, 423
Salone dei Mesi, 412
Salotto, 451
Salsomaggiore, 46
Salvi, Niccolo, 154
Salviati, Antonio, 390
Sambuca, 461
Sammartino, 207
San Antonio, 314
San Benedetto del Tronto, 451
San Carlo Opera House, 212
San Carlo Theatre, 212
San Carlo, 106
San Cataldo Church, 270
San Daniele del Friulli, 351
San Domenico, 405
San Dominico, 260
San Francesco d'Assisi, 279
San Francesco, 407, 430
San Giorgio Vecchio, 277
San Giorgio, 412
San Giovani cathedral, 277
San Giovanni al Sepolcro, 240
San Giovanni Evangelista, 415
San Giuliano, 62
San Giusto Hill, 345, 348, 353
San Lorenzo Maggiore, 207, 305
San Lorenzo Oratory, 270
San Marco, 224, 370, 421
San Maria Maggiore, 311
San Martino, 260
San Michele, 287
San Miniato, 427
San Niccolo cathedral, 286
San Nicola, 260
San Nicolo church, 273
San Paolo, 182
San Pietro Castle, 167

San Pietro church, 196
San Pietro, 179, 291, 308
San Remo, 392
San Remy, 286
San Salvo Marina, 197
San Satiro, 306
San Saturnino, 46, 285
San Sepolcro, 407
San Stefano, 261
San Tommaso church, 279
San Vitale, 408
San Vittore, 305
San Vittorino, 194
San Zaccaria, 365
Sanctuary of Fortuna Primigenia, 166
Sanctuary of Fortune, 166
Sanctuary of Saint Michael, 234, 232
Sangro Valley, 190
Sansepolchro, 95
Sansevero Chapel, 207
Sant Angelo, 219
Sant Apollinare Nuovo, 410
Sant' Abbondio, 314
Sant' Ambrogio; Venezia, 301
Sant' Eustachio, 466
Sant' Eustorgio, 305
Sant' Irene, 240
Sant' Maria Aprutiensis, 196
Sant' Onofrio, 291
Sant'Agostino church, 279
Sant'Andrea, 388
Sant'Angelo, 259
Sant'Elmo Castle, 206
Sant'Eufemian Church, 442
Santa Cecilia cathedral, 285
Santa Cecilia, 285
Santa Cesarea Therme, 240
Santa Chiara, 251
Santa Croce, 240
Santa Groce, 426
Santa Lucia, 212, 273
Santa Margherita Ligure, 395
Santa Margherita, 395, 396
Santa Maria a Mare, 196
Santa Maria Amalfitana, 237
Santa Maria degli Angeli, 441
Santa Maria dei Servi, 407
Santa Maria del Fiori, 421
Santa Maria della Neve, 289
Santa Maria della Salute, 376
Santa Maria della Strada, 191
Santa Maria delle Grazie, 305
Santa Maria di Castellebate, 224

Santa Maria di Collemaggio, 194
Santa Maria Maggiore, 185, 198, 314
Santa Maria Novella, 423
Santa Maria, 305
Santa Sabina, 119
Santi Cosma e Damiano, 285
Santi Vitale e Agricola, 407
Sapri, 224
Saracen's Joust, 89
Saracinesco, 165
Sardara, 46
Sardinia, 7, 19, 20, 30, 31, 43, 46, 51, 64, 76, 93, 94, 95, 100, 102, 173, 215, 253, 255, 260, 323, 458, 281-291
Sardinian Cavalcade, 95, 290
Sassari, 95, 286, 290
Sassi, 251
Saturnia, 46
Savona, 393
Savonarola, Girolama, 98
Scala Fenicia, 256
Scalinata dei Giganti, 348
Scanno, 198
Sciacchetra, 397
Scilla, 246
Scoppio del Carro, 94
Scrovegni Chapel, 379
sculptures, 142, 206, 229, 236, 288, 420
Segesta, 110
Selinunte, 279
Selva, Antonio, 127
Senigallia, 449
Sermoneta, 183
Sestri Levante, 396
Sezze, 183
Shelley, 145, 223
shellfish, 370
Sibari, 248
Sicilian cassata, 267, 461
Sicily, 7, 9, 12, 19, 20, 25, 31, 34, 43, 46, 48, 49, 76, 83, 93, 94, 98, 100, 110, 122, 127, 215, 243, 247, 248, 253, 254, 260, 263-279, 460, 483
Siena, 95, 114, 122, 458, 431, 432
Sigismondo Malatesta, 410
Sigmorelli, Luca, 439
Sila Massif, 247
Sila, 69
Silvi, 196
SIP, 302

Siren's Rocks, 257
Sirmione, 315
Sistine Chapel, 115, 149
ski, 39, 49, 55, 190, 193, 198, 247, 273, 323, 332, 378, 483, 477, 482
Soave, 378
Solfatara, 225
Son et Lumiere, 353
Sondrio, 307
Sorrento, 61, 218, 255, 257, 259
Spa of Bulicame, 179
spa, 225, 240, 259, 352, 119, 46
Spaghetti alla mozzarella, 214
spaghetti alla Pescatore, 214
spaghetti alla vongole, 459
Spanish Steps, 147, 154, 472
Spedale degli Innocenti, 123
Spello, 441, 442
Sperlonga, 183
Spoleto, 95, 442, 443, 444
Spotorno, 393
Spremute, 461
Spumatis, 466
St. Francis of Assisi, 435
St. Mark's Square, 367, 369, 371, 372
Stabiae, 217
Stabian Thermae, 209
Stanze di Raffaello, 149
Stelvio National Park, 55
stiacciato, 114, 123
Stilo, 248
Stradivari violin, 309
Stradivari, Antonio, 309
Strega, 461
Stresa, 313
Stromboli, 254, 263, 248, 272
stucco, 227
Subiaco, 165
Sud Tirol, 329, 335
Sulmona, 197
Superga, 323
Sutri, 175
Svevo, 100
Syracuse, 37, 110, 271

T
Talvera, 335
Tancredi Fountain, 240
Taormina, 279
Tarantella dance, 93
Tarantella, 241

Taranto, 37, 240, 241, 250
Tarquinia, 179
Tavola Rotonda, 197
Tavole Amalfitane, 220
Tavole Palatine, 251
Tavoliere Plain, 235, 236, 234
Teatro alla Scala, 302
Teatro Romano, 348
Telecommunications, 486
Telesio, Bernardino, 246
Temansa, Tommaso, 127
Tempio Malatestiano, 411
Tempio Voltiamo, 313
Temple of Antoninus Pius, 163
Temple of Apollo, 225
Temple of Caeres, 224
Temple of Castor, 163
Temple of Faustina, 163
Temple of Fortuna Virile, 143
Temple of Hera, 248
Temple of Hercules, 183, 197
Temple of Isis, 228, 229
Temple of Janus, 163
Temple of Jupiter, 166
Temple of Minerva, 144, 156, 441
Temple of Muses, 452
Temple of Neptune, 223
Temple of Pollox, 163
Temple of Rome, 163
Temple of Romulus, 163
Temple of Serapis, 166
Temple of Serpis, 225
Temple of Venus, 144, 163, 196
Temple of Vesta, 143, 163
Temples of Concord, 163
Temples to Apollo and Venus, 165
temples to the gods Apollo and Jupiter, 208
Teramo, 196
Tergestum, 345
Termoli, 191, 256
Terni, 442, 444, 445
Terracina, 183
Theater of Marcellus, 142
Theatre of Waters, 168
Therme of Sette Sapienti, 162
Tiber, 45, 135, 138, 143, 160, 435
Tibertinus, Loreius, 209
Tiepolo, 357
TIME, 486
Tintoretto, 125, 126, 147, 357, 366

Tipping, 486
Titian, 125, 142, 147, 154, 159, 203, 357, 370, 414, 426, 427
Tivoli, 162
Tocai, 344, 350
Todi, 444
Tomb of Volumni, 438
Tomba di Dante, 409
tombas de gigantes, 284
Torcello, 357
Tordi Valle, 482
Torino, 196, 317
Tornareccio, 198
Torre degli Asinelli, 407
Torre del Trivio, 169
Torre dell' Ore, 433
Torre dell'Aquila, 286
Torre dell'Orologio, 351, 367
Torre dello Sperone, 287
Torre di Porta Terra, 287
Torre di Sulis, 287
Torre Garisenda, 407
Torre Ghirlandina, 412
tortellini, 403
Tortoreto Lido, 196
Toscanini, 107
Tower of Milizie, 144
Tower of San Pancrazio, 285
Trains & Fares, 485
Trajan Market, 143
Trajan's Column, 143
Tramontano Fortress, 251
Trapani, 277
Tremiti Islands, 233, 256, 260
Trentino, 23, 43, 46, 57, 329, 332, 458
Trentino-Alto Adige, 43, 55, 483, 329-339
Trento, 45, 332, 333, 335
Trevi Fountain, 154
Treviso, 376
Trieste, 23, 37, 343, 345-350, 351, 352, 353, 375
Triton Fountain, 147, 154
Tronchetto, 361, 371
trulli, 238, 236
Tsentino wines, 466
Tura, 412
Tura, Cosimo, 412
Turin Shroud, 322
Turin, 36, 37, 52, 60, 126, 317, 478
Tuscan, 97, 420, 458, 459
Tuscania, 179
Tuscany, 21, 34, 43, 46, 64, 90

98, 114, 253, 390, 393, 397, 417, 420-429
Tusculum, 167

U

Uccello, 123
Udine, 344, 345, 347, 350, 351, 352
Uffizi, 421, 431, 115, 426
Ugni, 198
Umbria, 43, 435-445, 459
Ungaretti, Giuseppe, 100
Urbino, 451, 452
Urbs Salvia, 450
Useful Phrases, 488

V

Val Gardenia, 332
Vale of Tempe, 165
Valle D'Aosta, 323-327, 43, 46, 457
Valle Rendena, 332
Valley of Aniene, 165
Valley of Canopus, 165
Valley of Temples, 275
Valley of the Dragone, 220
Valli di Comacchio, 61
Vallo d. Lucania, 224
Vallone Fara San Martino, 198
Valpolicella, 378
Vanvitelli, Luigi, 227
Varese, 37, 307
Vasari, 426
Vasari, Giorgio, 431
Vasto, 197, 198
Vatican, 22, 87, 126, 148, 161, 392, 149
Vatican, 135, 138
Veio, 173
Velletri, 169
Venere, 196
Venetian, 251, 335, 344, 351, 352, 353, 370, 371, 333
Veneto, 43, 46, 329, 332, 343, 355, 376-381, 458
Venezia Giulia, 458
Venice Biennale, 95
Venice, 18, 21, 22, 37, 61, 95, 106, 107, 114, 115, 119, 122, 125, 126, 127, 345, 346, 349, 379, 380, 386, 395, 463, 468, 473, 355-376
Ventimiglia, 391, 392
Verdi, 107, 303, 309, 415
Vernazza, 397

Veroli, 185
Verona, 95, 99,
Veronese, 125, 357, 366
Vesuvio, 213, 218
Vesuvius, 48, 208, 213, 217, 259
Vetriola, 46
Via Appia, 146
Via Cappuccio, 305
Via Condotti, 472
Via Emilia, 399, 407, 415
Via Garibaldi, 387
Via Monte Napoleon, 306
Via Montenapoleone, 472
Via Porta Soprano, 389
Via Roma, 322
Via Romana, 420
Via Sant' Orso, 327
Via Tornabuoni, 423, 472
Via Veneto, 465, 472
Viareggio, 90, 93, 95
Vicenza, 379, 380, 376
Vico Equense, 218
Victor Emmanuel Monument, 143
Vieste, 232, 233
Villa Ada, 159
Villa Adriana, 162
Villa Aldobrandini, 168
Villa Borghese, 138
Villa Borghese, 159
Villa Carlotta, 314
Villa Cimbrone, 220
Villa Comunale, 206, 212
Villa Correale di Terranova, 219
Villa d'Este, 165
Villa Doria Pamphili, 138
Villa Ducale, 313
Villa Falconieri, 168
Villa Farnese, 175
Villa Floriana, 214
Villa Floridiana, 206
Villa Garzoni, 433
Villa Guinigi, 433
Villa Jovis, 256
Villa La Massa, 468
Villa Lancelloti, 168
Villa Manzoni, 314
Villa of Mysteries, 208
Villa of the Faun, 209
Villa of the Surgeon, 208
Villa Palagonia, 270
Villa Pallavicino, 313
Villa Reale, 433
Villa Rosa, 196

Villa San Michele, 258
Villa Scipione, 467
Villa Tarlonia, 159
Villa Torlonia, 168
Villa Torrigiani, 433
Villa Trieste, 248
Villa Tuscolana, 168
villas, 159, 214, 217, 256, 260, 291, 380, 395, 222
Villetta, 198
Virgil's tomb, 206, 214
Virgil, 15, 98, 212, 239, 240, 309
Visas, 485
Visconti, 106
Viterbo, 179
Vivaldi, 107
volcanic island, 253, 258
volcano, 259, 272, 48
Vulcano, 254

W

Water Pageant, 95
waterfalls, 165, 227
Weights & Measures, 485
Well of Saint Patrick, 445
White grottos, 258
white truffles, 323
wildlife, 183, 49, 247
Wine, 38, 391, 461, 34, 39, 167, 266, 279, 307, 322, 323, 349, 397, 430, 460, 473, 350, 344, 378
World Cup tournament, 478
World-Cup, 480
Worldwide Fund for Nature, 69

Z

zabaglione, 460
zuppa alla pavese, 308
zuppa di cozze, 214
zuppe di cozze, 459